MARKET RULES
Economic Union Reform and Intergovernmental Policy-Making in Australia and Canada

MARKET RULES

Economic Union Reform and Intergovernmental Policy-Making in Australia and Canada

DOUGLAS M. BROWN

McGill-Queen's University Press

Montreal & Kingston • London • Ithaca

M © McGill-Queen's University Press 2002
ISBN 0-7735-2286-7 (cloth)

Legal deposit first quarter 2002
Bibliothèque nationale du Québec

Printed in Canada on acid-free paper

This book has been published with the help of a grant
from the Humanities and Social Sciences Federation of
Canada, using funds provided by the Social Sciences and
Humanities Research Council of Canada.

McGill-Queen's University Press acknowledges the
financial support of the Government of Canada through
the Book Publishing Industry Development Program
(BPIDP) for its publishing activities. We also
acknowledge the support of the Canada Council for the
Arts for our publishing program.

Canadian Cataloguing in Publication Data

Brown, Douglas M. (Douglas Mitchell), 1954–
   Market rules: economic union reform and
   intergovernmental policy-making in Australia and
   Canada
   Includes bibliographical references and index.
   ISBN 0-7735-2286-7 (bnd)
   1. Interprovincial commerce – Canada. 2. Interstate
   commerce – Australia. 3. Federal government – Canada.
   4. Federal government – Australia. 5. Canada –
   Commercial policy. 6. Australia – Commercial policy.
   I. Title
   HD87.B76 2002   381'.5'0971   C2002-903247-1

Packaged for McGill-Queen's University Press by
Focus Strategic Communications Incorporated.
This book was typeset in 10/13 Baskerville.

Contents

Tables, Diagram, and Appendices

Abbreviations

ABS   Australian Bureau of Statistics
ACC   Australian Constitutional Convention
ACCC   Australian Competition and Consumer Commission
ACT   Australian Capital Territory
ACTU   Australian Council of Trade Unions
ACOSS   Australian Council of Social Services
AIT   Agreement on Internal Trade
ALP   Australian Labor Party
ANTA   Australian National Training Authority
ANZUS   Australia-New Zealand-United States Security Treaty
APEC   Asia-Pacific Economic Cooperation
BCA   Business Council of Australia
BCNI   Business Council on National Issues
BNA   British North America
CCC   Canadian Chamber of Commerce
CEC   Commission of the European Communities
CICS   Canadian Intergovernmental Conference Secretariat
CMA   Canadian Manufacturers Association
COAG   Council of Australian Governments
CMIT   Committee of Ministers on Internal Trade
EC   European Community
ECC   Economic Council of Canada
EPAC   Economic Planning Advisory Council
EMU   European Monetary Union
EU   European Union
FAG   Financial Assistance Grant
FMC   First Ministers Conference
FSRC   Federal-State Relations Committee [Parliament of Victoria]
FTA   [Canada-United States] Free Trade Agreement
GATS   General Agreement on Trade in Services
GATT   General Agreement on Trade and Tariffs

GBE	Government Business Enterprises
GDP	Gross Domestic Product
GST	Goods and Services Tax
IAC	Industry Assistance Commission
IC	Industry Commission
IPE	International Political Economy
ITS	Internal Trade Secretariat
JCPC	Judicial Committee of the Privy Council
MASH	Municipalities, Academic, Social, and Health Services
MC	Ministerial Council
NAFTA	North American Free Trade Agreement
NATO	North Atlantic Treaty Organization
NCC	National Competition Council
NCP	National Competition Policy
NDP	New Democratic Party
NEP	National Energy Policy
NEPC	National Environment Protection Council
NFA	National Food Authority
NIC	Newly Industrialized Country
NORAD	North American Aerospace Defence Command
NRTC	National Road Transportation Commission
NSW	New South Wales
OEC	Ontario Economic Council
OECD	Organization for Economic Cooperation and Development
PC	Productivity Commission
PQ	Parti Québécois
SPC	Special Premiers Conference
SPP	Specific Purpose Payment
SUFA	Social Union Framework Agreement
WA	Western Australia
WALA	Western Australia Legislative Assembly
WTO	World Trade Organization

Preface

This book examines the capacity of federal systems to adapt to changing conditions of governance in an era of globalization. It focuses on recent attempts by two older federations, Canada and Australia, to reform their "economic unions." Reform in both cases required collaboration among governments but had the potential to erode federal values such as diversity and flexibility.

Economic union is a regime of market rules embodying specific norms and institutions. The norms encompass economic and social values and objectives, such as degrees of liberalization, efficiency, and equity. The institutions include constitutional provisions and law-making and regulatory processes. Although they were part of the original rationale for creating the Canadian and Australian federations, these regimes came to be taken for granted. They were unable to deal with economic integration beyond their borders and contained equity and regional diversity arrangements that were unsustainable with increased international liberalization. Reform movements sought new market rules to increase economic competitiveness. The European Union's single market reforms, achieved through intergovernmental co-decision, became a prominent international benchmark for reform advocates.

In the first part of this book, I introduce a set of concepts to analyse the politics of institutional change in this comparative study. These include economic integration and liberalization as the specific forms of globalization, situating Australia and Canada within the international political economy with important consequences for reform strategy, outlining major differences in the federal design and historic development of the two federations, and the role and type of intergovernmental relations in federal systems generally and the two cases.

In the second part, I analyse the process and substance of reform. From 1979 to 1999, Canadian governments made several attempts at reform. They achieved only limited success through constitutional amendment but much more success through international trade agreements and the domestic Agreement on Internal Trade. In the process, they tackled comprehensively the barriers to a fragmented Canadian market. Yet weak institutional structures and significant exceptions to the new market rules reduce the effectiveness of the reforms.

Australian governments tackled economic union reform as part of a broad microeconomic agenda, mainly in 1990–95. Through diverse intergovernmental arrangements, Australians introduced powerful new principles affecting the whole economy, dealing with almost all of the barriers identified. Both federal states now have reformed economic unions that are more integrated than the European Union. However, the reform served to entrench neo-liberal values, restricting the room of all governments to intervene in their economies in the future.

These case studies, supplemented by recent European experience, also illustrate the emerging requirements for effective intergovernmental policy-making. These include the selective use of majority decision rules, improved enforcement of intergovernmental undertakings, non-centralized methods of regulatory harmonization, and formal institutions for national consensus building. Australia has surpassed Canada in meeting these requirements, but the will to collaborate within Australia has been wavering. Canada continues to avoid formalized relations and joint institutions capable of enforcing intergovernmental policy due to unresolved tensions in the federal society and concern about centralization and uniformity. In neither case do the new market rules upset the federal balance unduly, although this is more certainly the case in Canada. Both federations demonstrate a capacity to deal with complex policy-making in a context of multi-level governance, a strong comparative advantage in an age of globalization.

I have incurred many debts in the preparation of this work. Through interviews with seventy public servants and other experts in Australia and Canada, I gained an essential understanding of the policy-making process and its outcomes. Most of these interviewees must remain confidential, but their affiliation is listed in Appendix 2. Thanks also to many of these officials for providing me with key documents.

For other documentary information in Australia, I am grateful to Professor Cheryl Saunders and the staff of the Centre for Comparative Constitutional Studies at the University of Melbourne. I was also assisted by librarians at the Baillieu Library and Law Library of the University of Melbourne, the library of the Productivity Council of Australia in

Collins Street in Melbourne (thanks to Ann St. John), the Parliament of Victoria, and the staff of the former Federalism Research Centre at the Australian National University in Canberra. In Canada, the Stauffer Library and Law Library at Queen's University have been helpful, and the reading room of the Institute of Intergovernmental Relations at Queen's University has been an indispensable source of material.

Many academic and other colleagues have provided advice, listened to my arguments, read drafts, and provided leads to research. These include, in Australia: Brian Head, Glynn Davis, John Wanna, Ken Wiltshire, Ralph Mathews, Marcus Haward, Stephen Bell, Martin Painter, Hugh Collins, John Rimmer, and Lilian Topic. In Canada: David Cameron, Peter Russell, Ronald Watts, Robert Wolfe, Tom Courchene, Guy Laforest, David Schneiderman, Richard Simeon, and Robert Young. Bruce Doern kindly sent me an advance copy of his book, *Free-Trade Federalism*. I also had the benefit of comments on presentations of my work at the Department of Political Science, University of Melbourne; the Centre for Public Policy, University of Melbourne; the Australian Public Policy Network; the Federal-State Relations Committee of the Parliament of Victoria; the Department of Government at the University of Sydney; the School of Policy Studies, Queen's University; the Internal Trade Secretariat, Winnipeg; and Human Resources Development Canada in Ottawa.

I also owe a great debt to two institutional homes. The Centre of Public Policy at the University of Melbourne, directed by Brian Galligan, provided a welcoming base in Australia and access to public policy debate and expertise. He and Professor Cheryl Saunders of the Faculty of Law supervised my original dissertation and opened many doors for me. I would also like to acknowledge the assistance of Ellen Browne and Kate Robb. In Canada, I am grateful to Dr. Harvey Lazar, director of the Institute of Intergovernmental Relations at Queen's University for enabling me to continue in a supporting role as fellow at the Institute. Thanks also to Patti Candido, Mary Kennedy, Tom McIntosh, and John McLean. In an association that reaches back to 1978, I owe much of my understanding of federalism to former and current colleagues at the Institute and School of Policy Studies at Queen's, including Richard Simeon, Peter Leslie, Ronald Watts, Tom Courchene, Robin Boadway, Bill Lederman, Keith Banting, and Harvey Lazar.

Research for this work began as a doctoral dissertation, made possible in part by the financial support of the Social Sciences and

Humanities Research Council of Canada. I also wish to acknowledge the support of the Federal-State Relations Committee of the Parliament of Victoria (chair Honourable Michael John) – now regrettably discontinued – for a consulting contract that enabled me to complete a preliminary survey of Australian developments.

Finally, I thank my family for their continuing support. Richard and Julia Warren have been especially encouraging. To Daphne, Neil, and Norah: thanks for sharing my adventure in Australia. I could not have done it without your love and tolerance.

1 Federalism, Globalization, and Economic Policy-Making

INTRODUCTION

In the design and operation of states, a new age of federalism has arrived. States with long-standing federal systems are rediscovering the virtue of their federal arrangements, and new regional groups of states, such as the European Union, are also adopting principles of federalism. The reason for this renewed interest in federalism lies in the changed circumstances of governance at the end of the twentieth century – in a word, globalization. The global linking of economies, the intense interdependence of states, and the internationalization of policy are all characteristics of the era of globalization. Contemporary federalism is about managing interdependence and adapting to change with diversity and multi-level governance. This book explores the connections between federalism and globalization.

Federal government entails the sharing of sovereignty between the general and constituent governments of the federation. Policy outcomes are constrained by federal constitutions but are also mediated by the democratic and legal process. An important part of that process is a system of intergovernmental relations that responds to the need for flexible adaptation to changing conditions of governance. According to traditional theory, federalism offers a clear and comprehensive division of responsibility between orders of government,[1] but in revisionist theory and the practice in most federal countries, federal government is a competitive creature with considerable blurring of responsibilities and policy conflict.[2]

Federal government has not always been perceived to be flexible to changing needs. Earlier, during the Great Depression, dramatic changes in the conditions of governance challenged federal systems. Critics thought that federalism was obsolete in the drive to a more progressive and modern nation-state.[3] However, federal states rose to the challenge and constructed effective welfare states. Now, at the beginning of the twenty-first century, one may ask whether federal systems are once again capable of reform – of undertaking the reconstruction of the welfare state.

My argument is that even older federations (this work examines two of the oldest – Canada and Australia) are capable of responding to the changing requirements of interdependence and globalization. In making this argument, I address three major issues. The first is in the nature of the new challenge to federal systems. One of the more pressing public policy issues facing all nation-states, federal or not, has been how to respond to economic globalization, which, in specific terms, means that governments must respond to intensifying international economic integration and increasing economic liberalization. Integration draws national economies into larger, supranational regional and global markets. Liberalization constrains what governments can do to those markets. It both responds and contributes to integration. The key policy challenge of nation-state government is the task of adjusting the national economy to these new global conditions. In federal systems, all orders of government are engaged in this task.

A second major issue arises from the economic adjustment of the "national" economies in federations. Creating and sustaining a single market out of what are typically several pre-existing markets is one of the formative responsibilities of most new federations. But intensified economic integration beyond the boundaries of national economies – such as occurs with globalization – challenges the integrity of such economic unions and their markets. Thus, in federal systems, policy-making in response to globalization will inevitably include policy over the terms of the domestic economic union itself. Reform of the economic union is a task involving the very identity and balance of the federal union. Here, I examine the specific ways in which increasing international economic liberalization and international integration (since the early 1980s) have challenged the economic unions of federations – taking the cases of Australia and Canada – and generated an agenda for reform among policy-makers. In doing so, I conclude that the reform of the economic union – in effect the creation of a new set of market rules – is a prerequisite of successful economic adjustment.

The third major issue, then, is how federal states reform their economic unions. Historically, the chief ways have been unilateral central

government legislation, constitutional amendment, or judicial interpretation. However, for reasons outlined below, I argue that reform is
now most effectively done collectively by the governments of the federation through intergovernmental relations. The institutions and
processes of intergovernmental relations exist in federal systems to deal
with tasks that cannot be done by one government alone or, at the least,
to improve the collective decision making of each constituent government. Indeed, they reflect the reality that policy and policy-making are
as much concurrent as divided. The process and the outcome of policy-
making in federations must be done jointly for those many policy tasks
that cannot be neatly packaged and delineated. For many states, centralized decision making and a single set of economic rules might make
regulation of the market simpler and easier. But the results would be
too restrictive and counterproductive in cases where there is a diverse
regionalized economy and in the presence of decentralization to the
market more broadly conceived. In federal polities in which the decision-making process is inherently diversified and divided, a centralized
effort would be doomed to fail.

Thus, for reasons of policy effectiveness and political feasibility, economic adjustment policy, including reform of the economic union,
becomes a joint task in federal systems. Yet if it is a joint undertaking,
can it be done well, and how? Answering this question depends on
whether the processes of intergovernmental relations are capable of
joint policy-making. If they are not, a weak economic union may result,
which can contribute to economic adjustment problems.

In the literature on federal systems, there is a debate about where
intergovernmental relations can or should fit on a spectrum between
competition and co-operation. Intergovernmental coordination can be
loose or tight, and the appropriateness of competition or co-operation
can vary among policy fields. The design and operation of individual
federal systems prefigures the departure point on the competition–co-
operation spectrum, although in practice, governments have a degree of
strategic choice in the kind of relations they pursue. Until now, federal
systems have thrived by retaining this overall flexibility and diversity.

My goal in this book is to test the capabilities of intergovernmental
relations as practised in two federal states. By analysing the results of
recent intergovernmental relations in Australia and Canada, I conclude
that reform of economic unions depends on the capacity of intergovernmental relations to deliver jointly determined policy outcomes. My

work is, in essence, a process of discovery of what constitutes effective co-decision in the context of economic union reform. Federal theory suggests that it would be a process in which governments retain their independence and their flexibility. Economic integration theory suggests that to be effective, market rules must be comprehensive and uniform. Therefore, in this book, I explore: (1) the prerequisites for effective co-decision in a joint policy field; and (2) the nature of new market rules that result from such co-decision.

Before proceeding, a brief incursion to situate this analysis for the reader is warranted. This work is mainly about federalism as a form of state organization and its ability to respond to the globalizing economy with coherent policy results. It makes empirical generalizations about how the institutional structures of federalism shape certain types of economic policy outcomes. These institutions shape policy by structuring and restructuring the policy process itself and by working through the policy process in individual cases. Thus, my level of analysis is not about power systems as such, but about the structural use of power and its situational circumstances.

My paradigm is institutional or, more precisely, neo-institutional. I do not explain at length societal factors impinging upon institutions (such as globalization and other economic trends) nor the motivations and actions of individual players or groups within institutional settings (let alone voters, consumers, citizens, etc.). Yet I question the assumptions underlying dominant ideology within institutions and identify important analytical perspectives outside the institutional domain. Nonetheless, my approach is not primarily society-centred.[4] I view the state as autonomous from society, although clearly not disinterested.[5]

In this respect, my analysis will employ several analytical tools used by political scientists to demonstrate and explain state-society relations. The first of these is the issue of state capacity in order to understand the differing approaches of states to economic policy and to explain policy outcomes. Drawing on the Weberian concept of a strong state, several studies have undertaken comparative analyses of advanced democratic polities within a strong state/weak state framework.[6] These studies have found institutional features encouraging a strong pattern of state economic intervention (e.g., France, Sweden, and Japan) and features reinforcing a weak pattern of intervention (e.g., Britain, USA, Italy). This literature is significant for my work because it stresses the role that institutions play in mediating between societal forces (e.g., the global economy) and policy outcomes. Factors affecting state capacity include relative degrees of state fragmentation, such as federal forms of government.

A second analytical concept is the breadth of institutions as such. Here, institutions include not only official bureaus as such, but a broader universe of structures, all of which employ rules and bounded behaviour to some aspect of the state-society relationship. Of special importance to a study of economic policy is the idea that markets themselves are institutions. "Like public agencies, markets exist only within a certain organizational framework, and variation in that framework can profoundly affect their operation."[7] This is, of course, an old idea, going back to the political economy approach of Adam Smith. But it is one with great relevance to the current effort in many states to refashion the institutional structure of markets, employing ideology and interests not dissimilar to the liberal project of the nineteenth century.[8] As will be made clear, the "institution" of economic union in federal states is key to the market rules prevailing in these states and thus an important variable in this analysis.

A third analytical tool arises from the public choice approach, which views institutions in essentially pluralist terms. Employing the paradigms and methods of economics to political institutions and processes, this school takes rationality as the key assumption and, in general, deals with political preferences as given. Public choice perspectives have been enormously influential in applying market metaphors to the behaviour of individuals and groups within institutions – and to institutional rules and structures themselves. Within the public choice framework is an important theory of federalism and intergovernmental relations, applying principles of market-like competition, which will be examined more closely in this book.

Finally, a fourth analytical concept employed here is the significance of moments of institutional change in laying bare interests and power relations in a context in which "outcomes not only reflect but magnify and reinforce the interests of winners, since broad policy trajectories can follow from institutional choices."[9] In this respect, theorists Kathleen Thelen and Sven Steinmo outline three sources of institutional dynamism:

1 changes in the socio-economic context producing a situation in which previously latent institutions suddenly become salient

2 changes in socio-economic or political balance of power producing a situation in which old institutions are put in service of new ends

3 changes that produce a shift in the goals or strategies being pursued within existing institutions

As will be shown in the analysis that follows, all three of these forms of dynamism are present in the changes wrought to the institutions of economic union in contemporary federal states.

In working through these issues of state-society dynamics, one must keep in mind that the underlying political and policy concerns that consciously or unconsciously underpin any given theoretical position do change, often dramatically so, even within a decade. In this respect, any combination of theory and application is going to be bound to the preoccupations of the times – in the way that generals are said to be always fighting the last war. For example, it may be that the neo-institutionalists' offensive against society-centred approaches had already become obsolete by the 1980s. The preoccupation of the 1980s and early 1990s was not about social change or the ability (or not) of the state to respond to social stimuli (as it arguably was in the 1960s and 1970s). Rather, the preoccupation in much of the literature of the 1990s has been with the overreach of the state, with its fiscal crisis and its all-pervasive role in social and economic fields. As early as the 1960s, theorists in the public choice school stressed the perverse capture of the state by social interests.[10] In Canada, Alan Cairns, in a much-cited essay published in 1986, argued that "the traditional state-society dichotomy misleads, for it postulates a separateness that no longer exists."[11] He found in Canada and elsewhere a politicized society and an embedded state "caught in webs" of interaction. This embedding has prevented the state from taking a leadership role, bound by inherited decisions, trapped in the grooves of overused pathways. And to the then still very current theoretical concept of the autonomy of the state, Cairns countered that "the overriding reality ... is not state autonomy, but interdependence."[12]

As one commentary on the Cairns thesis suggests, the state must recover the boundaries of mediation.[13] Ten years on, the evidence of that recovery is all around us as the state redefines its relationship to society, particularly the global trend to reshaping the welfare state and liberalization of the economy. Cairns is still right about the interdependence of state and society, even if the state is now less embedded than before. Indeed, there may even be said to be a major political project pursued in most advanced capitalist states of a fundamental attempt at "disembedding." The leadership role assumed by the state is, in turn, redefining what is meant by the "strong" state. The direction and substance of these changes provide further grist for both society-centred and state-centred mills.

To conclude, my approach is primarily institutional. The focus will be on the ability of a specific set of institutions (federations, more specifically Australia and Canada as federal systems) to respond to a specific set of social forces (adjustment to economic globalization, more specifically integration and liberalization). Discussed below, Australia and Canada are chosen for comparison because they share similar colonial backgrounds, parliamentary institutions, and federal constitutions that were designed in the nineteenth century. The national economies of the two federations are now greatly exposed to economic globalization but in different regional circumstances. There are also significant institutional differences in the two federal systems.

In working out the comparative analysis of the two cases, I take the economic forces as largely given (i.e., exogenous variables), but I do not ignore the important influence that institutions have on the international and national economies. As noted, markets themselves are institutional structures. A main theme of this book is the ability of political agents, acting through one set of institutions – federal states and their processes of intergovernmental relations – to reform another set of political institutions – the economic unions of their federations.

RESEARCH METHODOLOGY

The following form a nested set of hypotheses tested in this work:

1 Increasing international economic integration and market liberalization forces economic adjustment on nation-states.
2 The process of economic adjustment in federal states requires the reform of their economic unions.
3 Reform of the economic union is most effectively achieved by intergovernmental policy process.
4 Intergovernmental policy process is capable of meeting the needs of economic reform where it can deliver jointly determined policy outcomes without compromising federal values.

I test these hypotheses by examining the recent experiences of two federal states: Australia and Canada. I explore in detail the intergovernmental policy-making process and the policy content of economic union reform. In broader strokes, I provide comparative assessments of constitutional design and evolution, the general political economy of federal-state (provincial) relations, and elements of the regional political economy. Background will also be provided on the place of the two national economies in their international settings.

This book thus belongs roughly in a literature on policy-making in federal systems. Nonetheless, the difficulty in making generalizations about federal systems has been well recognized. Indeed, Rufus Davis's frustrated attempt to find common threads in comparative federal studies led him to the subtitle: *A Journey through Time in Quest of a Meaning*.[14] His conclusions were pessimistic: federal systems cannot be easily reduced to common characteristics because each is a product of its founding and embedded within other institutional features and systems. This is especially so where theorists see federal institutions as basically reflective of unique federal societies.[15] Even the most resilient of state-centric theorists would have to recognize the importance of territorial polities tailored to the specifics of their time and space. Taken as a whole, each federal system is *sui generis*. As Ronald Watts puts it: "There is no single pure model of federalism that is applicable everywhere. Rather, the basic notion of involving the combination of shared rule for some purposes and self-rule for others within a single political system so that neither is subordinate to the other has been applied in different ways to fit different circumstances. Federations have varied and continue to vary."[16]

Comparative federal studies often run aground when focused too strongly on definitional issues or analysis of systems as a whole. Rather, as Bakvis and Chandler note, a more focused comparison on common operational practices and/or differing approaches to similar or common policy problems faced by federal polities is likely to produce more fruitful results.[17] This study accepts that advice in concentrating on relatively similar institutions within two federal systems and on a common set of policy problems.

Australia and Canada make a useful comparative set for a number of reasons, which may be summarized by reference to the strategies of "most similar" and "most different" in comparative inquiry.[18] On the most similar scale, the two states share many common aspects of political development and institutions: the history of British colonial development and a heritage of British parliamentary institutions, including the role of the Crown; responsible cabinet-style government; the Whitehall-type public service; and strong party discipline. They also have some aspects of social and economic development that are similar if perhaps only superficially: large continental-size territories with highly urbanized populations concentrated in very small parts of the territory; significant aboriginal populations; increasingly multicultural populations due to immigration; a regionally differentiated economy; and a sophisticated service-oriented industrial economy still strongly influenced by resource exports (for more detail on economic comparisons, see chapter 2). On the most different scale, there is the linguistic if not cultural homogeneity of Australia compared with the bicultural and bilingual composition of Canadian society, and the geographic proximity and dominance of the United States in economic and cultural life in Canada compared with the relative isolation (if increasing Asian orientation) of Australia. Another important difference is the climactic differences between the frozen northland and the subtropical antipodes, with effects on economic, social, and cultural life that are difficult to summarize but nonetheless real.

Comparative political inquiry that focuses on features other than federalism might count federalism itself as another element of "most similar" points of comparison between Australia and Canada. And, indeed, both countries have in common a federation and a federal political culture; their federal institutions are fused with similar parliamentary institutions; and they encompass unions of a relatively small number of constituent units (compared, for example, with the United States or India). Also, as I discuss more fully in chapter 4, both have an economic union at the heart of the initial rationale for union. But apparent similarities can conceal surprises. Key differences in the two federal systems and how they are adapting to change is the focus of this work. Thus, I examine the consequences of such differences as: the constitutional provisions for interstate trade (generally stronger in Australia); the form of allocation of legislative powers (concurrent in Australia, exclusive in Canada); the relative degrees of fiscal autonomy of the constituent governments (stronger in Canada); and, most crucially, the development and nature of intergovernmental flexibility (arguably more advanced in Australia).

The interplay of similarities and differences will be a leitmotif throughout the chapters that follow. As will become clear, the focal point of my comparative analysis will be the policy-making process for the reform of economic unions through intergovernmental agreement. Yet framing that specific case study requires considerable background on the points of convergence and divergence. In summary, three basic converging characteristics are important to my findings. First, both countries are medium-size, open economies faced with the challenge of economic adjustment to the global economic integration and liberalization. Second, both are federal states in which the policy tools of economic policy are divided among governments. Third, the task of reforming economic unions, in circumstances in which jurisdiction is concurrent, requires complex intergovernmental relations. The divergences are many and complicated, but it is in their detail that one may begin to see where general facts emerge, allowing one to make statements about the efficacy of federal government for economic policy-making in advanced industrial societies in an era of globalization.

The rest of this work is organized into two parts. The first part – chapters 2, 3, and 4 – provide the background to the economic policy field and the institutions of policy-making that are analysed here. Chapter 2 outlines more fully the specific challenges posed by international economic integration and market liberalization (globalization) to nation-states generally and federal systems more specifically. This entails a critical examination of the concept of globalization and its ideological usage. The discussion highlights the significance of recent European experience in integration, which has in the process redefined notions of integration, economic union, and federalism. The chapter ends by placing Australia and Canada within the international economy, stressing the differences in their exposure to international integration.

Chapter 3 introduces federal theory, dwelling on the role of intergovernmental relations to deal with adaptation in federal systems and with concurrent governance tasks. The chapter also discusses the concepts of economic adjustment and economic union in federal states and the connection between them. It stresses the significance of economic unions to the policy tasks of economic adjustment as well as the normative and institutional characteristics of federal economic unions.

Chapter 4 compares the "pre-reform" economic unions in Australia and Canada. I examine the historical design and development of the federations and their economic unions and the evolution and limitations of integration. The chapter provides an overview of the state of the economic union, about 1985, comparing Australia and Canada with the European Union. In this discussion, I provide an inventory of the remaining barriers to a single market in the two economic unions as a prelude to discussing the movement to reform. The chapter ends with a comparative analysis of the potential routes to reform, focusing on intergovernmental relations.

The second part of this book presents detailed empirical evidence of intergovernmental efforts to reform the economic union in Australia and Canada. Chapters 5 and 6 present a basic narrative of the reform process and outcomes in Canada, while chapters 7 and 8 do the same for Australia. This analytical narrative should contribute to a better understanding of an important set of recent intergovernmental relations in the two countries.

In Australia, the case begins in the mid-1980s, with debates over productivity and competitiveness in the national economy, leading to the push for microeconomic reform at the end of the decade. Australian governments used a specific intergovernmental process incorporating the Special Premiers Conferences (SPC) and subsequent meetings of the Council of Australian Governments (COAG) until 2000. I pay attention as much to reform of intergovernmental decision-making process as to substantive policy outcomes. In Canada, the debate over the internal economic union has been engaged over a somewhat longer time frame, beginning in 1979, with an unsuccessful attempt at constitutional reform to strengthen the economic union in 1980–82. The debate was taken up again in the mid-1980s as part of a broader issue of continental free trade and continued through another round of attempted constitutional reform in 1987–92. Finally, more direct intergovernmental efforts resulted in an Agreement on Internal Trade in 1994.

For the second half of this book, I have tapped two main sources of information as well as existing secondary commentaries. The first category of primary material is published and unpublished government documents providing evidence of the policy process and outcomes. This includes: major governmental and non-governmental studies; reports of commissions of inquiry, parliamentary committees, and quasi-independent public bodies; intergovernmental documents such as communiqués, policy papers, and agreements; federal and state/provincial legislation; and constitutional texts. Those documents cited directly are listed in the bibliography at the back of the book.

The second main source of primary information comes from approximately seventy interviews conducted by the author in Australia and Canada during 1997 and 1998. These were with key participants in the intergovernmental policy process at a variety of levels, including deputy ministers/secretary and assistant deputy minister/assistant or deputy secretary levels. While I was not able to interview politicians (it became too difficult to arrange), I did interview a cross-section of key advisors inside and outside of government, some retired, who played important roles in the more political side of the process in both countries. I made an attempt to get the perspective of at least two agencies within each government, usually the central agency of the Premier's or Cabinet Office as well as the treasury or the economic development ministry depending on where the chief policy participation for that government lay. Interviews with a cross-section of federal government officials were possible as well as most of the state and provincial governments, with some exceptions.[19]

The interviewees do not constitute any kind of scientific sample. They were chosen on the advice of key governmental participants and scholars and were persons who were occupying (or had occupied) major policy and advisory positions (including a few from leading academic and interest group institutions). The interviews lasted about an hour, often much longer, and followed a rough template of common questions tailored to the experience and position of the interviewee. There was no questionnaire as such, and all the interviews were off the record. As a whole, the interviews covered considerable ground, including such topics as: the rationale for reform; assessment of the federal system; specific reform objectives of governments; the nature of representations and pressures from social groups (including business); the intergovernmental negotiation process; and an assessment of the policy outcomes. Appendix 1 provides a general template of interview questions. Appendix 2 provides information on the interviewees' position, organization, and the date and place of interview.

The final portion of the book presents my conclusions through a sustained comparison of the two cases. It covers converging characteristics of process and political conditions that constitute successful intergovernmental reform. It summarizes the new market rules that resulted from the reforms in the two federations in comparison with the

European Union. And it draws conclusions about the significance of the developing (if differing) capacities for intergovernmental co-decision in Australia and Canada for the future of federalism. While the full measure of these findings must wait that chapter, a brief preview is warranted.

ઢ

My research shows that Australia has produced a more coherent and innovative set of reform processes. Many of the reforms will take a long time to take full effect, but the broad sweep of certain economic principles, such as those applied in the National Competition Policy (NCP), take Australia much further than Canadians have thus far dared to go. The mutual recognition of product standards and professional qualifications and the establishment of several new uniform regulatory schemes also constitute significant achievements. There has been an important trend toward co-decision through intergovernmental mechanisms – national results achieved through Commonwealth-state process.

This progress compares with Canada's strong reluctance to develop formally entrenched intergovernmental relations, given its more decentralized and less interlocked federal structure and its more divided federal society. There has also been the significantly complicating factor of Canada's attempted constitutional reform. Therefore, the outcomes of reform of the economic union as such have been not only more difficult to achieve in Canada, but also more watered down. This outcome will be illustrated in the negotiations leading to the 1992 Charlottetown Accord on constitutional amendments (which failed to obtain public consent in a referendum) and in the Agreement on Internal Trade (AIT) reached in 1994. While the terms of the AIT are more comprehensive than the reform outcomes in Australia, they do not appear to cut as deeply into existing patterns of government intervention. The language and structure of the AIT are strikingly similar to international trade liberalization agreements, including the reliance on mutually agreed dispute resolution processes. In any case, Canada continues to pursue more decentralized process and outcomes.

Still, my comparative assessment of reform outcomes finds substantially improved economic unions in both cases, more integrated in almost every respect than the current European Union. Moreover, reform is achieved as effectively by collaborative process and decentralized policy instruments as it is by centralized means and outcomes. In this respect, reform need not reduce federal flexibility and may indeed sustain it.

This comparative examination of recent attempts to reform the economic union in Australia and Canada feeds the final task: an assessment of the overall ability of each federal system to achieve reform. I conclude that a new paradigm of effective intergovernmental co-decision has emerged, evidenced by majority decision rules, enforceable commitments, non-centralized harmonization, and a collaborative notion of national policy-making. In my view, these conclusions would apply to most federal systems. If federal states do not adopt these new principles or do so only half-heartedly, they will be policy takers rather than policy shapers – weak states rather than strong ones. However, federal systems that adapt with this new paradigm of co-decision may more confidently meet the challenges of economic globalization.

2 Globalization, Liberalization, and Integration

The phenomenon of globalization discussed here is primarily economic and political. There are cultural and social aspects, but my focus is on the intensifying internationalization of the economy and the political structures that attempt to regulate it. Empirically, the phenomenon can be described as the increased degree of economic activity largely, but not exclusively, of private firms and individuals across national boundaries. This activity may be further described as:

1 increasing international trade in goods and services and increasing direct foreign investment
2 globally integrated production by transnational corporations and increased international networking and strategic alliances among firms
3 an explosion in international capital markets with transactions of greatly increased scope, speed, size, and fluidity
4 as a result of all of the above points, increased private sector competition for even the smallest of firms and markets[1]

This phenomenon, here simplified, arises from complex and contested causes. Technological advance in its broadest sense has been a factor in that it is now much easier to do business around the world due to the increasing diversity and lower costs of transportation and to the computation and telecommunication revolution. These technological factors in turn promote the increased trade and mobility of information as such, notably economic and financial information, enabling access for investors, entrepreneurs, and creditors to financial markets well beyond national borders. Now, many firms operate within a competitive environment in which they are freed from the constraints of the factor endowments of any one nation-state. Transnational corporations – not merely multinationals – pursue strategies for the research and development, finance, production, assembly, and marketing and distribution of goods and services, which can span several countries and regions if not the entire world.

Such generalizations can be taken too far, for the phenomenon of globalizing economic activity is highly differentiated by time and space. Some regions of the world, some countries, and even some regions within countries are more involved in this activity than others and often bear disproportionate benefits or costs. And even within the overall evidence of inevitable forward movement on a global scale, certain nation-states and regions have had a significant head start.

Even this thumbnail account is inadequate without noting the crucial role of political institutions in fostering and creating aspects of the new global reach of markets.[2] Thus, globalization is a political phenomenon as well as an economic one. The global market in which occur an ever-increasing number of transactions has been created and sustained by key political institutions. Following its dominant role in the victory of the Second World War, the United States and its allies led the way to create conditions for a restoration of international commerce – including such important institutions as the General Agreement on Tariffs and Trade (GATT) and the World Bank. At least within the reach of its hegemony (i.e., outside the state-controlled communist economies), "Pax Americana" and its institutions began a process that continued for the rest of the twentieth century. In some regions, such as Asia-Pacific, US hegemony has been declining, but the market-based economic system is as dominant as ever.[3]

For our purposes, the political aspect of globalization can be simplified into two related concepts. First is the movement to a greater degree of market *liberalization,* at all levels of political organization and economic regulation (i.e., national, subnational, and supranational). Second is the movement to intensify the *integration* of markets. (These terms will be further defined below.) International trade and capital liberalization agreements shape the growth of the world economy while, at the same time, removing national impediments to integration. In this respect, such institutional regimes are necessary multilateral responses to the forces of economic integration – shaping and regularizing what would otherwise occur in a more haphazard, but still relentless, fashion.

Yet globalization is not only an empirical phenomenon; it is also an ideological one. According to some critics, the "extreme globalization theorists" have pushed the concept as part of a new brand of economic determinism, tied integrally to their preference for "anti-political liberalism."[4] The extreme views have currency mainly among those on the right who see international liberalization as the basis for extended economic freedom at home as well as abroad, including an institutional bulwark against backsliding to state socialism. There is also the view of a shifting of economic sovereignty from states to consumers.[5] For those on the left, such views amount to ideological determinism – an attempt to assert capitalist hegemony on a global scale. However, to view political globalization as wholly a strategy of pursued class interests amounts to another form of determinism.

In sum, globalization is a useful and important concept, but two points of caution should be observed. First, there is the potential exaggeration of the empirical phenomenon: there may not really be a global economy, but rather an internationalizing economy still shaped crucially by leading national economies and national policy-makers. The differing paces and degrees of integration among markets for capital, labour, and goods and services are also significant, as are key differences among regional and national economies. (See, for example, the differential impact on Australia and Canada discussed later in this chapter.)

Second is the ideological thrust of the phenomenon and the extent to which it can be separated from the empirical evidence. Wherever possible, one should differentiate between the normative assertions of globalization theorists or advocates and the actual phenomena at hand. Also, two specific aspects of globalization are most relevant: intensifying international economic *integration* and the increasing scope and depth of international market *liberalization*. This book focuses on the institutional forms of both.

Wither the nation-state in this trend of globalization? There is, of course, a growing literature on the perforation and diminution of national sovereignty.[6] As Vincent Cable has written, globalization does not make the traditional nation-state redundant, but it has been eroding its power at a speed and intensity that differs according to the degree of exposure of individual nation-states to globalizing forces.[7] In this study, however, globalization will be treated as an important and, for the most part, independent variable. It is not assumed to be a single set of economic, social, or political conditions. But much of the analysis to follow is about how well federal state structures respond to the external challenges of globalization. And, to return to the discussion of state autonomy in the introduction, I hope to contribute to an assessment of the degree of which federal states in general, and Australia and Canada in particular, are strong or weak, as illustrated by their capacity to respond to the challenges of globalization.

ECONOMIC INTEGRATION AND LIBERALIZATION: INTRODUCTION AND GENERAL THEORY

Intensifying economic liberalization is the aspect of globalization that is seen most often as threatening of national sovereignty. The threat is universal: it affects federal nation-states as much as it does unitary ones. The degree of competition to which private actors are exposed hinges primarily on the degree of openness in the economy, in turn affected by the degree of liberalization within a national economy as well as with other national economies. In any case, it is argued, the ability of national governments to manage national economies is reduced. In this work, liberalization occurs within the context of integration. Liberalization is distinguishable from integration, even if often nested within an integration framework. It is not always easy to separate the effects of one from the other.

From our perspective, economic integration is an institutional phenomenon. It is a reshaping of the boundaries of economic activity by eliminating existing frontiers. Liberalization does not eliminate frontiers as such but attempts to make freer the markets within existing boundaries. Integration implies a more ambitious process, which, for purposes of the regulation of markets, transcends boundaries. To a point, liberalization can occur without integration and vice versa, but in both theory and practice, the two are intertwined. Integration is at least partly an exogenous variable, shaping the nature of ongoing liberalization within any national (or indeed subnational) economy. Discussed below, it is of some significance whether the institutions of integration shaping a national economy are global (e.g., the multilateral trade regime) or regional (e.g., a continental trade regime). Where a nation-state economy is integrated only on the more general international level, it has more room to undertake liberalization according to its own priorities and pace. Thus, when situating Australia and Canada within the world of liberalization and integration (see the last part of this chapter), Australia has more room to pursue its own path than does Canada, where the structure of internal integration is heavily influenced by the logic of its regional integration in North America.

Before pursuing the specifics of the Australian and Canadian cases, it is helpful to examine further the concept of integration. There are three reasons why it is important. First, as already noted, global and regional integration is a key external phenomenon to be examined. It is important to outline the significant aspects of integration and how it impinges generally and specifically on the two federal systems under review. Second, much of the literature on integration dwells upon the causes and effects of the most ambitious and influential exercise in political and economic integration: the evolution of the European Union. The EU is important to Australia and Canada as a trade and investment partner and as one of the most important regional powers in the current world economy. Even if the regional grasp of Europe does not extend fully to these two federations, they maintain important relations through bilateral and multilateral channels. More importantly, the European experience of integration, especially since 1985, has been an important influence in debates about federal types of governance and the economic union in Australia and Canada. Third, integration theory as such, largely but not only arising out of European experience, sheds light on the process and significance of integration as well as on the related concepts of interdependence and intergovernmental policy coordination (in turn, important concepts in the theory and practice of federal systems). The remainder of this chapter deals with each of these three aspects of integration, in reverse order. First is the general theory.

There are two branches of general theorizing about integration: one is rooted mainly in political science; the other, mainly in economics. Both have relevance here, but neither takes us much further than some useful concepts. The political theory of integration arose in Europe after the Second World War to deal primarily with the ongoing process of integration among Western European states. It was, as Peter Leslie puts it: "as much prescriptive and even strategic as it [was] analytical."[8] Despite valiant efforts to develop a general theory applicable to the integrative process universally, the focus of virtually all scholars was ultimately confined to the European case, reinforcing a conviction of *sui generis.* Among the various European camps of integration theorists were the federalists who, whether by philosophical first principles or by comparative and pragmatic application of existing models of federal government, promoted federal outcomes to European integration. Less ambitious goals were pursued by the functionalists and neo-functionalists who saw the European Community as evolving to meet sectoral or other broad functions, chiefly economic.[9]

This integration theory in political science is not particularly germane here, but its more universalist objectives have been absorbed into the literature on international relations, the international political economy, and interdependence (the newer literature on the European Community will be discussed below). The economists have focused more consistently on a generic notion of integration. Their concept is primarily on economic means and ends, although it is not without significance for politics. Thus, Jacques Pelkmans defines *economic* integration as "the elimination of economic frontiers between two or more economies." He stresses the notion of *market integration* as measurable economic behaviour in terms of the cross-border flows of trade and other factors, and, where goods or services are homogenous, price convergence. It is a concept rooted in neo-classical economics, drawing on the theory of the welfare effects of international trade and competition: "the fundamental significance of economic integration is in the increase of actual or potential competition."[10]

The economics literature on integration makes implied pluralist assumptions about what drives integration. In this view, integration is the handmaid of liberalization. This is not to suggest that the economists ignore institutions or the state, but rather that they see political integration as an essential part of economic integration, with intensity of liberalization being matched by intensity of institutional development. The literature employs a number of theoretical and descriptive typologies to underscore this point. Among these is the notion, generally drawn from historic practice, of integration proceeding through a series of stages.

For example, Bela Balassa employed a typology of stages in which economic integration proceeded from a free trade area through four more stages, each successively more advanced: customs union, common market, economic union, and (finally) total economic integration.[11] There have been variations on Balassa's theme and over time, some questioning of the usefulness of the stages theory. Also, different analysts use different terms in the context of different political and economic systems, so that one cannot assume that such terms as common market or economic union mean the same thing in every case. This is especially so when the terms enter political and everyday discourse beyond the academic discipline. For this reason, even though in this book I use the term economic union extensively, the term will be defined specifically to apply to federal states (see chapter 3).

There is a more fundamental blurring of distinctions, however. As Peter Leslie has recently argued, Balassa's typology has essentially outlived its usefulness. "The idea that there are successive stages of integration, that each of which provides a base upon which the participating states may decide to erect another story, must be jettisoned."[12] Historical events have moved past Balassa's 1961 formulations. The Canada-United States Free Trade Agreement (FTA), for example, incorporates not only Balassa's definition of a free trade area in goods, but provides a significant degree of liberalization in investment and services, reflecting the increasingly integrated nature of productive factors in the world economy. As described in table 2.1, Leslie goes on to outline a revised set of concepts under the general label of "aspects of economic union." (This typology will be applied in this work to compare degrees of economic integration in the European Union, Australia, and Canada.)

Without getting deeper into a discussion of typology, a few points are worth underscoring. First, despite the continuing revision of typologies, one should distinguish one aspect of economic integration from another and recognize that integration is as much a process as it is an end point. The typologies may be seen more usefully as marking characteristics of the process at any given point in time (and space). Second, and confusingly, popular and political discourses use the terms common market, free trade, economic union, and so on to describe not only points on an integration spectrum, but also as ideological rallying cries. Analysis should provide some rigour to the concepts used in political discourse but not at the risk of definitions that are entirely divorced from everyday discourse. Third, and related to the previous two, there is a distinct process of market liberalization and institutional formation that comes with each characteristic phase of integration. The important thing for our purposes is not to get caught up on the typology so much as to identify and analyse the markets and institutions that apply. This will be the task in the next chapter with respect to economic union in federal states.

A second important concept in the theory of economic integration is the classic dichotomy of *negative* and *positive* integration. Fritz Scharpf

Table 2.1 Leslie's Aspects of Economic Union

ASPECT	DEFINITION	CHARACTERISTICS/COMMENTS
TRADE AND INVESTMENT UNION	• Free or freer movement of goods, services, and capital among members; imposing discipline or harmonization on non-tariff barriers (e.g., subsidies).	• Often includes Common Competition Policy. • The new model for international trade agreements seeks deeper integration than GATT/WTO. • Usually found in confederal or federal polities.
LABOUR MARKET UNION	• Free movement of labour, possibly extended to all persons. • May provide for portability of social benefits and harmonized occupational and professional standards.	• In federal systems, usually takes the form of a constitutional guarantee of personal mobility. • Substantial room for diversity. • Relaxes or prohibits migration controls among members.
FOREIGN ECONOMIC POLICY UNION	• Includes a customs union but also a common policy on external non-tariff barriers. • Requires a single trade negotiating authority, increasing international influence.	• Can be a problem for some federal or confederal polities. • Would encompass all the issues negotiated in contemporary comprehensive agreements such as WTO.
MONETARY UNION	• Creation of a common currency or fixed parity among member currencies. • May provide for fiscal policy harmonization and common regulation of financial markets.	• Key component likely to be a central bank. • Practice in federal systems shows much diversity regarding extent of fiscal policy harmonization.
STRUCTURAL/ DEVELOPMENTAL UNION	• Joint action or policy on economic development. • Can include union-wide sectoral and regional policy; education and R & D.	• Creates strategic comparative advantage. • Leaves wide scope for central or decentralized program delivery.

Source: Leslie, 1998.

makes a distinction between negative and positive as "between measures increasing market integration by eliminating national restraints on trade and distortions of competition on the one hand [negative integration], and common ... policies to shape the conditions under which markets operate on the other [positive integration]."[13] To Scharpf's "national restraints," we would add subnational and regional. To varying degrees of completeness, negative integration provides for the free movement of goods, services, labour, and capital (the "four freedoms" in European parlance). The positive measures consist of the regulation of the economy and the provision of public infrastructure. They respond to the need to create a single market through active governmental intervention – especially in the developmental stages of economic integration.

As providing direct prohibitions against barriers to economic mobility, negative integration might simply be called "liberalization," whereas the positive integration seems to imply institutions broadly defined. But the negative/positive distinction is telling and useful. It resonates with conceptions of negative and positive rights and liberties. Moreover, it gets across the notion that the full creation of a free market involves the positive action of the state.

In his stages of integration theory, Balassa assumed that negative integration alone was needed to achieve the early stages, up to and including a common market. As Jacques Pelkmans points out, no stage of integration is without its positive elements. Each stage requires not only specific institutions of some sort (even if only dispute resolution mechanisms), but also a strong state generally in order to enforce the rules.[14] The distinction between negative and positive becomes heightened when the objectives of integration are in debate. The ideology of neo-liberalism may be blind to many forms of positive integration, while democratic ideology would stress the positive aspects of economic citizenship. At its crudest, this is the trade-off between efficiency and equity. As will be discussed in more detail below, in federal states, the trade-off between degrees of negative and positive integration becomes intertwined with the very essence of the federal bargain.

As Cheryl Saunders puts it, a definition of negative integration that precluded the role of regional (subnational) governments in shaping regional markets would "be a rejection of federalism itself."[15] At this stage, it is sufficient to flag the issue and note its significance not just for the theory of integration, but for the practical reform of economic integration in federal states. As I argue more fully below, different types of economic reform require more intensive forms of positive integration than others (e.g., competition policy compared with trade policy). The ability to deliver (or not) on requisite measures of positive integration will determine the shape of integration and liberalization achievable as a whole.

EUROPEAN EXPERIENCE

European integration has taken off since the mid-1980s and transformed not only the global economy, but also our understanding of integration and of international and supranational governance. In terms of economic liberalization, the achievement of a single market (with some qualification) has been unprecedented in its scope and scale among advanced industrial economies. European Union[16] institutions of integration have redefined the nature of federal governance, breathing life into previously moribund forms of confederal government,[17] indeed redefining the typology of federalism in the process. Of particular interest is the evolution of the European Community's method of decision making and the substance of the liberalization of the EU's internal market, a process launched in 1985. Both have galvanized the reform exercises in Australia and Canada. The European experience is also important for what can be said about the evolving nature of intergovernmental relations and institutional formation in an integration context. Lessons from this experience, with appropriate adjustment for the context, can be applied to intergovernmental relations in old-style federal systems.

It is important to stress that the relaunch of the integration project in Europe in the 1980s responded to a demand for the creation of a single market to enable the member states of the European Community to compete with its main trading partners, the United States and Japan, as well as the rising competition from newly industrialized economies. It coincided, in the wake of the early 1980s recession, with a revival of international economic liberalization. There were other concerns such as east-west security, democratization in southern Europe, and, later into the 1990s, the unification of Germany and political integration of Eastern Europe, but most analysts would agree (even if much is assumed) that economic liberalization drove the process in the 1980s. Peter Leslie provides a succinct summary of this background:

The Community was relaunched in the mid-1980s after a period of "Europessimism" during which non-tariff barriers multiplied. The relaunch occurred in large measure because competition from Japan and the United States demanded it. A more fully integrated Community would be a stronger competitor in a globalized economy. Thus, external economic pressures reinforced domestic pressures for deregulation and the extension of markets, leading to the dismantling of economic barriers among member-states. To achieve this goal, common policies in several areas were required, as were new limitations on the policy-making capacity of each of the new member-states. The steps that were proposed (and mostly implemented) were described as the Europe 1992 or Single Market program. Its aim was to create "a market without internal frontiers," dismantling all border controls among member states by January 1, 1993. To facilitate the reforms, institutional changes ... were made through a set of treaty revisions known as the Single European Act negotiated in 1985 and ratified in 1986.[18]

Thus, after 1985, the European Community sought more intensive liberalization because the removal of tariffs and quantitative restrictions in the 1950s and 1960s had not been sufficient. A diverse community of twelve members with significant disparities in productivity and income could remove such non-tariff barriers – and take the important symbolic step of actually closing frontier posts – only if it moved past the unanimity rules of community decision making. Thus, the *Single European Act* broadened significantly the scope for the use of qualified majority voting by which the Council of Ministers could approve a measure that would be binding on all member states.[19] This enabled the community to adopt about 300 new directives specifying the internal market reforms.

The resulting form of integration has had very far-reaching consequences. According to Loukas Tsoukalis, the European process confirms a model of ever-widening scope of economic integration from goods to services and capital, from economic to social policy. The "process can be viewed as a series of dynamic disequilibria which create the conditions and pressures for further extension and deepening."[20] The result has been a significant weakening of the influence of the member-states and, in particular, the nature of their national economic adaptation to the global economy. Tsoukalis cites a common aphorism: no more the possibility of Keynes at home and (Adam) Smith abroad. The spectrum within which national economic adaptation could vary –

from Sweden to Switzerland, from Denmark to Britain, from Germany to France – has shrunk dramatically. The competitive pressures have swept away much political and social differentiation. As Peter Leslie has noted, the *Single European Act* and the 1992 program "have given powerful impetus to the spread of neo-liberal ideology and practice," reflected not only in the specifics of internal market reform, but also in fiscal and social policy.[21]

The specific causes and effects of how and why European economic interests and governments sought and confirmed their newly liberal approach to economic management is well beyond the scope of this book. Yet it is important to underscore the role of changing perceptions of international competition and of neo-liberal ideas on the European experience as they have been so influential to the general concepts of liberalization, freer trade, integration, and microeconomic reform that have informed the reform efforts in Australia and Canada.

As noted, two aspects of the European experience have special relevance for our examination of the reform of federal economic unions. These are the community method of decision making and the substance of internal market reforms. Four key evolving institutions have shaped the EU to 1992 and beyond: the Council of Ministers, the European Commission, the European Parliament, and the Court of Justice. The Council of Ministers is the chief legislative body and represents each member-state equally, although it has a variety of decision-making rules, including qualified majority voting. The European Commission is the administrative arm of the EU and is appointed by the council; its role also is to propose legislation (directives) in areas of union competence, to execute council decisions, to be the legal guardian of the treaties, and to represent the EU externally. The European Parliament comprises directly elected members who share legislative power with the council. The Court of Justice is the final appeal for EC law and can mandate changes to member-state law.

Without getting into further detail, it is important to underscore a few points about the "federal" nature of these institutions, especially as they compare with the structure of federations such as Australia and Canada. The institutions are *confederal* in that by treaty, the member-states delegate competencies to the commission; yet it is more typically *federal* in the direct election of the European Parliament. However, the parliament must share the legislative function with the Council of

Ministers. Also, the parliament has no taxation powers. The Court of Justice plays a role similar to high courts in federal systems in having the final and binding appeal over jurisdictional disputes, but its purview does not extend to member-states' national law not covered by the union treaties. Nonetheless, its judgments, as well as the operating principle of *"acquis communitaire,"* perform a strongly integrative function.[22] The role of the commission is particularly unique in that it is not typical of the executive branch in parliamentary or presidential democracies but fulfills many functions of a permanent central civil service. And yet it relies greatly on the member-states to undertake its legislative program and indeed runs only a few programs directly. This limited role is reflected in the budget of the union that, as a whole, is still less than 1.5 per cent of union gross domestic product. Another important potential restraint on centralization in the union is the adoption of the principle of subsidiarity in which the union institutions are to take a minimalist approach to the exercise of its competencies, leaving as much room and discretion as possible to the member-states. In sum, the European Union is a new and very effective hybrid of federal-type government, but one in which the heavy hand of the state relies much more on the force of law than the power of the purse, an important consideration in a neo-liberal era.

The European institutions have gradually evolved to perform functions, which in more consciously initiated federations are assigned to the federal government from the outset. The genius of the union, especially since 1985, has been in reinventing intergovernmental relations as a more effective decision-making tool. In particular, the qualified majority voting has enabled the Council of Ministers to move beyond the stalemate of unanimity to reach decisions that do not have the consent of all but are binding on all. As noted, the confirmation of this feature in the *Single European Act* of 1986 broke the log-jam and made possible the relatively rapid passage of 300 directives to reform the internal market (see table 2.2). This issue of decision rules in intergovernmental relations is important, and I will return to it in the next chapter. But here, it is also important to note that from the perspective of federal theory, necessity has been the mother of invention. The union adopted these decision rules (which can still be very cumbersome compared with the bare majority decision rules of most parliaments) because it has no federal government as such. Europe may not want a federal government, but this begs the

Table 2.2 European Union Internal Market Reforms

A. PRODUCT MARKET INTEGRATION

Factor	Dismantled barriers (negative integration)	Common policies or approximation (positive integration)
Market Access		
• Tariffs.	• Abolished intra-EC.	• Common external tariff.
• Quotas.	• Abolished intra-EC.	• Selective national quotas remain.
• Voluntary export restraints.	• Prohibited intra-EC.	• None.
• Measures equivalent to quotas (regulations).	• Prohibited.	• Minimal approximation and mutual recognition.
• Indirect taxes and excises.	• Some abolition; tax frontiers remain.	• Value-added taxes on a single base.
Competitive Conditions		
• Industrial subsidies.	• Prohibited with major exceptions.	• Commission/court surveillance.
• Public procurement.	• Formal prohibition of discrimination.	• Major harmonization of procedures, broad scope.
• State monopolies.	• Prohibition of discrimination.	• n/a
• Competition policy.	• n/a	• Common policy extends to restrictive practice, abuse of dominant position, and regulation of mergers.
Market Functioning		
• Legal conditions.	• n/a	• Harmonization or unification of standards.

B. SERVICES, CAPITAL, AND LABOUR INTEGRATION

Services	• General free movement provisions for temporary service provision (with major derogations). • Right of establishment for permanent service provision (with major derogations).	• Separate treaty regimes for transport (Common Transport Policy), resulting in mostly complete liberalization except in air transport. • Financial services, only now being liberalized as monetary union approached. • Telecom and postal services required separation of regulatory and service provision; liberalization proceeding on telecoms.

Table 2.2 European Union Internal Market Reforms *(Continued)*

FACTOR	DISMANTLED BARRIERS (NEGATIVE INTEGRATION)	COMMON POLICIES OR APPROXIMATION (POSITIVE INTEGRATION)
CAPITAL	• Most restrictions removed in lead-up to European Monetary Union (for those who take part).	
LABOUR *Note:* "natural barriers" such as language, customs, and geography continue to keep labour mobility limited beyond national borders.	• National treatment afforded to migrant workers.	• Mutual recognition process under way for occupational standards and licensing. • Some movement toward minimal approximation of national labour market regulation.

Source: adapted from Pelkmans, 1997: table 5.1 and elsewhere.

question about whether existing federal states should adopt formal decision rules for their intergovernmental relations in addition to having a federal government in place.

The internal market reforms of 1986–92 are a second major feature of contemporary European integration of interest here. These reforms are the latest in a long list of integration steps – from the original customs union begun in 1958 to the monetary union, which only began to take effect in May 1998. But the achievement and focus of the internal market reform is germane to the reform of economic unions in federal states for a number of reasons. As in the two federations, the reform built upon a completed customs union and the existence of formal guarantees of economic mobility. Yet just as was the case in Australia and Canada (see chapter 4), the growth of non-tariff barriers in the form of subsidization, state monopolies, discriminatory procurement practice, excessive and protective regulations, technical standards, and so on had reduced the effectiveness of the original measures of negative and positive integration.

As shown in table 2.2, the internal market reforms of the EU tackled these non-tariff barriers across a broad range of markets for goods, services, capital, and labour. The measures encompass a great deal of dismantling of barriers (negative integration) but also much effort at common policies or a process of approximation of common policies (positive integration). Jacques Pelkmans notes, in particular, the special characteristics of the EU "regulatory strategy" that have made it possible to knit together the market structures of so many diverse member-state economies. In addition to the principle of subsidiarity, he notes the significance of two regulatory principles: "minimum approximation" and "regulatory mutual recognition."[23] These principles, in theory at least, provide a least intrusive and non-centralizing method for the harmonization of market structure. As such, they provide an important model for reform elsewhere. We will return to the detail of these reforms later in the discussion on the unreformed and post-reformed conditions of the federal economic unions of Australia and Canada.

Finally, before leaving this discussion of European experience, it is worth pursuing a few points about how the more recent European-style integration has been interpreted within political science theory. Theorists try to explain how the major achievements of European integration have come about and why member-states, some of which are major international powers, have surrendered part of their national economic sovereignty to such a degree. For simplicity's sake but also because they help to explain the forces of integration and reform in this work, I select two examples of a burgeoning literature on the European Union.[24]

One approach, taken by Andrew Moravcsik, is "liberal intergovernmentalist."[25] His take stresses the lumpiness of the achievements of European integration over time (i.e., only a few big steps forward such as in 1957–58, 1985–86, 1992, etc.). This lumpiness is the hallmark of a process driven by the interests of the member-states themselves and the relative power each brings to intergovernmental bargaining. Integration moves forward through such intergovernmental bargaining only when there is a sufficient calculus of member-state interests to proceed. Moreover, the institutional innovations of the union serve chiefly as an international regime for more effective bargaining of this type.

Thus, Moravcsik's approach is liberal, rooted in pluralist assumptions about rational state behaviour, national preference formation, and intergovernmental analysis of interstate negotiation. Even if one does not share his assumptions, his analysis of the process and dynamics of intergovernmental relations is quite useful. At this point, it is enough to draw out the key point he raises about how EU integration differs from other international regimes. Not only do member-states delegate sovereign powers to union institutions, but they also pool their sovereignty through the use of the qualified majority voting. The pooling function is taken in the expectation of "a stream of future substantive decisions," so that movement beyond the ad hoc and unanimous decision making prior to 1986 would produce "more decisions at a lower cost in time and energy."[26]

An alternative approach is illustrated by the work of Paul Pierson.[27] To him, the liberal intergovernmental theory does not sufficiently explain the constraining power of the EU institutions. He explains his focus on: "the gaps [that] emerge in member state control over the evolution of European institutions and public policies, why these gaps are difficult to close, and how these openings create room for actors other than member states to influence the process ... while constraining the room for manoeuvre of all political actors."[28] In his view, the liberal intergovernmental analysis assumes too much by way of state sovereignty and overstresses the instrumentality of institutions and the importance of intergovernmental bargains. Pierson posits a "historical institutionalist analysis" – it is the evolution of institutions taking a life of their own that matters. The evolutionary path itself has an enormous influence, "embedding member states in a dense institutional environment."[29] The institutional formation occurs mainly between the big intergovernmental bargaining episodes, and integration achieved in one area spills over to other areas, forcing unintended change. Eventually, a "path dependence" takes hold in which the member-states have made serious investments in the integration and would face a high (likely unacceptable) price of exit, thus eroding the rationalist assumption of voluntary co-operation.

From these two perspectives, I take two conclusions about the politics of European integration that may apply to the politics of economic reform in federal states. From Moravcsik's liberal intergovernmentalist approach, one can gain the insight of the importance of specific bargains and interest-pressure episodes in the substance and pace of change. There is a specific dynamic about attempts at institutional reform, particularly those resulting from intergovernmental negotiation – a set of conditions that can spell success or failure. Moravcsik's technique sheds light on these conditions, as discussed more fully in the conclusion. Pierson's historical institutionalist approach provides insight into the evolutionary effect of institutions beyond their initial creation, creating a pathway that shapes all subsequent uses of those institutions. In this respect, one can partly explain the possibilities of any given reform of the institutions of integration by the constraining features of existing institutions. One can also predict the success of any specific reform of integration by the attention paid to such institutional dynamics.

SITUATING AUSTRALIA AND CANADA

Having laid out the concepts of globalization, liberalization, and integration, and having introduced key aspects of integration theory as well as the empirical and theoretical aspects of recent European experience in economic integration, it remains to place Australia and Canada within the framework of these concepts. More discussion on the specific issues of federal economic unions and intergovernmental relations follows this chapter. Here, I summarize (without much reference to the federal nature of the two countries) the specifics of Australia's and Canada's respective positions within the international political economy.

What follows is a brief discussion of sameness and difference between the two countries and their international and economic positioning. This leads into a more pointed comparison of the challenge of regional and global integration faced by the two federations, providing background to the detailed comparative exercise that is much of the remainder of this book.

Similarities and Differences

First are some important historical convergences and divergences that shape the approach and positioning of Australia and Canada in the international political economy (IPE). Both became modern nation-states as federations of British colonies. Their position within the global economy in the nineteenth century was a secure but subordinate role within the second British Empire. However, from the mid-nineteenth century, Britain signalled its desire to move its colonies to economic self-reliance.

The colonial foundations of the two countries diverge in two important respects. First, as noted, Canada has its roots not only in the British Empire, but also the French. The British decided to govern the former French possessions by protecting the French language and civil law tradition as well as the Roman Catholic religion of *les Canadiens*. This sowed the seeds for the coexistence of two nations within a single state and later for a federal union as a way to sustain the political community. Despite the fact that both Australia and Canada have a considerable ethnic (multicultural and aboriginal) diversity in their contemporary populations, the French fact in Canada makes for very significant differences in social, economic, and political development, not least of which is a federation in which provincial autonomy is a vital operating principle. By contrast, Australia's is a more homogenous society, and its federal development is tilted more to a single nation-building process. (These aspects of federal design and dynamics are covered in chapters 3 and 4.)

The second key difference is Canada's symbiotic – some say dependent – development with the United States. The American Revolution forced the Tory refugees north to create two new colonies (Upper Canada and New Brunswick), setting the stage for the later confederation of the British North American (BNA) colonies. Canada shares the continent with the USA, across the longest undefended border in the world. North of the border is arguably the remainder bin of the continent's geography, certainly most of the rock and bog. Thus, it has been argued that Canadian governments have had to be more proactive in areas such as transportation and communication with a host of economic and political tools to overcome this geographic legacy and keep together a sparse east-west chain of provincial communities and regional economies.[30] Thus, participation in the American economy and culture has always been an ambiguous reflex for Canadians. Yet a trend to economic integration has been continuous for all of the twentieth century. Indeed, trade with the United States surpassed that with Britain as early as 1921.

Canada's sharing of the North American continent contrasts with Australia's continental isolation. While it has a close neighbour of considerable affinity in New Zealand, the dependency relationship and size differential is reversed. And, as for its other neighbours, the larger ones such as Indonesia are far away in both a geographic and a cultural sense. Until recently, Australians have not thought of themselves as Asian – indeed, quite the opposite. And, as discussed more fully below, the Australian economy may now be integrated into the East Asian region, but in a much more diffuse way than is the case within North America, where the overwhelming influence of the United States dominates the region.

The development of the two countries also has parallels in geographic scale and scope. The sheer size of territory controlled by the colonial power and the sparseness of aboriginal occupation led to a gradual but dispersed settlement pattern. There developed separate colonies with separate histories and therefore, societies with at least a minimum degree of diversity (although Canada is much more diverse with its originally dual settler nationalities). By international comparisons, both countries remain today not only sparsely populated, but highly concentrated in cities (over 80 per cent), and the cities themselves are geographically concentrated within their respective countries. These spatial characteristics have profound consequences for political development and practically guarantee a federal form of government if there is to be a united polity at all.

The evolved national economic systems in Australia and Canada are quite similar, again a legacy of British rule. With the exception of the French civil law tradition sustained in Quebec since 1774, the British North American colonies adopted English or British law, political institutions, and commercial practice. In North America, Canada would gradually be influenced by the somewhat separate development of capitalism in the United States. Yet both Canada and the United States are within the broad family of Anglo-American market economies. This is a significant characterization, one that assumes much more than can be discussed adequately here.[31] In a nutshell, the Anglo-American model is distinguished from the co-operative capitalism of Eastern Asia and Europe by a more purely Lockean commitment to political and economic liberalism. This entails a less encompassing role of the state and, more crucially in the twentieth century, less reliance on corporatist mediation of economic interests by the state.

Even so, this basic characterization can be overdrawn. For in both Australia and Canada (and much more so than in the United States of America or the United Kingdom), the state undertook a strong developmental role in the economy. This was highly appropriate in the geographic settings of vast undeveloped continents, where private capital was often unwilling or unable to invest in the infrastructure necessary to promote a market economy (railways, canals, electrification, ports). Yet well beyond the original conditions of developing economies, in both Australia and Canada, there would remain strong elements of a state role in economic development. In Australia, W.K. Hancock wrote famously in 1930 of the state in his country as a "vast public utility."[32]

State (federal and state governments) ownership and management of economic resources had far exceeded, in his view, the requirements of a developing economy. The same has been true for Canada, if to a lesser degree. Utilities such as electricity, water, and telephones have been in the hands of Crown corporations – at least in some provinces – for most of the twentieth century, and the state played a crucial role (if not always one of direct ownership) in key transportation sectors, notably transcontinental railways and airlines.[33]

If the economies that developed in Australia and Canada shared strong aspects of state-led development, it is also true that they both exhibit elements of staples-led dependency. In Canada, there has been, from the sixteenth century on, cod fishery, fur trade, lumber, wheat, minerals, hydroelectricity, and oil and gas, among others. In Australia, the list would include wool, gold, beef, minerals, coal, and forest products. Resource development and exploitation remain important parts of the two economies, disproportionately so among Organization for Economic Cooperation and Development (OECD) members. Although, historically, the staple exports generated a good deal of wealth, the contemporary image and reality of Australia and Canada is one of struggling resource producing giants. They both try to retain economic rents and living standards in a more competitive global market for resource products. Their resource dependency underlies a long-standing weakness in their competitive position.

Finally, Australia and Canada's common British heritage has also led to commonalities in their political status in the world community. As the United States gradually overtook Britain as the hegemonic power in the world economy, Britain's independent dominions came under the security umbrella of the USA. This process began in the First World War, strengthened during the Second World War, and was cemented by the Cold War. The international personalities of the two have been shaped by their membership in the Western alliance system – Canada in the North Atlantic Treaty Organization (NATO) and North American Aerospace Defence Command (NORAD); and Australia in Australia-New Zealand-United States Security Treaty (ANZUS). Moreover, both were enthusiastic participants in the post-war order led by the United States, being charter members of the United Nations, the IMF, and the GATT. Also, both countries have attempted, with varying degrees of success, to carve out what has been called a middle power status commensurate with their contributions to the strategic alliance and their growing prosperity and economic clout.

In Australia's case, there has also been the filling of a modest role left by a declining US security presence in the South Pacific. The idea of middle powers is contested, and this is not the place for that discussion, but it nonetheless expresses some measure of the self-professed identity of these two states.[34]

Comparing Regional and Global Integration

In the past three decades, certain trends in the status of the position of both countries within the IPE have accelerated. The basics of economic globalization have been discussed already. For these two economies, certain trends have been especially clear. The resource exporting sectors have faced more competition from new sources of supply in the developing world and as new and less resource-intensive technologies and alternative materials have been applied to manufacturing. As Peter Drucker has argued, manufacturing is less reliant now on resource inputs, and, as a result, resource prices have been in a long-term decline.[35] In Australian parlance, the country could no longer live off the sheep's back. The two countries' manufacturing sectors have also come in for new competition, first from the restored economies of Germany and Japan, and then from other Western European countries. From the 1960s on, new competition arose from the newly industrialized East Asian "tigers" of Korea, Taiwan, Hong Kong, and Singapore. By the 1980s, they were joined by Malaysia, Indonesia, Thailand, China, Mexico, Turkey – the list goes on. This competition first affected labour-intensive sectors such as textiles, clothing, and footwear but soon spread to consumer electronics, steel, ships, and autos, among others. Production processes had become transnational, but only a few transnational corporations were actually based in Australia or Canada. Even the service sectors have been a part of these secular economic trends. The degree and nature of tradable services has exploded, the application of technology has fostered greater competition for business services and a separation of service from manufacturing functions in firms, and productivity changes have begun to make their way through community and public services as well.[36]

In a generic sense, these trends would appear to have made identical impacts on Australia and Canada by the early 1980s: both had been part of the GATT process; both were Anglo-American-type capitalist market economies; and both had advanced, high labour cost structures.

Both were also close allies with the United States and Britain and were English-speaking societies (at least in the majority), thus increasing their exposure to a knowledge structure of competitive ideas and practices readily transmitted from United States and Britain. By increasing exposure to international competition, these factors undermined the position of the Australian and Canadian economies. Despite some spectacular years in the 1970s and early 1980s, when the price of commodities such as oil and grains soared, the terms of trade deteriorated. Resource business had to become more productive, shedding labour and shutting down uncompetitive operations. The crisis also hit manufacturing as national firms lost market share to imports; indeed, they became muscled out altogether in many sectors (e.g., televisions, shipbuilding), notwithstanding protective tariffs. Structural unemployment mounted, and the purchasing parities of the Australian and Canadian dollars eroded. Across the two economies, the pressure to adjust became paramount. With the onset of truly global financial markets in the 1980s, the pressures became unbearable as currency traders and bond markets made daily judgments about the competitiveness of national financial instruments and the fundamentals of the underlying national economies.

How could Australia and Canada compete in this globalizing economy? This became arguably the most important policy issue of the 1980s and led directly to the economic reforms of the 1990s examined in this book. The specific advocacy of the reforms and their details are covered below. For our purposes here, the context of liberalization and integration is especially significant: how these specifics differ between the two countries and how that context affects the economic adjustment strategy adopted by each.

In the 1980s, Australia faced a world of greater competition, with an economy still largely shaped by what has been called the "Australian settlement" of the first decade of the federation. According to Paul Kelly, the five pillars of the settlement were imperial benevolence, a "white Australia" immigration scheme, industrial protection, centralized wage arbitration, and state paternalism.[37] It was a regime underpinned by Australia's role within British imperial trade preferences and security protection, with Asian influence limited to trade patterns mediated by the British imperial presence. Yet if imperial benevolence had gone by the mid-century (although trade preferences were retained until Britain's entry to the European Community in 1973), the other four pillars crumbled only slowly over the next forty years. Most notably for Australia's exposure to competition, the level of tariff protection remained high by OECD standards until the late 1980s.[38]

But the pattern of trade had already begun to change. Raw and semi-processed resources still dominated the export mix. Conversely, finished goods dominated imports. By the mid-1980s, however, the value of manufacturing's share in exports had begun to grow relative to resource products, especially as prices for the latter declined overall. And some sectors such as agriculture began to make the transformation from trade in commodities to trade in finished food products. More significantly has been the steady replacement of trade with Europe by trade with East Asian countries. After the Second World War, trade with Britain collapsed (especially imports) and was replaced by trade with Japan and the United States, and much of this occurred before Britain's entry into the European Community. Since the 1960s, export trade growth has been led by Japan, but also Korea, China, Taiwan, Hong Kong, and the Association of Southeast Asian Nations (ASEAN) members. In general, Australia's trade is diverse, if increasingly Asian, and in chronic imbalance, running an overall balance of payments deficit in every year since 1981.

Clearly, Australia had been losing its competitive edge. More importantly, it had been losing it in the very region with which its market integration has been increasing. By the 1970s, Australians had to witness the apparent decline of their standard of living relative to Japan and Hong Kong. By 1984, the *Economist* was predicting that on recent performance, Singapore would overtake Australia within ten years, followed by Malaysia, Taiwan, and South Korea within a generation.[39]

According to a growing chorus of business, economic, and political advocacy, the solution to declining competitiveness lay in comprehensive economic adjustment. By the end of the 1980s, Australia adopted a strategy of adjusting the economy to better meet global competition, especially Asian competition. This strategy had both an internal and an external component. Internally, the strategy is a program of microeconomic reform. It seeks to do two things: first, to enhance the competitiveness of Australian business by maximizing the size and dynamism of the national base for doing business abroad; and second, to increase the level of competitive efficiency within the national market by eliminating anti-competitive practices (for more details, see chapters 4, 7, and 8). The external strategy has been for Australia to assert more influence over, and to advocate a more coherent shape of, regional integration. It has done this where it could in its own backyard through the bilateral agreement with New Zealand (the Closer Economic Relations and Trade Agreement of 1983). More broadly, Australia has attempted to promote regional integration through its strong advocacy of Asia-Pacific Economic Cooperation (APEC). It has been clear from the outset, however, that APEC is not going to attain, any time soon, the level of institutional integration that prevails in North America let alone Europe. For example, it has not reached even the elementary stages of free trade according to orthodox theory.[40]

For good or ill, then, Australia seems stuck with an external strategy that is fraught with risks. Market integration with Asia is uneven, diverse, and politically volatile. As the Asian financial crisis of 1997–98 demonstrated, the explosive growth of many East Asian economies may have been based on shaky foundations. Certainly, the Australian economy is vulnerable, if less so than most of its Asian neighbours, to the rapid movements of capital in and out of the region. More important in the longer term, putting its faith in the Asian region does not ensure that the marketplace will always be open or that the rules will be played as Australians would like them to be. Nor is it clear that APEC is the right forum, given that it embraces not only East Asian members, but also a growing number of American ones including Chile, Mexico, Canada, and the USA, or that Australia is really having much influence in it.[41]

Canada's regional integration is a study in profound contrast with Australia. As with Australia, Canada had its own post-Confederation "settlement" with some similar features.[42] The transcontinental economy took shape only slowly until 1879, when the federal government implemented a policy of protective tariffs known as the National Policy. The complements of that policy were the transcontinental Canadian Pacific Railway to ship the new staple of wheat eastward and manufactured products west, and a policy of rapid immigration to settle the west. Like Australia, the early federation relied on imperial benevolence as well as a degree of state paternalism and, until the 1960s, essentially European immigration. Finally, Australians consider their form of industrial relations, characterized by centralized wage arbitration by federal and state tribunals, to be an important pillar of their economic development. In Canada, as in the United States, a more decentralized enterprise-based collective bargaining has prevailed.[43]

The latter example underscores a more pervasive trend of Canadian economic development. For even with the National Policy of tariffs in place, trade with the United States continued to grow, mainly in resource products. Also, it was mainly US capital that built branch plants behind the Canadian tariff walls to service the Canadian market for finished goods. Indeed, the theme of free trade with the United States was never far from the surface in Canadian political history.[44] Market integration with the United States, always prominent in resource products, began to include finished products during and after the Second World War through defence production agreements and through the important bilateral concessions between Canada and the USA under the auspices of the GATT. Indeed, through this latter process, Canada's external tariff was steadily whittled away.

Another huge step in integration occurred in 1965 with the Autopact, a managed trade agreement affecting assembled automobiles and auto parts. From this date begins a strong and growing trend of intra-firm trade as a major component of bilateral trade with the United States (e.g., trade from the Canadian subsidiary of General Motors to the parent firm or other subsidiaries and vice versa). These developments also contributed to an increasing proportion of higher-end processed and finished products in Canada's overall trade mix. By the 1980s, then, Canada was already facing significant degrees of liberalization and market integration: through successive rounds of tariff concessions under the GATT and through intra-industry and finished product trade under the Autopact and other bilateral arrangements. In each respect, Canada was a more open and integrated economy than was Australia. Canada has had and still has a trade surplus both with the United States and with the rest of the world as a whole.

However, Canada's increasing market integration with the United States has meant increasing dependence on American trade policy. By the early 1980s, when Canada depended on the USA as a market for approximately 75 per cent of its exports, it could ill afford the "new protectionism" then emerging south of the border. Since the 1960s, the US manufacturing economy had endured waves of new competition from newly recovered European economies and the newly industrialized countries (NICS) of Asia. Following the 1981 recession, Canadian business also awoke to a declined level of competitiveness and productivity in the global economy and a renewed set of trade disputes with the

United States (for more details see chapter 5). By 1986, Canada began negotiations for a free trade agreement with the United States for two reasons: first, Canada sought secure and expanded access to the American market on which so many sectors of its economy depended; and second, it sought to use trade liberalization as the chief means of forcing economic adjustment to global competition (not only with the USA but also, more generally). Obviously, the United States also wanted the agreement partly to tame Canadian economic nationalism, but more importantly, to boost its global agenda for trade and investment liberalization then stalled in the interminable Uruguay Round multilateral trade negotiations.

There have been two regional integration agreements to which Canada has been a party. The Canada-United States Free Trade Agreement (FTA), in force since 1 January 1989, is the more important of the two for Canada in that it took greater effort and political capital to obtain and is more tailored to Canada's needs. The North American Free Trade Agreement (NAFTA), in force since 1 January 1994, is a trilateral deal with Mexico. As Mexico provided more threatening labour market competition for the United States, NAFTA was the more significant political event for the USA. For Canada, the main objective was to ensure that the new agreement did not erode the achievements of the FTA. The details of the two regional integration agreements are not germane here (see discussion in chapter 5 for their effect on the Canadian economic union). However, it is worth noting their unprecedented scope to include not only trade in goods, but also services and investment as well as important institutional features such as binding dispute settlement procedures for certain kinds of disputes.

Thus, Canada, like Australia, had by the late 1980s adopted a strategy for economic adjustment to global competition. Also, like Australia, Canada's internal strategy included microeconomic reform such as deregulation, privatization, and freeing the internal market. Unlike Australia, the external component – free trade – is much more important to the overall approach. As will be argued later (and this is not an original thought), Canada's industrial strategy now amounts to free trade.

To conclude, the difference between Canada and Australia's integration with the global economy can be summarized. While the two have strong similarities in economic structure, their geopolitical position differs significantly. Australia faces *diffuse market integration* from around the world and increasingly from East Asia. With the important exception of New Zealand, no one bilateral relationship is so important to Australia that it has sought institutionalized integration through bilateral means. This may also be due to Australia's continuing commitment to the multilateral process (i.e., GATT/WTO) that has served it well. Another factor may be the more collective, familial cultures of capitalism that prevail in its Asian neighbours (compared with Australia's Anglo-American business culture). Whatever the cause, Australia is left as a cheerleader for APEC where regional integration is yet to get beyond even elementary stages. This means, on the one hand, that Australia is free from the constraints of negative regional integration in which it, as but one of the smaller players, is unlikely to have a major influence. On the other hand, it leaves Australia room – or forces its hand, depending on one's perspective – to pursue unilateral liberalization in order to speed the pace of competitive adjustment. As I stress later, these circumstances of *diffuse market integration* and *low level of institutional integration* help to explain Australia's more direct and unilateral policy reforms dwelling on competitive conditions in its national economy.

Canada is a case of *concentrated market integration*. This market integration derives from a continental neighbourhood and a common (or at least very similar in relative terms) capitalist culture. Thus, when US actions threatened to erode the basis of liberal access to its market, Canada sought a more formal institutional integration. The resulting regional integration agreements are not nearly as advanced in institutional terms as the European Union. Yet the agreements were significant steps in the global movement to integration and have influenced the pace of integration in Europe and the Asia-Pacific, and the completion of the Uruguay Round. Unlike either Europe or Asia, however, Canada participates in a very asymmetrical regional relationship. The terms of integration are set more often by the United States than by either Canada or Mexico. After all, it is the US market that is chiefly in demand. Moreover, since so much of the Canadian economy (especially its goods-producing sectors) is integrated already to the North American continental market, the institutional integration of the FTA and NAFTA – even if mainly negative – sets the market rules domestically as well. This is why "free trade" is Canada's economic adjustment strategy: it leaves very little room for anything else. In contrast to Australia's diffuse and low-level regional integration, Canada's *concentrated and formal (if medium-level) regional integration* helps to explain why Canadian governments would apply the focus and form of free trade to their proposals to reform the Canadian economic union.

3 Federalism, Economic Unions, and Intergovernmental Policy-Making

ECONOMIC ADJUSTMENT POLICY IN FEDERAL STATES

In all industrialized democratic countries, there is an intense debate about policies of adjustment to globalization. For most countries, the question is one of removing barriers to the competitiveness of national business, mediating the effects of market liberalization, and integrating and adjusting social policy to new circumstances. In many cases, there is also the closely related task of paring back the state in fiscal terms to balance budgets, reduce tax burdens, or both. Setting aside for the moment fiscal and social policy implications, the cluster of policy instruments and sectors involved in economic adjustment policy is nonetheless large. It involves, among others: trade and investment policy, competition policy, the regulation of services including financial services, intellectual property, transportation regulation, energy market regulation, industrial relations, labour force training, and industrial and regional economic development and subsidization. At its most ambitious, economic adjustment policy can be akin to an overall "industrial strategy."

It is worth stressing that a strategic approach to the economy does not necessarily imply a high level of interventionism, at least as an end result. However, whether the state is overseeing and policing a free market or directing the economy in more precise ways, change from one regime to another requires the application of all the levers of power at the state's disposal. Of relevance here is the issue of strong versus weak states, noted in chapter 1. The so-called strong states such as France or Japan have taken a proactive, interventionist role in their economies, shaping and planning the industrial structure. Alternatively, theorists have seen Britain as a weak state regime, typical of the Anglo-American approach (to which Australia and Canada are also said to belong). Yet the Thatcher governments took a very strategic approach to reform of the national economy, using all the tools of a strong state in the process. The question remains whether federal states are strong or weak, to which we will return shortly.[1]

Another issue is whether globalization provides any room at all for an interventionist industrial strategy, as practised and theorized in Europe, Japan, and elsewhere until the mid-1980s. It might be said that outside of Japan and the United States, no state can manage an industrial strategy that is not aimed at liberalizing the economy; France and Sweden are two instructive examples.[2] This could be said to apply all the more so to economies such as Australia and Canada.

In this context, the issue becomes less one of creating an industrial strategy as one of promoting economic adjustment. Thus, the emphasis is placed, at the very least, on halting industrial protection and at the most, on actively adjusting economies. This is not to imply that there is no debate about whether and what kind of industrial strategy should be pursued, but that the ascendant view and that adopted by governments since the early 1980s has been adjustment to economic globalization. This outward focus is revealed in the way in which policy is subsumed by a discussion of "competitiveness."[3] Under this new economic policy orthodoxy, increasing international liberalization, and competition is assumed. It is also assumed that increasing or even sustaining economic growth and income at the national level depends on a monetarist stance to macroeconomic policy and a supply-side orientation to microeconomic policy. Trends in the latter field are especially important here.

Since the mid 1970s, and more especially since the early 1980s, industrialized economies have attempted to improve growth in their stagnated economies through productivity improvements across the full range of economic sectors. The renewed focus of microeconomic policies is on productivity at the firm or industry level. This trend draws on an increasing consensus among neo-classical economists that government interventions at the micro level were out of sync with monetarist solutions in macro policy. Moreover, the view is that decades of accumulated micro-interventions had resulted in regulatory capture by industry, heavy costs to consumers, the creep of political and bureaucratic bias in market decisions, and the destabilization of markets in some instances. The solutions lie in deregulation, privatization, and competition.[4]

The OECD's 1987 report, *Structural Adjustment and Economic Performance,* is an important example of reform advocacy. It focused on existing microeconomic policies as structural constraints to economic adjustment. Its program for change had considerable influence in policy circles and sought three broad sets of reforms. First, it advocated increased competition in product markets, necessitating reduced domestic price support for agriculture, increased liberalization of international trade, and more reliance on national competition. Second, the OECD pushed for improved responsiveness in factor markets, meaning more liberalized and integrated capital markets, more competitive labour markets, and a greater emphasis on education and training. Third, the report pursued reform of the public sector for greater efficiency and effectiveness, entailing a redefinition of the scope of the public sector (including the questioning of monopolies), the use of work incentives in social programs, and reform of the structure and level of taxation.[5] Finally, but crucially, it was argued that a successful microeconomic reform program had to proceed across a broad front. Change in international trade policy would be ineffective if factor markets were unreformed; the pace of reform in the private sector generally would be sclerotic if labour markets were inflexible and overregulated or if the tax structure and social programs were not also competitive.

Thus, microeconomic reform had to be comprehensive and, given the diverse nature of vested interests in the unreformed policy mix, bold and interventionist. To use a phrase of British political scientist Andrew Gamble, it is a project of a strong state to create a free market. At its most dramatic – as it was in Thatcher's Britain – the task seemed to entail taking on all aspects of the post-war economic and social order, including full employment, the collectivist welfare state, and corporatist partnership.[6]

If this agenda of economic adjustment is assumed, what about federal states in which the power to adjust and liberalize national economies is divided? Several commentators have argued the advantages of federalism in the context of global economic adjustment. In economist Thomas Courchene's view, as global liberalization favours markets and is therefore inherently decentralizing, federal polities with decentralized government are better able to adapt.[7] Federal government provides constituent government autonomy, which in turn can provide a variety of means and outcomes for local economic adjustment. This diversity and decentralization matches that of the marketplace, especially as it emerges within specific regional (i.e., subnational regions) settings. Analysts in the United States and Germany argue that microeconomic reform, in particular, is best done at the subnational level, which is closer to the action. Such reform erodes the policy prominence of central trade and industrial policies in favour of more localized solutions.[8]

On the other hand, as the market expands its scope and efficiency, it requires central institutions of greater scope.[9] Indeed, global and federal-state integration becomes mutually reinforcing in that a trend toward centralization of regulation is occurring in both cases. This argument stresses that federal institutions provide only a weak form of economic union where they retain barriers to economic mobility or allow the regionalization of factor markets in the first place. And even if, as Courchene and others contend, microeconomic adjustment is best done at the local level, such reform would be counterproductive if the reform principles and market rules were inconsistent and contradictory across the federal economic space. Thus, the extent, nature, and degree of consistency of economic adjustment in federal political systems are contentious issues. In fact, in the next section of this chapter, I lay out the case for why reform of the economic union as such in federal states is a key part of microeconomic reform. And, of course, the economic union reform process in Australia and Canada discussed in later chapters provides importance evidence of the effects of global and regional liberalization and integration on federal economic integration.

A second broad advantage of federal government in relation to economic adjustment is said to be the experience of federal systems with the political and institutional demands of integration at home, which can be applied to increasing integration abroad. In this view, federal systems provide just the sort of institutional and political "suturing" of governments and governance required.[10] As Canadian political scientists David Cameron and Richard Simeon put it: "Federalism is just one example of what we call multilevel governance, in which power and authority are shared among a wide range of institutions. These are not simply federal and provincial. Increasingly, they also involve local and regional governments and a vast array of international and supranational institutions ... new quasi-governmental players in the form of international tribunals, aboriginal governments, and NGOs. The world of multilevel governance is one of complexity, uncertainty, fluidity, and blurred boundaries."[11]

The European Union is an example of multi-level governance reaching from subnational to supranational. On the latter, Cheryl Saunders notes, "supranational" intergovernmental relations are not just international relations by another name, but an intermediate category of relations akin to confederal arrangements whereby regional or similar groupings of governments agree on joint regulatory and other functions.[12] As regional and global integration proceeds, supranational relations are taking an increasingly important role in both forming and, in many cases, constituting a form of political integration to regulate economic integration (see the discussion in chapter 2).

One consequence of multi-level governance is an extension of the familiar two-level games of domestic politics whereby domestic intergovernmental relations are played off supranational relations – and vice versa.[13] In the context of negotiated market liberalization, dual- or triple-level policy in the field of economic adjustment seems obvious. Barriers to trade or other factor mobility within a federal nation-state become international barriers to trade and mobility. Foreign trading partners often identify state or province-induced barriers to trade for removal in international trade negotiations. Even where they do not, the increasing degree of openness to foreign trade puts those barriers into question from the perspective of business attempting to compete both within and outside their national markets with foreign firms. Thus, trade and investment policy become a joint federal-state concern, and no government can afford to keep its strategic goals confined to separate levels of intergovernmental relations. In terms of policy process, methods and ideas learned at one level of relations may be readily adapted to another. It is not clear from recent experience in federal states whether their exposure to multi-level governance is an advantage or a disadvantage for economic adjustment. The answers lie in how well individual federal states cope with their conditions of multi-level governance. Part of the task here is to search for those answers.

In summary, federal institutions and political cultures are themselves undergoing much change as a result of globalization, integration, and liberalization. The causal arrow points both ways. If there is a great uncertainty about the implications of globalization for federalism, there is also uncertainty about the implications of federal responses to globalization. Some economic adjustment policy in federal states, as evidenced below, will point in the direction of increasing national uniformity and the concentration, if not centralization, of market power; other policy reforms point in the direction of greater diversity and flexibility.

Thus, an old debate about federalism and a coherent industrial strategy has been transformed. The new economic adjustment agenda emphasizes microeconomic reform, dwelling on the processes of deregulation, privatization, and competition. Even if these manifestations of global liberalization transfer power to the market, they still require a strong state in order to effect and to regulate the change – in other words, to institutionalize the new market rules. As just discussed, federal systems have some specific advantages and disadvantages in undertaking such a role. The recent attempts by two older federations – Australia and Canada – to undertake such reforms provides important new evidence to test the capacity of federalism in the era of globalization. The next two parts of this chapter provide further framework for analysing the capacity of federal systems to adapt by examining the specific role of economic unions and the role and nature of intergovernmental relations.

ROLE AND SIGNIFICANCE OF ECONOMIC UNIONS IN FEDERAL STATES

As I outlined in chapter 2, economic integration is a symbiotic process between the integration of markets and the institutions that regulate them. It entails both the degree of desired economic linkages and the appropriate process for maintaining and shaping those linkages through political and legal institutions. And, as noted, it involves both liberalization through "negative" measures and institutional integration through "positive" measures.

In this work, I define economic integration in federal states as an "economic union." As noted in chapter 2, this term is also used by the traditional integration theorists to describe the stage between a common market and total economic integration and one in which the harmonization of positive integration is added to the factor mobility of a common market. Peter Leslie uses the term economic union in a more generic way, encompassing one or all of five aspects of integration: trade and investment, labour market, foreign economic policy, monetary, and structural/developmental (table 2.1). Both typologies are useful but need further clarification when it comes to the specific use of the term "economic union" as applied to federal states.

First, it is certainly true that most, if not all, federations that have market economies (even some that did not such as Yugoslavia or the Soviet Union) approximate the economic union stage of Balassa's typology. The federal constitutions of Australia, Canada, the USA, Germany, and Switzerland provide negative integration through a customs union and a guarantee (in some cases, only partial) of labour and capital mobility. These constitutions also provide positive integration through central institutions that create common policies and a monetary union.[14]

Second, and drawing from Leslie's qualifications, all of these federations have elements of each of the five aspects of integration. Yet federations differ in the degree of integration achieved in any given aspect. Thus, for example, some federations provide for stronger mobility guarantees than do others (USA cf. Switzerland) or for more centralized fiscal policy (Australia), while others have stronger institutions of developmental coordination (Germany). Even in monetary unions, there is some scope in some federations for regionally determined money supply (USA).

Yet the concept of economic union in federal states goes beyond these typologies. To begin with, notions of integration that stress a gradual process, as in the European Union spanning some decades, do not capture the essence of federal integration in the older federations. The economic union was part of their original rationale and design. They exist in part to create a new economic and political space, although the dynamics can be quite different depending on whether the federation is bringing together units (USA, Canada, Australia) or decentralizing a unitary state (Germany, Belgium). For the two federations under scrutiny here – Australia and Canada – the economic union was and is part of a nation-building enterprise, creating unity in the presence of diversity in political and economic terms.

One may now take the next step to describe a federal economic union regime – i.e., to explore its normative and institutional context.[15] In normative terms, there are two related concepts: the creation or maintenance of a "national"[16] economy and the extension of economic citizenship. According to economic theory, federal economic unions create national economies in order to capture four types of economic benefits. These are:

1 *market integration:* the creation of a new, expanded economic space, achieving economies of scale and specialization in the process (although the latter may occur only over time)

2 *increased bargaining power:* greater influence or market power with reference to external countries and markets

3 *sharing of costs:* the ability to undertake defence expenditures and large developmental projects and other public goods

4 *pooling and sharing of risks:* federation as an insurance scheme, particularly in the context of regional economic diversity[17]

All four of these are important benefits, but at any particular point in time, one or the other may seem more important. For example, the benefits of the initial market integration, once achieved, may become taken for granted and can even be reversed as outlined in chapter 4. Pooling of risks is more salient during periods of rapid change in the terms of trade (e.g., oil prices in 1974–84), and sharing of costs is more obvious when expenditures are rising (e.g., wartime, building of the welfare state). Also, Maxwell and Pestieau refer to these benefits as the "surplus" of federal economic union and postulate that a federation would fail if the surplus were not achieved. This could occur if the national economy did not generate economies of scale and specialization due to the erection of interstate barriers. Another reason for failure might be an economic union seen to discriminate permanently in favour of one or more of the constituent units or if one or more units were the permanent beneficiaries of redistribution. Yet another reason for failure might be if the federated units could not find sufficient common ground on economic goals (or the trade-off with non-economic goals).[18]

Economic citizenship is a political and legal benefit of economic union. This concept is especially prominent in federal systems with a rights-based political discourse, whether there from the beginning (USA) or adopted later on (Canada). Thus, the economic union is seen as conferring certain rights of economic citizenship such as personal mobility, the right to work, and equality and fairness (non-discrimination) in employment, and in the provision of social services and public goods generally (see also below regarding the concept of "social union"). Economic citizenship may refer as well to the property rights of individuals and corporations throughout the national economy. Such economic citizenship can be seen as privileging liberal values and

Lockean principles of property, or it may be seen in more positive terms as enhancing economic opportunity for all. Such citizen-based or rights-based concepts of economic union are typically constitutionalized, but they can also infuse other institutional features of federations, not least of which is the ongoing interpretation of the constitution and other law by the courts. Economic citizenship is also a powerful political concept in that it speaks to the tension within federal unions between national (or federated) and provincial (or state) communities, begging the question as to which political community rights and obligations of economic citizenship adhere. And where the more purely economic benefits are obscure or contested, these political rationales for economic union can be even more important.[19]

In the debates over the reform of the economic union in Australia and Canada, discussed more fully in chapter 4, both sorts of norms will be in play. Canadian political discourse is more attuned and receptive to argument about economic citizenship due, as noted, to its rights-based political culture. Yet this may also be due, paradoxically, to Australia's more advanced state of economic citizenship since the early twentieth century. In other words, Australians take their economic citizenship for granted. In both federations, too, there had been concern about the erosion of benefits from a national market, concern heightened by increased international competition. Finally, in Canada's case, there is the political issue of the need for federalists to demonstrate to Quebecers the economic value of staying in the union.

Apart from their common normative context, federal economic unions share characteristic institutions. Six institutional features of federal systems in general are important in this respect and may be summarized briefly as follows:

1   A *common economic space* matches the territorial scope of the federal union itself. This includes explicit constitutional provisions for negative integration. The specific provisions can differ (see comparison of Australia's section 92 and Canada's section 121 in chapter 4), but at a minimum, they create a customs union.
2   A constitutionally protected *distribution of powers* between the general and constituent governments includes the allocation of key powers of economic regulation (i.e., positive integration). An important aspect is the extent of control retained by the constituent units over

their regional economies. Powers may be distributed concurrently or exclusively.

3 *Central executive and legislative institutions* are designed to form federal law and policies to give effect to positive integration. All federations incorporate at least some aspect of representation of the constituent units in these central institutions, including the second chamber of the federal legislature. Such institutions are vital in building consensus for federation-wide economic integration measures.

4 *Fiscal relations* among the governments amount to de facto power sharing. Their nature depends partly on the constitutional allocation of taxation and expenditure responsibilities. Most federal systems attempt to deal with "horizontal" and "vertical" imbalances among the constituent units and between orders of government. Relative fiscal power has a huge impact on governments' ability to undertake (and to thwart) positive integration.

5 *Intergovernmental institutions and processes* deal with the interdependencies of government policy (see next part of this chapter). Many aspects of positive integration such as common policies can be forged effectively only through intergovernmental collaboration.

6 *A system of courts* interprets constitutional provisions and arbitrates intergovernmental and other disputes. Case law has been an essential part of upgrading the terms of the economic union to meet the needs of evolving national economies.

These six institutional features have a combined effect within a single federal system that can be grasped only in its broader historical and constitutional setting. This is pursued in chapter 4 for Australia and Canada.

Before turning to these specifics, one more theme is crucial to the general picture. This is the obverse side of the coin of integration. Federal states operate not only to promote unity, of which economic union is a vital part, but also to preserve and promote diversity. Thus, there is, in practice, a constant tension within federal systems between unity and diversity and integration and autonomy. It seems obvious that these forces must be in balance if federalism is to endure, but comparative and historical analysis demonstrates much room for difference among federal states on where the point of balance lies, both normatively and empirically.

To take a prominent example of this balancing act, the distribution of powers between the central and constituent governments has an important effect on the degree of economic autonomy provided to constituent governments to pursue diverse and decentralized paths to economic adjustment. Over time, constituent governments can employ their autonomous powers to put brakes on economic integration created by the federal union in the first place, modifying economic efficiency for equity purposes. This autonomous counteraction arises due to the very success of federal economic unions in creating an integrated national economy with such effects as industrialization and urbanization. Equity demands result in competitive spending and regulating by federal and constituent governments as they seek to protect, subsidize, and otherwise intervene in regional and national markets. These equity-induced activities of government can run counter to the objectives of the economic union, reducing national efficiency.

The question is one of a balance between efficiency and equity goals. It is a balance that shifts over time and according to politically perceived economic and social needs. Indeed, the equity counterpart of economic integration may be part of an implicit federal bargain. This is especially so where perceptions of the costs and benefits of economic union are regionally disparate and thus politically problematic for a federal system. In this respect, the institutions of integration within federal states exhibit a "double movement" – now encouraging, now restraining the operation of a single market.[20] In their broadest sense, then, federal economic unions provide a framework for the ongoing process of making trade-offs between national integration and subnational (regional) autonomy.[21]

The nature of these trade-offs changes over time to respond to the requirements and development of national and regional economies and degrees of political and social integration. International pressures, whether the result of global or regional integration, challenge existing bargains within federal states regarding the economic union and policy trade-offs between efficiency and equity. Efficiency becomes an imperative, and equity may be subordinated to it. Federated national economies are drawn into integration frameworks that are much broader than the federal union; the central government may not be able to take the needs and sensitivities of the constituent units into account and may constrain the capacity of the units to strike their own balance between efficiency and equity.

Thus, globalization can be a centralizing force for federal systems. The market itself can be the centralizing force of economic activity in that it concentrates capital and production in some regions and metropolises at the expense of others, creating new regional disparities. And within federations, international integration can tip the internal balance by forcing the central governments to take an exclusive or primary role in mediating integration into larger entities and/or to use the rationale of external integration to increase their authority over the internal market. The role of mediator to regional or global integration becomes a core function of central governments in federal systems when so much else is delegated upward to supranational institutions and downward to subnational state and local governments.

Moreover, liberalization and integration at the international or regional level can conflict directly with the regulatory measures of the federal economic union. It may produce the political debilitating effect of making trade with regional or global partners freer than it is within the federation itself, with spiralling damage to the relative degree of trade done nationally. The bargain struck between equity and efficiency objectives in the federation may thus become unstable and require renegotiation to meet the broader integration of the global economy. Finally, the specific norms and institutions of the economic union may not be promoting effectively the required economic adjustment. This is especially so in light of the microeconomic reform agenda in OECD countries. For all of these reasons, reform of the economic union is a prominent contemporary issue in federal states.

Finally, in discussion of economic union, equity, and integration, there is the concept of a "social union." The term refers to the maintenance of harmonized social standards and programs, often in the context of fiscal and economic decentralization.[22] It also has resonance in the European Union's concept of "social Europe" and in "social charters" of social and economic rights more generally. In Europe, social democrats have attempted, with limited success, to match the EU's economic integration with a common and overarching social policy framework.[23]

The social union discussion in this work will be confined mainly to its use in Canadian debate. There, it expresses both general and specific concepts. More generally, it refers to the institutions and norms (cf. economic union) by which social cohesion and integration occurs. In this respect, it is similar – but with an emphasis on positive as compared with negative integration – to the notion of economic citizenship discussed above. More specifically, the Canadian debate has used the term in two separate contexts. First, in the 1990–92 constitutional negotiations, proposals for a "social charter" became expressly linked in proposed constitutional amendments to enshrine "Canada's social and economic union." Second, after 1995, Canadian governments negotiated a Social Union Framework Agreement (SUFA), with some implications for economic union reform. The term social union has not been used in Australia, but a strong sense of national standards for social programs is a key aspect of the federal system. Attempts to reform certain aspects of the social policy framework were part of the overall economic union reforms in Australia.

In summary, federal economic unions are a form of integration, imbedded in federal systems of government. As such, they form a regime with normative and institutional characteristics. The norms include the economic benefits of market integration, increased bargaining power, sharing of costs, and the pooling and sharing of risks. They also include the political benefit of economic citizenship, with its values of mobility and equality. The task of sustaining an economic union involves essentially ensuring that these benefits continue to be attained. The institutional characteristics of the regime include measures for negative and positive integration over a common economic space mediated by common political institutions including a central legislature, fiscal relations, the courts, and intergovernmental arrangements. And an important role of the institutional mediation of economic unions in federal states is to reach political bargains over efficiency and equity goals. Global and regional integration can undermine the norms, the institutions, and the political trade-offs integral to federal economic unions. The rest of this work outlines how this has occurred in the case of Australia and Canada and what the two federal systems have done about it. But first, we turn to the final discussion of this chapter – to set out the crucial role and nature of intergovernmental relations.

Role and Nature of Intergovernmental Relations

Governments in federal systems are separate and sovereign within their jurisdiction but nonetheless intersect one another, influence one another, and engage in direct conflict or co-operation. Thus, intergovernmental relations exist in all federal systems, and they are especially important as the practical, ad hoc means for adapting rigid constitutions to changing circumstances. It is useful at this stage to explore the role and nature of intergovernmental relations because they were the chief means by which Australia and Canada achieved economic union reforms (just as they played an important role in European Union integration as shown in chapter 2). More importantly, reform of intergovernmental relations themselves is an important part of the economic reform agenda in both federations. The relative capacities of federal systems to adapt their intergovernmental relations to current reform needs will affect their continuing ability to adapt to global and regional integration. Thus, this part of the chapter departs from the focus on economic change and policy response to consider in some detail the nature and evolution of the policy process. Subsequent chapters provide a more integrated discussion of policy substance and process.

Intergovernmental relations arise from a paradox of federalism. Federal systems were designed to divide and tame power, but detailed arrangements among governments blur jurisdictional responsibility and combine the power of governments. This paradox arises naturally from inherent tensions within federal institutions and values. Political theorist Daniel Elazar describes federalism as "self-rule and shared rule."[24] This description certainly fits the original conception in the United States Constitution of 1787 of separate, coordinate governments drawing sovereignty from the same American people: self-rule by the people through their state governments and shared rule by the people through a national government. The description also fits the concurrent nature of the contemporary American federal system. US state and federal governments are not only strong actors on their own, but they are also completely enmeshed in each other's activities: self-rule is in constant tension with shared rule. Moreover, shared rule takes place not only within the central government, but also between the central government and the constituent governments.

The self-rule and shared rule description also fits federal systems in general. All federations have a tendency toward both coordinate and concurrent government. *Coordinate* federal government implies separate but equal roles (stressing the use of "coordinate" as an adjective, meaning "equal in rank," and not to be confused with "coordinate" as a verb, meaning "to put into proper relations"[25]). Governments have distinct jurisdictions and policy responsibilities. The constituent units are not subordinate to the central government; each order is free to act independently within a federal constitution. Concurrent federal government implies shared and overlapping power. Citizens have access to alternative decision structures over ultimately the same policy responsibilities. Both forms of federalism can be engaged in an era of interdependence. In a coordinate mode, governments co-operate voluntarily from their separate but equal spheres. In a concurrent mode, governments compete in policy fields but can also co-operate when their competition becomes counterproductive.[26]

Coordinate and concurrent federalism can coexist within a single system, although over time, practice tends to emphasize one aspect over the other. Vincent Ostrom stresses that the original American design foresaw elements of concurrency alongside coordinance. He dwells on arguments in the Federalist Papers (mainly Madison) about the protections afforded the American people by two orders of government dealing with the same set of public affairs – in Ostrom's phrase, the "compound republic."[27] In this, he describes concurrent government as a form of competitive redundancy. It is a view that differs profoundly from the other basic response to concurrence just noted – i.e., co-operative relationships and collaborative federalism. However, Ostrom does not suggest that competition precludes co-operation, rather the reverse: "Co-operation and co-ordinated action among various agencies at different levels of government is the hallmark of federal administration ... A federal system of government with overlapping jurisdictions depends, then, not upon integrated hierarchy of command to gain co-ordination among diverse jurisdictions, but upon a variety of different co-operative and joint arrangements."[28]

Federal constitutions configure the tendency toward one mode of relations or the other. Australia has an explicitly concurrent form of division of powers. The Commonwealth's powers are explicitly enumerated. However, the states retain both residual powers and share many Commonwealth powers concurrently. By contrast, the Canadian federal system was designed for a maximum degree of coordinance, but the evolution of the de facto exercise of power has been in the direction of concurrency as well (for more on this comparison, see chapter 4).

Apart from this basic conceptual framework, some analysts have concentrated on what they call intergovernmental "working rules" within federal systems. Applying public choice theory, such analysis focuses on implicit rules as to who participates, the scope of allowable action, the norms of information exchange, how decisions are made, and how payoffs (costs and benefits) are allocated.[29] I do not adopt these rules in a rigorous way here, partly because I do not share all the public choice assumptions. Nonetheless, the way in which such working rules prefigure the role of intergovernmental relations is worth underlining. Where appropriate, I return in subsequent chapters to key working rules and their reform in Australia and Canada.

Another way of analysing these institutions is to track their organic evolution. From this perspective, contemporary intergovernmental relations has long antecedents. Historically, American federalism and most other federal systems around the world have passed through distinct phases of intergovernmental relations. Even in nineteenth-century America, the governments of the federation interacted and shared power much more than is commonly perceived. From the 1930s to 1975, power became increasingly shared. But the direction of that sharing, at least until the mid-1970s, has been to favour the centre. State and local government functions were increasingly compromised and controlled by congressional funding; political parties became increasingly more integrated and less differentiated by state politics; and cities bypassed the states for more direct relationships with the central government. Similar trends occurred in other federal systems against the universal backdrop (in both federal and unitary systems) of increasing national economic and social integration during the Depression and the Second World War and the building of the welfare state afterwards. Interdependence became the key condition in which all governments were drawn into a complex web of intergovernmental relations across virtually all aspects of government policy. In this era of "co-operative" federalism, it was assumed that trends to policy coordination, increasing uniformity, and greater central direction were unidirectional and unstoppable.[30]

The specific ways in which this co-operation has taken place differs substantially according to the overall institutional setting of federal systems, notably the nature of the separation of powers between the legislative, executive, and judicial branches. The American typology assumes the strictly separated roles of the legislature and executive at both the state and federal levels. The consequence of this compound separation is what has been called a "marble cake" – a matrix of relationships in which state governors and legislators as well as local governments pursue separate, direct relations with agencies in the federal administration, the president and White House staff, and both houses of Congress.[31] In federal systems with Westminster-style parliaments, such as in Australia and Canada, the executive dominates intergovernmental relations as legislative and executive power is fused in responsible cabinet government. Compared with the American marble cake, intergovernmental relations in parliamentary federations are layer cakes: relations are essentially monopolized and controlled at each level of government by cabinet ministers including first ministers such as premiers or prime ministers. As Martin Painter notes, parliamentary federalism sets up "wholly distinct governing systems" in which "the original arm's-length relationship remains intact. Adversarial politics and joint administration co-exist as a matter of course."[32]

Despite these fundamental institutional differences, however, co-operative federalism everywhere has exhibited a similar set of functional and flexible arrangements. These have included joint discussion and information sharing, joint planning and deliberation, legal and financial mechanisms to induce state and local government spending in areas of national concern, and the establishment and enforcement of national standards to promote economic and social integration. Co-operative federalism has produced characteristic benefits and costs. Foremost among the benefits is the achievement of otherwise unattainable goals by joint means. Governments may prefer to take unilateral measures, but when those fail or when governments lack the nerve or political support to pursue them, governments seek co-operation. Another benefit is the promotion of harmonized or standardized policy results across jurisdictions. This became especially vital for the development of welfare state policies when the delivery of policy was clearly in state hands, but federal redistribution was deemed essential. Another benefit is the elimination of destructive competition (a "race to the bottom") and counterproductive conflict, most obviously seen in economic development and regulatory standards.[33] Finally, the avoidance of the duplication of effort and funding was also seen as a major benefit.

The costs of co-operative federalism are the obverse side of the coin. The first is the blurring of accountability and political visibility through joint arrangements. Citizens find it difficult to know what government is responsible for what aspect of a co-operative program, and indeed, no single government can be held accountable. Thus, critics in the public choice perspective liken co-operative federalism to a cartel of governments colluding against the public good. Another cost is the suppression of diverse policy outcomes. This is the flip side of harmonization and standardization. Harmonization can be measured in degrees and can be a race to the bottom or to the top.[34] The results are partly dependent on whether decision making can get past lowest common denominator outcomes, typically found where a loose consensus is all that intergovernmental relations can manage. (I discuss this issue further in chapter 4 in relation to the specific processes of intergovernmental relations in Australia and Canada.) Co-operation also limits the scope for experimentation and local flexibility. Finally, for each individual government, co-operation is costly in terms of time and control (especially as compared with internal consensus making).

In many contemporary federal systems, co-operative federalism is still a vital aspect of intergovernmental relations. Its importance has declined since about 1975 as governments have reduced their expenditures and their regulation of the economy. But it has also been in retreat for normative reasons. Dwelling on the shortcomings summarized above, two rather contradictory critiques of co-operative federalism have emerged. The first is the theory of competitive federalism; the second is what may be called the rationalist or managerial critique of federalism.

In its simplest terms, competitive federalism is about restoring a measure of competition to intergovernmental relations. One of its chief proponents, economist Albert Breton, sees the competition in both the neo-classical sense of price competition and the Schumpterian sense of new ideas and processes pushing aside the old. Competition allows entrepreneurial governments to appeal for public allegiance. The outcome is deemed to be politically more efficient in producing better public goods, greater diversity and experimentation, and less collusion. In fact, Breton expressly denies the applicability of economic arguments for co-operation. In his view, governments should not be deciding whether or not to co-operate, but how to allow citizens to exercise their rights and express their preferences.[35]

Competition in the political economy in general has been a dominant theme in the public choice literature. Charles Tiebout's influential article introduced the idea of public expenditure competition among state and local governments in the United States.[36] In this sense, citizens would vote with their feet to choose the most efficient mix of spending and taxing for their needs. This "interjurisdictional" competition – i.e., state versus state, locality versus locality – is a horizontal feature of competitive federalism. There is also a vertical aspect of federal versus state competition. As noted above, James Madison argued that such vertical competition was a chief virtue of the American design. The two types of competition are related in that overly close co-operation between federal government and the constituent governments, such as over national standards, can foreclose the room for competitive diversity among states. In John Kincaid's terms, co-operative federalism in the United States leads to a form of mediated competition only in which the states get to "compete" for federal funding.[37]

The competition theorists rest on assumptions about liberal pluralism and market behaviour that are not shared by all. Indeed, Ostrom admits that the political efficiency of federal competition is counterintuitive to notions of bureaucratic efficiency. This latter concept is the chief concern of the other major source of criticism of co-operative federalism – that of managerial rationalism. For those in this school, the arguments of competitive federalism are too subtle by half. They would tend to share the criticism that co-operative federalism is collusive and complicated. But their solution is radically different. For them, it would be best to return to a form of classical, coordinate federalism in which governments required less intergovernmental co-operation in the first place and where bureaucratic tasks such as policy development, program management, and service delivery could be rationalized in one order of government or the other. They argue that the coordination achieved by co-operative federalism is too partial to be effective. Where harmonization is deemed essential, managerialists seek central control. In any case, the managerialists argue that there should be little or no competition for scarce public resources.[38]

The rationalists assume that conflict is counterproductive and that coordination is essential. Theirs is, at root, a hierarchical concept. For them, the problems of federal government arise from an excess of concurrency, and the solution lies in reducing what is commonly referred to as "overlap and duplication." According to Gordon Brown, the costs of overlap and duplication are assessed in terms of standard accounting efficiency as well as economic efficiency more broadly conceived. From the "accounting" perspective, the costs are:

1 direct redundancy creating waste in public resources
2 conflicting objectives, in which the effects of competing programs cancel each other out or render a joint program difficult to evaluate
3 coordination costs, which include the time, bureaucratic resources, and political capital expended in constant meetings and communication with other governments
4 lost economies of scale assuming that these exist in the public sector

There are two broader economic efficiency concerns: the potential oversupply of public goods implied by overlap and duplication, and the inherently conservative nature of policy response in a federal system where power is divided.[39]

Thus, the critics of competitive federalism and the managerialists differ radically in their prescriptions. As Stephen Schecter concludes: "The basic difference between federalism and managerialism, and hence the tension between them, has to do with ends and limits. The end of federalism, in the American system at least, is liberty; the end of managerialism is efficiency. In this sense, the challenge of *public* management consists largely in directing the 'gospel of efficiency' to the constitutional ends of limited government."[40] Managerialists are unwilling to take the competitive federalism leap of faith that the political market will clear. Instead, they posit a faith of their own. Yet their views resonate with those who seek to shrink the state, particularly to cut deficits and debt. As will be outlined in chapter 4, the managerialist critique has become prominent in both Australia and Canada, helping to shape the movement for reform of intergovernmental relations and the economic union. By comparison, the political advocacy of competitive federalism is less obvious. The views of the public choice school in America have influenced a rhetoric of returning to the concurrent roots of federalism. Ronald Reagan campaigned on returning power to the states and reducing the burden of co-operative arrangements. In practice, the federal government during his terms as president reformed fiscal transfers only by cutting them, increased federal pre-emption of state law, and passed a fresh set of unfunded congressional mandates onto the states.[41]

In order to summarize this discussion and to set up a template for assessment and comparison of intergovernmental relations in the remainder of this book, table 3.1 sets out a typology of intergovernmental relations. Drawing on the distinctions made above between *coordinate* and *concurrent* federalism and the practice of co-operation and competition, one may build a three-way classification of contemporary intergovernmental relations. On the left side of the table is a description of *competitive* relations in which the concurrent nature of federalism is used to full effect and where the requirements of interdependence are met through the unmediated action of a political market. In the middle panel are described co-operative relations where concurrency is tamed through harmonization, either voluntary or constitutionally required. On the right is *rationalization* where coordinate federalism is maximized, concurrency is minimized, and harmonization, where unavoidable, is achieved through central dominance. Table 3.1 summarizes the characteristics of each of these forms of relations in two ways: basic characteristics and typical benefits and costs.[42]

Taken together, the two panels portray the differing emphasis placed in each mode of relations on the various values of federal systems. Competitive relations emphasize liberty and autonomy and downplay conflict management. They are characterized by the multiple occupation of a policy field and rely on a political market for coordination or harmonization. Conversely, rationalization emphasizes control, efficiency, and certainty, while downplaying diversity. It seeks a single, consolidated occupation of a policy field, mandatory harmonization, unified decision making, and minimal spillovers. The middle path of co-operative relations places value on conflict avoidance, problem solving, harmonization, and bargaining. Less prominent are concerns about redundancy, autonomy, and certainty. While co-operation is voluntary, the occupation and achievement of harmonized results in a policy field is mediated through agreement, not left to the chances of the political market.

The characterizations in table 3.1 are ideal types. In practice, federal systems will exhibit a mixture of types, with a predominance of one type over another. Over time, governments may shift the emphasis to meet the needs of changing circumstances. As discussed above, the middle

Table 3.1 Typology of Intergovernmental Relations

BASIC CHARACTERISTICS

COMPETITION	CO-OPERATION	RATIONALIZATION
• Competitive occupation of policy field. • Coordination by "unseen hand" of market. • Policy-making by unilateral thrust and riposte.	• Mediated occupation of a policy field • Coordination by voluntary agreement • Policy-making by consensus or negotiated decision making.	• Consolidated, single occupation of a policy field. • Coordination by mandatory consolidation. • Policy-making by unilateral, unified decision making.

TYPICAL BENEFITS AND COSTS

COMPETITION	CO-OPERATION	RATIONALIZATION
• Maximum citizen responsiveness. • Diversity, flexibility, innovation in policy outcomes. • Policy convergence over time (a race to the bottom or to the top?). • Duplication and overlap. • Conflicts eroding legitimacy. • Coordination costs for citizens. • Autonomy maintained.	• Voluntary joint action • Harmonization of objectives and possibly outcomes. • Partial coordination at costs for governments. • Blurred accountability and visibility • Reduced intra-government consistency. • Minimizes overlap and duplication. • Reduced citizen responsiveness (government collusion). • Loss of autonomy for both parties (or pooled sovereignty?).	• Jurisdictional certainty. • Maximum coordination at minimum cost. • Uniform results. • Minimum conflict. • Maximum accountability. • Intra-government consistency. • Quick results. • Minimum spillovers, duplication, and overlap. • Loss of flexibility, innovation, diversity. • Low level of citizen responsiveness. • (Can be) loss of autonomy for one order of government.

Sources: Breton, 1985; Fletcher, 1991; Fletcher and Wallace, 1985; Kenyon and Kincaid, 1991: Kincaid, 1991; Leslie, 1987; McRoberts, 1985; Moravcsik, 1993; Painter, 1991; Painter, 1995; Scharpf, 1988; Sproule-Jones, 1993; Watts, 1999.

path of co-operative relations has tended to prevail for much of the past century, but now reformers seek either more competitive or more rationalized relations.

In some respects, the three modes illustrate segments of a spectrum, with movement possible along the spectrum and only subtle differences of shading from one point to another. As already noted, federal systems combine coordinate and concurrent elements. Campbell Sharman notes a "double ambiguity: ... on the one hand, intergovernmental relations is a manifestation of the open and competitive interaction of governments in a federation, and on the other, it can be seen as a way of suppressing such open competition."[43] Within any given policy area, relations may be predominantly of one type, but overall, there may be considerable mixture of the three (this will be shown in the case of relations over economic union reform discussed in later chapters). There is also the important consideration of choice among the three modes. The advocates of competitive federalism clearly wish to promote new forms of relations but may be prevented from doing so by social and institutional factors that constrain that choice. Nor can one type alone illustrate a given federal system. As Rufus Davis warns, taxonomy is better suited to rocks than to federal systems.[44] Nonetheless, a cursory examination of the American system shows a strong affinity with competition, while the German system seems locked into its co-operation.

As noted, the purpose of introducing this discussion and the typology here is to provide an analytical framework for assessing the intergovernmental reform process in the remainder of this work. The chief question to be addressed is which type of relations achieves the most effective results in terms of economic reform. The answer will differ from federal system to system, while some elements of "best practice" will emerge of relevance to federal government in general. In chapter 4, I apply this analysis to the pre-reform state of intergovernmental relations in Australia and Canada. In the concluding chapter (9), I reapply it to the reformed process and draw further conclusions for federal systems in general.

To conclude here, it is sufficient to return to the theme that contemporary federal systems face the task of adjustment to international economic liberalization and global integration with multiple jurisdictions and fragmented authority. The managerialist response to this challenge would be to create centralized regulatory authority or uniformity of responses among constituent governments. Competitive federalism critics would worry that such reform would erode federalism and its flexible and diverse pattern of adaptation. It is my hypothesis that comprehensive policy reform, such as that involved in changing the rules of economic union, can be accomplished only through intergovernmental collaboration. Thus, the reform process fits more surely in the "co-operation" mode. And the process may still leave room for movement between the three modes of competition, co-operation, and rationalization. In any case, Australia and Canada provide a test of the ability of intergovernmental relations to deliver such coherent reform. They also provide an experiment of the effects of such reform on the evolving federal systems themselves.

4 Comparing Pre-Reform Economic Unions in Australia and Canada

DESIGN AND DEVELOPMENT OF THE ECONOMIC UNIONS OF AUSTRALIA AND CANADA

In chapter 3, I introduced the concept of a federal economic union and its characteristic institutional features. These include: a common economic space and institutions for negative and positive integration, imbedded in a federal constitution with a protected distribution of powers; central executive and legislative institutions; and fiscal relations, intergovernmental relations, and a system of courts. One cannot understand the need for and significance of reform without understanding the basic shape and evolution of the economic union regimes in Australia and Canada. In the following discussion, I provide detail for readers unfamiliar with either or both of the Canadian and Australian federal systems. The discussion here is organized into seven sections:

1 Federal Origins
2 Basic Constitutional Scheme
3 Territory and Constituent Units
4 Rules for Negative Integration
5 Federal Economic Powers
6 Provincial/State Powers
7 Evolution and Limits of Integration

In each section, I discuss Canada first, then Australia, also drawing comparisons between the two.

Federal Origins

The founders of the Canadian federation of 1867 sought an economic union among the British North American colonies. Britain's repeal of the Corn Laws in 1846 and the Americans' abrogation in 1866 of the Reciprocity Treaty of 1854 impressed the colonists with the need to find new markets. Confederation was a way to provide the conditions for a consolidated and potentially expandable domestic market. Still, economic integration was not the only objective of the union. Defence concerns were also prominent, as was the broader constitutional objective of many in the Province of Canada (now Quebec and Ontario) to get out of the straitjacket of the unitary constitution imposed in 1841. However, if motives were multiple, the political visionaries who negotiated Confederation foresaw a new transcontinental economy as a result.

Despite advocacy in Canada West (now Ontario) for a new unitary state, only a federal union would satisfy the other colonies. In particular, the French-speaking and Roman Catholic population of Canada East (Quebec) sought the protection of a federal constitution for its specific interests, including its language, civil law, religious education, and social services. Nonetheless, in the compromise to create the federation, most, if not all, of the key features necessary to create an integrated economy – at least in nineteenth-century terms – were vested in the Dominion (federal) government. The federal government inherited the colonial governments' strongly entrepreneurial role in economic development, extending a tradition of "defensive expansion" vis-à-vis the United States.[1]

Economic union also motivated the creation of the Australian federation. Indeed, in the 1891 convention, which initiated the long negotiation, economic union figured in two of the four principles adopted to guide the process.[2] Agreement on the details took some time to reach, however, given the fundamental division of interests on the overall trading position of the proposed union between free trade states led by New South Wales and protectionist states led by Victoria. A high external tariff would require an internal customs union if it were not to be undermined. As the customs duty was the principal revenue source for the uniting colonies, its consolidation in the central government would also require a financial settlement to compensate the states. As with Canada, however, there seems to have been no doubt that Australia would be a federal union, given the strong position of the existing colonial governments and an economy that revolved almost completely around the colonial capitals.

Basic Constitutional Scheme

The Canadian constitution married parliamentary institutions to a federal distribution of powers with the aim of creating a much stronger and potentially more centralized system of government than the American one, without the US constitution's formal separation of powers. However, the federal bargain in Canada was not able to reconcile completely the competing tendencies in the 1860s for, on the one hand, a strong political union designed to create economic integration in the interests of the dominant economic elites and, on the other, a decentralized system rooted in important religious, ethnic, and other differences.

Over time, the constitution of 1867 has permitted wide variations in federal and provincial power as the balance swung between unitary and confederal tendencies. Change occurred through judicial review, institutional practice, fiscal arrangements, and intergovernmental relations. Moreover, events such as two world wars and two long phases of severe depression, interspersed with periods of rapid growth and prosperity, drove the evolution of the system, overwhelming various elements of the original design.

Australian federalism is similarly wedded to parliamentary institutions, with important differences. Australia in the 1890s was a significantly more democratic political culture than Canada in the 1860s. This is reflected in the actual framing of the constitution by a directly elected convention and its subsequent ratification by the people in a referendum (and the continuing requirement of a referendum for any amendment). It is also shown in the role of the Senate, elected on a statewide franchise, on different terms than the federal lower house and with therefore stronger legitimacy over time as a house of review as compared with the appointed Canadian Senate.

The most important design difference between the two federations is the distribution of powers. Australia consciously chose the American system of concurrent federal and state powers, with the states holding the reserve of powers, over the Canadian model of mostly exclusive federal and provincial jurisdiction and the reserve held by the centre. The great irony is that this choice was made because the Australian founders thought that Canada was too centralized. Whether this was a misapprehension of the Canadian constitution or an accurate portrayal of the Canadian federation circa 1890 is not important here.³ What matters is that Australians thought that the states' rights would be most effectively protected by their reserve powers. They did not foresee the centralizing dynamic inherent in a scheme in which there is no effective constitutional check on the expansion of Commonwealth (federal) legislative authority in its concurrent fields. And in the absence of such a specific protection for state legislative room, the High Court has not gone out on a limb to invent one. The result of the concurrent powers scheme has been not only centralization, but also an overlap and concurrency of governmental roles.⁴

Territory and Constituent Units

Both federations inherited substantial territory. To the four original Canadian provinces – Ontario, Quebec, Nova Scotia, and New Brunswick – were later added three other British colonies: British Columbia (1871), Prince Edward Island (1873), and Newfoundland (1949). An even larger accretion of territory came in the 1870 purchase of Rupert's Land from the Hudson's Bay Company, comprising the entire watershed of Hudson Bay north of the US border and westward to the Continental Divide. From this territory, the provinces of Manitoba, Saskatchewan, and Alberta were formed. The Arctic islands were acquired later through a British act of Parliament. Thus, the Dominion of Canada had, almost from the beginning, a huge internal empire.

As a federation, Canada has a small number of diverse constituent units. The ten present-day provinces differ widely in territorial size and population: at one end of the scale is Prince Edward Island, with a territory of 5,600 square kilometres and a population in 1998 of 135,000; at the other end is Ontario, with a territory of 1,068,000 square kilometres and a population of 10.7 million, 37 per cent of the Canadian total. Quebec, the only province with a French-speaking majority and homeland to 80 per cent of French-speaking Canadians, comprises over 7 million people, a quarter of the total Canadian population – a proportion that has been declining slowly in recent decades. Most of the Canadian population occupies a narrow ribbon of land 8,000 kilometres (5,000 miles) long, hugging the United States border. This distribution of population, its uneven linguistic composition by province, and great differences in size among the provinces have had important consequences for the notion of provincial equality and autonomy as the federation has developed.

Australia's continental territory was intact upon federation. All the state boundaries had long since been fixed. Indeed, the only major issue was whether the federation would include New Zealand, which had been represented at the 1890–91 Australasian Federation Conference. Geographical distance, historic difference including different relations with aboriginal peoples, and a sense of social superiority (on New Zealand's part) seem to have kept New Zealanders out of the union. And on the continent, some elements of the constitutional carve-out were incomplete, including the evolving status of the Northern Territory and the creation of the Capital Territory.

While Australia has some small overseas territories, the constituent units of the federation as such are confined to the six states. For many intergovernmental purposes, the two mainland territories join the states. While the Australian Capital Territory (ACT) and the Northern Territory do not have the same legal status as the states and are even more dependent on the Commonwealth financially, the Northern Territory is bigger than most states geographically, and the ACT's 1998 population is over half that of the smallest state. All this is to stress that like Canada, the Australian federation has a relatively small number of constituent units, but the range of differences among them is not as great.

Rules for Negative Integration

Canada's 1867 constitution contains what is often called the Common Market clause; section 121 guarantees the free movement of goods among provinces without tariffs.[5] It covers goods only; thus, it falls far short of a comprehensive prohibition on the erection of barriers to the free movement of goods, services, persons, and capital. Moreover, the courts have interpreted section 121 even more narrowly as prohibitive of fiscal measures only, preferring to handle disputes over regulatory barriers to integration on the basis of the distribution of powers. At the time of Confederation, section 121 was nonetheless significant in securing a customs union. A companion provision, section 122, deprived the uniting provinces of their customs and excise revenues, creating a huge hole in the finances of the Maritime provinces, in particular, for which they had to be compensated.

Second, the constitution prohibits the provinces from levying indirect taxes (sections 91(3) and 92(2)). The courts have interpreted these provisions narrowly to ban provincial customs and excise-type taxes but not to prevent general sales taxes levied on the consumer of goods and services.

A third and more important constitutional provision dates only from 1982. Section 6 of the *Canadian Charter of Rights and Freedoms* guarantees that every citizen and permanent resident has the right to move and take up residence in any province and to pursue a livelihood, with exemptions for preferential employment policies in areas of high unemployment and saving provincial residency requirements for social service entitlements. While the section does not extend to corporations, it may yet be interpreted to extend to the economic activity of out-of-province persons without having an in-province presence.

By contrast, Australia's constitution provides a more comprehensive set of provisions to guarantee mobility in the common economic space. These include: section 92, the interstate free trade clause; section 90 to provide exclusive Commonwealth power to levy duties of customs and excise; section 117 regarding equal treatment of out-of-state residents; and sections 51(2), 51(3), and 99, which prohibit the Commonwealth from discriminating among the states in taxation, bounties, or more general preferences. These sections have given the courts much work, in particular section 92, the most litigated provision in the entire constitution. Section 90 is an important counterpart to section 92 in that the exclusive control of customs is essential if there is to be a customs union to go along with the Common Market.

Jurisprudence on section 92 has covered two themes: first, broad free market principles; and second, free trade within the federation. Beginning with its decision in *McArthur v. Queensland* (1920),[6] the High Court found that section 92 conferred an individual right or immunity for traders from restrictive state and (later) Commonwealth laws and other government actions. The high-water point for the individual rights/free market doctrine came in the 1949 *Banks Nationalisation* case. Over the years, the courts have struck down state and Commonwealth law across a wide swath, including transportation schemes, agricultural marketing, labour regulations, bank and airline nationalization, price controls, and even firearms and wildlife regulation.

In applying section 92 for economic union purposes, the High Court distinguished three aspects of section 92: "trade," "commerce," and "intercourse" (the latter referring to the general movement and communication of persons and businesses across state boundaries). Yet the court struggled to find a consistent interpretation of where section 92 begins and ends in regulatory terms. And as just noted, its application often had little to do with creating or sustaining a single market as such. Indeed, legal scholar Michael Coper argues that the expanded libertarian scope of section 92 departed from the founders' intention of internal free trade. His argument contributed to the decision of the High Court in *Cole v. Whitfield* (1988) to rein in the broader interpretation.[7]

The judgment in *Cole v. Whitfield* has a number of important consequences for the movement for economic union reform in Australia. First, it reinforced a moderate interpretation of section 92 as less than a set of individual economic rights but more than a prohibition of fiscal barriers alone. The new interpretation, that section 92 would be violated only by "discriminatory burdens of a protectionist kind," appears to have broad political support and stresses the economic union as its primary goal. Second, the judgment leaves room for the exercise of the Commonwealth trade and commerce power (see below) in that it recognizes a greater legitimacy for certain forms of economic regulation. Ironically, the court provides this room for government intervention just when political trends were moving in the opposite direction. Third, the court recognized that federal legislation could still be "discriminatory" if it regulated interstate trade but not intrastate trade. As a solution, the court proposed the co-operative adoption of laws by the Commonwealth and the states to cover the whole field of economic activity. Indeed, broad national schemes of economic regulation are likely to be entirely safe from section 92 challenge *only* if they arise from joint intergovernmental decision.[8] The court made this important legal argument in the early stages of intergovernmental co-operation on economic union issues.

The impact of *Cole v. Whitfield* on the economic union debate is reinforced by another timely High Court decision in *Street v. Queensland Bar Association* (1989). This judgment considerably strengthened the meaning of section 117 to make it a clear prohibition of discrimination on the basis of residence, permanent or otherwise. In Justice Brennan's words, section 117 can now be seen as conferring a "constitutional right." Moreover, Brennan made an important link between sections 92 and 117, between economic and social integration. With respect to section 117, he contends: "It is a guarantee of equal treatment under the law. The guarantee supplements the freedom of interstate intercourse, which is secured by s. 92. Sections 92 and 117 are the constitutional pillars of the legal and social unity of the Australian people, just as ss. 90 and 92 are the constitutional pillars of national economic unity."[9] This decision thus also reinforces constitutional notions of economic union at an important juncture in Australian federal history.

Federal Economic Powers

The Canadian distribution of powers is largely determined by the two long lists of exclusive powers for each of the federal (section 91) and provincial (section 92) legislatures. There is also a small list of concurrent powers (section 95) covering agriculture and immigration, contributory pensions plans (section 94A added in 1964), and interprovincial trade in natural resources (section 92A added in 1982). The residual power as such lies with the federal parliament. The most important federal powers for the purposes of positive economic integration have been the section 91 preamble, which provides a plenary power for "peace, order, and good government" and section 91(2) on the regulation of trade and commerce. Other important federal powers are: 91(2A), unemployment insurance (by amendment in 1949); 91(3), the raising of money by any mode or system of taxation; 91(14), currency and coinage; 91(15), banking, incorporation of banks, and the issue of paper money; and 91(10) and (12), navigation and shipping. These powers constituted a nineteenth-century attempt to consolidate in federal hands the infrastructural needs of a transcontinental customs union. Nonetheless, it was assumed that much, if not most, local economic activity would be unaffected by the federal powers and that matters of land settlement could be dealt with concurrently.

The trade and commerce power (section 91(2)) has been interpreted narrowly – especially in judgments, beginning with the 1881 *Parsons* case – by the Judicial Committee of the Privy Council (JCPC), which, until 1949, was the final court of appeal for all Canadian cases. That judgment set the stage for a clear distinction between interprovincial and intra-provincial trade, emphasizing federal jurisdiction over the "flow" of trade only. The court made its narrow interpretation in view of the clear conflict with the provincial power over "property and civil rights" (section 92(13)). The courts particularly sought to split the obviously overlapping subject matters of the two provisions into two coordinate spheres. In *Parsons*, the judges found trade and commerce to have two aspects: first, the regulation of interprovincial or international trade per se; and second, the "general regulation" of trade.

This second branch lay dormant until 1989, when the Supreme Court of Canada began to fill in the blanks, with possible long-term consequences for the centralization of economic regulation. In *General Motors v. City National Leasing* (1989), the Supreme Court set out a doctrine for the application of a general regulation of trade, providing federal legislation met certain tests. Chief Justice Dickson, writing the unanimous decision, drew upon three tests from a previous case *(Vapor)* and added two more. In sum, they are:

1 the presence of a "general regulatory scheme"
2 the "oversight of a regulatory agency"
3 a concern "with trade as a whole rather than with a particular industry"
4 that "the legislation should be of a nature that the provinces jointly or severally would be constitutionally incapable of enacting"
5 that "the failure to include one or more provinces or localities in a legislative scheme would jeopardize the successful operation of the scheme in other parts of the country"[10]

The importance of this new doctrine is first, that in applying this test, the Supreme Court declared that the federal *Competition Act*, as amended in 1975 and 1986, lay within this dicta of "general regulation" despite its application to intra-provincial trade. This decision reversed a century of Canadian governments having to rely on the federal power over the criminal law (with its much more onerous burden of proof) to enforce competition policy. Second, the court's new doctrine (partly evident in its 1983 judgment in *CN Transportation)* affected the debate over Canada-United States free trade by encouraging the view that the federal government might be able to proceed without the agreement of the provinces (this issue is discussed in chapter 5). Third, the dicta identify the nub of legal issues surrounding economic regulation in a federal state. The last two conditions in particular – that the federal government would be able to act if the provinces were incapable of doing so or if the failure to include one or more provinces would jeopardize the entire scheme – set a high bar for intergovernmental coordination for new forms of economic integration.[11]

Unlike its regulatory powers, the Canadian federal government's taxing and spending powers have not been as constrained. Its tax power is essentially unlimited in form. Moreover, the federal government has claimed a spending power (i.e., the legal ability to make expenditures even in matters of provincial jurisdiction) said to match its full taxing capacity. While the courts have upheld the spending power, its use has been controversial. It has contributed substantially to intergovernmental tensions, especially with Quebec, as the federal government intervened in cost-shared and direct program funding across a broad front of social programs since the 1940s. Less controversial has been a system of unconditional equalization payments to the poorer provinces, introduced in 1957 and altered frequently since. Another important trend since 1977 has been to bundle together payments for previous cost-shared programs into large block grants to all provinces.

In contrast to Canada's substantial but constrained federal powers, the powers of the Commonwealth in Australia have had few restraints. The long list of explicit powers assigned, albeit concurrently, to the Commonwealth by section 51 is similar in content to Canada's section 91. It includes notably: 51(I), trade and commerce with other countries, and among the states; 51(XXIII) and (XXIV), banking and insurance (except where established by the states); 51(XX), foreign corporations and trading or financial corporations formed within the limits of the Commonwealth; 51(XXIII) and (XXIIIA), invalid and old-age pensions and other direct social benefit plans; 51(XXIX), external affairs; and 51(XXXV), conciliation and arbitration for the prevention and settlement of industrial disputes beyond the limits of any one state.

In the first two decades of federation, these powers were balanced against the states' reserved power, section 107, and the doctrine of governmental immunity. With the *Engineers* case of 1920, however, these two defences were overturned, and since then, the High Court has read federal powers very broadly. Indeed, *Engineers* held that as long as federal legislation covered the field, it could be upheld over state legislation. The resulting centralization of legislative power has been deemed inevitable, and there has been no indication that the court will significantly change its tack on this interpretation of concurrency.[12]

Thus, the federal regulatory powers over the economy established in 1901 have grown. According to constitutional scholar Leslie Zines, after

1920, the reach of Commonwealth jurisdiction could extend not only to international and interstate trade, but also to manufacturing, mining, agriculture, and much domestic commerce. The courts found that it also extended, by the late 1930s, to cover most, if not all, labour relations in the country. Michael Coper defends the trend as indicating "the desirability of the policy of integration of the Australian nation."[13]

Over time, the emphasis in jurisprudence and legislation has varied from one head of federal economic power to another. The primary federal power, section 51(I) for trade and commerce, has been read by the courts as extending only incidentally to intrastate trade. The courts have also upheld a distinction between "inter" and "intra" state (e.g., *Concrete Pipes* case, 1951), influenced by jurisprudence on section 92. Indeed, until 1988, section 92 provided an important brake on the use of section 51(I) (see discussion above). Since 1971, the Commonwealth has relied more on the corporations' power (section 51(XX)) and the external affairs' power (section 51(XXIX)) to uphold their economic regulation, with mixed results. For example, the courts found the corporations' power supported the federal *Trade Practice Act* but did not extend to the actual process of incorporating firms (the *Incorporations* case, 1990). This forced the Commonwealth to negotiate a new co-operative legislative scheme with the states.

In the 1980s, the external affairs' power has been interpreted very broadly, essentially to allow the Commonwealth to pass any legislation that purports to implement a treaty that it has signed, regardless of its effect on state laws (e.g., *Tasmanian Dam* case, 1983). It has considerable legal (if not political) potential to enforce trade and other international economic policy on the states. Nonetheless, as tools of economic regulation, both the external affairs' and corporations' power are blunt instruments, incapable of providing precise rules for economic integration.

A second major aspect of federal power over the economy is the Commonwealth's fiscal capacity. As Cheryl Saunders argues, the original federal bargain did not include a lasting financial settlement, but by depriving the states of their chief source of revenue in 1900, the constitution laid the ground for a continuing and chronic vertical fiscal imbalance.[14] It does so by granting the federal government both plenary taxing powers and an explicit power to make grants to the states (section 96). Meanwhile, the states' fiscal capacity has been narrowed. Section 90 on excise taxes has been interpreted broadly to prohibit the states from levying sales or consumption taxes as well as direct taxes on production. No such legal bar exists for states levying income taxes, but the Commonwealth has successfully kept the states out of the income tax field by making their restraint a condition on the receipt of intergovernmental grants, a practice crucially upheld by the High Court in 1942. Thus, the vertical imbalance became a circular problem. As Saunders puts it: "the taxation imbalance which necessitates revenue redistribution is now itself the product of the grants power."[15] For the states, there has been little direct political incentive to get into the tax field, perceiving little room and lacking co-operation among themselves on a common approach.

In two important ways, the Commonwealth made it easier for the states to accept national fiscal leadership. These are the innovations of the financial agreements on borrowing, with the associated institution of the Australian Loan Council begun in 1927; and fiscal equalization applied to Commonwealth general purpose grants and according to formulae determined by the Commonwealth Grants Commission established in 1933. While neither of these institutions has been without controversy among sometimes restive states, they at least provided a safety net of redistribution and stabilized debt management to all states through difficult years. Both have had important equity and efficiency consequences for the national economy, underpinning the generally positive role played by fiscal federalism in national economic management. In the movement to reform the economic union in Australia, however, these advantages would be weighed against the mounting costs of vertical fiscal imbalance.

Provincial/State Powers

In their list of exclusive powers, the Canadian provinces retained control of "property and civil rights in the province" (section 92(13)) and thus over the law of contract and most private law. In this context, federal powers over subjects such as banking were exceptions to the more broadly stated provincial jurisdiction. The provinces also kept important roles in economic development through their legislative control over the management and sale of public lands (section 92(5)), reinforced by provincial proprietary rights over "all lands, mines, minerals, and royalties," confirmed by section 109. The provinces also have power to incorporate companies "with provincial objects" (section 92(11)) and retain power over local works and undertakings (section 92(10)), with the important exception of works declared by the federal parliament to be to the national advantage. The provinces also have jurisdiction over "all matters of a merely local or private nature in the province" (section 92(16)). The latter has been interpreted as a sort of provincial plenary power comparable to the federal power for "peace, order, and good government." Moreover, the provinces controlled most fields that brought government into direct contact with individual citizens: hospitals and charities, education (subject to guarantees of rights for religious minorities), the administration of justice (although the criminal law itself is federal), local prisons, and municipal institutions.

In addition to this extensive and exclusive list of provincial legislative powers, there are few constitutional constraints on provincial taxing authority. Those that exist include immunity from taxing federal property (but not employees) and a prohibition, as noted above, on the levy of "indirect" taxes, a provision that has been interpreted narrowly and has not prevented the provinces from levying retail sales taxes. The provinces also enjoy other revenue sources such as personal and corporate income taxes, resource royalties and other rents, and property taxes. As in Australia, a system of intergovernmental grants from the federal government has reduced (much less severe) vertical fiscal imbalance as well as provided equalization payments to the have-not provinces. While important disparities remain, the relative fiscal autonomy of the Canadian provinces is vital to understanding their ability to flex the legislative muscle provided by the constitution.

It is important to stress, as well, that this large grant of powers to the provinces has been generally upheld by the courts as a matter of maintaining federal balance. This trend began in the late nineteenth century under the judgments of the JCPC, overturning the early judgments of the Supreme Court of Canada. Indeed, by the 1930s and 1940s, the extent of court protection of the provinces was considered by some as so extreme as to be turning on its head the founders' intentions for a relatively strong central government. Moreover, the courts interpretation focused on determining the "pith and substance" of legislation before it in an attempt to award the subject matter to either the federal or provincial parliaments, but rarely to both.[16] Another logical extension of the courts' classical approach to the distribution of powers was the decision of 1937 in *Labour Conventions* by which the federal power to enter into treaties was found not to extend to their implementation where matters of provincial jurisdiction were concerned. In the famous words of Lord Atkin, "while the ship of state now sails on larger ventures and into foreign waters, she still retains the watertight compartments which are an essential part of her original structure."[17] This differs significantly from Australian jurisprudence noted above, particularly the *Tasmanian Dam* case (1983) in which federal legislative jurisdiction was held to extend to the implementation of any treaty the Commonwealth signed.

As for Australia, given the trends to centralization of legislative and fiscal power described above, one is tempted to ask "what's left?" for the states. In fact, the states were left with quite a bit in 1901. As Leslie Zines notes: "Subjects which Australians in the late nineteenth century associated with government regulation and administration, such as Crown lands, education, health, railways and roads, local government, police, mining, factory laws, the licensing of occupations, and the general criminal law, were not subjects of federal power and therefore were, prima facie, exclusively within State power."[18] Only after *Engineers* in 1920 did Commonwealth legislation begin to influence manufacturing, agriculture, and labour relations, among others. Still, much regulatory clout continues to reside with the states. Most important, perhaps, the executive prerogatives of the state governments have been largely preserved so that their pre-federation role in government enterprise continued and in some respects, expanded to cover large areas of the economy: notably railways; public transport; ports; and electrical, water, and gas utilities. They also continued to play a leading role in primary industries through their control over land and minerals. And from a political perspective, the states retained formal control over many areas of public life closest to the electorate: local government, education, health, and social services.

Nonetheless, the latter set of functions underscores the weakness of the states in the building and sustaining of the welfare state, particularly since the Second World War. Already losing to the Commonwealth some of their clout over wages and working conditions, the states' fiscal incapacity made them vulnerable to Commonwealth blandishments and conditions in the social policy field. As noted, the states have been kept out of the two most lucrative tax fields: income and consumption. What remained for them was a collection of minor, generally regressive, taxes with little room for growth (with the exception of gambling revenues). This included payroll levies, financial institution duties, stamp duties, and business franchise licence fees. And as recently as August 1997, the High Court ruled that the latter taxes were in effect "excise" and thus could no longer be levied by the states. The judgment helped to precipitate a wide-ranging discussion of tax reform options (discussed in chapters 7 and 8).

In any case, the constitution leaves the states chronically dependent on the Commonwealth for 39 per cent of total revenues on average in 1997–98, of which almost half is tied to specific purposes under Commonwealth legislation. This vertical fiscal imbalance is claimed by its critics to lead to a variety of problems at the state level. These include: excessive overlap and duplication of government services, lack of responsibility and accountability in shared programs, lack of flexibility and diversity among the states, discouragement of disciplined financial management, and rigidity with respect to tax reform.[19]

In conclusion, there are few state rights constraints on federal economic powers in Australia or at least many less than in Canada. Still, the states are important political and administrative players. Few comprehensive schemes of national integration could prevail in the face of sustained state opposition. And, as outlined next, the states have not been prevented from continuing many aspects of the regional economic development they had pursued as colonies.

Evolution and Limits of Integration

Constitutional design is one thing; political development over time is another. The histories of Canada and Australia as federations demonstrate interplay between economic integration and political development, shaping in quite different ways their already differing constitutional legacies. A basic sketch of this interplay is important for the analysis that follows.

In both Australia and Canada, national economic integration promoted a new pattern of economic activity that concentrated wealth and population. This integration created a political reaction to reduce the territorial and class inequities of industrialization and urbanization through central redistribution. It also involved attempts by the constituent governments to promote regional economic development. In the process, there emerged a conflict, sometimes latent, between the efficiency and equity objectives of the federal union.

Canada's east-west transcontinental economy – deliberately shaped by federal transportation, trade, and immigration policy – came to be characterized by a distinctly regionalized division of labour. Manufacturing dwindled in the Maritime provinces and became increasingly concentrated in Ontario and Quebec. In the Western provinces, resource production – wheat, lumber, minerals, and later hydroelectricity and oil – remained the driving force behind economic development. The regional differentiation generated or perpetuated large disparities in wealth and population densities. As a result, a diverse range of regional and ideological protest movements emerged, producing demands for a reorientation of federal economic policy and compensation for the effects of past policies.

The twentieth-century Canadian welfare state can be seen in part as a response to regional and social inequities spawned by national economic integration. The features of the federal equity response included: (1) direct federal payments to Canadian citizens (e.g., universal old-age security payments); (2) a complex and decentralized system of fiscal arrangements with the provinces; and (3) direct spending to promote regional economic development.[20] The intergovernmental transfers, in particular, became the chief means for establishing federation-wide social programs of comparable design and quality. These equity developments, built up slowly from the early 1940s, reached their peak by 1982. The overall framework can be termed a Canadian "social union." It became unravelled in a context of severe fiscal constraint due to an escalating debt at the federal level and by a neo-liberal policy framework arguing for less regional and personal dependence on the state, privatization of public enterprise, and tax cutting.

Equity, however, is not just about redistribution; it is also about regional balance within the economic structure itself. The federal government's powers have been used primarily for the former and not the latter. In other words, federal *allocative* powers (those used to create economic wealth as opposed to redistributing it) have been applied mainly for the purposes of national integration and not regional balance. Yet redistribution, no matter how generous, could never be sufficient where it was the allocative and not the redistributive role of the federal state that was in dispute. At one time or another, Canadians in all provinces have blamed federal allocative policy for their economic problems, viewing direct federal regional development programs, for example, to be only a minor counterbalance to the prevailing tendencies of overall federal regulatory strategy (e.g., protectionist tariffs). The provincial governments were ready-made articulators of such grievances and came to apply their own significant regulatory powers to counterbalance federal policies.

Thus, there has been a significant history of provincial attempts to use their economic powers (particularly ownership and management of natural resources) and their fiscal capacity to pursue regionally based economic development strategies. This trend began as early as 1900 with Ontario's attempts to regulate value-added production in resource sectors. It continued through Quebec's Quiet Revolution of the 1960s, aimed in part at making Quebecers *maîtres chez-nous* in the provincial economy, to efforts in the 1970s involving all provinces to varying degrees. As a result of this trend, non-tariff barriers in the Canadian economic union proliferated. Specific provincial measures included: subsidies, investment controls, agricultural marketing boards, liquor board practices, procurement preferences, resource management policies, and service regulation. Federal policies – such as those for transportation rate structures, agriculture, and regional and industrial development – have also been considered non-tariff barriers. These policies ultimately provoked a counter-reaction of federal government proposals to eliminate interprovincial barriers to trade and thus restore the economic union.

In summary, by the early 1980s, the Canadian federal system had demonstrated the limits to which it could be stretched in the name of both integration and equity. The strongly entrepreneurial role of the state, in federal hands in 1867, had come to be in bitter dispute by the 1970s and 1980s. This conflict placed limits on the ability of either order of government to continue to shape economic development and, in the case of the federal government, to promote economic integration.

The key differences in the pattern of integration and equity in Australia as compared with Canada is that integration has been more easily achieved and that the conflict over equity has been less dramatic. The national economy in Australia has not forced as great a specialization of regional roles. The economic geography of the individual states was more similar from the beginning (five states had well-developed, concentrated metropolises with extensive agricultural hinterlands) and continues to converge. And, of course, Australia's continental isolation did not introduce the conflicting dynamic of east-west versus north-south patterns that prevails in Canada. This is not to suggest that regional economic differences do not exist – e.g., the isolation of Tasmania and Western Australia; the greater reliance on manufacturing in Victoria and New South Wales; Sydney's emergence as an international service centre, and so on. But region and regionalism have simply not been as important.

More significantly, Australia has "policy-induced" reasons for its relative degree of regional convergence. Economist Thomas Courchene estimates that Australia's regional income disparities, based on 1991 data, are four times less than in Canada. He notes four policy factors contributing to the difference:

1   the centralization of wages and other working conditions through the operation and influence of industrial relations tribunals (no such system exists in Canada)
2   the system of fiscal equalization in operation for a much longer period and encompassing a much more comprehensive scope than Canada's
3   a wider scope of social benefits paid directly by the Commonwealth, notably for welfare (compared with the diverse provincial benefit pattern in Canada)
4   the comparatively much reduced capacity of the states in regulatory or fiscal terms to intervene to fragment the economic union[21]

As we have seen, all four of these factors arise from the constitutional design and its interpretation. In putting these features into practice, however, Australians show an appetite for national standards and what the Germans call "uniform living conditions" that are undoubtedly stronger than in Canada. In the process, the redistributive role of the state comes to be more heavily centralized. However, the Commonwealth has not taken, to anywhere near the same degree as in Canada, a direct role in ameliorative regional development programs. This seems likely because the disparities are not as great and have much less political salience.[22] And this is partly due, of course, to the Commonwealth's role in inducing uniformity in the first place. The national desire for uniform standards, the propensity to equity through regulation (especially in the labour market) and fiscal equalization, and the strong central role in social programs all contribute to what might be called a substantial Australian "social union."

The Commonwealth's equity role leaves the states even more dependent than the provinces in Canada on regulatory power if they are to respond to local concerns and interests in promoting regional economic development. Yet again, they do so in a context in which federal regulatory power is more sweeping. But one need not exaggerate the differences. The states have tended to fall back on their most direct role – often termed "state socialism" – of owning and running key sectors of the regional economy such as electricity generation, transmission, and distribution; water works; public transportation; railways; and port facilities, among others. As with the provincial non-tariff barriers in Canada, these state economic activities would come under increasing scrutiny as the national economy became exposed to international competition. Their existence has long detracted from national economic efficiency, but at least the efficiency-equity trade-off has been made in Australia. As in Canada, the domestic integration-equity bargain would be undone by increasing global economic integration.

Summary

The intent of this overview of the design and development of the Australian and Canadian federal systems, encompassing their economic unions, is to provide a foundation for the detailed discussion of economic union reform to come. The federations have some converging features in the significance of economic union to the original founding and its application to territory of continental scale, and the federal institutions are similarly wedded to parliamentary institutions. But here the similarities end. Comparing the scheme of distribution of powers, rules of negative integration, and federal and provincial/state powers, the federations diverge. Canada is considerably more decentralized in design and in practice, with the provinces' wider regulatory discretion being reinforced by fiscal capacity. Australia's concurrent powers scheme has developed in a more centralized way, reinforced by central fiscal dominance. Moreover, the interplay of politics and institutional formation produces in Australia a federation more valuing of uniform results and central direction, although the states retain considerable political and administrative clout. Canada's politics have been more regional and linguistic and have been influenced by the centrifugal force of the United States. These factors reinforce institutional tendencies to provincial autonomy.

Thus, in both federal systems, the design and the effect of the economic union competes with other federal values and institutions. In the late 1980s, the courts began to re-examine the intent and operation of the economic union rules – notably *Cole v. Whitfield* (1988) in Australia and *General Motors* (1989) in Canada. As discussed later in this chapter, such legal developments alone were insufficient to tackle economic union reform. It would take a much more concerted political effort to break free of well-established institutional patterns.

State of Economic Unions, 1985

By the 1980s, the Canadian and Australian federations had both experienced several decades of intensifying national economic integration. Indeed, by the measure of the original intention and shape of economic union implied in the nineteenth-century design, each federation had achieved considerable success. Yet the 1980s also witnessed a wave of advocacy for the reform of the economic union. The calls for renewing the single national market arose in part from the balkanization that had occurred through state and provincial intervention and ownership in the economy and, in some cases, federal redistributive and regulatory policies. But they also arose, as noted in the two previous chapters, from the pressure of new forms of economic liberalization and integration beyond the boundaries of the federation. The new competitive conditions and the neo-liberal ideology that accompanies them created an agenda for reform.

Before addressing the perceived deficiencies in the economic unions, it is useful to summarize the specific characteristics of the existing degree of integration. A full comparison cannot be made between the two economies for the simple but telling reason that Australia does not keep statistics on indicators of the economic union to the degree to which Canada does. Nonetheless, a set of "stylized facts" can be constructed.[23]

By 1984, the greater part of economic activity in Canada was still consumed within individual provinces, but international and interprovincial trade accounted for more than one-third of total economic output, including interprovincial at 18 per cent of GDP. Inputs to the economy also showed the greater importance of interprovincial sources than international, especially for services and in the pattern of trade in those goods long protected by tariffs. Labour mobility was also well advanced in Canada, among the highest of any OECD country and almost as high as in the United States; labour flows were judged to be high enough to make a significant contribution to market adjustment. Finally, capital mobility, as measured by the degree of corporate concentration in Canada, was significant.[24]

In terms of balance of trade, an important regional pattern also emerged in Canada. All of the provinces traded more with Ontario than even with neighbouring provinces, illustrating not only the size and diversification of the Ontario economy, but also its especially strong position in financial services and consumer goods. Indeed, in 1984, Ontario was the only province to import more from foreign markets than it did from the rest of Canada. And while intra-provincial and interprovincial trade was more important in gross terms for all provinces, some provinces demonstrated a markedly greater degree of integration with the international economy (e.g., British Columbia and Newfoundland), whereas others were even more dependent on interprovincial trade – notably Nova Scotia, Quebec, Manitoba, and Alberta (the latter due to oil and gas shipments within Canada). Labour mobility also showed distinct regional patterns. Quebec's French-language majority was much less likely to move to other provinces, and since 1961, only three provinces have been net recipients of migration: Ontario, British Columbia, and Alberta. By the early 1980s, a decade-long trend of westward movement of population had been confirmed.[25]

Australia's GDP composition in the 1980s showed an even higher dependence than Canada on trade within individual states and thus less reliance on international and (most notably) interstate trade. This reduced exposure to trade overall in the Australian economy relative to Canada was despite the acute export dependence of many sectors. It also seems clear that interstate trade was significantly truncated by the state government monopolies in several sectors and by weak transportation linkages. Interstate labour mobility, at or near 5 per cent, approached Canadian levels but with no major regional differences in the propensity to migrate comparable to Quebec's French-speaking population. There was, however, a similar trend in migration to the north and west. For example, Queensland and Western Australia (WA) were net recipients of migration from all the other states since the mid-1970s.[26]

The balance of trade showed a strongly regional differentiation in that the resource-rich states of Queensland, WA, and, to a lesser degree,

Tasmania had an internal trade deficit (importing more through inter-state trade than they exported) but an external trade surplus (exporting more internationally than they imported). The situation was reversed for New South Wales and Victoria. South Australia's trade both within and outside the country tended to be in balance. The overall pattern demonstrated not the tenable or untenable position of any given regional economy per se, but the important roles played by individual cities and states in the economic union. Thus, Sydney and Melbourne tended to be the entry points for imports, which were then distributed throughout the country. Similarly, these cities dominated corporate concentration and foreign direct investment.[27]

In conclusion, by 1985, both Canadian and Australian economic integration was indeed highly advanced and, if economic theory is to be believed, contributed significantly to national income and efficiency. The emergence of regionally differentiated roles within the economic union only serves as further evidence that the state and provincial economies were highly interrelated. Thus, the four types of economic benefits typically accruing to economic unions had obviously been obtained (recall the discussion in chapter 3). Market integration had occurred in most, if not all, sectors; the former colonies had greatly increased their bargaining power in international markets; the costs of significant infrastructure and other joint public goods had been borne; and there had been a pooling and sharing of economic risks, dramatically proven through wars and depression.

In sum, the extent of these benefits is worth bearing in mind as the focus inevitably shifts to the remaining barriers to integration or to backsliding trends. The perception of economic observers differs: some see the glass as half empty, other as half full. Yet the goal of completing the economic union in both cases would not have been as urgent if the base of existing integration was less significant. In other words, if there was a lot to be gained by an increased degree of economic integration, there was even more to lose by an increase in market fragmentation.

A second conclusion concerns the regionally different roles and impacts of economic union integration. These differences would show up in governmental positions on reform objectives. For example, one would expect that states or provinces that trade much less within the country than abroad, or that perceive the terms of internal trade to be chronically disfavouring them, will have less incentive to maintain or expand the federal economic union. Conversely, states or provinces with greater dependence on internal trade and with the terms of such trade shifting in their favour would be early advocates of reform. If this premise were borne out, one would expect, in the Canadian case, provinces such as Ontario and Quebec to be strongly in favour of an improved economic union (for slightly differing reasons); outlying provinces, such as British Columbia or Newfoundland, would be expected to be indifferent or hostile. In Australia, one would expect New South Wales, and to a lesser degree Victoria, to be keenest on a more integrated economy; Western Australia and Queensland would be expected to be less enthusiastic, even hostile, to reform.

As will be shown, the actual constellation of interests proved more complicated as ideological and other considerations came into play. Among these, a key new variable was the linkage of economic union reform to international trade and competitiveness. Thus, regions that would benefit less from the federal economic union per se might find advantage nonetheless in enhanced national integration aimed at improving overall national competitiveness. The goal would not be so much to enable firms in Perth, for example, to compete with those in Sydney, but to create national conditions that improve the ability of companies in both Australian cities to fend off foreign competition or improve their export position. This means, in Canadian parlance, that east-west need not be at the expense of north-south.

One may now turn to the state of the economic union in more definable policy terms as a prelude to introducing the specific context of reform in each country. Table 4.1 provides the details of existing integration and remaining barriers for Canada in 1985 (i.e., before the negotiation of the Canada-US Free Trade Agreement), Australia in 1990 (before the intergovernmental reforms), and, as a further point of comparison, the European Union after the single market reforms were completed in 1992. Some of these features have already been noted in the discussion above on constitutional design. However, by placing specific provisions, policies, and practices in a direct comparative context, one can get a comprehensive picture of the state of the economic union. What also emerges is a detailed blueprint for reform. Indeed, the sources of information of these details are, in most cases, influential major studies by authors whose specific aim had been the advocacy of economic union reform.

It is appropriate to compare the two federations with the EU in 1992 because in that year, the EU completed an integration process begun as

Table 4.1 Pre-Reform State of the Economic Union

ASPECTS OF ECONOMIC UNION	CANADA, 1985		AUSTRALIA, 1990		EUROPEAN UNION, 1992
	EXISTING INTEGRATION	REMAINING BARRIERS	EXISTING INTEGRATION	REMAINING BARRIERS	INTEGRATION AFTER REFORM
TRADE AND INVESTMENT UNION	• Prohibition of fiscal barriers (customs and excise).	• Quantitative restrictions in agriculture (supply management).	• Prohibition of fiscal barriers (customs and excise).	• Different product standards by state.	• No intra-EC tariff, but domestic tax frontiers.
• Goods.	• Single jurisdiction for product labelling.	• Discriminatory procurement practices.	• Basic non-discrimination in government procurement.	• Poorly integrated state railway systems.	• No quantitative restrictions.
	• Integrated transportation structure (airlines, railways, degree of highway harmonization).	• Discriminatory pricing and distribution of alcoholic beverages.	• Constitutional prohibition of fiscal discrimination among states.	• Differing highway regulations.	• Formal non-discrimination on procurement, moving to harmonized process.
		• Discriminatory rail freight rates.		• GBEs restrict trade and competition in energy, transport, and utilities.	
	• Single but restrained federal competition policy.	• GBEs restrict trade and competition in utilities sectors.	• Section 92 prohibits most types of agricultural marketing schemes (until 1988).	• Industrial and agricultural subsidies.	• Common Competition Policy.
		• Discriminatory pricing, oil and gas; restrictions on trade in electricity.		• Significant gaps in coverage of federal competition power.	• No trade discrimination by member-state monopolies.
		• Industrial and agricultural subsidies.			• Formal prohibition of subsidies; surveillance of member-state practice.

Table 4.1 Pre-Reform State of the Economic Union *(Continued)*

ASPECTS OF ECONOMIC UNION	CANADA, 1985		AUSTRALIA, 1990		EUROPEAN UNION, 1992
	EXISTING INTEGRATION	REMAINING BARRIERS	EXISTING INTEGRATION	REMAINING BARRIERS	INTEGRATION AFTER REFORM
TRADE AND INVESTMENT UNION • Services.	• Banking. • Insurance market harmonized. • Transportation. • Telecoms harmonized. • Federal competition policy (see above).	• Discriminatory procurement practices. • Securities market not wholly integrated. • GBEs restrict competitive services in telecoms, electricity. • Differing provincial regulation of professional services.	• Banking, insurance (but not including state-owned banks, insurance). • Telecoms.	• GBEs restrict competition in banking and insurance. • GBEs restrict competition in telecoms, electricity, other utilities, and transport (rail, ports). • Protective regulation of shipping. • Differing regulation of non-bank financial sector. • Differing regulation of professional services.	• Common Transport Policy (liberalization except for air). • Telecom integration under way. • Right of establishment for service provision (with major derogations).

Table 4.1 Pre-Reform State of the Economic Union (*Continued*)

ASPECTS OF ECONOMIC UNION	CANADA, 1985		AUSTRALIA, 1990		EUROPEAN UNION, 1992
	EXISTING INTEGRATION	REMAINING BARRIERS	EXISTING INTEGRATION	REMAINING BARRIERS	INTEGRATION AFTER REFORM
TRADE AND INVESTMENT UNION • Capital mobility.	• Monetary union (see below).	• Lack of coordination in securities markets. • Restrictions on investment in resource sectors; performance requirements on investors. • Restrictive investment policy for pension plan (Quebec) and resource revenues (Alberta). • GBE monopolies restrict private investment. • Subsidies to business by provincial and (where region-specific) federal governments.	• Monetary union (see below). • Single securities regime.	• State banks may restrict capital mobility. • GBE monopolies restrict private investment. • Business subsidies by states.	• Exchange controls and related capital restrictions removed. • Subsidies controlled and monitored. • Investment controls remain in many national sectors.

Table 4.1 Pre-Reform State of the Economic Union (*Continued*)

ASPECTS OF ECONOMIC UNION	CANADA, 1985		AUSTRALIA, 1990		EUROPEAN UNION, 1992
	EXISTING INTEGRATION	REMAINING BARRIERS	EXISTING INTEGRATION	REMAINING BARRIERS	INTEGRATION AFTER REFORM
LABOUR MARKET UNION	• Constitutional guarantee, except for affirmative action employment programs. • Generally portable social benefits.	• Federal unemployment insurance benefits differ regionally. • Occupational standards and licensing not harmonized. • Differing labour relations law. • Differing educational standards.	• Constitutional guarantee. • Universal access and portability to social programs.	• Inadequate harmonization of occupational standards and licensing. • Some divergence in labour relations law.	• Freedom of entry and exit. • Mutual recognition for occupational standards. • Minimal approximation of national labour relations law.
FOREIGN ECONOMIC POLICY UNION	• Federal external affairs power (but implementation limited to federal jurisdiction). • Single trade negotiating authority; informal consultation with provinces.	• Potential for partial or inadequate treaty implementation.	• Broadly interpreted federal external affairs power. • Single trade negotiating authority with consultative mechanism with states.		• Common Trade Policy. • Common Foreign Policy.

Table 4.1 Pre-Reform State of the Economic Union (*Continued*)

ASPECTS OF ECONOMIC UNION	CANADA, 1985		AUSTRALIA, 1990		EUROPEAN UNION, 1992
	EXISTING INTEGRATION	REMAINING BARRIERS	EXISTING INTEGRATION	REMAINING BARRIERS	INTEGRATION AFTER REFORM
MONETARY UNION	• Currency union since 1867. • Central bank since 1934. • Fiscal harmonization via centralized income tax collection (except Quebec) and equalization.	• Inadequate harmonization of consumption taxes. • Low level of budgetary policy coordination.	• Currency union since 1901. • Central bank since 1959. • Fiscal harmonization via centralized tax regime; equalization; coordinated borrowing.	• Moderate level of budgetary policy coordination.	• Most but not all member-states in EMU (monetary union) (1998). • EMU requires high level of fiscal and budgetary coordination.
STRUCTURAL/ DEVELOPMENTAL UNION	• Strong federal role in initial infrastructure. • Redistribution via federal spending power. • Federal regional development policy (constitutional provision). • Federal sectoral, industry policy.	• Strong provincial role in regional economic development. • Separate provincial sectoral, industrial policies.	• Strong federal presence in economic development. • Commonwealth power to make grants to states.	• "State socialism" – government enterprise.	• Structural funds. • Common Agricultural Policy. • Regional and sectoral policies.

GBEs: Government Business Enterprises

Sources: For Canada – Canada, 1985; ECC, 1991a; Leslie, 1996a. For Australia – IAC, 1989; Daley, 1992; IC, 1994. For the EU – Pelkmans, 1997; Leslie, 1998.

early as 1985. Intensifying European integration and its clearly articulated targets were a well-known foil for the advocates of single market reform in Canada and Australia in the late 1980s and early 1990s. The European experience is also the inspiration for Peter Leslie's "aspects of economic union" typology, which I adopt for table 4.1 (see also table 2.1). Under each of Leslie's five aspects, I provide a shorthand description of the key applicable features of existing integration, existing barriers, or, in the EU case, the achieved degree of integration by 1992. (Further comment is reserved for chapter 9, where I will compare the reformed economic unions of Australia and Canada with the European Union.)

Table 4.1 first compares aspects of the *trade and investment* union in Canada 1985, Australia 1990, and the EU 1992, covering, in turn, goods, services, and capital. Next it compares the *labour market* and *foreign economic policy* unions, then the *monetary* and *structural/developmental* unions. In each aspect, the features of existing integration are set out in comparison with remaining barriers to a single market. The point here is not to dwell on the distinctions between one aspect of the economic union compared with another – although some of those distinctions are important and will be taken up in later chapters. Rather, it is to draw the reader's attention to the juxtaposition between the "existing integration" and "remaining barriers" columns. Typically, the former refers to long-standing integration achievements, most dating back to the founding of the federation. As such, they are difficult now to measure in terms of economic benefit and are clearly taken for granted in ongoing economic decisions. The "barriers" column, however, is more specific and refers to practices identified by reform advocates including business associations, economic think-tanks, and academic analysis. Many constitute long-standing grievances for a specific group or region of the country. In this sense, the barriers are not new. But the perception that they erode national competitiveness is what made the "single market" issue prominent in Canada and Australia in the late 1980s.

As relatively small economies opened to competition from regional and global integration, by the mid-1980s, Canada and Australia could no longer rest on the laurels of what were – in theory, quite comprehensive economic unions. As non-tariff barriers to international trade proliferated throughout the world in the 1970s and 1980s, trading partners identified existing barriers to the national economic unions in

Australia and Canada as being barriers to their trade as well. At home, these barriers in and of themselves might be tolerable. They certainly reflected political balancing as shown in the above discussion about regional autonomy and equity. However, such barriers came under increasing domestic scrutiny where the incomplete single market reduced national competitiveness overall.

In what has been termed the "garbage can" phenomenon, public policy analysts note that problems and solutions are not often matched to produce coherent policy change. The opportunities for policy choice are like sorting through a garbage can full of unconnected problems and solutions, each put there over time.[28] Thus, it is useful to compare how both the problems and solutions were framed in this two-federation set. Australia and Canada shared many common problems. These included quite specific barriers to trade, often in the form of differing regulatory practices and standards, affecting goods and services but also labour. In both countries, the single market became fragmented by the removal from competition of many sectors through the creation of state monopolies or discriminatory investment or procurement policies. They also had a common problem in the inefficient provision of basic infrastructure through fragmented state-controlled systems. And there was a common distortion of efficiency and a protection from national and international competition through a variety of subsidy practices.

Yet within this common set, the Australian agenda for reform stressed the *barriers to national competition.* Reform focused on the practices of government business enterprises (GBEs) and on the requirements of national transportation, communication, and other utilities infrastructure as inputs to the competitiveness of other sectors such as agriculture and manufacturing. This emphasis appears time and again in the major studies published on microeconomic reform between 1989 and 1993.[29] As outlined more fully in chapter 7, the Commonwealth government had achieved much economic reform on its own by 1990, but the significant barriers remaining were mainly in state hands. The agenda for reform as taken up by Australian governments shared the concerns of the economic reform studies, but it was also much broader.

Canada's concerns tended to be focused less on national competition as such as on *barriers to internal trade* per se, thus concentrating on tradable sectors in the economy. The geographic and economic incentives to trade with the USA in particular were immediate. The list of policies to be reformed is longer, although probably not more significant than in Australia, and dwells on both discriminatory provincial policies as well as federally induced barriers to trade. In addition, the rhetoric for reform in Canada is cast more openly in terms of the economic union and economic citizenship, tied up as well in the politics of federal unity.[30]

As for the solutions, one may recall the conclusion I reached in chapter 2 that the two economies faced different situations in the international political economy in which the competitive shortcomings created by these barriers would be expressed and evaluated. In Australia's case of diffuse market integration and low-level institutional integration, no single trading partner had emerged to influence specific terms of reform. In this respect, Australia was free to pursue a unilateral approach to reform. The reform agenda coalesced around competition policy because it was a key horizontal policy field, affecting potentially all sectors of the economy, thus exceeding the more limited prospects for reform through sectoral approaches. Comprehensiveness became a key aspect of the economic agenda, which meant that once the Commonwealth government had achieved much of what it could do on its own, it saw little choice but to involve the states in order to complete the job.

In Canada's case of concentrated market integration and formal, regional institutional integration, trade relations with the United States had an enormous effect on the framing of both the problem and the solution. Internal barriers to trade were more quickly identified as the problem when they were also irritants for the dominant trading partner. And ultimately, agreements inspired in form and content by international trade liberalization treaties would become the solution to the perceived problem.

In any case, in both countries, reform would clearly have to involve both the federal and the state or provincial governments. The question arises as to the role of intergovernmental relations in the specific economic union reforms proposed. As pursued in the chapters that follow, an economic reform agenda became entwined with more general reform of the federal system in both federations. In Australia, a general malaise in the federal system became identified as part of the problem. Reformers focused on such problems as vertical fiscal imbalance, Commonwealth overreach in programs, the centralist trend in judicial decisions, and dysfunctional intergovernmental relations (especially the premiers conference). If the governments were to tackle together the microeconomic reform agenda, they would have to lift their inter-governmental game. This provided the potential for a comprehensive negotiation in which both orders of government would have consider-able room to manoeuvre.

For the Canadians, reform of the economic union could not be sep-arated from the general issues of national unity and constitutional reform as they have been played out in the past thirty years. The agen-da of strengthening the economic union became an instrument in the larger mega-game, although only as a pawn in the early stage. Broader regional and linguistic politics were implicated throughout, including the role of Quebec electoral politics and pending referendums on Quebec secession from the union. Within this broad set of issues, the nature and effectiveness of intergovernmental relations as such, includ-ing specific advocacy of its reform, also played a significant role.

Thus, we come to the final piece of background required before launching into the detail of the reform process itself. The next section examines the nature of intergovernmental relations in Australia and Canada prior to the reforms and why process reform in and of itself would also become important.

INTERGOVERNMENTAL RELATIONS AND THE CAPACITY FOR REFORM

Change to the economic union in federal systems can come through various means. Indeed, it is not self-evident that intergovernmental negotiations should be adopted as the main means to achieve reform. Conceptually, there are three alternative routes to reform:

1 The aggressive pursuit of central authority to enact the needed reforms. This authority could be sought through such actions as fed-eral legislation, conditional spending, expansion of jurisdiction in the courts, and political advocacy. This option assumes that the con-stituent governments would also pursue their own, uncoordinated reform initiatives to the extent to which central initiatives leave them any room.

2 The amendment of the constitution to strengthen the terms of neg-ative economic integration and/or to expand the scope of federal regulatory power for positive economic integration.

3 The agreement between the federal government and the states/ provinces on a joint set of measures (within the existing constitution) for reform in both jurisdictions.

The first option fits within the competitive role of intergovernmental relations discussed in chapter 3 (see table 3.1): the unilateral pursuit of priorities by the federal government and a similar independence of action by the constituent governments. The goal, especially from a federal government perspective, would be rationalization as an end result. Pursuit of this option requires strong political support and generates intense conflict, neither of which may be sustainable over time or the whole of the reform agenda.

Options 2 and 3 are similar in that both require the agreement of the constituent governments (or their electorates in a referendum) or at least most of them, according to constitutional amendment formulas. The end result of option 2 is a wholly new regime that could change permanently the basis for intergovernmental relations. As with option 1, rationalization is often the goal envisaged in constitutional reform, particularly in the economic union field.

Option 3 is the most resolutely co-operative of the three routes to change in that both the process to achieve change is co-operative as well as the ongoing outcome. Even here, one might use co-operative agreement to achieve a rationalizing result, but unlike constitutional amendment, this would be easier to revise or reverse.

In the actual cases of Canada and Australia, the three options posed above are present, if more subtle and complicated in practice. In Canada, all three options would be in play, sometimes simultaneously, with option 3 ultimately emerging with the most results. As discussed more fully in chapters 5 and 6, the federal government sought constitutional amendment, option 2, to strengthen the terms of the economic union. Only when this option failed to achieve all but a few of its objectives did the federal government turn to a mixture of options 1 and 3. In Australia, the federal government also briefly considered option 2, but the most co-operative route of option 3 was ultimately chosen, with strong overtones of option 1. The details are provided in chapters 7 and 8.

The choice of intergovernmental negotiation to produce comprehensive economic union reform has merit conceptually based in the concurrent nature of the task. As explored in chapter 3, concurrency –

the joint occupation of a policy field – is an integral part of the design of federal systems. Concurrency can be explicit or can rise implicitly in policy fields where the action of both governments is required. Economic union, both as a set of constitutional rules and as a policy field, exhibits strongly concurrent characteristics. In fact, it may be so concurrent that reform can be made only with the consent of all the parties to a federal union.

With the right kind of processes, intergovernmental relations can produce the kind of concurrent, substantive results needed for economic reform. The recent European Union experience provides the chief evidence of this point but, of course, in the context of being a confederal process without a federal government as such at the table. Are the Australian and Canadian federal systems similarly capable of producing reform through intergovernmental means?

In chapter 3, I proposed a typology on intergovernmental relations (see table 3.1) that suggests a spectrum of relations from competition to co-operation to rationalization. As is clear from the first part of this chapter, both federations provide wholly distinct governing systems at the federal and state or provincial levels – parallel rather than interlocking as in Germany. Both systems have been designed for a degree of arm's-length relations. Yet in comparative terms, Canadians have developed a more decentralized and competitive federalism, with a strongly concurrent de facto exercise of powers. This is so despite the attempts of the founders to create a more centralized and less overlapping system. By contrast, the Australians began with a more de jure concurrent system, but they have developed over time a more centralized system with strong elements of take-it-or-else coordination. Thus, recent Canadian experience occupies mainly the competition and co-operation types, while Australian experience has increasingly occupied the co-operation and rationalization types.

The propensity of a system to occupy different points on the spectrum arises from diverging social and institutional factors including values of federalism. But the instruments of executive federalism (the means by which both federations conduct intergovernmental relations) and their success or failure in historical circumstances have been important, too. Both provide clues to the type of intergovernmental relations pursued in the two federations and whether they could be expected to produce coherent reform results.

A major rationale for the Canadian federation has been the protection of a national French-speaking minority and the preservation of the autonomy of provincial communities. As discussed earlier in this chapter, this value is reflected in the original coordinate design of exclusive provincial powers and in the constitutional protection of linguistic and religious rights. Canada has remained a highly federal society, given the persistent survival of francophones, the resurgence of aboriginal identity, strong regional identities, and a newer multicultural pluralism. As a consequence, Canadians seem more tolerant of conflict, even while they occasionally shrink from it, and seem to recognize it as the price to be paid for diversity. Yet Canadians are deeply divided about the needs and values of national unity and integration and those of local and ethnic communities. The conflict includes intergovernmental relations. Canadians continue to debate the goals, means, and style of intergovernmental relations. Thus, no one mode of relations can prevail for long.

Australia's federal values differ in degree and kind from Canada's. As noted above, there is obviously less of a federal society, despite a more recent and similar resurgence of aboriginal identity and multicultural diversity. Regionalism is much less pronounced, and there is a high value placed on uniformity, fairness, and equity. Unlike Canada or the United States, there are no entrenched individual or group rights and much less recourse to rights discourse in the political culture. And yet there is some recognition of the values of citizen responsiveness and liberty through the dual occupancy of sovereignty. Nonetheless, the development of national integration and nation building over the past century has led to what political scientist Campbell Sharman calls a "closed, bureaucratic, and collusive" type of relations, fitting more closely and more stably into the co-operation type than the Canadian system.[31]

Apart from social factors, permanent institutional factors also affect the type of intergovernmental relations in Canada and Australia. I have already noted Canada's distribution of powers. Canada has few "joint decision traps" created by mandatory constitutional provisions for co-operation, although governments sometimes fall into temporary traps of their own making (e.g., the Meech Lake Accord ratification process).[32] However, the few areas of formal concurrency in the constitution (agriculture, immigration, pensions, and natural resource pricing) have spawned intensively co-operative intergovernmental regimes. Without these regimes, federal paramountcy would prevail, leaving no room for the occupancy of the field by the provinces (indeed, this is what occurred in the immigration field for most of the twentieth century).

The situation is reversed in Australia. The large scope of concurrent legislation, combined with centralist judicial interpretation of the rules of federal paramountcy, have induced co-operation across a much wider scope of policy than in Canada. The other key difference is the much greater vertical fiscal imbalance in Australia compared with Canada. This has created the need for greater co-operation (some would say coercion) in federal-state relations over spending programs and fiscal transfers generally. Nonetheless, as political scientist Martin Painter points out, in both federations, intergovernmental co-operation is essentially conditional and voluntary. For the most part, governments co-operate as a conscious tactical choice, not because they must.[33]

An institutional feature shared by the two federations is "executive federalism." Donald Smiley, who coined the term, defined it as "the relations between elected and appointed officials of the two orders of government in federal-provincial interactions and among the executives in the provinces, in interprovincial interactions."[34] Indeed, executives essentially monopolize intergovernmental relations. This arises from the characteristic of parliamentary government in which all the agencies of each government are integrated into "a single hierarchy with the executive at its apex."[35] The Westminster conventions of a cabinet responsible to Parliament, combined with strong party discipline, create a fusion of executive and legislative power. Cabinet ministers, and especially first ministers, can pursue relations with their counterparts in other parliamentary governments, confident that they can speak for and with the support of a majority in Parliament. While Canadians invented the conditions for executive federalism by being the first to marry federal with parliamentary institutions, similar aspects of executive federalism may be found in Germany, India, Malaysia, as well as Australia.[36]

Executive dominance shapes the typical outcomes of intergovernmental relations in several ways. First, executive federalism assumes minimal involvement by ordinary legislators and a monopoly by cabinet ministers and their unelected officials. This pattern holds true in both Canada and Australia, even if on occasion parliamentary debate intervenes. In both systems, the political level of relations is but the tip of an iceberg of bureaucratic structures, lending to overall practice a strong dose of bureaucratic norms. The tendency to bureaucratic collusion is reinforced by the development of specialized intergovernmental agencies within each government. These agencies improve intra-government coordination but may increase jurisdictional conflict. Executive dominance also tends to exclude or limit the role of interest groups in policy formation (the democratic limitations of executive federalism are discussed below).[37]

Direct intergovernmental relations are also influenced by the role of other institutions of national integration and conflict management, notably central institutions such as the second chamber of the federal legislature. Canada's appointed house of patronage, the Senate, does not represent the provinces either directly or indirectly in the federal parliament. This encourages provincial ministers to assume a role of representing their province's perspective on national issues. Australia's Senate, while elected on the basis of a state franchise and with equal representation per state, has functioned since federation as a house of review and of parties, not primarily as a "house of the states." Nonetheless, the Senate in Australia has more legitimacy to represent the interests of the states compared with the much weaker legitimacy of the Canadian Senate. This legitimacy may have kept state government leaders from taking the national stage sooner and more often. However, in both countries, the design and operation of the second federal chamber has not precluded direct intergovernmental relations and indeed has contributed to the potential for the latter to become an important *national* decision-making forum.

Both federations were founded in an era of classical federalism when there was much less interdependence than today. In the German federation founded in 1949, for example, there is a formal institutionalization of intergovernmental relations as an integral part of the constitution. There has been no such constitutional recognition of the institutions and processes of executive federalism in Canada. Australia's constitution is a bit more explicit, providing for agreements covering external borrowing, which led to the establishment of the Australian Loan Council (section 105(a)), and for the now-defunct Interstate Commission (section 101). But as in Canada, the constitution is silent on the main tasks of executive federalism, leaving them ad hoc and unformalized until the reform agenda came along. This lack of a formal role prevents the worst aspects of what Fritz Scharpf identifies as a "joint decision trap" in the German case.[38]

The combined impact of these structural characteristics creates a strong potential capacity for intergovernmental policy collaboration in Canada and Australia. Indeed, the executive dominates. Other structural factors reinforce this dominance: strong party discipline, only partially federated party structures, and the small number of governments. The executive orientation suggests that these systems would be likely to gravitate to a co-operative mode of relations in our typology. On the other hand, when combined with the lack of formal recognition of intergovernmental mechanisms, executives can choose to hold off the entrapments of excess co-operation. This is especially so where electorates interpret the latter as collusion against their interests. After all, electorates are still clearly separated. Governments reserve their stronger and more effective political signals for their own electorates through unilateral actions designed for them rather than through complex intergovernmental arrangements. Thus, there is room for competitive relations as well.

Finally, two criticisms of executive federalism limit its legitimacy and its effectiveness as a decision-making institution. First is the criticism of executive federalism on democratic grounds. Critics question the representativeness of executive federalism (which is typically not as socially representative as is a legislature) as well as the limited accountability and access for both the general public and legislatures. In Canada, this criticism has contributed to the demise of constitutional reform packages produced by executive negotiation and eroded the legitimacy of intergovernmental relations in general. While the issue of accountability and involvement of Parliament and of interest groups is of some concern in Australia, it has not been as salient on the political agenda. Overall, the critics may credit executive federalism with more power and effectiveness than is merited, but ironically, the presence of the critique can reduce that very power and effectiveness by eroding its legitimacy.[39]

A second criticism stems from the typical institutional status and decision rules of executive federalism as practised in Australia and Canada. As noted, intergovernmental relations are recognized only minimally if at all in the constitution. In the absence of formal establishment, the processes of intergovernmental relations are ad hoc and rudimentary. Thus, the states and provinces nurse grievances about the lack of regularity and shallow nature of consultation with the federal government. Agendas are set unilaterally; meetings are held only when the federal government wishes. Similarly, the federal government sees meetings as merely a chance for the states to gang up on the centre instead of resolving real problems.

The lack of formal status leads to the lack of formal rules of procedure. Thus, executive federalism falls back on two types of decision rules: consensus and unanimity. Where consensus is the norm, the results can never be precise and rarely be binding, even in a moral or political sense. Where unanimity is required, agreement is simply harder to achieve with attendant increased "transaction costs" and a propensity to "exchange relations" – i.e., horse-trading among the parties.[40] Another typical cost is the awarding of extra benefits to the last to sign on. The lack of alternative, formal voting rules does not always present a problem. When all that is required of executive federalism is the exchange of views and information, such as when governments occupy a competitive mode, decisions as such are not taken. But if substantive joint results are required and time is limited, the lack of formal voting rules other than unanimity or consensus (such as a simple or qualified majority) will restrict what can be achieved.[41]

Voting rules in intergovernmental relations are not unknown in Canada and Australia. Since 1927, the Australian Loan Council can take decisions under the "Financial Agreements" by a majority of votes, whereby the Commonwealth gets two votes plus the chair's "casting vote." In 1980, governments adopted a majority voting rule for the ministerial council of the Co-operative National Companies and Securities Scheme and in 1984, for some roles of the National Crime Authority Intergovernmental Committee. In Canada, there are the rules of the Canada Pension Plan, an intergovernmental scheme in a concurrent policy field, where changes to the agreement can be made only with the agreement of the federal government and two-thirds of the provinces comprising two-thirds of the Canadian population. Also, since the adoption of the *Constitution Act, 1982* and its explicit set of constitutional amending formulas, a majority of seven provinces having 50 per cent of the total Canadian population is required for many constitutional changes. Nonetheless, until the advocacy of reforms of intergovernmental relations related in part to the economic union reforms discussed in subsequent chapters, formal voting procedures did not apply except in these few cases.

Another consequence of the lack of formality of intergovernmental relations is the status of intergovernmental agreements. Both federations make extensive use of a variety of forms of agreement. For the most part, they are political documents, their chief function being communication and administrative guidance. However, increasingly, governments have sought more precise instruments through the use of legal terminology and legislative ratification and enforcement. Overall, Australia has made more frequent use of legislative entrenchment than has Canada. However, in both countries, intergovernmental agreements come up against the norms of parliamentary sovereignty. Parliaments will not be bound by intergovernmental agreements as such, even while passing legislation to give them effect. And intergovernmental agreements can rarely be litigated.

In summary, I return to the question posed above of whether the two federations were well equipped to pursue economic union reform through intergovernmental collaboration. The answer is that the unreformed institutions of executive federalism have not been well equipped for sustained decision making and policy implementation. In terms of the typology of intergovernmental relations in table 3.1, this would limit the achievements that are possible under a fully co-operative mode. It would also make the joint determination to establish a rationalization regime more difficult. This is not to say that governments could not achieve policy outcomes, but it does mean that the tendency would be to fall more frequently onto the competitive mode to do so. The tendency of Australian and Canadian intergovernmental relations to occupy different places on the competition-rationalization spectrum illustrates the force of path dependency in the institutions of federalism in these two countries. Nonetheless, when political imperatives emphasize co-operation and when the forces of change threaten autonomy and federal balance, the pressure will be on governments to find more effective ways to do business together.

Such pressure built steadily in both countries in the 1980s movement to reform their economic unions. Yet if the recent past had been any guide, the prospects for change were not good. In Australia, intergovernmental relations on economic issues were overshadowed by issues of fiscal transfers and social programs, which had begun to deteriorate in the 1980s. Important sectoral economic issues emerged during the 1970s, such as corporation law and offshore resources. Still, governments would have no experience with a comprehensive agenda such as microeconomic reform until the 1990s.

By contrast, economic regulatory issues were prominent features of Canadian intergovernmental relations in the decade before 1985. The competitive pattern of economic development, the conflicting regional interests in energy pricing and development, trade and investment policy – all were sites of severe intergovernmental conflict. As Canadian political scientists Chandler and Bakvis note, the inability of Canadian governments to "get their act together" on a national industrial strategy became an obsession in some quarters.[42] In 1978–79, governments attempted to produce a common economic development strategy through an intensive set of intergovernmental relations including First Ministers Conferences. This effort ended in failure.

Yet the more the federal government attempted in frustration to deal with economic matters on their own, the worse relations grew. Policy objectives diverged, and the incentives for compromise became less obvious. Thus, by 1985, observers were not optimistic that a way to more productive relations in the field of economic and industrial policy could be found.[43] In summary, in neither country did the recent past offer a promising start for economic reform through intergovernmental relations. The question remains whether the constituent governments of the two federations – as did their European Union counterparts – had reached the stage where the calculus of their interests would force them to adopt mechanisms to improve their capacity for co-decision.[44]

Conclusion: Institutional Change and the Test of Reform

To this point, I have set the stage for what follows on the actual process and outcomes of economic union reform. Before launching into those details, it is helpful to recall my discussion in chapter 1 about how moments of reform illuminate institutional structure and functions. Three sources of change in institutions can be identified.[45] The first source occurs when previously latent institutions become salient. The terms of the economic union, taken for granted by governments and society for so long, had clearly become a salient political issue by the 1980s. And regardless of whether reform would be intergovernmental or not, the rise of the federal economic union as an issue becomes, ipso facto, an intergovernmental issue.

The second source of change is when old institutions are put to new ends. This holds true for our case where economic unions designed for national integration have to address regional and global integration. This issue came to a head in Canada with the negotiation of the

Canada-United States Free Trade Agreement. Economic integration and liberalization had been building for some time until then but became more urgent thereafter. In Australia, the microeconomic reform agenda, of which economic union reform is part, arose with urgency following the mid-1980s balance of payments and currency crisis. From this crisis onward, Australians collectively seemed to realize that they could not avoid greater regional and global integration.

Third, change occurs when the goals and strategies of established institutions are transformed. In both countries, the advocates of economic union reform sought to tilt the balance achieved between efficiency and equity – in place for decades if not a century – in favour of efficiency as defined in neo-liberal policy prescriptions. Many also sought to change the balance of power generally within the federation.

Thus, we come to a test of reform – of both economic unions and of intergovernmental relations – in the two federations of Canada and Australia. In both cases, one is intrigued by how agreement is reached on far-reaching changes that limit the jurisdiction of the states and provinces. What were the incentives, the side issues, and the overall political context by which such voluntary agreement took place? Or was there an element of coercion or external determination at work? These issues are pursued in the next part of this book, chapters 5 to 8. In the process, I focus not only on the outcomes of economic union reform, but also on the type of intergovernmental relations that produces reform and the effect of the reforms on the federal system, which will affect the ability to choose among relation types in the future.

The movement to reform the Canadian economic union took place episodically over a twenty-year period. Throughout that period, the issues and focus of the movement underwent significant changes as domestic economic union reform became caught up in broader constitutional contests and in the policy-making of international integration. The Canadian experience is more complicated and drawn-out than Australia's. This does not mean that the results in Australia are any less impressive – on the contrary. However, the narrative and analytical line is somewhat longer for the Canadian story compared with the Australian one.

This chapter and the next are organized in the chronological order for the four main episodes of reform. The first part of the chapter covers the "patriation round" of constitutional negotiations, 1976–82. The second part covers the preliminary efforts at intergovernmental reform and the impact of international trade negotiations, 1983–92. The third part deals with a second attempt at constitutional reform, 1991–92. Chapter 6 covers the negotiations leading to the Agreement on Internal Trade (AIT) of 1995 and its subsequent implementation. The discussion of each of the four chronological episodes is organized in the same way, with an initial brief overview of events followed by an analysis of the process dynamics and an assessment of outcomes.

FIRST REFORM ATTEMPT, 1976–82: PATRIATION ROUND

Overview of Events

With the election of the Parti Québécois (PQ) government in Quebec in November 1976, the first phase of attempts to reform the Canadian economic union began. Canadians had attempted for some years to undertake constitutional reform, primarily to patriate the constitution from the United Kingdom. However, with the PQ election began a much more comprehensive effort to change the federal bargain as a way of meeting Quebec's aspirations and to neutralize nationalist sentiment in that province.

From 1976 to 1980, federal governments attempted without success to reach agreement with the provinces on constitutional reform. Following its election victory in February 1980, the Liberal government under Pierre Trudeau managed the federalist victory in the Quebec referendum campaign of May 1980, during which he promised swift action to renew the federation. Yet Trudeau attempted to achieve this renewal very much on his own terms, dealing with the provinces only if he could control the agenda or until events forced him to compromise.

The constitutional debate proceeded through three acts. Act one was a set of intergovernmental negotiations in 1980 during which a large and complex agenda for constitutional reform emerged, including aspects of reform of the economic union. This act ended when it became clear that consensus between the provincial and federal governments would be impossible. Act two began with Trudeau's unilateral patriation and amendment proposal, including a *Charter of Rights,* but with very little of the provincial agenda for reform. A year of bitter standoff on this proposal ended when the Supreme Court ruled in September 1981 that while under the strict legal letter of the law the amendments could be passed without the consent of the provinces, conventional practice required the agreement of a substantial majority of them. This led to act three when Trudeau compromised to reach an intergovernmental agreement on constitutional amendments in November 1981. Fatefully, that agreement did not include the government of Quebec. In April 1982, the Queen proclaimed the *Canada Act.* Thus, the *Constitution Act, 1982,* including the *Charter of Rights and Freedoms* and other reforms, became law.

This set of constitutional changes included very little on the terms of the economic union as such. While fundamental to the underlying sources of conflict, the economic union became a pawn in the larger power struggle. To Canadian governments for whom the tools of economic intervention were still used actively and contested bitterly, the stakes were too high to impose greater discipline in favour of economic integration. The participants in the debate, however, did make powerful arguments about the need to return to first principles of economic integration, about the linkage between integration and federal unity, and about the consequences for Canada's international economic position of a fragmented internal market. These ideas laid the foundation for future reform efforts.

Dynamics of the Process

In recent decades, the Canadian federal system exhibited a potentially destructive dynamic of intergovernmental competition and inter-regional rivalry. Debate about the role of the state in the economy and specific economic development and industrial policies intensified in the late 1960s and through the 1970s. Governments and other interests in society began linking constitutional reform strategies with economic policy goals.

In the debate to reform the constitution after 1976, several specific issues related to economic policy emerged. The formal agendas included provincial demands on the following: clarification of provincial ownership of natural resources and their jurisdiction over related aspects of interprovincial trade; regulation of telecommunication; jurisdiction over fisheries; ownership and management of offshore mineral resources; indirect taxation; and the use of the federal declaratory and spending powers. The federal government placed on the agenda the following: the issues of personal mobility rights (and, possibly, property rights) as part of a *Charter of Rights;* the principle of fiscal equalization and principles regarding regional development; and an item it called "powers over the economy." This last item was a deliberate attempt by the federal government to balance the provincial demands in the area of resources and trade.[1] However, the federal government's constitutional priorities lay essentially elsewhere, particularly with a made-in-Canada amending formula and the *Charter of Rights.*

The issues related to the economic union came rather late in the day to the constitutional agenda, without much, if any, prior intergovernmental discussion.[2] The federal government put forward its views in a position paper released in July 1980. *Securing the Canadian Economic Union in the Constitution* sets out the federal case on the following lines. First, the Canadian economic union was shown to be deficient in several respects. Even the provisions of the European Economic Community and the GATT were claimed to be stronger than the Canadian constitutional rules. Yet this was a specious argument based on comparing specific barriers but ignoring other more important aspects of integration such as the monetary union. Second, the rise of regional trading blocks and Canada's small domestic market meant that Canadians could increasingly ill afford a fragmented national economy. Third, it argued, the economic reasons for integration, while compelling, are not as important as the political and national unity reasons – i.e., providing citizens with equal rights and fair treatment across the country.

The paper outlined three proposals for constitutional amendment to reform the economic union: (1) to entrench the mobility rights of citizens; (2) to revise and expand the Common Market clause (section 121); and (3) to broaden the federal trade and commerce power (section 91(2)) to encompass all matters necessary for economic integration.[3] The federal government wanted to proceed with all three reforms, but it expressed a one-sided view of the problem. While the position paper admitted that federal policy was responsible for some of the barriers to economic mobility, Ottawa clearly saw the provinces as the main culprits.[4] Thus, the federal government proposed that its parliament be provided with a wider leeway for derogations from the revised section 121 than would the provincial legislatures. Also, as the federal government intended to expand section 91(2), the trade and commerce power, the likely effect would be to decrease the room for provincial jurisdiction (e.g., over property and civil rights and possibly regulation of natural resources).

The provinces levied several formal objections to the federal proposals during the negotiations. They objected to the assumption by Ottawa that only the federal government and not the provinces could act in the national interest on economic issues. The provinces thought that the proposed remedies were far worse than the disease. And they were concerned that the amendments would exacerbate regional disparities. More directly, the dissenting provinces (i.e., all but Ontario) had strong reservations about empowering the courts and not legislatures to rule on economic integration issues, an important argument given that it tied in with many provinces' similar concerns with a *Charter of Rights*. But apart from these, there was a more visceral and immediate reaction from provinces to what they saw as an attempt to trump their own constitutional amendment proposals to consolidate provincial economic power, notably over natural resources.[5] In any case, as a direct result of these disparate views, the parties were too far apart to reach consensus on constitutional amendment by September 1980.

In Trudeau's unilateral reform package that followed, only one part of the federal agenda on the economic union went forward – the mobility rights provisions that would come to form section 6 of the *Charter of Rights and Freedoms*. These provisions survived the final stage of intergovernmental agreement in November 1991, as did two other amendments (discussed below) that bear to some degree on the economic union. On the whole, however, the "powers over the economy" item became a sacrificial lamb. The Trudeau government proceeded only with those items for which it thought it could carry the country as a whole or with minimal compromise with the provinces. The "powers over the economy" issue was too new and too divisive to gain such support.

Assessment of Outcomes

As already noted, these constitutional amendments did not deal significantly with economic union issues. Notably, they did not include a strengthened federal trade and commerce power, nor did they expand the Common Market provisions. Nonetheless, three parts of the 1982 amendments are important to the economic union.

First is a new section on equalization and regional disparities: Part III, section 36, *Constitution Act, 1982*. This section commits the federal parliament to making equalization payments but does not entrench a formula for so doing. It also commits the federal and the provincial legislatures to the pursuit of equal opportunities for Canadians to further economic development to reduce disparities and to provide essential services of reasonable quality to all Canadians. While probably not justiciable, section 36 provides at least a benchmark for equity principles – all the more noticeable in the embrace of neo-liberal principles in the years that followed 1982. In this sense, this amendment contributes to the equity side of integration.

Second is the confirmation of a concurrent provincial power clarifying jurisdiction over natural resources and interprovincial trade (in a new section 92A, *Constitution Act, 1867*). This amendment had been keenly sought by Saskatchewan and Alberta following the loss of important legal cases in the Supreme Court of Canada, which constrained the exercise of provincial regulation affecting interprovincial trade in resources. The new concurrent power would preserve some room for the provinces to have comprehensive resource management legislation. It applies to non-renewable mineral resources as well as renewable resources such as forests and hydroelectricity. It would not prevent federal legislation, which would have paramountcy, and thus could not have prevented the federal government's 1981 National Energy Program (NEP) (see the next part of this chapter). However, by underpinning and confirming important aspects of provincial natural resource control, the amendment went some way to alleviating provincial alienation and concern about judicial centralization. In this respect, it contributed to federal balance but did little for integration as such.

Finally, and most importantly in terms of actually strengthening the economic union, were the provisions of section 6 on mobility rights in the new *Charter of Rights and Freedoms*. This section established a clearly justiciable set of rights and filled a major gap in the rules of negative integration. It guaranteed freedom to move and to pursue a livelihood. And while it applied to natural persons only, not corporations, the courts' subsequent interpretation of section 6 seemed to be leaning toward providing protection to economic activity taking place in a province but not resident in it.[6]

In conclusion, this first phase of the debate over the reform of the economic union coincided with an important episode in the struggle over the constitutional identity of the Canadian federal state. A more perfect economic union became a part, but ultimately not a crucial part, of the Trudeau-led attempt to redefine Canadian nationality and in the process, marginalize Quebec nationalism. The results demonstrate the risks in choosing constitutional amendment as a reform vehicle; obviously the stakes in such "mega-politics" are high. The ability to get agreement on lasting reform becomes that much more difficult. The economic union issues were nonetheless integral to the federal government's constitutional strategy to nullify and blunt the demands from Quebec and the other provinces for greater economic autonomy. As a tactical device, the federal proposals succeeded, but the federal position poisoned the atmosphere for a more neutral discussion of the issue on its own merits. Thus, for the next decade, the provinces would view any further discussion of the economic union issue in terms of a centralist power grab. Ottawa's position tended to reinforce this perception as it continued to be unwilling to curb its own ability to intervene in the economy. It would take the 1981–82 recession and the colder climate of international competition of the rest of the decade to convince Ottawa that its own interventionist powers over the economy would have to be curtailed as well.

FREE TRADE AND RENEWED REFORM EFFORTS, 1983–92

Overview of Events

In the period following the 1980–81 recession, Canadians battled over two approaches to economic development: renewed economic nationalism versus free trade. The Trudeau government responded at first with an increased dose of economic nationalism: a protective domestic energy regime (the National Energy Program), stronger foreign investment review, and an emphasis on *dirigiste* megaprojects with specified regional economic spinoffs. In the process, it alienated many of the provinces for which the aggressive federal policies left little room for manoeuvre, as well as the American investment community and government, which saw the need for less, not more, restrictions on economic activity in North America. This strong regional and continental reaction to Canadian economic nationalism contributed to the election of the Conservative federal government under Brian Mulroney in 1984 and the adoption of free trade as policy in 1985–86.

International liberalization proceeded through three venues. Bilateral trade negotiations with the Americans were initiated in mid-1986 and resulted in the Canada-United States Free Trade Agreement (hereafter FTA), signed in October 1987 and coming into effect in 1989. After that, trilateral negotiations with the USA and Mexico, begun in 1992, resulted in the North American Free Trade Agreement (hereafter NAFTA), coming into effect in 1994. Third, negotiations in the Uruguay Round of multilateral trade negotiations, begun in 1986, resulted in a broad set of new agreements and the establishment of the World Trade Organization in 1993 (hereafter WTO), with agreements coming into effect in 1995. Of the three, the original FTA is more important politically as it marked the more dramatic departure from past policy. The test of that policy change came in the general federal election of October 1988, fought mainly on the free trade issue. The victory of the Conservatives enabled the FTA to pass its last legislative hurdle in Canada and weakened trade policy critics for the subsequent debates over NAFTA and the WTO agreements.

By putting an institutional framework on continental and global economic integration, these international agreements changed fundamentally the context of the domestic economic union as well as undermined many of the policy instruments sustaining it. They did so partly by removing some barriers to the Canadian economic union, which were also international trade barriers. Moreover, the agreements forced adjustment to liberalization, placing a greater emphasis on national competitiveness. And they reinforced other political trends to adopt neo-liberal economic policy with reduced stress on subsidization and regulation. Thus, soon after the last episode of attempted reform in the 1980–82 constitutional debate, pressure built again for comprehensive domestic reform.

In June 1985, governments began a slow-moving series of intergovernmental efforts to deal with the domestic internal barriers. Yet over the next five years, governments could move very little past an initial consensus despite discussion at every Annual Premiers Conference (provinces and territories only) from 1986 to 1991 as well as the First Ministers Conferences on the Economy in 1985 and 1987 (i.e., including the federal government). The governments achieved two sectoral agreements covering government procurement and beer in 1991 and 1992 and some regional initiatives. Still there was no comprehensive, institutionalized liberalization of barriers to interprovincial trade. The failure of these domestic intergovernmental efforts, especially when juxtaposed to the success of liberalization at the international level, sets the stage for a renewed effort at constitutional reform in 1991–92 (discussed in the last part of this chapter).

Dynamics of the Process

Let us proceed to the two fronts of reform: the domestic intergovernmental effort and the international trade negotiations. Here, we concentrate on important aspects of the reform process for each.

To begin with, independent analyses of the policy challenge of reforming the economic union played an especially important role in this phase. Two sets of studies were influential in setting the terms of the debate. First was a set of papers published by the Ontario Economic Council (OEC), providing the most comprehensive assessment to date of the current state of the economic union.[7] One of the papers, in particular, provided an exhaustive catalogue of thirty-eight different types of provincially induced barriers to trade, and an appendix detailed 544 individual subsidy programs by the provincial and territorial governments.[8] The studies cast doubt that the full costs of barriers could be counted accurately, although they put their own estimate conservatively at 1 per cent of GNP – neither overwhelming nor insignificant. What's more, these studies also buried the notion that only the provinces were to blame for distortions to the national economy, finding federal interventions to have an even greater impact on the economy.

The 1985 Report of the Royal Commission on the Economic Union and Development Prospects for Canada, chaired by former federal Minister of Finance Donald Macdonald, also became very influential in the debate. Its most prominent recommendation was that Canada's best prospects for economic development lay in a policy of free trade with the United States. The Macdonald report also focused on the economic union, exploring not only issues of negative integration, but also of positive integration including national economic regulation, fiscal federalism, and inter-regional redistribution.[9]

In its analysis, the commission tended to downplay the issue of interprovincial barriers per se, except in the broader context. The chief economic rationale for reducing barriers was not seen to be the economic costs of the barriers themselves, judged to be small, but the effects they had on international competitiveness. The political rationale of enhancing economic citizenship was also seen as important. As discussed in chapters 3 and 4, this concept stressed personal legal rights and benefits such as mobility and equality of treatment and opportunity.

In retrospect, the Macdonald report recommendations formed an early blueprint for domestic intergovernmental agreement in Canada. Some of these concepts culminated in the Agreement on Internal Trade of 1995 and are thus important to summarize here. They were as follows:

1 A limited amendment of the "Common Market" clause (section 121, *Constitution Act, 1867)* to cover services.
2 A negotiated intergovernmental code of economic conduct, covering barriers to trade, non-discrimination of persons by province of residence, externalities of provincial programs, and national economic infrastructure. The code could be entrenched in the constitution once sufficient experience with it is gained.
3 A formal Council of Economic Development Ministers, with a mandate to negotiate the code of economic conduct and to appoint a federal-provincial commission on the economic union. The commission would undertake studies, receive complaints from individual

and corporate citizens, and make recommendations to the ministerial council.

In conclusion, the Macdonald report broke with the previous federal government position of 1980 to pursue integration chiefly by amending section 121 to ensure the enforcement by the courts. Instead, it would rely more on the negotiated code, applied to the federal and provincial governments, avoiding the courts wherever possible. In the Royal Commission's view, the courts were ill equipped to deal with complex economic issues and with the need to maintain sensitive regional and federal-provincial balance. Yet, by putting its eggs in an intergovernmental basket, the Royal Commission placed the chance for reform in the hands of an unreformed process of intergovernmental relations (recall the discussion in chapter 4). It did review the need to upgrade the machinery of executive federalism, but opted in its recommendations for a minor degree of formalization. There is no discussion in the report of the need for improved decision rules. Still, together with the OEC study, the Macdonald report provided the main intellectual and policy foundation for a non-constitutional approach to the reform of the Canadian economic union.

This leads to the second major feature of the process: the conditions for renewed intergovernmental collaboration. As discussed in chapter 4, the federal government and the provinces had failed to reach substantial agreement on economic issues in 1972–84 because the goals and instruments of intervention were still in bitter dispute. By the time the Macdonald Commission reported in 1985, a new Conservative government under Brian Mulroney had been elected, which was committed to both a more collaborative approach to the provinces and a neoliberal approach to the economy.

In particular, Mulroney sought to emphasize co-operative deregulation, program downsizing, and internal liberalization rather than the interventionist economic development of previous regimes. General consensus on these goals emerged from First Ministers Conferences on the Economy held in February and November 1985. This consensus is reflected in an intergovernmental position paper released in June 1985 that identified the elimination of internal trade barriers as an objective.[10]

Soon after the release of that document, the governments established an intergovernmental task force to review barriers. It reported in turn to a federal-provincial ministerial conference that attempted in June 1986 to launch comprehensive reform along the lines proposed by the Macdonald report. However, the provinces were nervous about how far the process should or could go and agreed to only a scaled-down version.[11] This position went forward to the Annual Premiers Conference (i.e., provinces and territories only) in August 1986. There, the premiers agreed: "to a moratorium on new barriers to interprovincial trade subject to compelling considerations of provincial economic development; to establish a permanent mechanism to reduce existing trade barriers; to develop an inventory of barriers; and to define a set of Guiding Principles for reducing barriers."[12]

During the next few years, even these commitments would not be adhered to. The moratorium on new barriers was not honoured. A sectoral approach dealing with existing barriers in procurement, beer, transportation, and employment produced only limited results in the first two sectors. There was insufficient commitment to sustain an inventory of barriers. Work never began on the set of guiding principles. By late 1991, after five years of on-again, off-again effort, governments had very little to show for their discussions.

In conclusion, the commitment to intergovernmental reform came slowly and ultimately too late for results in this format. This happened simply because the process did not have a high enough priority for the governments concerned. The federal-provincial agenda was crowded with other issues, which not only prevented the internal trade barrier exercise from receiving a higher priority, but also shifted the very ground on which the federal and provincial governments were dealing. One of these bigger priorities was the Meech Lake Constitutional Accord. This agreement did not deal with the economic union per se, but would have shifted the intergovernmental balance of power (see the last part of this chapter). The other major priority, of course, was the FTA and other trade negotiations. It would seem that governments held back in making concessions to freer trade at home so long as domestic policies were at issue in the international arena. Why concede on a national scale when such bigger stakes were involved? Besides, as will be illustrated next, the international forum enabled the Canadian governments to achieve much reform of the domestic economic union without direct domestic trade-offs and within the larger context of global and regional integration and its broader pattern of benefits and costs.

We now turn more directly to the international arena. Canadian governments made much more progress with Canada's international liberalization agenda. As noted, Canadians had begun a historic reversal of economic nationalism in favour of free trade. They did so for both defensive and offensive reasons. Defensively, they sought to get on the inside of American protectionism. Canada was more severely affected by US contingency protection than any other country. The Canadian business community thus embraced the objective of more secure access to the American market, which quickly evolved to support for a comprehensive free trade agreement. As an offensive strategy, free trade was a means of attaining global competitiveness, notably for the manufacturing sector, reversing its century-old position in favour of protection.

The bilateral negotiation process illustrated overwhelmingly the domestic nature and the multi-level games of contemporary trade policy-making. At one level were Canadian and American federal governments negotiating trade concessions and a new set of rules. Yet each side had to also contend with complex domestic political processes over which they had only partial control. In the US case, this entailed Congress as well as the states and industry and labour. In Canada, relations with the provinces became the most important second level, although industry consultation was also important. Conflicts and consensus at one level quickly spilled over to the other. Only the two federal governments actually had to conduct negotiations in two "games," but all players had to watch carefully developments at all levels. In Canada's case, as discussed below, a worrisome issue became whether the provinces would agree to trade liberalization in areas of their jurisdiction. And in terms of the Canadian economic union, the pace and substance of change at the international level would drive domestic negotiations.

The substantive policy results of the international negotiation and their effects are dealt with below. Here, it is important to record three outcomes of the process as such. First, the momentous decision to enter the negotiations was proof that the old style east-west Canadian integration was in relative decline. Quebec's position proved to be pivotal in this respect. Traditionally protective of its "soft" sectors of footwear, clothing, textiles, and furniture, Quebec's vulnerability to international competition had been gradually eroded through successive rounds of tariff cuts through the GATT. By 1985, Quebec was ready to embrace a more open position. The change of one of the two largest provinces from a net protectionist to a net liberal approach made a big difference in the national calculus. Alberta, British Columbia, Saskatchewan, New Brunswick, and Newfoundland joined Quebec in strong support for a free trade agreement. Ontario alone remained mainly opposed, while Manitoba, Nova Scotia, and Prince Edward Island were ambivalent. Alberta, in particular, saw free trade as a means to neutralize federal intervention in its own economy, given the bitter recrimination over the Trudeau government's National Energy Program (NEP). These regional positions held roughly the same for the negotiation of NAFTA.

Second, the Mulroney government needed the political support of the provinces to proceed with the negotiations and for broader public acceptance of the final result. As discussed in chapter 4, this was due not only to the important role of regional representation in national politics played by provincial governments (their premiers especially), but also to the fact that the negotiations covered a broad range of issues in provincial jurisdiction. Provincial subsidies, government procurement, liquor board practices, agricultural marketing boards, and the regulation of services and investment were only the most prominent of the provincial measures potentially on the table if there was to be a comprehensive agreement with the USA.

Thus, the political requirement for provincial support and the presence of so many provincial policies on the bargaining table gave the provinces a strong hand to negotiate a major role in the bilateral negotiation process itself. The provinces had already been consulted during the Tokyo Round of multilateral trade negotiations and over trade disputes with the European Community.[13] The Macdonald Commission had foreseen the need for close provincial collaboration in the bilateral negotiations with the United States (and indeed, in the long term, a process of provincial ratification of trade agreements).[14] After some intense jockeying for position in the first half of 1986, the federal and provincial governments agreed on a set of modalities for "full provincial participation" in the Canadian trade negotiation process. These included: meetings of the first ministers every three months for the duration of the bilateral negotiations; consultations with the provinces on the negotiation positions to the Americans in advance; confidential monthly meetings of senior provincial officials with Canada's chief negotiator, Simon Reisman; and formal consultation with provincial cabinets prior to signing any agreement.[15]

These intergovernmental arrangements were essentially consultative, not deliberative. The provinces met their minimal requirements for input and information; the federal government retained control over the Canadian negotiators and ensured that only they would be at the table with the Americans. Nonetheless, the federal-provincial consultations, conducted in secret over highly sensitive issues requiring trust on both sides, worked remarkably well. Without these arrangements, the provinces (or at least eight of ten) would not have had the confidence to back the federal position. Without that backing, it can be argued, the Canadian negotiating position with the Americans would not have been sustainable, given the high degree of controversy generated by the negotiations in the Canadian media and public. During the negotiations for the NAFTA (1991–93) and the WTO agreement (1986–93), a similar set of domestic intergovernmental consultations took place, although they were less intensive at the political level.

This complex consultative process delivered other benefits. For the federal negotiators, it increased political support and knowledge of federal objectives in sensitive regions while providing in-depth knowledge of regional industry and provincial policy and administration. To the provinces, it provided a crash course in the ideology, jargon, and technical detail of international trade negotiations. In each province, a small but significant group of officials became knowledgeable about trade issues and about how trade agreements are crafted. This experience would ultimately lay the basis for the intergovernmental negotiations leading to the Agreement on Internal Trade.

Assessment of Outcomes

This phase in Canadian economic union reform is characterized by a dichotomy of results. Against Canada's success in international negotiations is set its failure on the domestic front. At least the issue had reached the intergovernmental agenda. Even the name of the game came to reflect that priority (the first ministers in 1987 relabelled the group of ministers to deal with the issues the Committee of Ministers on Internal Trade (CMIT) from the earlier title of Economic Development Ministers). However, the domestic process delivered too little too late. It would be superseded in 1991 by more ambitious constitutional reform negotiations.

As for the international trade agreements, one can assess their impact in three ways. First is the effect of the actual provisions on the ability of the federal and provincial governments to maintain internal barriers in the Canadian economy. Second is the effect on the relative balance between federal and provincial powers. Third is the effect on the policy environment for government intervention. In these assessments, I place special emphasis on the FTA as the first and most controversial of the three agreements.

The FTA broke new ground in terms of international trade agreements by dealing with such matters as services, investment, and the temporary entry of businesspersons. It was also designed to meet the specifications of regional free trade agreements in article XXIV of the GATT, and thus, its provisions are mainly prohibitive: it is a classic instrument of negative integration, providing very limited capacity for common regulation (i.e., positive integration).

Table 5.1 provides an overview of the existing internal trade barriers in Canada implicated by the FTA (as well as the NAFTA and WTO agreement). About half of the internal barriers are reduced in whole or in part by the FTA alone. In some cases, the international barrier and the interprovincial one were the same. The removal of an irritant in bilateral international trade is thus also a freeing up of interprovincial trade. This is especially the case for federally induced barriers to trade, such as tariffs and export controls and discriminatory pricing for oil and gas. By prohibiting intervention to discriminate against American goods, services, and investment, the federal government would, in practically all cases, be denying itself the ability to undertake discrimination within Canada. The most controversial example was export taxation of oil and gas that would prevent the federal government from reimposing the two-price petroleum regime, which had been the most odious aspect of the National Energy Program (NEP) of 1980–85 for Alberta and other petroleum-producing provinces. (The Mulroney government had by early 1985 dismantled the NEP in any case, but the FTA makes it more difficult for future governments to reverse that policy.)

The effect of the FTA on the provincially induced barriers to trade is not quite so clear-cut. The FTA applies to the provinces the following provisions:[16] chapters 5 on national treatment, 7 on agriculture, 8 on wines and spirits, 9 on energy, 12 on exceptions to trade in goods, 14 on services, and 16 on investment. The provinces are expressly exempted from chapter 6 on technical standards, 13 on government procurement,

Table 5.1 International Liberalization and Canadian Internal Barriers

NATURE OF EXISTING BARRIER	FTA (1989)	NAFTA (1994)	WTO AGREEMENTS (1995)
GOODS			
• Quantitative restrictions in agriculture (supply management).	• Not covered.	• Not covered.	• GATT 1994 Agreement on Agriculture turns quotas into tariffs, to be reduced over time.
• Discriminatory procurement practices.	• Chapter 13 for federal by government alone, coverage by entities listed.	• Chapter 10 mandates negotiations by 1998 to cover provincial entities.	• Plurilateral agreement mandates negotiations that may cover provincial entities.
• Discriminatory pricing and distribution of alcoholic beverages.	• Chapter 8 applies to wine and spirits; prohibits discriminatory price markups and mandatory bulk blending. Beer exempted.	• Chapter 3 prohibits mandatory bulk blending.	• No specific measures.
• GBES (Crown corporations) restrictions on competition.	• Chapter 20 reinforces GATT commitment to non-discriminatory practice by government monopolies; fair compensation for expropriation.	• Chapter 15 extends and broadens commitments of the FTA.	• No specific measures.
• Discriminatory pricing of oil and gas; restrictions on trade in electricity.	• Chapter 9 reinforces GATT provisions to rule out discriminatory supply and export taxes. Allows incentives for exploration and development.	• Chapter 6 extends to Mexico but reduced in scope cf. FTA.	• No specific measures.
• Industrial and agricultural subsidies.	• Chapter 19 provides binding dispute resolution panels applied to national laws on subsidy-countervail. A working group to negotiate new subsidies code (later abandoned).	• Chapter 19 – similar provisions to dispute resolution in FTA.	• New code on subsidies as part of Agreement on Subsidies and Countervailing Measures (does not cover agriculture).

Table 5.1 International Liberalization and Canadian Internal Barriers *(Continued)*

NATURE OF EXISTING BARRIER	FTA (1989)	NAFTA (1994)	WTO AGREEMENTS (1995)
SERVICES			
• Securities markets not integrated.	• Chapter 17 provides national treatment to banking but does not extend to provinces.	• Chapter 14 on financial services does extend to provinces.	• Financial sector covered by new GATS, providing at minimum most-favoured nation status, transparency, and mutual recognition; national treatment only where specified by specific parties.
• GBES restrict competition in service sectors.	• Chapter 20 (see above).	• Chapter 15 (see above).	• GATS article VIII prohibits discriminatory practice by monopolies.
• Discriminatory regulation of professional services.	• Chapter 14 covers engineering, accounting, management consulting, and architecture. Existing provincial measures grandfathered. Mandate for further sectoral liberalization.	• Chapter 12 prohibits residency as requirement for professional services. Existing provincial measures grandfathered.	• Not covered.
CAPITAL			
• Investment restrictions.	• Chapter 16 provides national treatment (but grandfathers provincial measures). Prohibits some types of performance requirements. Cultural industries specifically exempted.	• Chapter 11 broadens FTA coverage and deepens obligations, including providing direct access for investors to dispute resolution process. Prohibits more types of performance requirements. Some provincial measures grandfathered if scheduled.	• Agreement on Trade Related Investment Measures prohibits some types of performance requirements, sets general rules.

Table 5.1 International Liberalization and Canadian Internal Barriers *(Continued)*

NATURE OF EXISTING BARRIER	FTA (1989)	NAFTA (1994)	WTO AGREEMENTS (1995)
LABOUR			
• Occupational standards and licensing.	• Regulation of professions not covered, but Chapter 15 eases temporary business access.	• Chapter 16 provides for temporary business access.	• 1993 ministerial decision mandates negotiations for "movement of natural persons." GATS provides for mutual recognition.
• Labour relations standards.	• Not covered.	• North American Agreement on Labour Cooperation (a side deal to NAFTA) commits parties to comply with existing national and subnational laws and standards to avoid "social dumping." Independent commission to monitor compliance but applies to Canadian provinces only if a majority of them agree.	• Not covered.

FTA   Canada-United States Free Trade Agreement
GATT   General Agreement on Tariffs and Trade
GATS   General Agreement on Trade in Services
GBES   Government Business Enterprises (Crown Corporations)
NAFTA   North American Free Trade Agreement
WTO   World Trade Organization

REFORMING THE CANADIAN ECONOMIC UNION, 1976–92 • 129

and 17 on financial services. Yet chapters 14 and 16 affect the provinces only prospectively in that existing "nonconforming" measures are "grandfathered." And there are other more specific exceptions in chapter 12, such as for beer and the export of logs.

In summary, the FTA did remove or dramatically reduce the trade-distorting effect of a number of the more important policy instruments of the Canadian state, among them (federal) procurement policy, energy policies, and investment controls. Nonetheless, for all the controversy about the role of the provinces in the negotiations and the lengthy agenda of potential items within provincial jurisdiction, it is surprising how little the FTA impinged directly on provincial jurisdiction. Even so, the exact extent of the provincial jurisdiction affected was a matter of some legal debate at the time.[17]

This last point leads to the issue of the effect of the FTA on the federal-provincial balance of power. As noted in chapter 4, treaties negotiated by and signed for Canada by the federal government cannot be implemented in matters of provincial jurisdiction without provincial consent. That consent would include provincial legislation if necessary. This legal understanding has been in place since the 1937 Privy Council ruling in *Labour Conventions*. However, by the 1980s, considerable legal opinion, yet to be definitively tested, was of the view that the subject matter of international trade agreements such as the proposed FTA would come under an expanded definition of the federal trade and commerce power (recall the discussion in chapter 4 about the trend of Supreme Court judgments). Some legal commentators even foresaw the negotiations as leading to an overturning of *Labour Conventions* itself.[18] Thus, there arose the potential that the federal government would seek to implement the FTA within Canadian law in a way which would test the limits of its jurisdiction and precipitate a constitutional challenge. One notes the parallel with the role of the Commonwealth government in Australia over its litigation in the *Tasmanian Dam* case. Long-term jurisdictional gains could come from such a legal strategy – of enormous significance to the operation of the Canadian economic union, let alone the federal treaty-making capacity.

This issue haunted the bilateral negotiations with the Americans. Ontario had opposed the agreement openly. Indeed, Liberal Premier David Peterson won re-election in September 1987 in part due to his opposition to the (then) potential agreement. Could Ontario alone block the agreement by refusing to implement an important provision?

Could the federal government unilaterally impose the FTA on a dissenting province? The most likely test of this jurisdictional issue came with the Ontario government's initial refusal to implement the provisions of chapter 8 – to open its wine market to American competition. California wine producers, which had the ear of President Reagan, had long targeted the discriminatory pricing and distribution policies of the Canadian provincial liquor monopolies. The Liquor Control Board of Ontario was reputed to be, by virtue of its monopoly, the largest single purchaser of alcoholic beverages in the world. Though small in the overall agreement, the obligations on the provinces in chapter 8 were thus rather sensitive politically.

Despite advice from some quarters to impose the FTA on the provinces with the full force of the law, the federal government took a less intrusive route in its implementing legislation.[19] The bill included what amounted to legislated warnings about federal jurisdiction and included provisions for implementing chapter 8 if the provinces failed to comply. However, when the Ontario government finally settled with the federal government on an adjustment package for its grape growers and wine industry in March 1989, the threat of a provincial legal challenge faded. In summary, then, the federal government was able to achieve the implementation of the FTA without formal recourse to the instruments in its implementation bill. No province has yet challenged the federal legislation. This does not mean that the provinces thought they would lose their case, but surely the risks would have been perceived as high. The province of Ontario chose wisely to keep its views out of the courts rather than risk a permanent loss of jurisdiction. The province came to a similar conclusion in 1994 when the then NDP government dropped a planned court challenge to NAFTA.

If the de jure balance between the federal and provincial governments remains to be tested, what about the de facto balance? As is clear, the FTA neutralizes federal intervention much more than it does provincial. By curbing the federal government more comprehensively than the provinces, the FTA is perceived as decentralizing. Thus, some critics predicted that despite the specific provisions of the FTA, the logic of integration would lead to the harmonization with US policies or elimination of Canadian social programs such as medicare, unemployment insurance, and regional development. This view was especially prominent during the period from 1987 to 1990 (and beyond), when many Canadians opposed what they perceived as the further decentralization of the Meech Lake Constitutional Accord. To this argument about decentralization, others countered that the full force of liberalization would soon affect the provinces in any case. This would come through the general ideological climate or by further liberalization as specified in various negotiations mandated in the FTA or by NAFTA and GATT Uruguay Round negotiations. In any case, analysts on both sides of the ideological divide would agree that international trade agreements create a powerful alternative to formal constitutional reform in reforming the economic roles of government in the federal state. In this view, through continental integration, the American market becomes a powerful force on Canadian economic policy.[20]

Finally, the specific effects of the two other trade agreements may be summarized briefly. As outlined in table 5.1, NAFTA reinforced the FTA by extending its liberalization in services, investment, and temporary business entry to Mexico. But NAFTA also deepened the integration. It included a chapter on intellectual property rights, not in the FTA; had a tighter regime against "performance requirements" for investors; mandated further liberalization of financial services; and required more transparency of the provinces in their grandfathering of existing laws. Like the FTA, NAFTA did not touch cultural industries or agriculture, nor did it attempt a new code on subsidies.[21]

Most significantly for the provinces, however, NAFTA included as "side deals" two agreements on labour and environmental standards. In order to prevent "social dumping," these agreements provided new regional commissions to monitor the compliance of existing labour and environmental law by national and subnational governments within North America. The side deals are replete with limitations and exemptions and are intended to ensure compliance with existing laws rather than to integrate them in any way. Nonetheless, they constitute an important departure. According to one study, the provinces were intensively involved in their negotiation, much more so than the main agreement.[22] Also, the agreement on environment is brought into effect for Canada only if the provinces collectively agree. In so doing, it sets out a novel (in Canadian terms) decision rule by which the agreement's provisions are triggered on the assent of two-thirds of the provinces having among them 55 per cent of GDP. A dissenting province can "opt out." There are similar arrangements for the labour law side deal.

By building on the GATT regime, the WTO agreements are, of course, much more extensive geographically than the FTA and NAFTA. However, they borrow from the FTA and NAFTA their approach to liberalization in services, investment (notably regarding monopolies and performance requirements), and intellectual property. The WTO breaks new ground in agriculture and in subsidies and countervailing measures, and both these agreements affect the provinces deeply. The former takes the import quotas underpinning Canada's federal-provincial supply management schemes for dairy, eggs, and poultry, changes them into tariffs, and then cuts them by 36 per cent over five years. Further cuts in these politically sensitive sectors can be expected in future agriculture rounds.

The new agreement on subsidies imposes discipline on WTO parties by categorizing subsidies into those prohibited outright, those actionable by countervail, and those non-actionable (but open to dispute resolution). In particular, the new code clarifies but limits the scope of acceptable regional development assistance. These provisions will shape policy in all government programs of assistance to industry, primary producers, communities, and specific regions. Finally, a "plurilateral" agreement reached by the Uruguay Round commits the provinces to negotiations on government procurement.

In conclusion, the achievement through the FTA of a significant degree of continental integration – reinforced by NAFTA and the WTO agreement five years later – placed new pressures on the Canadian economic union. First, by removing specific barriers to international trade, the regional and global integration measures put direct and indirect pressure on the remaining barriers to the internal market. The scope, the time frame, and even the legal drafting of the international agreements would drive the agenda for internal trade. These effects would be seen most clearly in the Agreement on Internal Trade (see chapter 6). As will become clear in later chapters, this development contrasts strongly with Australia, where the burden of reform must be carried entirely by domestic arrangements, contributing to a more centralized result.

The agreements also boost cross-border north-south trade in separate regions. In this respect, British Columbia's future economic adjustment may be primarily with markets in the US Pacific Northwest rather than with the rest of Canada, Ontario with the adjoining Great Lake states, and so on. Such intensifying regional market integration in Canada, even if of longer-term economic effect, spawned considerable political controversy. Not only business associations, but also social interests and political parties, noted the debilitating effects of what was perceived to be more open market with the USA than within Canada. Of course, this is the perception only, not the reality. I have argued already that the Canadian economic union sustains a much greater degree of integration than the FTA or NAFTA ever could. Still, the pace and direction of reform at the international level seemed incongruous compared to the slow progress at home. Such concerns would become even more pronounced with increased anxiety over national political unity in Canada. And since north-south trade is, in fact, growing more quickly than east-west, the dynamic effect may be to increase the divergence within the regionalized Canadian economy.[23] This could make positive integration more difficult in the Canadian economic union of the future. Therefore, the long-term effect of north-south integration is important to the Canadian economic union, a point to which we return in the concluding chapter.

SECOND ATTEMPT AT CONSTITUTIONAL REFORM, 1991–92: CANADA ROUND

Overview of Events

The story begins with the defeat of the Meech Lake Accord in 1987. This constitutional initiative had been designed expressly as a "Quebec Round" of constitutional amendments to redress Quebec's failure to be a part of the 1981–82 constitutional settlement. After about a year of negotiations, the first ministers (of all the provinces as well as the federal government) reached unanimous agreement on a set of proposed constitutional amendments in May 1987, meeting at a government retreat at Meech Lake near Ottawa.

The Meech Lake Accord answered five "minimal" Quebec demands, although none of them addressed economic union issues as such. The five constitutional reforms proposed in the accord were:

1 an interpretative clause recognizing Canadian duality and the "distinct society" of Quebec's francophone majority
2 explicit recognition of the federal spending power along with curbs on its use in areas of provincial jurisdiction
3 entrenchment of an agreement on the exercise of the concurrent jurisdiction in immigration

4 a guarantee of the existing convention that three of the nine justices of the Supreme Court of Canada would be from Quebec's civil bar
5 a veto for Quebec on constitutional amendments affecting national institutions

In order to get the unanimous agreement of all provinces (ultimately needed to pass the accord through all the legislatures), the leaders also agreed to grant to all the provinces the veto over amendments demanded by Quebec and extended to all provinces a role in the appointment of Supreme Court justices and of senators. The accord also mandated annual First Ministers Conferences.

This deal became unravelled during the three-year time limit required for its ratification by the federal and all of the provincial parliaments. Many Canadians opposed the accord as too decentralizing; some objected to the "distinct society" clause for its potential to provide greater leeway for Quebec's francophone majority over minorities in that province; and aboriginal groups objected to the lack of recognition of their needs. Many also objected to the executive federalism process taken to reach the accord, which was seen as secretive and collusive.

The rejection of the accord came at the end of six months of highly emotional and visible debate. Indeed, francophone Quebec interpreted the rejection as a direct insult. Premier Bourassa's Liberal government withdrew from further intergovernmental relations. What had begun as a low-key and modest effort at accommodation ended in a highly charged failure, opening the floodgates of Quebec nationalism, arguably shut since the failure of the 1980 referendum. Poll results showed a majority in Quebec in support of sovereignty by early 1990.

The road from Meech Lake to the Charlottetown Accord of August 1992 was long and difficult. A new Canada Round of constitutional discussions was launched, intended to embrace both Quebec as well as the diverse critics of Meech. This round also ended in failure, but not before a wide-ranging agenda of constitutional reform had been proposed and debated.

Events moved quickly in Quebec. By January 1991, the governing Quebec Liberal Party endorsed the Allaire Report, which proposed sweeping reforms, much more decentralizing than Meech.[24] In March 1991, the Quebec National Assembly endorsed the Belanger-Campeau Report,[25] setting a deadline for reform that either there would be "offers" of reform to the federal system for Quebec to assess and put to a referendum in the province by October 1992, or there would be a referendum on sovereignty instead. The goal, in the famous words of a prominent Quebec constitutional advisor, Léon Dion, was to put a "knife to the throat" of the rest of Canada.[26]

The debate engaging the rest of Canada took several stages. First, governments, interest groups, and academics undertook a broad effort to redefine the issues and the foundation of a new federal position. Then, the federal government released proposals in September 1991, followed by proposals from Ontario and some other provinces. Next came public consultations on those proposals, culminating in an all-party federal parliamentary committee report in March 1992. Multilateral negotiations then ensued, involving the federal government, all provinces but Quebec, the two territorial governments, and representatives of four national aboriginal organizations, meeting from March to July 1992. Through this latter process, the parties reached agreement on 12 July 1992. The final stage in the negotiation process, bringing Quebec back to the table to reach agreement prior to the Quebec referendum, began in August 1992. The negotiations were completed at Charlottetown on 28 August 1992, with unanimous agreement among the governments and aboriginal leadership on a proposed set of constitutional amendments and related political undertakings.

In this entire debate, as detailed below, the economic union at first played a prominent role, but the role declined as the process spun to its conclusion. The Charlottetown Accord tackled such issues as an interpretative clause on Quebec's distinct society, Senate reform, the federal spending power, and the self-government of aboriginal peoples. But on the economic union, the only constitutional amendment proposed was a new set of principles to guide the "social and economic union."

At Charlottetown, the first ministers agreed to submit the new agreement to a referendum not just in Quebec, but in all of Canada, to be held on 26 October 1992. The Canadian people defeated the Charlottetown Accord by an overall vote of 54.4 per cent. Quebecers voted against it by 55 per cent, but there were even greater majorities opposed in Manitoba, Alberta, and British Columbia. The reasons for the electoral rejection are complex, but they may be summarized on the grounds that the Charlottetown Accord delivered too little to Quebec for its liking and too much to Quebec for other Canadians, notably those in the West. The modest achievements on the economic union were not prominent in the debate and, according to polling analysis, would have swayed few votes.[27]

The public associated the agreement with the Mulroney government, then at only 14 per cent support in public opinion polls, and distrusted the overly complex and compromised agreement. Moreover, the referendum campaign marked a signal failure of political, business, and social elites to convince the electorate to accept the product of their accommodation. In sum, six years and seemingly endless rounds of discussion of constitutional renewal ended in defeat for the proponents of reform.

In conclusion, economic union played throughout this episode in a variety of ways. First is the attempt within the Canada Round itself to deal with economic union issues. Second is the post-Charlottetown context, which led directly to the negotiation and successful conclusion of the non-constitutional Agreement on Internal Trade (discussed in the next chapter). Third, economic union reform became important to national unity overall as an exhibition of the ability (or not) of the federal system to renew itself, as well as underpinning the nature of continuing economic integration (or not) should such efforts fail and the federal union dissolve.

Dynamics of the Process

Two major political and economic factors contributed to making the economic union an important issue in this round of constitutional debate. First, as noted above, free trade dominated much of the economic policy agenda in the 1985–95 period. The Canada Round coincided with a sharp recession in 1991–92, especially in Ontario, which increased anxiety about economic globalization and political opposition to further liberalization. Yet most political and business elites seemed convinced that the logic of globalization and liberalization had to be extended through NAFTA and Uruguay Round negotiations abroad and by whatever forum became available at home. As a key senior federal official during the Canada Round put it, a "strong intellectual convergence" emerged around the need for competitiveness, for reducing the scope of government intervention, reducing government deficits and debt, and removing barriers to the single market.[28]

The advocacy of economic union reform linked to a neo-liberal agenda is seen most clearly in the views of major national business organizations such as the Business Council on National Issues, the Canadian Manufacturers' Association, and the Canadian Chamber of Commerce. Of course, labour, social interest groups, and left-wing political parties opposed the economic union issue as couched in such terms. These views were championed officially by the NDP government of Ontario elected in September 1990 under Premier Bob Rae. The Rae government made a "social charter" (later to be changed to a social "union" for reasons discussed below) one of its bottom line objectives of constitutional reform. Ontario did not seek to link directly the social and economic union agendas, but the former was a way to redress what the province saw as a federal agenda tilted in favour of neo-conservative ideology.[29] As Canadian political scientist Miriam Smith notes: "The social charter idea had its origins in the same forces of globalization that propelled the constitutional agenda of business. The proposal drew its inspiration in part from the experience of the European labour movement with the 1989 social charter, which had been an attempt to provide a counterweight to the 'marketizing' effect of the European Community 1992. In the Canadian case, the social charter was seen as a means of countering the increased liberalization that had begun with the FTA and threatened to accelerate under NAFTA."[30] Indeed, the economic *and* social union, as constitutional agenda items, illustrate a common phenomenon in political agenda formation: the rise to prominence of issues coinciding with the opportunity to pursue them – this time an open-ended constitutional forum. As shown below, however, the existence of the opportunity to debate the issues in a constitutional "mega-game" only exacerbated the search for solutions.

The second factor driving the economic union issue was the same concern as in the Patriation Round of strengthening federal powers over the economic union as a quid pro quo for the expected decentralization of powers to the provinces. In the climate of opinion following the collapse of Meech Lake, virtually all observers assumed that there would have to be a major decentralization of jurisdiction to Quebec to keep it within the federation.[31] This is certainly the message that came out of Quebec itself. Most prominent of these signals was the governing Liberal Party's own Allaire Report, which proposed that Quebec control regional development, industry and commerce, language, communication, unemployment insurance, agriculture, and income security, among others. Outside Quebec, the debate concerned the issue of whether there should be decentralization to Quebec alone or to all the provinces. Some provincial governments such as Alberta also wanted decentralization, while others such as Newfoundland did not seek new powers but would insist that what would be offered to Quebec would be offered to all (the latter position having strong resonance in the Canadian public outside Quebec).

In this debate, Ontario distrusted Ottawa's neo-liberal agenda. In its view, the federal government's deficit-cutting efforts had been penalizing Ontario, in particular, through certain unilateral changes to intergovernmental fiscal arrangements. Thus, the Rae government's priorities for reform included greater certainty for future intergovernmental arrangements and championing both the social union and the economic union agenda as a way of neutralizing the effects of more provincial powers, which it did not seek but could not refuse. The Ontario government was supported by many left-leaning centralists who sought to ensure that Quebec's decentralization agenda was blunted by measures to enhance pan-Canadian identity and citizenship.[32] In any case, both those who applauded major decentralization and those who wished to limit it argued in favour of economic union reform as a counterweight to ensure that existing degrees of economic integration were preserved, if not extended.[33]

The issue of economic union also became important in this round in light of the growing support for Quebec sovereignty after the rejection of Meech. This led most Quebecers to stress the need to maintain economic and financial ties with Canada come what may. Of course, federalists pointed to the economic union as one of the chief benefits of the federation, arguing for improvements to the functioning of the economic union as a way of shoring up Canadian unity. On the other side, the sovereignists premised their project on strong continuing economic relations with the rest of Canada. While there was immediate skepticism about this PQ position in the rest of Canada, prominent economic analysts nonetheless recognized that the potential costs of economic disintegration could be enormous. If reform of the economic union were needed to sustain the federal regime, even if the direct benefits were small, the avoided costs would be significant.[34] Even so, the need to make the argument that the federal union held significant economic benefit for Quebec put reform-minded federalists in a somewhat schizophrenic position of having to defend a set of institutions and, at the same time, arguing for their overhaul.

All of these aspects of the economic union issue were reflected in the federal government's proposals for reform, released in September 1991 in the document *Shaping Canada's Future Together: Proposals*. Indeed, the economic union formed a centrepiece of the new federal position. While careful to stress that the existing Canadian economic union was already strong enough to provide substantial benefits, the background paper to the economic union proposals identified the standard pathologies of barriers and inefficiencies. It stressed that in recent years, "the balance between the perceived costs and benefits of internal barriers has begun to change"[35] relative to Canada's trade competitors, now including the European Union, and relative to other federations. It acknowledged (as discussed in the previous part of this chapter) that effort since the mid-1980s to reduce barriers had produced only modest results. According to the document, the solution lay in improving constitutional instruments for both negative and positive integration.[36]

The new proposals established two goals for improving economic integration: "We must enhance the operation of our internal market. We must improve the harmonization and co-ordination of economic policies."[37] Among its reform proposals were the following:

1 Broadening section 121, the Common Market clause, to include the "four freedoms" of movement for persons, goods, services, and capital. These freedoms would be subject to derogations for dealing with regional disparities or laws declared to be in the "national interest."

2 A new exclusive federal legislative power, section 91A, for the management of the economic union. However, legislation under this section would have to be approved by two-thirds of the provinces having together 50 per cent of the population (see Council of the Federation below) and allow dissenting provinces to opt out temporarily.

3 Harmonization of the budget planning process though agreement with the provinces and the joint development of a set of guidelines for fiscal and monetary policy coordination.

4 The entrenchment of a Council of the Federation as a permanent intergovernmental forum of federal, provincial, and territorial governments. The council would have three formal roles: to vote on proposed federal legislation under the new section 91A; to vote on guidelines for fiscal harmonization and coordination; and to vote on the use of the federal spending power on new Canada-wide shared cost programs and conditional transfers in areas of exclusive

provincial jurisdiction. The decision rule in all cases would be the "7+50" rule drawn from the constitutional amending formula (*Constitution Act, 1982*, section 38(1)).

In retrospect, these proposals marked the high-water line of the tide of economic union reform in this round. They came under immediate attack from Quebec and elsewhere, forcing the federal government to retreat to the much-diluted position of the Charlottetown Accord. The story of how these proposals got transformed is not essential here. Instead, a few conclusions can be drawn about how the demise of the federal proposals illustrates underlying tensions on the economic union issue.

First, the proposals for new federal legislative powers (a new section 91A), even if subject to intergovernmental co-decision, were seen as too blunt and sweeping. Critics stressed concerns about federal balance. In a game in which the ultimate goal of most players was to reform the federal system to make Quebec feel more at home, concern over the federal balance trumped arguments for more intensive positive integration.

Second, the proposals for better negative integration, the changes to section 121, had greater staying power and survived in diluted form almost to the end of the process. Yet important concerns shaped the debate. The role of the courts in interpreting a new section 121, and therefore second-guessing federal and provincial legislation on behalf of the national market, worried governments and interest groups still reeling from the policy upheavals of the courts' interpretation of the *Charter of Rights and Freedoms*. Thus, by March 1992, support died for new, broadened, and detailed constitutional provisions that could be interpreted and applied by the courts. The other controversy about the federal proposal lay with the idea of derogations. Business groups wanted no derogations at all, while many provinces and other interests loaded onto the proposal a list of additional derogations to protect legislation in areas such as public health and safety, agricultural supply management, public monopolies, etc. (compare GATT articles XIV and XX). When at the end of the negotiations Quebec could not agree to even a watered-down constitutional amendment to section 121, the governments agreed to pursue the matter through a non-constitutional "political accord." Attached to that text were ten different types of derogations.[38] In sum, one may say that social interest groups and some of the provinces succeeded in taming the proposed negative integration measures for purposes of equity and regional balance.

The same arguments against court-made policy through a strengthened section 121 came to be used effectively against any new social charter as well. The social program activists who fought against the constitutional entrenchment of neo-liberal values thus had to jettison their own preferences for entrenching justiciable social values.[39] The result was the twinning of "social and economic union" in a statement of general principles only, to be part of an expanded section 36 of the *Constitution Act, 1982.*

Finally, the proposal for intergovernmental co-decision through a Council of the Federation ran into a post-Meech mood of antipathy to executive federalism in any form due to its perceived lack of representativeness and accountability (see discussion in chapter 4). And some doubted that there was sufficient trust among governments, particularly Quebec, for binding votes in the proposed council.[40]

In conclusion, many of the obstacles to reform in a constitutional venue that had been expressed in 1980–81 resurfaced in 1990–91. Concerns about a federal power grab, court-made policy, and the effect of stronger integration measures on regional autonomy and equity all helped to sink the economic union provisions. Despite an impressive and building consensus on the need for economic union reform, particularly given the success at the international level, the high-stakes forum of constitutional politics could not deliver. Instead, as Peter Russell points out, the final result is "barren," as amendments to section 121 were deleted from the main text of the accord and relegated to a "political accord." The federal government had failed to achieve its own apparent priority in the intergovernmental negotiations.[41]

Assessment of Outcomes

This round did not produce any tangible reform of the Canadian economic union. It was an all-or-nothing sort of process. The most important political outcome of the Canada Round thus came in how the issue of economic union continued to be framed and in the delimiting of the further options available to reformers. The first of these political outcomes is the most obvious – that at least for some time, the constitutional amendment route to reform would be closed. The Canada Round had absorbed significant amounts of political and other resources, the federal government under Mulroney faced a year at most before the next election, and politicians and the public turned to mounting fiscal and economic problems.

Analysts began to rake the coals of the Charlottetown Accord nonetheless for ways of proceeding in a "non-constitutional" fashion to renew federalism, including the economic union. They would find the "political accord" attached to the Charlottetown agreement as a possible blueprint, even though these accords were officially as dead as the Charlottetown Accord itself.

Clearly, some analysts had been disappointed by the failure to achieve more substantive provisions in the Charlottetown text. Yet the broader view was that there was more virtue than necessity in proceeding with reform primarily outside the constitution.[42] Constitutional provisions would have required the continual interpretation of the courts, a role few were anxious to thrust upon them. This is a view common among the government participants in the Canada Round as well.[43] Instead, the political accord's approach would have been to create an independent intergovernmental agency responsible for four roles related to the reduction of discriminatory barriers to internal trade. The roles of the new agency would be: "(a) mediation and conciliation; (b) determination that a prima facie case exists (screening); (c) final determination on a case; and (d) dispute resolution, which would be binding on governments."[44] The courts would presumably play a role *in extremis* only.

The bare bones text of the political accord also reinforced two other aspects of the context for future negotiation. First, it continued to put an emphasis on what could be termed a GATT-style type of agreement. It would enshrine the four freedoms along with the commitment not to erect interprovincial trade barriers (parts (1) and (2)). But these principles would be followed by a set of derogations – i.e., the agreement would not apply to certain types of laws (e.g., regional development) or for certain other public purposes (e.g., public security, provision of social services, etc.) (parts (3) and (4)). This approach of establishing general rules as well as detailed derogations would become the architecture of the Agreement on Internal Trade, albeit expanded to a 220-page text covering 18 chapters.

Second, such a political accord would have to rely on the unreformed decision rules and other processes of intergovernmental relations (recall the discussion in chapter 4). A constitutional proposal to entrench intergovernmental agreements had died with the Charlotte-town Accord. To reach any new agreement on the economic union, the governments would have to fall back on established practice by which intergovernmental agreements were essentially non-justiciable, unenforceable by the courts, and non-binding on legislatures as such, and where intergovernmental agreement could proceed only on the basis of consensus.

Finally, the process of the Canada Round left some specific political legacies for the future negotiation of the issue. The business community and economic think-tanks had awoken to the issue and were not about to let it go.[45] As discussed in the next chapter, these interests pushed hard to keep economic union reform on the post-Charlottetown agenda. And yet in this context, their advocacy would be unfettered by the countervailing advocacy of social interest groups that had pursued the social charter. The latter interests took note of the ensuing negotiations on the Agreement on Internal Trade, but with the constitution off the table and the stakes thus lowered, the social interest groups concentrated their advocacy on other issues such as fiscal policy. Only after the severe cuts to intergovernmental fiscal transfers in the 1995 federal budget would the provinces (not social program activists) seek a new understanding with the federal government on the social union. Ultimately, this took shape in the Social Union Framework Agreement (SUFA) concluded in 1999 (and discussed in the next chapter).

The Canada Round process had also laid bare the ambiguous position of the federal government. Initially bullish about economic union reform, particularly in light of potential decentralization of powers to the provinces, the federal government advocacy lost its bite. Some have put the blame for this on federal leadership. They especially point to Joe Clark, who as federal minister in charge, took a particularly conciliatory approach without a strong federal "bottom line." In any case, the federal position became diluted, but so too did the content of the reform package in terms of the transfer of powers to the provinces. It seems that much of the energy of the federal team in the latter stages of negotiation dwelt on limiting the remaining scope of decentralization. More fundamentally, the federal position throughout this round was torn between its role as reformer of the economic union and as defender of national unity sensitive to public opinion in Quebec.[46]

The national unity subtext would continue to be a dominant factor in the next round. The Conservatives lost the 1993 federal general election to the Liberals, led by Jean Chrétien. However, the sovereignist Bloc Québécois, led by Lucien Bouchard, took a majority of the federal seats in Quebec, enough to form the official opposition in Parliament. A provincial election in Quebec was expected in 1994, and in the two years prior to that election, the sovereignist Parti Québécois led in the public opinion polls. This provided a compelling time frame for the Liberal government in Ottawa to proceed with policies to demonstrate the strength of the federal system and with reform through non-constitutional means. Reform of the economic union became an obvious candidate, and governments sought to achieve results before the next Quebec election. In pursuing this approach, federal leadership would continue to be caught between the demands for economic union reform and the political realities of federal-provincial relations.

Thus, in comparison with Australia, Canada's reform efforts were dominated by constitutional politics from 1980–92. This may have been appropriate to the circumstances: the terms of the economic union are an integral part of the federal system and major change, whether done through formal constitutional amendment or not, should be considered as part of a broader constitutional consensus. Yet the stakes are higher and the symbolism more enhanced in a constitutional amendment process as such. Australia's reforms, covered in chapters 7 and 8, were achieved at a more "mezzo" level of relations. This enabled governments to reform the process of intergovernmental relations as well as the substantive provisions of their single market without the high stakes of constitutional principles and permanent change being implicated. As seen in the next chapter on Canada's most recent phase of reform, Canadians would have more success in a non-constitutional intergovernmental format as well. However, underlying constraints within the federal society, including Quebec's uncertain status, would continue to affect the shape of reform.

6 Canada's Agreement on Internal Trade, 1992–99

OVERVIEW OF EVENTS

The negotiations for the Agreement on Internal Trade (AIT) arose from the context, discussed in chapter 5, of an external policy of new international trade agreements and from the domestic experience of failed constitutional reform. The negotiations that led to the doomed Charlottetown Accord at least helped to define the scope of the reform to be tried next – i.e., an intergovernmental agreement focusing on non-justiciable provisions. Constitutional amendment as a route for reform was blocked and discredited, but governments were still under pressure to demonstrate that the federal system was capable of renewal. Internal trade became one of the most commonly cited issues for reform by non-constitutional means after October 1992.

In returning to a non-constitutional bargaining table on the economic union issues, the governments quickly embraced what may be called a "free trade agreement" paradigm for their efforts. As noted in chapter 5, by the early 1980s, the Macdonald Royal Commission and other reports had laid the intellectual foundations for a "GATT-style" domestic intergovernmental agreement in Canada. With the FTA already in place and negotiations completed or reaching completion on NAFTA and the WTO agreement, governments and business advocates turned their attention to the domestic front. The free trade agreement paradigm was also adopted because many in the federal and provincial governments were familiar with its devices and jargon (i.e., the trade policy community). While powerful and effective, this paradigm was often inappropriate for the domestic purposes of a federal economic union and brought with it narrow ideological baggage.

Also, one should not imply that the social consensus on internal free trade was universal. Groups opposed to the FTA and NAFTA also opposed the AIT for similar reasons.[1] However, unlike the Canada Round when social interest groups and labour became mobilized to ensure that their concerns were addressed, they seemed to have run out of steam on the AIT. This may have been due to the low profile of the negotiations but also to an impression that the stakes were less high compared with constitutional reform and to the preoccupation of such groups with more direct fiscal policy advocacy during the period of the AIT negotiations (1993–94). Governments addressed some of these concerns in the Social Union Framework Agreement reached in 1999.

The negotiation of the AIT also took place during a period of sharp political transition. After Prime Minister Mulroney's resignation as Conservative leader early in 1993, the new leader, Kim Campbell, called a general election for October but led the governing party to disastrous defeat to the Liberals under Jean Chrétien. In Quebec, meanwhile, the Liberal government faced a provincial election ultimately called in September 1994. The Parti Québécois won that election and held a referendum on sovereignty on 30 October 1995 in which their proposition was defeated by the incredibly narrow vote of 50.6 per cent. Canada had come to the brink of breakup. Many argued that the failure of Meech and Charlottetown in the previous five years had led to this result.

This fluid political climate contributed nonetheless to a widespread governmental consensus that progress had to be achieved on the economic union issue and that such progress could bring political benefit to the participants. The AIT negotiations began in March 1993 and were completed within fifteen months (by June 1994). It is remarkable and rare for intergovernmental negotiations to be conducted through a period of such electoral and political turmoil.

This period began as early as March 1992, when the Canadian first ministers committed their governments to work toward the accelerated reduction of internal trade barriers, without specifics as to form of agreement or its scope, but to finish their work by 31 March 1995. A ministerial council, the Committee of Ministers on Internal Trade (CMIT), met several times. Senior officials, called chief negotiators, pursued the detail of the negotiations, convened by an independent chair, Winnipeg businessman Arthur Mauro. By June 1993, the CMIT released a list of eleven sectors to be included in the agreement as well as a list of other intergovernmental forums that would be involved in the negotiations. These were, in essence, the intergovernmental councils at the cabinet minister level (hereafter "ministerial councils") for agriculture, labour market, consumer protection, environment, financial institutions, and transportation and highway safety. Finally, on 28 June 1994, the CMIT was able to announce an agreement in principle followed by a formal public release of the agreement at a first ministers' meeting of 18 July 1994. The AIT took formal effect on 1 July 1995.

The agreement comprises six parts (see table 6.1 for a list of the eighteen chapters.) More analytical detail will be provided on these provisions later in this chapter. Here, only a brief description will suffice for the discussion to follow.

- Part I sets out the broad operating principles of the agreement, the extent of obligations, and the general definitions of key terms used.
- Part II consists of a single article (#300) that underscores that the AIT is a normal intergovernmental agreement of the Canadian federation and is not to be construed as a proposed constitutional amendment. It confirms that "Nothing in this agreement alters the legislative or other authority of the Parliament or of the provincial legislatures ... or the rights of any of them under the Constitution of Canada."
- Part III provides a set of six general rules meant to guide internal trade overall, adopting principles used commonly in international trade policy. These are: (1) reciprocal non-discrimination; (2) right of entry and exit; (3) no measures to constitute obstacles to internal trade; (4) certain measures permitted that are inconsistent with the last three rules if they are "legitimate objectives" as defined by the agreement; (5) the reconciliation of standards by harmonization, mutual recognition, or other means; and (6) transparency in the application of legislation, regulation, procedures, and policy.
- Part IV is a set of eleven chapters containing specific rules divided into two types (see table 6.1). Horizontal chapters cover types of economic activity that cut across industrial sectors, while vertical chapters cover an individual sector, often broadly defined. The horizontal chapters are those on procurement (chapter 5); investment (chapter 6); labour mobility (chapter 7); consumer-related measures and standards (chapter 8); and environmental protection (chapter 15). The vertical chapters are agricultural and food goods (chapter 9); alcoholic beverages (chapter 10); natural resources processing (chapter 11); energy (chapter 12); communication (chapter 13); and transportation (chapter 14). The AIT is designed so that the rules in the horizontal chapters trump the provisions of the vertical

Table 6.1 Agreement on Internal Trade: Chapter Headings

Preamble

PART I – GENERAL	
Chapter One	Operating Principles
Chapter Two	General Definitions

PART II – CONSTITUTIONAL AUTHORITIES	
Chapter Three	Reaffirmation of Constitutional Powers and Responsibilities

PART III – GENERAL RULES	
Chapter Four	General Rules

PART IV – SPECIFIC RULES	
Chapter Five	Procurement
Chapter Six	Investment
Chapter Seven	Labour Mobility
Chapter Eight	Consumer-Related Measures and Standards
Chapter Nine	Agricultural and Food Goods
Chapter Ten	Alcoholic Beverages
Chapter Eleven	Natural Resources Processing
Chapter Twelve	Energy
Chapter Thirteen	Communications
Chapter Fourteen	Transportation
Chapter Fifteen	Environmental Protection

PART V – INSTITUTIONAL PROVISIONS AND DISPUTE RESOLUTION PROCEDURES	
Chapter Sixteen	Institutional Provisions
Chapter Seventeen	Dispute Resolution Procedures

PART VI – FINAL PROVISIONS	
Chapter Eighteen	Final Provisions

chapters (at least most of the time) and that the specific rules trump the more general rules of chapter 4.[2] Unless otherwise covered in a sectoral chapter or by the general exceptions, all governmental measures affecting trade in goods and services and the mobility of persons and capital would be subject to the general rules. As discussed more completely below, these chapters serve to fine-tune the obligations of the agreement in the context of the specific sectors or issue areas. In so doing, however, they provided great scope for limiting the application of the general rules in the form of exceptions, temporary non-conforming measures, and emergency safeguards.

• Part V provides for rudimentary administrative apparatus similar to routine intergovernmental processes in Canadian executive federalism. The AIT establishes a ministerial council, the Committee on Internal Trade (although governments would continue to call it the Council of Ministers on Internal Trade (CMIT)), to supervise the overall implementation of the AIT. The CMIT does not have any authority over other ministerial councils named by various sectoral chapters. The CMIT is to make decisions and recommendations "by consensus" only. Chapter 16 also sets up a secretariat to provide administrative and operational support. Chapter 17 provides two routes of dispute resolution: one is for government-to-government disputes; another is for private party-to-government disputes. Both entail a staged process of notification, consultations, panel review, and final implementation including retaliatory action. In the end, neither process is binding legally on the parties.

- Part VI is a set of "final" provisions for some general exceptions for regional development programs and the non-application to measures related to aboriginal peoples, cultural industries, the financial sector, taxation, and measures affecting national security. Chapter 18 also mandates future negotiations to extend the agreement, specifically to fill in chapter 12 on energy, which the governments left blank because they could not reach agreement. Other provisions throughout the text provide for a lengthy process of continued negotiation and implementation. This agenda covers such issues as procurement by Crown corporations and by publicly funded provincial entities such as hospitals, universities, and municipalities; reconciliation of occupational standards; and further liberalization in agriculture.

In summary, the agreement is complex and comprehensive. Its basic architecture bears strong similarities to the twenty chapters of the FTA and the twenty-two chapters of NAFTA. The AIT also covers similarly broad economic ground including services and investment as well as goods and, of course, surpasses the international agreements in its treatment of labour mobility. Despite its many achievements, however, the agreement was greeted with some derision when first announced. This is partly due, as discussed more fully below, to expectations raised as part of negotiating tactics by the governments themselves. The adoption of the free trade agreement paradigm also led to invidious comparisons of specific provisions in the AIT with chapters in the FTA or NAFTA, stressing the loopholes in the former. Comments also emphasized the unfinished business and the lack of a legally binding process.[3] This initial reaction would deepen over time to a more serious critique among business advocates and academic analysts as well as the media when the full import of the many tortuous compromises in the AIT became realized (discussed in the third part of this chapter). In any case, the media and others recognized in July 1994 that the agreement came together as quickly as it did – possibly too quickly – in order to provide substance to "renewed federalism" in the face of the pending Quebec election.

This generally uncharitable assessment of the initial AIT has become reinforced in the slow pace of implementation and further negotiation since 1994. While the official AIT has been amended twice,[4] the improvements have been mainly technical and cosmetic. By the summer of 1997, fully three years after the initial signing, many parts of the agreement remained unimplemented. Deadlines for undertakings to be completed in the first twelve and eighteen months after 1 July 1995 have come and gone. As a result, the federal government came under some pressure during the 1997 general election campaign to back its position on completing the AIT with a legal challenge to recalcitrant provinces.

In conclusion, there remains a substantial conflict of views, both inside and outside the government in Canada, on the AIT as negotiated and as being implemented. The debate amounts partly to the difference between a glass-half-empty and a glass-half-full perspective. Yet, as will be shown in the rest of this chapter, these views reflect underlying regional conflict of interest and deep-seated disagreement over the normative goals of the Canadian economic union. These conditions were reflected in differences within and among the governments during the negotiations on how far to push the free trade paradigm in a domestic setting. The conflicts are embedded in a less than ideal AIT and in its less than effective implementation.

DYNAMICS OF THE NEGOTIATION

The outcomes of the AIT are better understood when one apprehends the positions of the parties and the process of negotiations. Here, I concentrate on three aspects of the process:

1 General Positions of the Governments
2 Key Negotiation Issues
3 Process of Reaching Agreement

The governments' positions coming into the negotiations were shaped by a variety of factors.[5] Individual provinces' views reflected their position in the regional political economy, which change very slowly over decades. They also reflected differing views of the objectives of the negotiations based on party affiliations of the government. In some cases, the specific characteristics and capacities of key government departments and ministers also played an important role.

Based on historic positioning discussed in chapters 2 and 4, one would expect Ontario and Quebec to take the strongest positions in favour of reform, with the Western and Atlantic provinces being more skeptical. However, in the context of "free trade" as the dominant policy mode for most governments, strong commitment to trade liberalization in the international arena tended to reinforce commitment to domestic free trade in the AIT negotiations (e.g., the positions of Quebec, Alberta, New Brunswick, Manitoba, and the federal government). Similarly, skepticism of trade liberalization on ideological grounds, such as expressed by the New Democratic Party (NDP), tended to affect the position on internal trade as well (e.g., Saskatchewan and British Columbia). Ontario's position is more complicated. While governed from 1990 to 1995 by the NDP and opposed to NAFTA, Ontario recognized that its traditional regional interests lay in a stronger economic union. Indeed, as the negotiations proceeded, Ontario Minister of Economic Development Frances Lankin came to take an increasingly dominate role in favour of a strong AIT. This contrasts with the position of British Columbia, where its regional position of chronic internal trade deficits reinforced its partisan skepticism. The BC government could not be convinced that there was any benefit for it.[6]

Another important aspect of the governments' positions is notable mainly in its absence. Constitutional jurisdiction and normative views of federalism played much less a role in these negotiations than has been the case in intergovernmental negotiations on the constitution, discussed in chapter 5. Indeed, much of the relative success of the AIT negotiations may be due to the fact that such normative positions were often left aside. For example, Alberta, one of the most aggressive provinces in terms of provincial rights over the past thirty years, was the most prominent advocate of a strong, comprehensive agreement. In this position, it sided most often with the federal government over the scope and depth of the proposed agreement. Other provinces did lead a rearguard defence of provincial autonomy, but they justified their positions, at least in interviews with this author, not so much in terms of normative views of federalism as in the need to continue to protect especially vulnerable regional economies or sectors or to protect the role of governments in social policy.[7]

In all of this, the federal role was the most complex. Federal government advocacy was important in securing the initial commitment to the negotiations, with a key role played by Conservative Minister of Industry, Science, and Technology Michael Wilson in the early stages from March 1992 to June 1993. This federal role embraced two aspects: (1) to push for a maximum degree of liberalization to match its own microeconomic agenda for the country; and (2) to be a neutral facilitator to resolve differences among the provinces. Yet to its credit, the federal government did not return in general to the position it took in the early 1980s, that the agreement should bind the provinces more fully than the federal government. Federally created barriers to trade would be covered as fully as provincially created ones. There remained a lingering suspicion among some provinces, British Columbia especially, that the federal government was bent on a centralist agenda.[8] In any case, the provinces were not about to leave federal neutrality to chance. Throughout the negotiations, Alberta, in particular, sought to ensure that the federal role in the agreement would be as one party among the others, with no special role to enforce the agreement and no special privileges in its implementation and administration.[9] This more neutral federal role was reinforced by the federal government itself in the stance taken in the prenegotiation period by its chief official Robert Knox and later by the appointment of Arthur Mauro from the private sector as an independent chair.[10] This characteristic of the federal government as an equal party and not a dominant senior partner in intergovernmental arrangements, while not always present in the Canadian style of collaborative relations, appears to have been key to achieving results in the economic policy field. It is especially distinguishing in comparison with Australia.

Otherwise, the federal role was conflicted internally between hawks in favour of a strong agreement (e.g., Ministry of Industry John Manley and other right-of-centre cabinet members) and the doves concerned with the sensitivities of federal-provincial relations (notably ministers from Quebec and officials in the Privy Council Office). Some provinces such as Ontario also detected in the federal position a protective and strategic concern for the smaller and weaker provinces (the four Atlantic provinces, Manitoba, and Saskatchewan), particularly in its acquiescence on exemptions for regional development.[11] As noted below, the doves had the ascendancy as the end-game approached.

In summary, based on the author's interviews with negotiation participants, four categories of player positions stood out.[12] The first category was one of true believers, those willing to go the furthest in terms of scope, depth, and legal bite of internal liberalization. In this camp were Alberta, Manitoba, and, for the most part, the federal government. The second category was one of skeptics, parties who would come to the table reluctantly and sign off at the end of the day mainly out of concern for national unity. This camp included British Columbia and Saskatchewan. In a third category was Ontario on its own. Its clear objective interests were for maximum liberalization, but for ideological concerns, it resisted giving the agreement any institutional strength. Finally, the fourth and largest category was one of pragmatists, those that sought carefully managed reciprocal arrangements as much as general liberalization. While always inside the tent, they were looking for a special deal. This group included Quebec, the four Atlantic provinces, and the two territorial governments of Northwest Territories and Yukon. It is true that Quebec, led by the federalist Liberal Party for the duration of the negotiations, had the most pressing political need to reach an agreement in a doomed electoral effort to demonstrate that federalism works. And Quebec officials note that this constraint meant that Quebec could not refuse a deal overall. However, the perception of other provinces was that Quebec worked both sides of the liberalization/protectionist fence with great skill.[13]

In any case, these categorizations, while not airtight, demonstrate the markedly different approaches and objectives going into the negotiations. They help to explain the often confusing and compromised results. Compared with the Australian governments' negotiations (see the next chapter), the Canadians' positions demonstrate a wider range of regional views and a less dominant and more internally conflicted federal government. In turn, these conditions contributed to an agreement that has less internal consistency and less centralization than outcomes in Australia. In the latter case, the states' views are less diverse, and their main differences were with the federal government, which had a more consistent internal position and a stronger bargaining position.

Key Negotiation Issues

A few key issues at the negotiating table illustrate how the positions of these competing camps played themselves out. Here, I focus on: (1) the overall architecture of the agreement; (2) the extent of the exceptions; and (3) the institutional apparatus, including the dispute resolution mechanism.

Two basic options were posed for the overall architecture of the agreement. The initial position proposed by some federal officials, and strongly supported by Ontario, was for a brief text setting out general principles for reciprocal liberalization of internal trade together with a mechanism for resolving disputes. In their view of this option, Ontario and British Columbia reflected an ideological concern that the agreement should not be too sweeping in its proscription of government intervention and should concentrate on reciprocal concessions in a minimal package. The other option, strongly favoured by Alberta and Manitoba as well as by many in the federal government, was for an international-style agreement of chapters, based on a relationship between general rules and more specific sectoral rules. It was an architecture that appealed to the experience of the trade policy wonks in both orders of government but which would have made the intergovernmental generalists nervous.[14]

In any case, there was a consensus that the agreement be as comprehensive as possible in its coverage of the economy; all parties recognized that a sector-by-sector negotiation would take too long and had not worked in the past. The first ministers, in particular, made it known that they wanted to see results across twelve specific sectors. The preference for a comprehensive negotiation seemed to have settled the matter of the agreement being comprised of several chapters. Ironically, the multiple chapter architecture provided more scope for fine-tuned deal making and thus, appealed to the more pragmatic participants such as Quebec. As noted already, the specific rules would trump the general rules in the final AIT. Thus, the advocates of a minimalist agreement feel some vindication in that their approach may have been less open to protectionist manipulation. However, the advocates of the big-style agreement remain convinced that, over time, the rules-based approach will produce liberalization that is both deeper and broader than a minimal, reciprocity-based agreement would have allowed.[15]

A second issue that illustrates basic differences is the extent of exceptions in the AIT. It is likely that even a minimalist agreement would have had its exceptions and areas of non-application. This is suggested by the fact that the liberal core of the AIT, chapter four on general rules, still includes as one of six rules the allowance for measures inconsistent with liberalization if their purpose is a "legitimate objective" as defined by the agreement. This device, borrowed from GATT, makes it clear that the agreement is not to apply to seven specifically listed categories of public policy. These are: public security and safety; public order; protection of human, animal, or plant life or health; protection of the environment; consumer protection; protection of health, safety, and well-being of workers; and affirmative action programs for disadvantaged groups.[16] However, as Canadian political scientists Bruce Doern and Mark MacDonald explain, the AIT provisions turn international trade practice "on its head" by allowing the legitimate objectives as excuses to avoid non-discrimination, whereas in GATT, such measures are allowed only if there is "national treatment."[17] There is much room to manoeuvre between "non-discrimination" and "national treatment." In any case, the legitimate objectives are prevented from becoming truck-size loopholes by the provision that such measures must not "impair unduly" economic mobility, must not be more trade restrictive than necessary, and must not be a disguised restriction on trade.

The inclusion of the "legitimate objective" provision does not come as a surprise given the background of previous negotiations on economic union reform. Something like it appeared in the various drafts of amendments to the constitutional Common Market clause, section 121, during the Canada Round. And in the AIT negotiations, it became a bottom line demand for the NDP governments in particular. The "legitimate objective" rule does not appear to be terribly controversial, although one commentator is concerned with the "elastic" quality of the definition.[18] However, it is one of the more clear and comprehensive acknowledgements in the AIT of the concerns of social interests with the scope and intent of free trade.

More controversial were the proposals to exempt from the AIT certain types of measures or economic activity. Such derogations constituted in many cases "deal breakers" for the various negotiating parties.

Moreover, decisions on what to include or not in the AIT were made by consensus and under the operating principle that "nothing is agreed until everything is agreed." These operating rules provided individual governments with an incentive to hold out for concessions. For example, Newfoundland insisted on retaining its ban on the export of unprocessed fish (a wrinkle it had also obtained in the FTA). New Brunswick insisted on the general exception, within limits, for regional development. Quebec insisted on the cultural industries exception. Ontario, Saskatchewan, and BC insisted on the limited application of the procurement chapter in health, social services, and education as well as to Crown corporations. Several provinces insisted that substantial liberalization in agriculture be left to another round. The list goes on.[19]

Against such positioning, governments that tended not to have protectionist bottom lines, such as Alberta and Canada, railed as best they could. By most accounts, this listing of exceptions threatened to overwhelm the agreement in the last weeks of the negotiation. The federal minister, John Manley, objected very strongly to the broad scope of the regional development and cultural industries exemptions. In so doing, he forced the issue to the first ministers level, but without much success. Those in favour of the liberal goals of the AIT remained hopeful that the cumulative effect of the derogations would not damage the agreement unduly. These considerations weighed heavily in the end-game process, discussed below.

A third example of negotiating issues is the institutional apparatus of the AIT. In this case, the positions simplified into two camps. In the first camp, the federal government and Alberta pushed hard for an AIT with a strong, independent institutional component. This would include a ministerial council fashioned along the GATT Council lines, with a strong supervisory role over the dispute resolution process and the agreement as a whole. They also proposed an independent secretariat with the capacity to undertake a research and policy role as well as to assist the ministerial council in administering and implementing the agreement. Their preferred dispute settlement mechanism would be binding on the parties in its final decisions, provide full access for private parties, and allow the awarding of costs and damages to private parties if they won. All of the other governments, to a greater or lesser degree, were in favour of a more minimal package of institutional supports. They were distrustful (especially Ontario and Quebec) of the idea of a strong, independent secretariat. They were not willing to give a ministerial council authority over other ministerial councils implicated by the agreement; and they did not want any elements of legal process to intervene in what they saw as the properly political and bureaucratic process of dispute resolution. Moreover, these positions were in keeping with what most parties sought as an intergovernmental political agreement, not some form of binding legal contract. Indeed, Ontario officials saw a legally binding dispute resolution process as simply not appropriate in a federal state.[20] And on an issue that would arise mainly after the AIT was negotiated, governments did not even consider the idea of decision rules for the management of the agreement, other than consensus. According to some participants, the idea of new decision rules would have been a "non-starter" in the context of the failure of the Charlottetown Accord.

This minimalist position on the institutional and dispute resolution provisions prevailed even though the federal government took some aspects of the issue "down to the wire."[21] The motivations of the minimalists were mixed: some resisted what they feared would be federally dominated central institutions; others feared ideologically driven institutions; still others were just not convinced that the status quo required so much change. As one participant put it, the more rules in the agreement, the less likely were the parties to want to hand over their interpretation to tribunals.[22] As a result, the secretariat is small and understaffed; the Committee of Ministers on Internal Trade (CMIT) as the overseeing ministerial council has no decision rules and no mandate to override other ministerial councils; and the dispute resolution system provides only limited private access and does not make its final decisions binding on the parties.

Process of Reaching Agreement

Finally, the actual process of reaching agreement, particularly in the end-game, demonstrates clearly how structural institutional and political factors can shape intergovernmental outcomes.

The first of these structural factors arose with the ultimate deadline of early July 1994 to reach agreement before the Quebec election, which Premier Daniel Johnson wanted to hold in the early autumn. The other first ministers shared this deadline in so much as they wished to be seen as demonstrating substantial agreement on revising the federation before this vote. Yet they may have also read in the polls the strong possibility of defeat of the Liberal government of Quebec after two terms in office, and they may have feared that a new government would derail the negotiations. Still, the Quebec election did provide the leverage of a firm deadline for the successful final negotiations.[23]

It is tempting to conclude that the election deadline gave the Quebec government more power at the negotiating table; after all, an agreement that seemed against Quebec's interests would be counterproductive for federalists. And, indeed, the AIT text did reflect strong sensitivity to Quebec concerns. It exempted cultural industries, and it did not deal with energy (where the main bone of contention was over "wheeling rights" for electricity transmission, a subject of a long-standing and bitter dispute between Quebec and Newfoundland)[24] nor with agriculture supply management, another extremely sensitive political issue in Quebec. Participants from other provinces saw Quebec negotiators as extracting many other small concessions to avoid political embarrassment at home.[25]

Yet Quebec officials did not share this view of their role. They saw the electoral deadline as putting them under pressure to get a deal at all costs. A more measured perspective may be that Quebec was a constructive if tough negotiator, strongly in favour of the basic objectives of the AIT but sensitive in certain areas.[26] One cannot deny, however, that the impending Quebec election, the rising support for sovereignty, and the pressure to demonstrate progress toward renewed federalism all contributed to a heightened awareness of the Quebec position. This would be especially so for the federal cabinet in that it did not back up its minister of industry in a tougher negotiating stance.

Whatever the judgment on Quebec's role, the deadline did compress the time available to sort out difficult issues that could not be resolved between the chief negotiators and other separate negotiating tables such as agriculture and energy. This raises a second important structural factor in the final stage of the negotiations. As noted, the governments sought a comprehensive agreement covering as much of the economy as possible. However, this objective begs the question as to whether the negotiators had whole-of-government coordination for their efforts. Such coordination is essential for multi-faceted, comprehensive negotiations. One recent analysis stresses the fact that the AIT negotiations were a rare case of "macro multi-field policy negotiations" in Canadian intergovernmental relations.[27] The negotiations leading to the Charlottetown Accord dealt with a wide range of ministerial portfolios; and in the late 1970s, governments dealt with a similarly broad scope of economic sectors. But never had Canadian governments attempted such an ambitious, single agreement requiring the detailed input of ministerial councils.

Success in this endeavour depends on central agency control of, and direction to, the negotiators (or a similar mandate awarded to a line agency), on cabinet consensus on priorities, and on the willingness of the first minister to exercise political clout. In only two of the negotiating parties – Alberta and Quebec – were the minister responsible and chief negotiator based in a central intergovernmental agency. Elsewhere, the industry ministry took the lead role, while central agencies participated in the team or kept a watching brief. This pattern rendered whole-of-government coordination more difficult. Only if the chief negotiator had superior access to the cabinet and the first ministers could such internal differences be overcome.

All of the specific rule chapters had to be signed off by the ministerial council responsible, in some cases the CMIT, but in other cases, the ministerial councils for labour, agriculture, energy, environment, and so on. If there were disagreements between these groups and the CMIT or the chief negotiators, they would have been resolved ultimately by the first ministers. In recent Canadian constitutional negotiations such as the Meech Lake and Charlottetown Accords, the first ministers were personally involved for weeks at a time. However, in the AIT negotiations, the first ministers did not spend much time at all (perhaps because of the very failure of the recent constitutional negotiations). The political turmoil of leadership contests and elections would have made extensive first ministers meetings difficult to arrange in any case. The outcome is that the AIT negotiations suffered from a weak degree of whole-of-government coordination. All but the most sensitive political issues were left to the chief negotiators and the several ministerial councils.

A final significant constraint, already noted, was the convention of intergovernmental relations that demanded unanimity based on consensus. This convention would have been felt even more strongly in the context of a "show of national unity" to Quebec. Indeed, this factor is said to have tipped the balance in favour of signing the AIT in British Columbia's case, where Glen Clark, the minister in charge of the negotiations (and later premier), had advised against it.[28] The requirement

to have everyone on side merely gave every player the potential of holding out for some concession or other.

These constraints of weak coordination and the lack of effective decision rules are illustrated by the role of the federal minister and chief
hawk for a strong AIT. According to press reports, John Manley fought
a rearguard "damage control" during the last phase of the negotiations
as one derogation after another was added to the draft agreement. At
one point, he threatened to impose a text on the provinces by federal
legislation, exercising the federal trade and commerce power. Such a
move would have destroyed the negotiation process, and with that in
mind, cooler heads prevailed in Ottawa. As Giles Gherson wrote in the
Globe and Mail, Manley's legal threat came too late: "imagine a less
opportune moment [than the pending Quebec election] for Ottawa to
poison the atmosphere with a war over trade ... The odds favour accept-
ing a half-baked deal."[29] Once the negotiations had reached the point
of no return, Manley realized too late that the architectural choice for
a rules-based and multi-chapter agreement had become a framework
on which to hang protectionist exceptions. At this stage, Manley might
have been better advised to keep his reservations to himself since his
objections made the subsequent selling of the AIT more difficult.
Instead, he communicated his disappointment to the policy community and the media, many of whom were scathing in their initial assessment of the agreement.

In summary, the end-game of the AIT negotiations reflected the conflict between policy positions of a minimalist versus maximalist type of
agreement, less versus more institutional support, and a comprehensive
and principled versus a managed approach to liberalization. The origin
of these positions lay in part in different regional and jurisdictional
interests but also in the diverse perspectives and experiences of three
policy communities that came together in these negotiations (i.e., the
regional development and industry policy community; the trade policy
community; and the intergovernmental relations community).[30] This
diversity of views posed a significant challenge to the negotiators, but on
top of that was laid the additional constraints just described regarding
Quebec's role in the federation, the difficulty of sustaining whole-of-
government coordination, and the unreformed decision rules of
Canadian intergovernmental relations. Some prominent players, such
as federal Minister of Industry John Manley, tried to break free of such
constraints. But as discussed more fully in the concluding chapter of

this thesis, such efforts are doomed to fail if process reform is not made an integral part of the overall reform from the very beginning.

This point will also become clearer after the next two chapters on the Australian reforms, which included an attempt to improve the way that intergovernmental business was conducted. The Australian first ministers were able to exert stronger whole-of-government and inter-governmental coordination through their new forum of the Council of Australian Governments (COAG). In the process, they streamlined the role and input of ministerial councils and in some cases, improved their ability to make co-decisions. Thus, the Australian governments now have the potential to move more quickly on economic reform because they have adopted new rules for intergovernmental relations.

ASSESSMENT OF OUTCOMES

The AIT may be assessed in parts as well as its whole. My analysis examines four significant features of economic union reform as well as a summary assessment. The four features are:

1 Agreement Architecture
2 Negative Integration
3 Positive Integration
4 Institutions

Agreement Architecture

As noted, the AIT conforms, at least superficially, to the international trade agreement model. Governments adopted the model due to its familiarity, its popularity, and its relevance for the more decentralized negotiating mode envisaged. Having failed at constitutional reform, Canadian governments were willing to try a rules-based instrument but shied away from an agreement that would be based primarily in a new corpus of law. Not for them the European Community model of centrally drafted directives adjudicated by a central court.

Of course, the AIT is a domestic agreement, not an international one. The parties are not sovereign states. Discussed in chapter 4, there already exists a national economy and a whole apparatus of federal economic integration for which the AIT functions to plug gaps and to provide rules for future use. Thus, specific comparisons with international agreements must be made cautiously. As noted above, the internal design of the AIT rules reverses the pattern in international agreements by making the specific rules trump the general ones rather than vice versa. The critics have made other comparisons with the texts of the FTA and NAFTA that are not entirely valid in an internal trade context. And yet throughout the agreement, the influence of international institutions is ubiquitous since the text borrows from GATT texts, the FTA, NAFTA, and even the Treaty of Rome.

As legal scholar (now Justice) Katherine Swinton notes, the AIT is written in legal language but is not designed to be litigated.[31] In her view, this outcome reflects Canadian opinion that judges are not well suited to making economic decisions. There also prevails in Canada a "Charter phobia" whereby governments are reluctant, as seen in the Canada Round discussions, to entrust the courts with a new set of policy levers. Thus, despite the extensiveness of the AIT, it remains, in essence, a non-binding intergovernmental political agreement within the conventions of Canadian federalism. There has been no agreed approach to entrench the agreement in statute law. Unlike Australia, no attempt has been made to introduce uniform legislation let alone legislation of any kind in every jurisdiction. Four provincial legislatures – Alberta, Quebec, Nova Scotia, and Newfoundland – followed the federal parliament in passing legislation to implement the AIT in their jurisdictions. But nowhere have the legislatures and courts been given a specific role in enforcing the AIT, and, as Swinton would argue, legally enforceable intergovernmental agreements are not generally in the Canadian tradition.

In Swinton's view, the negotiators could have drafted the AIT with more specific statutory language but deliberately chose otherwise.[32] Legal scholar Robert Howse argues that the existing federal implementing legislation could be considerably strengthened.[33] In my view, however, new federal legislation would very likely be challenged unless it had the agreement of all the provinces, which seems unlikely. As discussed earlier in this book, the Supreme Court of Canada is prepared to expand the interpretation of the federal trade and commerce power if the circumstances permit. However, the federal government has seen fit, since the mid-1980s, to avoid jurisdictional disputes over trade and commerce, preferring to manage these issues through intergovernmental means.

If the AIT is a hybrid between an international type of trade agreement and a Canadian type of intergovernmental agreement, some commentators have been damning on that very point. Armand de Mestral claims that the AIT is a confusion of paradigms, neither GATT nor federalism, and since it is not grounded in any constitutional or statute law, its obligations are meaningless in his view.[34] Other commentators have similarly dwelt on the limitations of a "voluntary" agreement.[35] One need not partake fully of these views to acknowledge that the Canadian negotiators have struck on an odd mix: to establish a detailed set of legally drafted rules over 230 pages and yet treat the result as a non-justiciable political agreement. This contrasts with the Australian approach to intergovernmental reform as discussed in the next chapter, where there is no attempt at a comprehensive agreement, but most of the individual agreements are implemented by statute.

Negative Integration

The AIT goes a very long distance to closing the remaining gaps in the economic union in terms of specific trade prohibitions. Thus, its contribution to negative integration is significant. As outlined in table 6.2, the AIT covers, at least to some degree, nine of the twelve major types of remaining barriers in the Canadian economic union identified in the early 1980s (recall table 4.1). Of those that require negative integration, this includes the partial elimination of discriminatory procurement practices, the elimination of almost all discriminatory pricing and distribution of alcoholic beverages, the prohibition of a broad range of investment restrictions and discriminatory subsidies, the prohibition of residency and related requirements for professional services and occupational licensing, and guaranteed access to telecommunication networks. More important than these specific cases is the enshrining in chapter 4 of the "classic" expressions of negative integration applying to all goods, services, persons, and capital. These embody in domestic language the national treatment and most-favoured nation principles of international law.

The biggest gaps in terms of economically significant barriers are the failure to deal with the quantitative restrictions of agricultural supply management and the failure to agree on a text for a chapter on energy, particularly to deal with barriers to hydroelectricity transmission. By 1994, Canada had only begun to tackle its agricultural quotas under the new rules of the WTO, and most governments were content to let that process carry the burden for a few years yet. As of

Table 6.2 AIT and Canadian Internal Trade Barriers

NATURE OF EXISTING BARRIER	AIT (1995) PROVISIONS
GOODS	
• Quantitative restrictions in agriculture (supply management).	• Article 903 commits ministers of agriculture to a review on further liberalization consistent with international trade obligations (no progress yet).
• Discriminatory procurement practices.	• Chapter 5 removes most barriers for direct government procurement, to be extended within a year to the MASH sectors and to listed Crown corporations (GBES). (This deadline missed but essentially completed by early 1998.) • New national electronic tendering system and harmonized bid protest system.
• Discriminatory pricing and distribution of alcoholic beverages.	• Chapter 10 removes most barriers but grandfathers some wine protection to be phased out by 1998, consistent with the Canada-EC agreement.
• GBES (Crown corporations) restrictions on competition.	• Chapter 5 commits governments to not intervene in procurement policies of Crown corporations. • Chapter 6 maintains ability to establish monopolies, but consistent with chapter rules including reciprocal non-discrimination, prohibition on residency requirements, performance requirements, etc.
• Discriminatory pricing of oil and gas; restrictions on trade in electricity.	• Not covered. (Energy chapter missing, not yet signed.)
• Industrial and agricultural subsidies.	• Chapter 6 Code on Incentives disciplines certain types of subsidies, but chapter 18 allows generally available regional development subsidies. Chapter 6 does not cover agricultural subsidies.
SERVICES	
• Service markets not integrated.	• Chapter 4 General Rules applies to all services unless otherwise provided. These rules include reciprocal non-discrimination, right of entry and exit, no obstacles, reconciliation of standards, and transparency. • Specific rules for communication (chapter 13) and transportation (chapter 14) providing access to and use of telecommunication and transportation networks and public services, but exempts public transportation. Chapter 18 exempts cultural industries, energy services, and financial services.

Table 6.2 AIT and Canadian Internal Trade Barriers *(Continued)*

NATURE OF EXISTING BARRIER	AIT (1995) PROVISIONS
• GBEs restrict competition in service sectors.	• Article 1304 specifically prohibits public telecoms from engaging in anti-competitive behaviour. (See also above under GOODS.)
• Discriminatory regulation of professional services.	• Personal mobility covered by the General Rules of Chapter 4.
	• Chapter 7 on Labour Mobility provides for harmonization of occupational standards through mutual recognition (not fully implemented).
	• Chapter 6 prohibits residency as a requirement for investment or the establishment of business.
CAPITAL	
• Investment restrictions.	• Chapter 6 prohibits most forms of direct restrictions, including local presence and residency requirements, performance requirements, and discriminatory incentives to business.
	• Code on Incentives provides disciplines on use of financial and other incentives.
	• Provides for reconciliation of corporate registration and reporting.
LABOUR	
• Occupational standards and licensing.	• Chapter 7 provides for a process of mutual recognition (in progress).
• Labour relations standards.	• Not covered. Differences in labour standards and codes (i.e., industrial relations) specifically exempted from Chapter 7.

AIT	Agreement on Internal Trade
EC	European Community
GBEs	Government Business Enterprises
MASH	Municipalities, Academic, Social, and Health Services

early 2001, there has been no sign of the broader liberalization of interprovincial trade in agriculture. The failure to tackle this most egregious set of internal barriers has left some participants cynical about the process (e.g., officials in British Columbia). The main political consideration continues to be to avoid exposing Canadian farmers to interprovincial competition until they are forced to compete internationally. In this calculus, the economic costs to consumers seem to have been discounted.

There is more hope for agreement on the hydroelectric issue. A chapter on energy has been drafted and would liberalize the market for interprovincial electricity transmission and distribution.[36] However, the parties have still not formally agreed to include the new chapter. And in this case, too, international considerations have been driving the results. Since 1992, the US Federal Energy Regulatory Commission (FERC) has been liberalizing the US electricity market. It has demanded that Canadian utilities seeking direct access to their market (i.e., no longer required to sell to a bordering utility) must provide reciprocal access. Thus, in order to pursue a lucrative export strategy in the US, the provincial governments that own and control electricity utilities are now willing to contemplate granting to their Canadian competitors the rights to sell power through another jurisdiction (called "wheeling rights") denied them for decades.

Finally, much of the commentary of the negative integration aspects of the AIT dwells, understandably, on the derogations from these rules. But it cannot be doubted that the great bulk of the Canadian economy now and especially in the future would be covered by the general rules, not the specific derogations. The latter are, in the phrase of one Quebec official, "local ripples on the main pond."[37] The concern of the provincial negotiators to protect specific policies and sectors, particularly under the guise of regional development, led to an unnecessarily complicated and obfuscated agreement. A simpler approach would have been to adopt a WTO-type text disciplining subsidies in a blanket way, focusing not on the purposes of regional development, but on removing trade-distorting instruments.[38] Just the same, one must place the regional development exception in its proper context. As political analyst Donald Lenihan notes: "The desire to preserve a place for regional development ... reflects more than parochialism: it also reflects a recognition by some parties that, while harmonization is generally a good thing, too much of it will undermine diversity – which is fundamental to Canadian federalism."[39]

Positive Integration

The AIT provides also for a good deal of positive integration. It establishes a series of processes for the governments to harmonize both regulations and standards, although it leaves the task to the same intergovernmental forums that drafted the specific rules during the negotiations. Thus, while article 405 of chapter 4 refers to the general objective of reconciliation by "harmonization, mutual recognition, or other means," the devil is in the details of the various chapters on labour mobility, consumer protection, agricultural and food technical standards, telecom regulations, transport standards, and environmental protection. The pace and substance of positive integration in these fields will be determined, unless pushed specifically by first ministers, by the separate ministerial councils.

Regulatory reconciliation in the AIT borrows heavily from concepts used in the European Union. As legal analyst Alex Easson has demonstrated, the AIT envisages two levels of reconciliation: (1) harmonization or mutual recognition of standards and standards-related measures; and (2) co-operation on regulations. However, the use of the instruments is tentative, often confused and, in his view, deeply flawed by the fact that the intergovernmental decision bodies will operate without decision rules other than consensus (compared with the qualified majority voting that enabled much of the EU reconciliation to take place).[40] Also, the use of mutual recognition is voluntary. Unlike the EU in which mutual recognition of standards becomes the default if negotiations fail, in the AIT, the default position is the status quo. On both of these points (mutual recognition as default and majority decision rules), the Australian agreements would conform to the more effective EU model, while the Canadian model in the AIT is a weaker version. In the Canadian case, this means that completion of specific work plans for reconciliation and harmonization can and has dragged on for years.

In sum, to achieve negative agreement through the AIT, one needs only a set of rules and an effective dispute resolution process. However, positive integration depends on a sustained process of intergovernmental negotiation and political will to put in place new regulatory regimes. As discussed more fully in the last part of this chapter, that sustaining will has not always been available since the AIT has come into force. As a blueprint for reform by harmonization, the AIT provides an ambitious agenda, covering such key areas as occupational standards and environmental and consumer protection. If the parties had adopted the European procedural reforms of mandatory mutual recognition and majority decision making, progress on this agenda would have matched the AIT's potential.

Institutions

Related to the effectiveness of the instruments for positive integration are the institutions meant to promote them. The basic nature of the AIT institutions has already been noted. The agreement establishes a minimalist secretariat and the rather weak overseeing role of a ministerial council, the CMIT. It also adopts a GATT-style dispute resolution mechanism, with the more privileged position granted to governments rather than to private parties and with panels to review disputes and to make non-binding recommendations. These institutional features arise, as noted above, from the conflicted interests and positions of the parties (i.e., that only a minority of the governments wanted strong independent institutional apparatus). They also arise from the consensus developed from the very beginning (indeed, during the previous constitutional negotiations) that disputes over internal trade matters should be settled primarily by governments and not by courts.

These realities have not stopped several academic commentators as well as business organizations from attacking the weak institutional structure and proposing improvements. Typical of one end of the spectrum of views are those of legal scholar Robert Howse who makes clear his preference for stronger federal jurisdiction over the economic union either through constitutional amendment or through aggressive federal litigation of the provinces in the courts. He distrusts the institutions of executive federalism, including the many opportunities provided in the AIT for governments to come to a quiet resolution of internal trade disputes behind closed doors. Howse would have preferred to increase the transparency and citizen access to the dispute resolution procedures wherever possible. In addition, he makes the intriguing assessment that at the end of the day, a private party could still take a government to court if it failed to implement the recommendations of a dispute resolution panel. The latter would provide important and compelling evidence in "a parallel constitutional claim that the offending measure is outside the jurisdiction of the province, either as an interference in interprovincial trade or because it has an impact beyond the province's boundary."[41]

Other analysts have been more supportive of the dispute mechanisms in the AIT. A federal official involved in the drafting notes that the negotiators sought to maximize the opportunities for alternative dispute resolution rather than use the courts. The negotiators wished to discourage private sector harassment of governments through too easy access to the process.[42] Still, constitutional analyst Patrick Monahan sees the potential for such harassment as unfounded. He, too, supports the strong emphasis on government-to-government consultations, but Monahan sees executive federalism in a more positive light than Howse does. "Governments will be more likely to agree to dismantle trade barriers voluntarily if they are permitted to explore possible compromise solutions in an informal setting away from the media spotlight."[43] Finally, Doern and MacDonald point out that the dispute settlement provisions include not only the chapter 17 general process, but also, as detailed in other chapters, several sector-specific processes that must be undertaken first. This "matrix" structure of dispute resolution lengthens the process considerably.[44] In any case, the AIT may evolve, as did the GATT, into a political-legal hybrid. While the GATT dispute mechanisms had been designed in 1947 to facilitate the quiet diplomacy of governments to pursue essentially political solutions to disputes, over the years, the role of the GATT panel has been to create a clear line of international trade law more or less binding on future cases.

Summary Assessment

As stated above, the AIT is a glass half-empty or half-full, depending on one's perspective. For some, the measure of achievement is a measure of expectations. For example, critics who expect little of nation building from intergovernmental decision making would look for reasons to justify their pessimism in the AIT.[45] The compromised nature of the agreement, with its many derogations, invites such criticism, but a more pragmatic assessment would stress the governments' relative success after such a long period of failed attempts.[46] Indeed, many participants in the negotiations, perhaps being defensive about the results, stress that the important achievement is not the details of the AIT so much as its symbolic value. The AIT denotes a sea change from the competitive interventionism of the past. It institutes a rules-based regime to replace the de facto rules of strong provinces preying on the weak. And it provides a forum for continued consultation and negotiation. In making such assessments, government negotiators also stress the gap between the rhetoric of the flawed economic union and the reality of the problems. They would argue that those most disappointed in the

AIT exaggerate the extent of the problem in the first place. This observation is even more valid given the continuing analytical controversy about the real extent of the costs of alleged barriers and the competing values to be balanced, such as national efficiency and citizenship versus provincial diversity and autonomy.

In addition to the above assessments, I return to the more prosaic examination of the alleged barriers themselves. Recalling table 4.1 on the pre-reform state of the economic union, I examined the chief remaining barriers in Canada and Australia. Of the twelve key barriers in Canada, most have been reduced in some way but not removed entirely by one or all of the three international trade agreements to which Canada has become a party in the past decade (see table 5.1). The AIT makes further progress on nine of these barriers and promises future liberalization in two more (see table 6.2). Yet in almost all cases, the "barriers" are not expressed in numerical values that, like tariffs, can be reduced and eliminated by a simple formula. They are typically a set of laws, policies, and administrative practices that are more amenable to incremental reform or require a long process of reconciliation and harmonization. Thus, even to note that a barrier has been "reduced" or "eliminated" requires some exercise of judgment, if not bias. Nonetheless, from my reading of the evidence, I conclude that the AIT builds upon the trend of recent international liberalization to substantially reduce or eliminate most of the long-standing barriers to internal trade in Canada. This achievement is in addition to its broad, if more modest, success in establishing an institutional framework for the better functioning of the economic union in the future.

Finally, one may assess the AIT in the context of the longer-run efforts in Canada to reform the economic union. The AIT could not have been achieved in the late 1970s when the advocacy for reform began. Economic union reform was too implicated in the broader struggle for dominance in the federal system, a struggle that reached an impasse of sorts only in the aftermath of the Canada Round of constitutional negotiations. This is not to imply that constitutional issues are far from the surface, but one key to the success of the AIT has been the facilitating and non-aggressive role of the federal government seeking a partnership with the provincial governments. Jurisdictional issues were kept at a distance. The AIT has not been perceived as a vehicle for centralization, and, indeed, the nature of its architecture and its institutional support exemplify a decentralized approach to economic union reform. This outcome stands in contrast to the more uniform and centralized outcome in Australia (see chapter 8).

The other major change since the 1970s has been the attitudes of all governments toward intervention in the economy. The AIT was negotiated at the peak of public concern and governmental priority over budgetary deficits and mounting federal and provincial debt. The mindset of the negotiators arose from a consensus of liberalization and deregulation, reinforced by the lack of funds to pursue the expensive subsidization of the past. Moreover, the model for trade liberalization posed by the FTA, NAFTA, and the WTO agreement seemed to fit, *mutatis mutandis,* the needs of internal trade liberalization. As discussed in chapter 5, the success of these trade agreements led to public acceptance of similar instruments in the domestic realm.

In sum, the AIT, in my view, is a significant achievement of Canadian federalism, all the more so for having been concluded so soon after the failures of constitutional reform. As a set of reforms of the economic union, the new agreement deals comprehensively, if not always effectively, with the remaining requirements for negative and positive integration. It does so in a way that complements and completes the liberalization and integration of the three international trade agreements dealt with in chapter 5. And it fills the gaps – if through non-binding, political means rather than legal and constitutional instruments – in the original terms of the Canadian economic union.

EPILOGUE: IMPLEMENTATION AND CONTINUED NEGOTIATIONS, 1995–99

The AIT is both an end and a beginning. As discussed above, the unfinished business included the extension of the procurement chapter to the municipal, health, and education sectors and the completion of the listing of covered Crown corporations. It also included the major review of agricultural policies in conjunction with international commitments, the missing energy chapter, and several specific working groups on harmonization or mutual recognition as well as a revised Code on Incentives. The success of this agenda depended upon effective institutional support as well as continuing political will. The disappointing pace of further reform since the actual signing of the AIT indicates that the political will to go the final distance has been waning. It also reinforces the many criticisms that the institutional mechanisms are too weak. To discuss fully the ongoing specifics of the implementation would mire us in detail that can be found elsewhere.[47] Instead, I wish only to make a few salient points about what the post-agreement phase has done to the substance and dynamics of economic union reform in Canada.

The first point to make is that the AIT machinery is in use and that it may simply be taking longer than most had hoped to have beneficial effect. Senior government officials (the "internal trade representatives") meet quarterly, and to the end of 2000, the Committee of Ministers on Internal Trade (CMIT) had met seven times since the AIT was signed. Some participants feel that the ministers do not meet often enough and that the first ministers are not interested, but the lack of progress is not due merely to a lack of meetings. The secretariat is functioning now, although at a minimum level of staff and funding. The dispute settlement mechanisms have been used frequently, with twenty disputes registered in the first nine months and a total of eighty-four in the first five years. Nonetheless, the AIT came under damaging scrutiny in 1995–96 when New Brunswick refused to agree that a dispute with British Columbia should be submitted to the agreement's resolution mechanisms. New Brunswick had provided an employee training incentive to the courier firm UPS to encourage it to expand its operations in that province at the alleged expense of employment in British Columbia. New Brunswick excused its actions by claiming that they were taken after the AIT was signed but before it was to come officially into effect. It also argued that the rules affecting locational incentives in the AIT were vague. British Columbia disagreed, but the other parties to the AIT could not force New Brunswick's hand to send this dispute to the formal channels. Nonetheless, as former federal official Robert Knox notes, the episode has rendered ineffective the Code on Incentives, which is a key part of the investment chapter and an important part of the AIT for British Columbia.[48] The disagreement certainly has done little to increase BC's attachment to the agreement.

On the other hand, the dispute settlement provisions have worked as intended in an important dispute over federal legislation banning a gasoline additive MMT from interprovincial trade. The details are not important here except to note that the dispute involved a federal and not a provincial measure and that important regional and industrial interests as well as health and environmental issues were at stake. The MMT dispute has been the first to go all the way to a panel report. The panel reported in favour of the complainant provinces and against the federal government, and soon after, Ottawa announced that it would repeal the offending legislation. This has set an important precedent about how governments should respond to AIT panel reports.[49]

The more difficult and controversial aspect of the implementation process has been the unfinished negotiations. As noted already, the record on obligations under the AIT has been a long list of missed deadlines. This issue began to come to a head in late 1997, two years after the AIT came into effect, when it was obvious that much foot-dragging was taking place. After some strong lobbying from business groups, the provincial premiers issued at their annual meeting an uncharacteristically detailed communiqué about the need to get on with the agenda, particularly on the MASH (municipalities, academic, school, and health sectors) negotiations, the energy chapter, a revised code of conduct on incentives, and agriculture. Meanwhile, the federal minister, John Manley, as co-chair of the CMIT, refused to hold meetings until specific good news could be announced and began the same sort of legal sabre-rattling that had accompanied the final push in the 1994 negotiations.

In February 1998, the provincial governments were finally able to announce agreement on the extension of the procurement chapter to the MASH sectors. But they did so by allowing British Columbia to opt out. BC did not veto the amendment as such but would not be a party to it, so the extended national market for procurement in the MASH sectors would not include BC. The province extracted a price for its lack of veto by insisting that the extension would not apply to health and education services (cf. goods). To what extent this development will become a precedent for asymmetrical application in years to come is unclear. BC is marginalized in the Canadian economic union by geography and its predominant trade orientation to the Asia-Pacific region. Thus, BC's opt-out, while serious, does not radically alter the economic benefits of the agreement to Canada as a whole. In this case, there is a strong similarity in the role played by Western Australia in the Australian economic union. The situation would be entirely different if it were Ontario or Quebec objecting to the amendment. Indeed, their lack of participation would mean no amendment at all. Apart from the economic issue, more serious may be the continuing political significance of British Columbia apartness, not sharing fully in the symbolic citizenship of the evolving economic union.

The unfinished negotiations issue has also led to a significant split among the governments about the scope and pace of "renegotiations."

The split is largely along the same lines as in the original negotiations between the hawks and the pragmatists. The hawks (the federal government, Alberta, and possibly Manitoba) are anxious to improve on the AIT as soon as possible. This could be done by continued refinement of existing provisions or by a second round of formal negotiations to remove some derogations, strengthen the institutions, and to broaden and deepen the liberalization. In this sense, one Alberta official cites the common analogy used about the GATT/WTO rounds: trade policy is like riding a bicycle where forward momentum must be sustained or else you lose your balance.[50] In this stance for continued negotiation, they have the strong support of the Canadian Chamber of Commerce, in particular, to improve private access to the dispute mechanisms and to make the panel report recommendation findings binding on the parties.[51]

On the other hand, the doves are united in their opposition to a second round any time soon. The smaller provincial governments are finding it hard enough to implement the complex AIT and to staff the several working groups already under way; they tend to resent the clamour for more negotiations as attempts to reopen the overall agreement. Larger provinces such as BC and Ontario continue to be highly skeptical of the AIT in any case, Ontario, in particular, seeing more merit in dealing bilaterally with Quebec and others outside the AIT framework.[52] Finally, a certain reform fatigue has taken hold in Canada (as it has in Australia – see chapters 7 and 8) based on the costs of economic adjustment. This contributes to a low sense of urgency on the AIT. In any case, once the initial agreement was signed, the issue fell off rapidly as a political and bureaucratic priority in most governments.

In summary, there may now be some question as to whether the political and policy commitment to the 1995 AIT is sufficiently strong for its full implementation, let alone a second round of negotiations. If the implementation continues to drag on, pressure will mount on the federal government to intervene legally. During the June 1997 general election campaign in which the Liberal Party won a second majority government, the Conservative, Reform, and Liberal parties all spoke about getting tougher with the provinces. In the intervening three plus years up to the most recent federal election of November 2000, which returned the Liberals for a third majority, the government has not taken a tough stance, at least publicly. How a tough line would be put into practice is not clear. It might involve federal intervention in private litigation against a specific provincial measure to test again the limits of the Common Market clause in the constitution (section 121, *Constitution Act, 1867*) or of the federal trade and commerce power (section 92, *Constitution Act, 1867*). (The latter is proposed by the Canadian Alliance Party, currently the official opposition in the federal parliament.)

Yet playing the legal card is risky. In such games, typically the winner takes all. If intended to back up the AIT, such a tactic might destroy the good will needed to make it work. Moreover, the extension of federal jurisdiction that might occur from such litigation would help with negative integration but is unlikely to make much headway in positive integration. As Australia's constitutional and intergovernmental history attests, the presence of much stronger constitutional guarantees of internal free trade does not rule out the need for continued efforts at positive integration. Finally, in Canada, for reasons of national unity, the federal government may be no more prepared now to take aggressive unilateral action against the provinces than it was in 1994.

Thus, one may be tempted to conclude with political scientists Janine Brodie and Malinda Smith that the "[Chrétien second term] federal government does not appear to have either the jurisdictional power or the political consensus necessary to enforce trade liberalization domestically."[53] In their view, the Chrétien government has already abandoned the AIT. In my view, this assessment is overdrawn. The federal government may not have the will to take the provinces to court on its own, but if there is private litigation in the future spawned by disputes under the AIT, it may have no choice but to intervene to protect its jurisdiction. And despite Manley's frustrations, there is no evidence that Ottawa has abandoned the undramatic, plodding work of implementation.

One potential means for rekindling the interest in the AIT and further economic union reform is the Social Union Framework Agreement (SUFA), signed by the federal government, all the provinces (except Quebec), and two territorial governments in February 1999.[54] The six-page agreement deals, as the title indicates, with a set of framework principles and other undertakings. Part 2 of SUFA refers to "mobility within Canada" and ties freedom of movement of Canadians to the social union principles. It commits governments to eliminate within three years "any residency-based policies or practices which constrain access to post-secondary education, training, health and social services, or social assistance." The SUFA also commits governments to ensure full compliance by 1 July 2001 with the mobility provisions (chapter 7) of the AIT.

Potentially, these SUFA undertakings demonstrate increased political support, firmly rooted in Canadian public opinion, for negative and positive integration of economic mobility. The twining of the economic and social union agendas could shore up both regimes. However, in practice, SUFA remains a loose political agreement requiring extensive sectoral intergovernmental negotiations to take effect, in particular, in the sensitive health care field. Such negotiations are proceeding slowly, if at all. In the meantime, the consequences of Quebec's absence from the SUFA are yet to be realized, although one notes that its objections to the text were not based on the mobility provisions but on the use of the federal spending power (part 5).[55] In sum, it is too early to tell how the SUFA will impact on the AIT implementation.

In any case, as discussed above, by focusing on the empty parts of the glass, the critics have ignored the full parts. Even if the pace is slow, the fact is that the AIT is being implemented. The attention is understandably on the highly visible unfinished business and exceptions in the agreement and not on the long-standing barriers that have been removed. Like an iceberg, much more lies beneath the surface – in the historic commitment to a rules-based regime, the uncontroversial coverage of so much of the economy, and the departure by all governments from decades of trade distorting behaviour and expectations.

No doubt the flaws in the original AIT, particularly its slow and compromising decision-making processes, have become magnified by the controversy surrounding its implementation. These flaws illustrate the limitations of the intergovernmental route to reform in Canada. As shown in this chapter, the conventions of Canadian intergovernmental relations have not been for binding, legally enforceable agreements nor for effective decision-making institutions such as would result from entrenched decision rules. The Canadian governments did not attempt to reform the process of intergovernmental relations while negotiating the AIT, nor did the federal government have the political strength to enforce such reform. This is understandable given the context of the recent failure at constitutional reform. Indeed, for over thirty years, the trauma of constitutional dissent and failure has prevented Canadian governments from upgrading their more prosaic intergovernmental machinery. In Australia, where mega-political constitutional stakes have not been in play, reform has been more sensibly able to include the process of intergovernmental relations as such, as detailed in the next two chapters. More definitive comparisons between the reform processes and outcomes in the two federal systems will be drawn in the final chapter.

7 Microeconomic and Intergovernmental Reform in Australia, 1990–99

Australian governments achieved a significant reform of their economic union in the 1990s. The reform encompasses many separate initiatives but with a consistent theme to broaden and deepen competition in the national economy. The agenda for change included the process of intergovernmental relations: financial relations among governments, their respective roles and responsibilities, and their ability to reach common decisions. As with chapters 5 and 6, the next two chapters present and analyse the empirical evidence as found in key documents, interviews with policy-makers and other observers, and academic and media commentary. Due to the complexity of the reforms but also to the distinctness of chronological episodes in the reform process, I begin this chapter with an overview of the reform process and its outcomes. I then proceed to analyse the reform process, leaving an assessment of the reform outcomes to chapter 8.

Overview of Events

The reforms produced by the Australian governments are numerous and complex and can be fully understood only in their detail.[1] Here, I begin with a bare narrative, leaving further details to the second part of the chapter. My narrative follows periods of federal leadership since the pace and substance of reform changed so dramatically with each succeeding prime minister. (In this section, a summary of each specific area of reform is provided following the main headings. Readers familiar with this detail can skip it without missing the analytical focus).

Prior to the concentrated reform efforts of 1990–95, Australians considered their constitutional options with respect to the economic union and fiscal federalism. Two major processes produced detailed recommendations for constitutional amendment. The Australian Constitutional Convention – consisting of appointed delegates of the federal, state, and territorial parliaments as well as local government representatives – met on and off between 1973 and 1985. However, it did not succeed in creating sufficient consensus or political momentum to move forward amendments dealing with economic union. The Constitutional Commission, a federally appointed body of experts meeting from 1985 to 1988, dealt exhaustively with economic union issues. Its final report recommended several important constitutional amendments, which, if approved by referendum, would have constituted a major strengthening of the economic union, albeit through a significant centralization of power. However, the commission had little political clout of its own, and there was little indication that the recommended changes had widespread support in the federal government, let alone among the states or the public at large. These two episodes of constitutional consideration did serve to broaden the debate on economic union issues. They also served to make governments and other interests realize that it would be better to proceed to reform through intergovernmental means.

Hawke Initiative (July 1990–November 1991)

The intergovernmental reform process started with the prime minister's speech on 19 July 1990 to the National Press Club, "Towards a Closer Partnership." Robert Hawke promised to hold a Special Premiers Conference (SPC), and, following some months of communication and negotiation with the states, he convened the conference on 30–1 October 1990. The opening words of the communiqué from this meeting convey the breadth of the reform objectives: "Leaders and representatives acknowledged that past inefficiencies can no longer be tolerated and that changes are needed to make the Australian economy more competitive and flexible. An internal part of any micro economic reform strategy is a more effective public sector. Leaders and representatives therefore declared their intention to use this unique opportunity to maximize co-operation, ensure a mutual understanding of roles with a view to avoidance of duplication, and achieve significant progress towards increasing Australia's competitiveness."[2]

Another SPC followed on 30 July 1991, with Hawke in the chair. Each of these two meetings covered an agenda of over a dozen substantive items, and the discussions ranged over two days. A senior steering committee of officials met more frequently between SPCs. Ministerial councils and working groups of officials were mandated to consider issues and report back to the SPC. This process continued to the end of 1991. The SPC scheduled for November 1991 became a states-and-territories-only meeting when Hawke, then in the midst of a party leadership challenge from Paul Keating, withdrew his participation. The November meeting communiqué nonetheless indicated a substantial degree of interstate consensus. The meeting helped to keep the reform process going at the state level during the political transition in Canberra.

Eight major initiatives were put in place in this important initial phase:[3]

1 *Rail reform:* Agreement to establish a National Rail Corporation, with states as shareholders, to provide interstate rail freight operations on a national network. Formalized in Commonwealth legislation *(NRC Act,* 1992).
2 *Road transport:* Establishment of the National Road Transportation Commission, authorized to provide advice on uniform road charges and regulations and vehicle licensing regimes (initially for heavy vehicles only), formalized in a co-operative legislative regime (e.g., Commonwealth's *NRTC Amendment Act,* 1992).
3 *Electricity:* National Grid Management Council established with a mandate to develop a competitive market for electricity, with first attention to southern and eastern Australia.
4 *Performance monitoring of government business enterprises (GBEs):* Under the chair of the Industry Commission head, governments set up a steering committee on performance monitoring measures.
5 *Food standards:* Agreement to establish a National Food Authority (later extended to New Zealand), formalized in Commonwealth legislation *(NFA Act,* 1991).
6 *Disabilities services:* Agreement to transfer to the states full responsibility over accommodation- and employment-related services for the disabled, with the Commonwealth paying all additional costs. State

legislation passed complementary to a new *Commonwealth Disabilities Services Act,* 1991.

7 *Fiscal federalism:* Two working groups established to examine taxing powers and tied grants. The groups produced reports endorsed by the states but not the Commonwealth.

8 *Intergovernmental process:* Governments agreed to follow improved procedures for Financial Premiers Conferences, and to deal with non-financial matters in the series of Special Premiers Conferences.

In sum, the actual agenda was broader and reform potentially more comprehensive than at any subsequent stage, encompassing microeconomic reform and a significant review of fiscal federalism. The governments also launched what they called a review of program "roles and responsibilities" intended to reduce duplication and overlap, mainly in social programs. And the agenda included improved process for intergovernmental relations. The momentum for reform was strong. A large trade-off for microeconomic reform in return for fiscal and program responsibility reform seemed plausible.

First Keating Government (December 1991–March 1993)

On 11 May 1992, Prime Minister Keating convened a first ministers meeting on reform, called a Heads of Government (HOG) meeting, apparently to distinguish it from the Special Premiers Conferences chaired by his predecessor. In that meeting, the governments agreed to create a formal Council of Australian Governments (COAG) to include: the Commonwealth prime minister, the six state premiers, the chief ministers of the Northern Territory and the Australian Capital Territory, and the president of the Australian Local Government Association. The first meeting of COAG as such took place on 7 December 1992. The HOG and COAG meetings continued with a large agenda, but crucially, they did not include significant discussion of fiscal reform, certainly not to deal with the vertical fiscal imbalance. As before, the first ministers were the tip of the iceberg of an extensive set of ministerial and senior officials meetings.

Four major reforms were initiated:

1 *Mutual recognition:* Agreement on the mutual recognition of the regulation of trade in goods and of occupations, formalized by

legislation in all jurisdictions in 1993–94 except in Western Australia, which did not enact legislation until 1995.

2 *Non-bank financial institutions:* Agreement reached on a co-operative legislative regime among the states only, establishing uniform regulation of building societies and credit unions, overseen by the National Financial Institutions Commission. An interstate agreement to cover uniform credit laws was reached in 1993.

3 *Environment:* Intergovernmental Agreement on the Environment (IGAE) was reached in 1993, which mandates co-operation in nine appended schedules covering: data collection, resource and land use assessment and approval processes, impact assessment, national environmental protection, climate change, biodiversity, national estate, world heritage, and nature conservation.

4 *Intergovernmental process:* The establishment of COAG, as noted, and the rationalization of ministerial councils.

In sum, the main task of the governments in this phase was to complete reforms initiated under Hawke's leadership. However, fiscal relations reform was taken off the table, ultimately reducing the scope of the reform of program responsibilities.

Second Keating Government (March 1993–March 1996)

Prime Minister Keating continued to chair four more COAG meetings before the March 1996 election in which his government was defeated. These meetings were held on 8–9 June 1993, 25 February 1994, 19 August 1994, and 11 April 1995. The list of agenda items continued to grow, with the June 1993 meeting notably dominated by the native title issue in the aftermath of the High Court decision in the *Mabo* case, which was an issue extraneous to the reform agenda. The Commonwealth government also added to the agenda the issue of potential constitutional reform, notably the issue of a republican head of state.

Another important development in this period was the establishment on 19 July 1994 of a separate Leaders Forum of state premiers and territorial chief ministers – to meet once or twice a year, without their Commonwealth counterpart. The Leaders Forum met in November 1994 and again in November 1995. The forums were designed to discuss broader federal-state and national issues, including the progress of the COAG reform agenda. The leaders also dealt with a variety of issues in state jurisdiction alone.

Six major reforms were either completed or launched in this period:

1 *Competition policy:* Governments agreed in February 1994 to a set of principles to govern a new National Competition Policy (NCP). The major elements of the policy, finalized by April 1995 and passed by a uniform legislative scheme later that year, included the following:

   i. A substantial increase in the scope of the Commonwealth's *Trade Practices Act* (TPA) to include types of business formerly under state jurisdiction.

   ii. A Conduct Code Agreement by which the states agree to apply the TPA in their jurisdiction to cover the prevention of anti-competitive practices by state GBEs and unincorporated businesses. The agreement also provides for consultation with the states over appointments to the new Commonwealth regulatory agency, the Australian Competition and Consumer Commission (ACCC).

   iii. A Competition Principles Agreement to govern the policies of the Commonwealth and the state governments in an effort to promote further economic competition. It covers five aspects: (1) a consistent approach to the reform of price oversight mechanisms; (2) an agreed approach to applying the principle of "competitive neutrality" to government practice with respect to GBES as compared with private firms; (3) an agreed approach to the structural reform of public monopolies; (4) a review of all Commonwealth and state legislation to remove anti-competitive provisions; and (5) a new national access regime for monopoly infrastructure and service providers, to take precedence over state regimes if they do not perform. The agreement also specifies the states' role in the creation and procedures of a new policy agency to implement broad competition policy, the National Competition Council (NCC).

   iv. An Agreement on National Competition Policy and Related Reforms, the final political linchpin of the policy. It provides a schedule of payments to the states in order to compensate them for revenue losses due to private competition with their GBEs. Attached to the payments are conditions that the states must keep to a schedule of reform, including not only the specific provisions in the NCP, but also previous COAG commitments covering electricity, gas, water, and road transport. The payments are estimated to total $AUS 2.4

billion over eight years. The agreement also commits the Commonwealth to maintain a real per capita guarantee of financial assistance grants on a rolling three-year basis.

2 *Gas reform:* Agreement in 1994 on a framework for gas industry reform for "free and fair trade," to begin implementation in 1996.

3 *Water reform:* Agreement in 1994 on a Water Resource Policy to introduce pricing and other reforms to water utilities and resource management processes.

4 *Environment:* Establishment of a National Environment Protection Council in 1994 under Commonwealth legislation, providing for co-decision on specified environmental matters, including mandatory standards.

5 *Borrowing:* Agreement on a revised Financial Agreement covering the external borrowing of the states and the role of the Australian Loan Council (ALC). The agreement confirmed an evolving process of deregulation and greater transparency, leaving the ALC with a much-reduced role in economic policy coordination.

6 *Intergovernmental process:* Agreement on principles and guidelines for national standard-setting and regulatory action by ministerial councils and other intergovernmental bodies.

Howard Era (March 1996–)

To the end of 2000, Prime Minister John Howard, leader of the Liberal-National coalition government, had chaired four COAG meetings. The meeting held on 14 June 1996 came back to back with the Annual Premiers Conference on financial matters – a practice that had been avoided by Howard's predecessors. The inevitable spillover of short-term financial issues onto the longer-term agenda was the result. Another COAG meeting scheduled for November 1996 was cancelled, apparently due to an election campaign in Western Australia. The Howard government let another year pass before convening its second COAG meeting in November 1997, and more time passed again before the April 1999 meeting covering tax reform. The latest meeting was held in November 2000. The prime minister has also met informally with the premiers, for example, to discuss native title issues as a result of a December 1996 High Court decision in the *Wik* case.

The election of the new federal government in 1996 also created initial uncertainty about the scope of the continuing agenda for reform.

Overall, there has been a decline in the number and intensity of meetings with the states. In the meantime, however, the Leaders Forum continued to meet on 12 April 1996, 27 September 1996, 7 March 1997, and 31 October 1997.

Five major reforms have been achieved thus far under COAG auspices:

1   *Mutual recognition:* Agreement in 1996 to extend the mutual recognition agreement to New Zealand, including New Zealand membership in the decision-making ministerial council.
2   *Gas reform:* Agreement on National Gas Pipeline Access, reached in 1997.
3   *Intergovernmental process:* Agreement in June 1996 to establish a formal Treaty Council consisting of the state premiers (not territories) and the Commonwealth, as well as a standing committee of senior officials. Governments also agreed to a set of principles and procedures for Commonwealth-state consultation on treaties.
4   *Tax reform:* In April 1999, governments agreed to the terms for introducing a federally collected Goods and Services Tax (GST), the proceeds to go to the states on an equalization basis. In return, the states withdrew from nine types of consumption taxes and were no longer to receive Financial Assistance Grants.
5   *Natural resource management:* In November 2000, governments endorsed a wide-ranging national action plan, to be followed soon by an intergovernmental agreement, covering issues such as land salinity and water quality.

Apart from these decisions, there was a large agenda of ongoing discussions and intensive implementation programs in areas such as performance benchmarking of government business enterprises (GBEs), electricity and gas markets, rail networks, and other aspects of the competition agenda. Also, COAG meetings have covered a broad scope of issues unrelated to the microeconomic or intergovernmental reform agenda as such – e.g., aboriginal title and reconciliation, illicit drugs, gambling, and marine safety. As part of the November 1997 COAG, the Treaty Council met and, among other items, endorsed the Commonwealth's negotiating position prior to the Kyoto multilateral conference on climate change. Otherwise, the GST agreement remains the most important initiative in this period. It is a significant development, but coming so late cannot be counted as an integral part of a comprehensive reform approach.

Summary

These 1990s economic union reforms cover enormous ground. They introduce powerful new principles, which will take years to apply fully. And they will result in deeper integration of the Australian economic union, reaching practically every sector of the economy. They do so through an impressive array of intergovernmental instruments, with varying effects on the continuing room for the flexibility of federalism in Australia. The broader public sector reform – notably changes to the roles and responsibilities of governments and the fiscal federalism underpinning those roles – turned out to be much more modest. The decentralization inherent in this latter agenda, important ultimately to counterbalance the more centralizing and uniformity-inducing characteristics of the reformed economic union, remains unfulfilled. In addition, reform of what may be called the "social union" has not been a significant part of the governments' work. Finally, the new intergovernmental mechanisms are significant achievements, even if their current use is sporadic and selective. They will prove to be of lasting value to the evolution of the economic union and to Australian federalism more broadly.

Further assessment of the substance of these reforms can be made after a more detailed discussion of the dynamics of the process, to which we now turn. Already it is clear, however, that the reform agenda was broader than in Canada. Moreover, it achieved its basic objectives in a much shorter time frame. The context and explanation for these differences is explored below.

DYNAMICS OF THE PROCESS

The 1990s reform process is the most comprehensive attempt at public policy change by intergovernmental means and the most complete examination of the federal system since the founding of the federation. To better understand the dynamics, I focus briefly on four aspects:

1 Reform Policy Community and the Converging Agenda
2 Attempted Constitutional Amendment and Unilateral Reforms

3 Intergovernmental Reform Process 1990–96: Changing Positions
4 Intergovernmental Reform Process 1990–96: Negotiation Dynamics[4]

Reform Policy Community and the Converging Agenda

As discussed in chapter 2, the movement for reform arose from economic changes impinging on Australia since the early 1980s. Changes in the international political economy had left Australia facing intensified but diffuse market integration, with the prospects for only low levels of regional institutional integration. Thus, economic adjustment focused on internal microeconomic reform and not primarily on trade liberalization as it did in Canada.

While pursued and implemented by governments as such, a much broader set of interests and actors has been engaged in the microeconomic reform process.[5] Most of what follows in this chapter deals with the intergovernmental policy-making process, but it is useful first to place that process in the larger context of the policy-making network. Australian political scientist Elizabeth Harman identifies five clusters in the competition policy community which, with some adaptation, can be applied more generally. The first and key cluster is the Commonwealth government actors. The most important political actors were the prime minister and treasurer, while the main ideas and much of the strategy for reform came from senior officials in the federal government's central agencies. During the Hawke-Keating Australian Labor Party (ALP) governments, views on reform within government were by no means uniform, and the left factions of the ALP cabinet and caucus posed frequent problems. The latter's concerns were significantly mollified by the Hawke and Keating governments' formal alliance (cemented by their "accords") with the labour union movement, led by the Australian Council of Trade Unions (ACTU).[6] I will discuss the dynamics of the federal government's reform leadership more fully below.

The second key cluster consists of the state and territorial governments. Their commitment and positions on reform reflect their regional interests and, to a lesser degree, partisan positions. The personal relationships of the state leaders were also a factor, as were certain senior officials and the varying capacities of the individual state governments to formulate policy and conduct negotiations. I deal with the detail of these differences below as well.

A third cluster in the policy community consists of organized business and other interests that formed a key and relatively consistent advocacy for reform from outside government with a strong capacity to the keep governments on track. The leading player in the cluster is the Business Council of Australia (BCA), formed in 1983 from two other organizations. It has grown into a formidable lobby, with membership of all the largest firms and supporting a considerable think-tank.[7] For most reform positions, the BCA would have the allied support of the Australian Chamber of Commerce and Industry and the National Farmer's Federation. To these would be added the business media, key academics, and a few think-tanks devoted to economic reform (although the most important semi-independent sources for economic and policy analysis in favour of reform came from the Commonwealth government's think-tanks, the Economic Planning Advisory Council and the Industry Commission.)[8] As the details of specific reform were debated, individual industrial sectors and firms became opposed or wary of reform measures but not enough to shake the overall reform advocacy of the peak national organizations. As discussed more fully below, the zeal for reform in all of these organizations did begin to wane by late 1995.

The fourth cluster of interests consists of consumer groups, welfare and environmental organizations, and other public interest groups and coalitions. It came into the process only once it was well launched but was influential enough to have its views taken into consideration, through both formal and informal consultative means. This cluster did not oppose reform so much as seek to ensure it was balanced in terms of the broader interests. The cluster became engaged with considerable effect in two key sets of reform: the National Competition Policy and the GST.

The fifth and last cluster consists of the ACTU and the individual labour unions, which were distrustful of the general thrust of microeconomic reform and strongly opposed to specific features. The ACTU leadership was, of course, highly integrated with the federal political leadership until the ALP lost power in 1995. This gave the ACTU an important bargaining position with respect to parts of the ALP reform agenda (buttressed by the left factions of the ALP), but this did not extend through the whole of it. For example, as Harman notes, the ACTU seemed to have had no effect on the Keating government's desire to move ahead on competition policy.[9] Individual unions had even less influence on the reform agenda.

From this characterization of clusters, it should be clear that the reform agenda began with the engagement of the first and third cluster (i.e., mainly the federal government and business), spreading later to the states and to public interest/social advocacy groups, and lastly, and mainly in opposition, to organized labour. The Hawke government proceeded first with reforms that opened the national economy to international competition, notably the floating exchange rate and tariff reduction. In turn, this led to broader domestic adjustment to ensure that industry remained competitive. Thus, the focus shifted beyond the specific adjustment of manufacturing and resource sectors to public and private sector inputs that influenced the competitive position of industry. This focus led the Commonwealth to specific reforms in its own jurisdiction, such as the deregulation of airlines and telecommunication, education and training, and industrial relations, among others. At the same time, the Commonwealth government and its in-house think-tanks began to concentrate on the large part of the reform agenda in the hands of the state governments.[10] This part of the reform agenda included: further industrial relations deregulation; extension of trade practices (competition) law to all parts of the economy; pro-competitive regulation of state-based utilities and infrastructure (electricity, gas, water, public transport, ports and shipping, rail and road transport); and a broad-based reduction or harmonization of regulation of trade among the states, including trade in goods and services and professions.

As if this agenda implicating the states was not large enough, the push for microeconomic reform was extended to the public sector at large. Government business enterprises (GBEs) became obvious candidates for reform, as implicated in their anti-competitive practices. But the entire role and form of government came under attack. This meant greater fiscal discipline, pressure for balanced budgets, debt reduction, and tax reform. It also entailed making government operations more efficient, in tune with pro-competitive practices in the private sector. Reformers also targeted federal-state fiscal relations to reduce vertical fiscal imbalance and its perceived inefficiencies and as an incentive for other single market reforms.

This broader agenda (often termed pejoratively as "economic rationalism" or "managerialism") had the support of the strong business community and agriculture. Together with the federal government's quasi-independent think-tanks, they pushed forward a sophisticated reform program.[11] However, the social interest groups, while supportive of broad microeconomic reform, opposed much of its public sector counterpart, especially in relation to program and service cutbacks, the reduction of community service obligations for GBEs, and the erosion of entitlements to the poor and other disadvantaged groups. The agenda would place ALP governments, especially at the state level, in difficult positions and provoked the opposition of public sector unions.

In any case, collectively, these interest clusters set the stage for a wide-ranging economic reform agenda encompassing both the private and public sectors. By 1990, the Hawke government had initiated or completed most of the reforms possible within its own jurisdiction, so the remaining reform agenda was in state hands or could be achieved comprehensively only by a joint effort. Such a broad agenda implicating both orders of government need not be completely coordinated, and in any case, coordination can be tight or loose (compare table 3.1). In the absence of coordination, however, governments would proceed on their own schedules of reform, which in the case of economic union may make progress difficult if not impossible.

Recall that chapter 4 discussed the basic options open to both Canada and Australia in reforming their economic unions. These were: (1) the unilateral exercise of federal and state authority; (2) constitutional reform; and (3) intergovernmental agreement. Just as in Canada, Australians debated how best to proceed, with many in the federal government, in particular, doubting the efficacy of intergovernmental cooperation in view of the past record. Thus, it is important, before examining the specific dynamics of the reform option ultimately adopted with considerable success (number 3 above), to understand more clearly why the other two options failed (numbers 1 and 2 above).

Attempted Constitutional and Unilateral Reforms

Chronologically, Australians dealt first with the second of these options, constitutional reform, in two phases in the late 1970s and 1980s. In each phase, there was both a specific process for debate on constitutional issues as well as proposals put before the Australian people in referendums (held in 1977, 1984, and 1988). The constitutional debate, while dealing with significant economic union and fiscal federalism concerns, also ranged much more broadly, covering parliament and elections, the role of the Governor General, a bill of rights, external affairs, the judiciary, the distribution of federal and state powers, and intergovernmental relations,[12] among other issues. Thus, somewhat like Canada, economic union considerations in Australia had to compete with other constitutional priorities. Moreover, Australia's constitutional reform efforts seldom took on the significance and salience of parallel episodes in Canada such as the patriation round and the Meech Lake and Charlottetown Accord processes, discussed in chapter 5.

The difficulties of constitutional reform process in Australia are beyond the scope of this study, but suffice it to note a few points of context. Constitutional reform advocacy in the 1970s and 1980s emerged from two somewhat contradictory motives.[13] The first is the long-standing advocacy to "modernize" the Australian constitution, led largely but not exclusively by Labor Party federal governments and the progressive legal community, focused on furthering central regulatory power, reforming central institutions, and entrenching individual rights. The second force for change have been the state governments, which sought constitutional reform chiefly to improve fiscal federalism. The two strands of reform are not entirely incompatible, and some commentators thought a grand compromise possible.[14] However, they tended to be championed in the political arena by competing sides of the partisan divide.

This was so especially after 1983 with the Commonwealth Labor government under Hawke and, to a lesser extent, the Labor governments of the states on the one hand and the Liberal-National opposition and non-Labor state governments on the other. In this contest, constitutional processes and proposals tended to become captive to shorter-term political expediency.[15] This expediency is seen most clearly in the disjuncture between the slow-moving constitutional deliberations of conventions and commissions compared with the shorter-term partisan considerations in referendum planning, coinciding with national elections. None of the referendum proposals of 1977, 1984, or 1988 dealt with the core issues of economic or fiscal reform, but the outcomes of these efforts, particularly the massive defeat of the 1988 proposals, dulled the appetite for advocacy of constitutional amendment. However, the constitutional discussion did raise important issues about reform, as shown in the detail of the two main processes.

First were the deliberations of the Australian Constitutional Convention (ACC) from 1973 to 1985. An initiative at first of the states but joined by the Commonwealth (which also insisted on the strong representation of local government), the ACC was a forum of appointed delegates: sixteen from the Commonwealth parliament, seventy-two from the state parliaments, four from the territorial assemblies, and twenty representatives of local government. It met in six plenary sessions over the twelve years of its life and spawned a large number of committee and subcommittee reports. Among the issues germane to this study, it tackled fiscal issues such as tax powers and fiscal transfers; economic union issues such as the scope of the federal powers over trade and commerce, corporations, industrial relations, and external affairs; the Common Market provision, section 92; and intergovernmental issues such as the interchange of powers.[16]

The ACC process made many recommendations, but of the issues noted above, none proceeded to referendum with the exception of a proposal on the interchange of powers in 1984. The ACC itself seemed to reach consensus in 1984 on the need to correct vertical fiscal imbalance. For example, it sought a loosening of the conditions of specific purpose grants (a reform that did not require constitutional amendment). But it also recognized that other needed reforms, such as a redefined Common Market clause, section 92, would be too controversial to pass. It seems that toward its end, the convention bogged down in partisan and federal-state disputes. Indeed, the Commonwealth government acted specifically in 1985 to wind up the ACC, launching its own process through an appointed commission of experts as a strategy to move constitutional debate away from state concerns.[17]

The second attempt at comprehensive constitutional review, the Constitutional Commission of 1985–88, took on the issues of economic union and federal economic management more directly but ultimately, with no greater success in terms of constitutional amendment. One of five advisory committees established, the Advisory Committee on Trade and National Economic Management, held hearings and undertook detailed analysis of the issues. Its report and the final report of the Constitutional Commission remain the most important statements of the advocacy for centralization of positive integration and the improvement of negative integration in the Australian economic union, through constitutional means.[18] The advisory committee had proposed sweeping change, recommending a new head of federal power, which they would call "matters affecting the national economy." The commission found that prescription too broad but made several recommendations of its own, which included:

1 to amend section 51(I), the federal trade and commerce power, by deleting its restriction to international and interstate trade alone
2 to amend section 51(xx), the federal corporations power, to include incorporation as such and the regulation of financial markets and services
3 to amend section 51(xxxv) to cover the entire field of industrial relations
4 to amend the provisions dealing with the interstate commission to enable the courts to mandate inquiries into trade and commerce matters

The commission decided against amending the crucial parts of section 92 because of the new interpretation given the section by the High Court in *Cole v. Whitfield* (see the discussion in chapter 4). The latter decision, unanimous by the court and following an extensive review of all the preceding judgments on section 92, came down just before the commission completed its own final report. In the commission's view, the new judgment "largely conforms" with its own view of how the section should be interpreted, obviating the need for amending its key provisions.[19] And in the whole area of fiscal relations, the commission acknowledged a "feeble desire" for reform, confining its specific recommendations for constitutional amendment to the important change to section 90 on excise tax, proposing that it become a concurrent power.

These recommendations, if accepted by the Commonwealth and if approved by the required national and state majorities in a referendum, would have eliminated the need for much else by way of economic union reform. The result would have been an enormous centralization of power as well. However, the commission itself had little political salience and could not on its own convince the Commonwealth parliament to proceed. Indeed, the Hawke government apparently did not even bother to respond in detail to the commission's final report. Instead, it decided to proceed to referendum on four issues, none of which dealt with economic union.[20] The four referendum questions dealt with parliamentary terms, fair elections, the role of local government, and certain rights and freedoms. All four were soundly defeated in 1988.

In addition to the Hawke government's rejection of its brainchild, the commission's report received no open political endorsement elsewhere. The coalition parties at the federal level had opposed the process from the beginning, as had the states that were not consulted on its appointments and distrusted its motives. Still, the commission's widespread consultative process enabled various interests to raise concerns about the fragmented economic union, calling for a more integrated and uniform approach to business regulation, road transport, financial services, restrictive trade practices, consumer protection, company formation, and industrial relations.[21] This contributed to a growing chorus of calls for reform.

In sum, the option of constitutional amendment as a means to reform the economic union suffered several flaws. The constitutional debaters saw economic union as only one of a large number of constitutional issues, while the Commonwealth government did not think of it as a political priority when choosing which proposals to put before the people in a referendum. The latter process has been, historically, an onerous one in itself. A referendum must win both an overall national majority and in a majority of the states. This has seldom occurred. And as political scientist Brian Galligan points out, Australian voters have never agreed to constitutional amendments perceived as centralizing Commonwealth power or jeopardizing the position of the states.[22] The constitutional reformers themselves also recognized that for much of the economic reform agenda – such as fiscal issues, the Common Market clause, and industrial relations – the better strategy would be to agree on flexible non-constitutional measures. Alternatively, they could leave the task to the High Court, as was done in the case of section 92. Others noted that in an age of interdependence, any attempt to clarify governmental roles and responsibilities by constitutional amendment would be both impossible and undesirable.[23]

Thus, Australian governments were reduced to the two remaining options: unilateral reform and intergovernmental agreement. The federal government was clearly tempted to proceed unilaterally. Indeed, in areas such as industrial relations, no serious attempt at co-operation was ever made as the Commonwealth preferred to proceed on its own – discussed more fully in chapter 8. However, a unilateral approach to reform depends nonetheless on political determination and support as well as a strong legal brief. For both political and legal reasons, the Commonwealth decided to proceed with a co-operative, intergovernmental process. A unilateral route to reform through Commonwealth legislation would have been challenged in the courts where, the trend of recent cases notwithstanding (see discussion in chapter 4), it is unlikely that the Commonwealth would have won. In fact, within the scope of one reform area, such an outcome had already occurred in the fate of proposed federal legislation on companies regulation, struck down by the High Court in the *Incorporation* case, 1990.

Just as importantly, the states embraced rather than opposed the Commonwealth's general analysis and goals for microeconomic reform. Senior state policy-makers shared the sense of economic crisis that placed economic competitiveness at the top of the national agenda. They felt the same international competitive pressure for change and were the recipients of direct and specific advocacy from business organizations, particularly the Business Council of Australia.[24] And they were already undertaking significant reform within their own jurisdictions. States such as New South Wales (NSW) led the way in industrial relations reform, and Victoria soon followed with fiscal and expenditure reform and the privatization of utilities. Indeed, as Australian political scientist Martin Painter notes, among the states, "the pressure to outdo one another in microeconomic reform intensified in the national and international political and economic climate of the 1990s."[25]

The multiple and varying agendas for reform at the Commonwealth and state levels produced (then and now) a laboratory of experimentation, emulation, and competition. Indeed, as some have pointed out, federalism itself is a reform vehicle by providing such a competitive and diverse policy environment.[26] However, there arose a broad consensus that in some areas of reform, a coordinated approach was essential. For new rules of competitive behaviour, in particular, only a wide-ranging forum including all governments and covering all areas of economic intervention would produce the desired results. It would be especially important to avoid the special pleading that would inevitably occur in a piecemeal, sectoral process.[27] Commonwealth jurisdictional sabre-rattling might have been effective to help set the stages for such a broad-based negotiation, but unilateral federal measures could not on their own deliver the needed reforms. The states did not need to be convinced to sing the notes of reform. What they needed was some way to ensure that their tunes would be in harmony. The time had come for a concerted effort at intergovernmental collaboration.

Finally, the states had other reasons to be drawn into comprehensive reform discussions with the Commonwealth. The states felt increasingly squeezed fiscally. Without relief on the fiscal front, particularly to ease the vertical fiscal imbalance, they could not be expected to undertake costly reform in their own backyards.[28] Moreover, reform of federal-state roles and responsibilities provided the important link between federalism and microeconomic reform by "establishing the incentives that allocate our nation's resources."[29] Long-standing state concerns with fiscal federalism thus combined with managerialist concern about overlap and duplication and the blurred accountability and effectiveness of tied grant programs. From the states' perspective (and that of many independent observers if not the Commonwealth), the proposed reforms implied a basic trade-off. The Commonwealth would get more uniform regulation and a reduction of the states' intervention in the economy, while the states would get a new dispensation on their expenditure responsibilities and the revenues to fund them.[30] As discussed below, this potential trade-off came undone in late 1991 with Paul Keating's challenge to the Labor leadership, but not before it played a role in launching the reform movement.

One other factor important to the converging reform agenda and its successful launch was the favourable alignment of political forces. This included the personal role and influence of Prime Minister Hawke, a bipartisan intergovernmental commitment to reform, and a powerful set of interests in central government agencies. Hawke won an unexpected fourth term of office in March 1990, steeling his resolve to finish his reforms by bringing in the states. His personal style as a conciliatory leader is also key; he liked to bring people together to collaborate on decisions and to make deals. By 1990, the Commonwealth Labor government faced Labor governments in all the states but New South Wales, where Premier Nick Greiner was an unusually strong reform supporter. Thus, from the beginning and in a tone set from the top, all the governments adopted a collaborative, consensual approach. In this environment, a "central agency club" dominated by a few key senior officials also played a vital role in pushing the reform agenda.[31]

Intergovernmental Reform Process, 1990–96:
Changing Positions of the Government Players

Governments have long-standing interests that change only slowly. But intergovernmental negotiations are also conducted by elected leaders and their senior officials and advisors, whose personal and political interests influence their positions. In these intergovernmental negotiations, the long-standing interests of the Commonwealth and its varying expression by the political leadership was a key factor. The power imbalance in the federal system in Australia is such that the states alone cannot force a reform agenda without strong participation and direction from the Commonwealth. Yet within the confines of some consistency of interests and approaches, it is Canberra's position that changed most dramatically over the life of this reform episode, with important consequences for the results.

As noted above, Hawke's personal commitment and initiative was pivotal in the initial launch of the reform process. He recognized the need for a break from the past and, ironically, for what followed, saw a bold intergovernmental initiative as bolstering his leadership rivalry with Paul Keating. To Hawke can be credited the creation of a new venue (the Special Premiers Conferences) and the broadened agenda for reform. On the other hand, Keating assumed Commonwealth leadership in December 1991 partly by attacking Hawke's "new federalism." He condemned Hawke's initiative as a "surrender of powers" and a "dismembering of the national government."[32] Yet Keating also saw himself in the mould of a reformer, if considerably less conciliatory in style than his predecessor and from a more traditionally centrist position. Thus, under his leadership, the Commonwealth dropped any real intent to reform fiscal relations and reinforced a view of roles and responsibilities reform that stressed new quasi-market means to retain and reassert Commonwealth control over social and other programs. Keating's biggest intergovernmental accomplishment came in the economic regulation field, notably the National Competition Policy (the dynamics of that case are reviewed below).

Finally, John Howard's personal antipathy to a comprehensive collaborative approach with the states changed the dynamics of the reform movement once again. He and his government were elected in 1996 in part on a wave of public fatigue with reform and took a narrower view of microeconomic issues.[33] Moreover, Howard took a less bureaucratic and more personal approach to relations with the states. For example, one of his early achievements at co-operative action, tough gun law reform, took place totally outside the COAG framework.[34] The coalition government proceeded with many other reforms of its own but – with the key exception of tax reform – on a more piecemeal and less collaborative basis. The reform process as a tightly coordinated, comprehensive set of negotiations essentially ended with the Howard election. And as discussed below, by that time, the reform movement was losing steam in any case.

In sum, the direct political leadership of the federal government played a vital role in initiating and sustaining the Australian intergovernmental reforms. The full nature of how and why Commonwealth leadership changed over the period in review cannot be told fully here (and indeed is still being played out to some extent). Still, the underlying context includes the perceived benefits and costs of a more collaborative approach to government – a topic addressed in the final chapter comparing Australia's reform record and process with Canada's.

In comparison with the Commonwealth, changing political leadership at the state level mattered less. From July 1990 to April 1995, most state governments did change hands, and by the end of Keating's period in office, he faced more Liberal premiers than Labor. However, none of the elections significantly derailed the reform agenda once the commitment to proceed had been established. The election of Richard Court's Liberal government in Western Australia (WA) in 1993 brought a sometimes reluctant player to the table. WA would take an outlyer position on mutual recognition and the environment and delayed progress on rail reform. But it took a leadership role for the states in its position in favour of competition reform.[35] On the other hand, the 1992 election of Jeff Kennett as premier of Victoria delivered a more consistent champion of reform. In sum, partisan labels did not seem to have been a determining factor in the states' reform agenda, although they did affect the pace of implementation.

Regional differences among the states were more pronounced, although not as much as in Canada. For the purposes of these negotiations, the states may be divided into three camps. The first camp contained the three relatively prosperous eastern states of Victoria, New South Wales, and Queensland, of which the economic interests are for a more integrated economy and for more fiscal and program autonomy. There are important differences among them, such as Victoria's continued vulnerability to declines in the manufacturing sectors compared with Sydney's unique international service economy. But the states' common interests are apparent, reinforced by their proximity to a Sydney-Melbourne-Canberra axis among policy and business elites.[36] Moreover, decision makers in these three states would be especially open, politically and intellectually, to the sustained reform advocacy of the business-led policy network (the third cluster noted earlier in this chapter).

In a second camp are the two fiscally mendicant states of South Australia and Tasmania; their interests converge in their heightened dependence on Canberra (fiscally, this would include the two territories as well). This dependency reduced their interest in certain forms of fiscal and program reform and would make them more vulnerable to the economic and fiscal costs of microeconomic reform, particularly competition policy. Also, Tasmanian officials noted that smaller states found it more difficult to provide the professional resources to participate fully in the comprehensive negotiations.[37]

Tasmania also belongs in a third camp with Western Australia as geographically separate from the other states and thus having less potential benefit from greater national economic integration. Indeed, the separateness of Western Australia emerged as an especially important division in the negotiation outcomes. Like British Columbia's position in the Canadian economic union, WA can afford to be outside the national consensus, and the economic union can afford to have it missing – to a point.

Overall, however, based on this author's interviews with participants and available accounts of the process, the differences among the states and territories in their negotiating positions was not as significant as their differences as a group with the Commonwealth. Their interests were certainly less diverse than those of the Canadian provinces. Thus, the main conflicts would be between an overall states position and the Commonwealth position, largely on jurisdictional and fiscal terms.

Intergovernmental Reform Process, 1990–96:
Negotiation Dynamics

As suggested in the narrative above, the 1990s intergovernmental reform episode took on three distinct phases: the initial launch, a middle period of sustained reform, and a third period in which the reform movement ran out of steam. There would be little story to tell if the reform process collapsed with Keating's assumption of Commonwealth leadership. As promising as the previous eighteen months of negotiations had been, many initiatives had not truly jelled, and very little would have been accomplished had the process ended there. Keating himself was genuinely committed to reform, but on his own terms. He enraged the states by reneging on Hawke's promise to tackle vertical fiscal imbalance. Still, the states' commitment to deep fiscal reform at this stage has to be questioned. While all states shared similar concerns about the tied grants, only a few – most consistently Victoria and New South Wales – were seeking major tax reform. Nonetheless, all states experienced an increasing sense of fiscal insecurity. Keating knew this and exploited it by calling the states' bluff in his delivery of a revenue guarantee in 1992 and later in 1995 by sealing the agreement on a National Competition Policy with the financial compensation package.[38]

By taking tax reform off the agenda, Keating was responsible for a narrowing of the scope of potential reform of program roles and responsibilities in that realignment in that area was unlikely without a major transfer of fiscal resources. Keating distrusted the "roles and responsibilities" exercise discussed above, reflecting the deep antagonism toward it within the ALP caucus and the big spending Commonwealth departments.[39] Nonetheless, as Martin Painter argues, by taking fiscal issues off the table, the governments actually improved the prospects for overall co-operation on the remaining agenda. "The failure to resolve this issue through the SPC and COAG was the exception that proved the rule: as an issue, it was out of kilter with the co-operative rationale and norms of the new institutions."[40] The Howard government's later success in reaching agreement with the states on a new GST is unrelated to the broader reform agenda. Moreover, the agreement is proof that fiscal reform need not be packaged with other reforms in order to take place.

The question remains – what kept the states in the game once Keating had narrowed the scope of reform? The answer is that microeconomic issues had stand-alone merits for the states. All state leaders were under enormous pressure from the business community to produce reform, and the media had raised high expectations of results. An influential group of senior central agency officials also looked to comprehensive reform as the only means to achieve change in reluctant and powerful line departments and government enterprises. Thus, both politicians and officials recognized that progress in such difficult areas as competition policy required an all-in approach, without which special interests would win the day in any given state.[41] And perhaps some state leaders felt they could eventually leverage the Commonwealth back to their agenda – some obviously counting on an electoral upset in

1993. Finally, once the state and territorial leaders began to share the national stage with the Commonwealth prime minister, they did not want to leave it. They benefited personally and politically from being seen to be acting in the national interest. This was another motivation that Keating understood and exploited.

The proof of sustained reform is in the outcomes as outlined in the next chapter. However, it helps to illustrate the process by commenting on the negotiation of one of the most important outcomes, the National Competition Policy (NCP). Here, the governments stayed the course through three years of acrimonious negotiations – and three separate COAG sessions – to produce an imaginative and complex set of reforms. Interspersed with the federal-state meetings were extensive consultations and, of course, a good deal of political lobbying by the non-governmental actors. The pro-reform lobby of business and agriculture, led by the Business Council of Australia (BCA) and the National Farmers Federation (NFF), succeeded at several crucial junctures to keep the reform momentum going. This included their July 1994 endorsement of reform in a joint statement with the federal government and their strong representations to the state governments in early and late 1994 when their support appeared to wane.[42] It seems certain that the depth and breadth of the NCP reforms are due to a large degree to their continuing pressure. Social interests such as Australian Council of Social Services (ACOSS) and the Australian Federation of Consumers also sought and obtained consultations on the detail of the NCP reforms. They had an influence on the guiding principles of the new regulatory process and how it treats public interest issues and on consumer representation on the main regulatory body, the ACCC.

However, our continuing focus here is on the intergovernmental aspects of the negotiation. One analyst contends that the NCP negotiations were "dominated by Canberra and appeared top-down, centralist, heavily managed and relatively closed" – so that the states had "little room to manoeuvre against the Canberra juggernaut."[43] Yet the states did make significant gains. First, the agreement to pursue a co-operative approach is in itself a significant achievement in that it forecloses the Commonwealth from implementing a unilateral reform program.[44] The states conferred powers on the ACCC through amendable state legislation, not a permanent referral of jurisdiction to the Commonwealth as recommended in the influential Hilmer Report. In addition, the states got a veto over any further changes to the Common Competition

Code embedded in the *Trade Practices Act*. Second, the states achieved agreement on a flexible approach, according to their own agendas, on price oversight mechanisms, competitive neutrality toward GBEs, and the structural reform of monopolies. Third, the states as a whole gained a veto over appointments to the ACCC and NCC (i.e., a majority of states would have to approve) and co-decision on the NCC's work plan. Finally, the states forced the Commonwealth to go out on a limb to bring together the financial compensation package.[45]

For its part, the Commonwealth got the states to agree to a complicated and long-term set of undertakings that constrained considerably their economic and fiscal policy options. The new national policy, while flexible in some areas, retained considerable bite in such aspects as the default national access regime for monopoly service providers. It succeeded in centralizing the administration and enforcement of competition law in the ACCC. And the fiscal compensation agreement, regardless of the flexible state agendas for implementation, provided firm dates for keeping the states' feet to the fire – not just on the terms of the NCP agreements, but on a broader COAG agenda. Thus, there may be truth in the claims of some participants that few state and territorial leaders understood fully the terms of the new policy, let alone its long-term consequences.[46] However, this example (and others) demonstrates the considerable give-and-take of long intergovernmental negotiations.[47] The policy outcomes would have been much different if the Commonwealth had chosen not to pursue reform co-operatively with the states.

Finally, as already noted, the sense of a linked and comprehensive agenda for reform has dissipated since the 1996 federal election. This was due to the personality and political agenda of John Howard, the coalition government's specific experiences with the states since its election, and a more secular sense of the decline of the urgency of reform.

Howard's leadership style has already been covered. One result of his low-key and non-bureaucratic approach to intergovernmental relations is that the Commonwealth has reduced substantially its whole-of-government coordination of reform efforts. This had important implications for reform prospects in programs such as health, discussed in the next chapter.

The new government might have come around eventually to the intergovernmental reform spirit, but its experiences in the first two years proved otherwise. Its first COAG meeting, described in the press as a "debacle," saw Howard and his treasurer, Peter Costello, back down from a proposed reform of wholesale taxes in the face of state opposition. Their plans to transfer responsibility to the states for many housing, health, and education programs also ran aground on the Commonwealth's fiscal position of significant grant cutbacks.[48] Thus, it seems that the initial agenda of the Howard government for some speedy changes soured the mood for more comprehensive reform, for which they had little taste in any case. And, as noted, Howard managed to convene only two full COAG meetings to the end of 1998. As a result, journalist John Short declared COAG to be "dead."[49] This is an exaggeration, but if not dead, COAG was very ill.

Last, the reform movement itself has run out of steam. In terms of microeconomic issues, even the business press has been questioning their commitment to economic rationalism in recent years.[50] Reform fatigue became a real political phenomenon as the rise of Pauline Hanson's One Nation Party attests (see the discussion in the next chapter regarding implementation of the NCP). No reform period is unlimited, and many of the changes introduced by the governments since 1990 have now become routine and bureaucratized. The issue in 1999–2000 was not so much whether comprehensive reform should or can be renewed as whether the governments could stay the course to complete the many commitments already made.

Two initiatives led by the Howard government since 1998 demonstrate that the opportunity and the need for a collaborative approach will continue to arise. First, the Commonwealth's tax reform initiative since August 1998 has been a very substantial reform. Indeed the states' support has been essential for the Commonwealth's selling of the GST. The resulting intergovernmental agreement, including an important role for co-decision by a ministerial council, illustrates a further use of the new machinery. So, too, does the COAG agenda of November 2000, which dealt most notably with a new national action plan (to be followed up with an intergovernmental agreement) on natural resource management, to tackle the serious environmental problems of dryland salinity and associated water quality. On the broader economic reform agenda, however, the governments seem committed at most to the plodding implementation of those reforms upon which they have already agreed. Overall, Australia is not going irreversibly in the direction of collaborative federalism; there is plenty of room left for competition between the federal and state governments and among the states.

Conclusion

Several aspects of the politics of the reform process in Australia may now be summarized. First, by process of elimination, governments chose the option of a comprehensive intergovernmental approach to reform. By the late 1980s, governments had ruled out constitutional amendment. There seemed little prospect for governmental consensus or public approval of the reforms proposed by constitutional experts, particularly after the failure of the modest set of constitutional amendments in the 1988 referendums. The option of unilateral action by the Commonwealth government was not entirely abandoned, but as a general strategy, it entailed too much political and legal risk. Fortunately, the states also supported coordinated reform as better able to withstand entrenched interests inside and outside their governments.

Second, any reform momentum needs some lasting substantive policy rationale beyond short-term electoral considerations. At first, this rationale – particularly for the states – seemed to be the trade-off of state involvement in the federal microeconomic reform agenda in return for fiscal and program reform according to the states agenda. It later became more simplified as microeconomic reform for its own sake. In any case, what drove the pace and depth of reform was an ongoing calculus about whether the incentives for political collaboration outweighed the incentives for competition. And in that calculation, governments' decisions can be fully understood only in relation to their position in a broader policy community, some elements of which – particularly key business and other interest groups – had an important impact on the pace and shape of policy outcomes.

Third, federal political leadership is vital to any reform effort. Overall federal-state reform cannot easily proceed without bipartisan support – implicitly in the federal parliament, explicitly among the state governments. This condition prevailed in the early phase of the reforms but is part of the reason for the faltering reform movement by 1996.

Lastly, reform cannot go on forever; if it does, it ceases to be reform. Any set of dynamic forces eventually becomes routinized, and in this case, is owned more by the bureaucratic process than the political. The marshalling of forces to coordinate reform is not easily sustained, and there is a limit to collaboration unless all other political and bureaucratic systems are to become subservient to it. In this respect, Australian governments have not yet created a "joint decision trap" from which they cannot be freed. The chief policy difficulty with the notion of an end to the reform process is that it comes too soon, before commitments can be fully implemented and tested.

These process conclusions are reflected in the substantive reform outcomes to which I turn in chapter 8. I also return to reform process in the context of a more direct Canada-Australia comparison in the final chapter.

8   Reform Outcomes in Australia

The reform outcomes produced by intergovernmental agreement in Australia are contained in several undertakings and range over a broader set of policy areas than the single comprehensive Agreement on Internal Trade in Canada. Thus, I divide this chapter into three parts to address the following:

1   Reform of Intergovernmental Relations
2   Fiscal and Social Policy Reform
3   Microeconomic and Related Reform

I conclude with an overall assessment of the effects of the reforms on the economic union in Australia.

REFORM OF INTERGOVERNMENTAL RELATIONS

Part of the reform agenda has been to change the very process of intergovernmental relations. Governments came to a collective assessment that these means were not up to the task of producing the substantive reforms they desired. The procedural changes are thus an important and permanent legacy of the 1990s reforms in Australia. The reforms fall into five categories, each of which merits analysis and assessment:

1   First Ministers and Whole-of-Government Coordination
2   Ministerial Councils and Co-Decision Mechanisms
3   Mutual Recognition
4   Uniform Legislation
5   New National Agencies

Genuine reform requires the commitment and hands-on decision making of the heads of government. (Hereafter, I will use the Canadian term first ministers.) Without the strong initial and ongoing commitment of first ministers and their political oversight and control of bureaucratic coordination, reform does not happen. The Australian intergovernmental reform process is notable for the heavy involvement of its first ministers, beginning with the Special Premiers Conference (SPC) in 1990. First ministers needed to meet in a new format in the early stages of reform to break free of the narrow and conflicted agenda of the traditional premiers conferences as well as to assert whole-of-government coordination across a broad agenda.

After 1992, COAG became the pinnacle and management forum for all intergovernmental relations – at least until 1996. It dealt not only with the ongoing reform agenda, but also with other issues gravitating to it, such as native title and the republic. The June 1996 decision to formally establish a Treaty Council as a sort of subset of COAG is also potentially important but may be only window dressing. Also, the Leaders Forum – the states- and territories-only meetings – became what Painter calls an "unintended consequence" of reform.[1] While some observers have wondered if the Leaders Forum still has a purpose, state participants see it as an important means of sustaining reform when the Commonwealth's commitment is flagging.[2]

As shown above, the effectiveness of COAG depends on the political will and leadership of the Commonwealth prime minister. And COAG can accomplish more when it meets frequently. First ministers met fifteen times on the reform agenda during the past seven years (including the Leaders Forum). This is more significant when one considers the numbers of ministerial councils, steering committees, and working groups that the first ministers have spawned (see diagram 8.1 for the overall organization scheme). As a consumption of total government resources, this process may not be all that significant, but at its peak, it has tied up extensive time and attention of senior officials and political leadership.

These first ministers meetings still operate by consensus decision making. Australia has not adopted the European Union's Council of Ministers model whereby the peak intergovernmental body takes votes. COAG has produced very substantive results, as the communiqués from

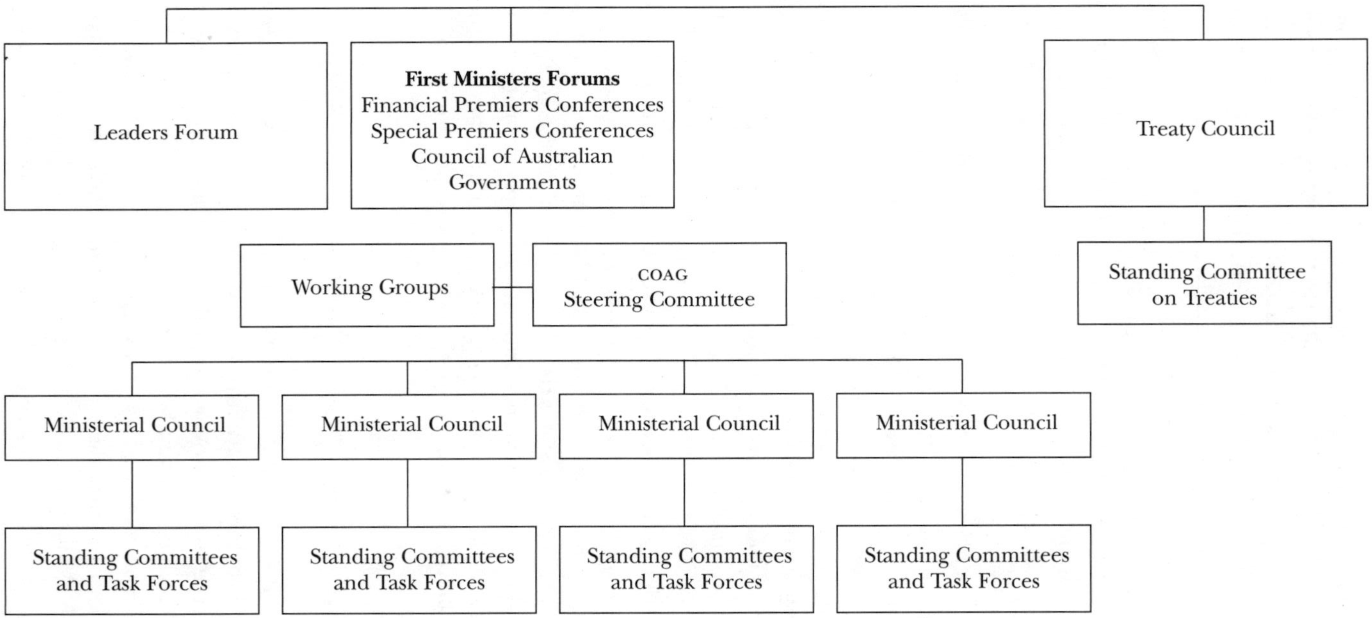

Diagram 8.1 First Ministers and Whole-of-Government Coordination in Australia

the meetings make clear. However, each decision is only a commitment that must be backed up by an Order-in-Council or legislation within the leaders' respective cabinet and parliament. The first ministers did endorse improved mechanisms of co-decision for selected ministerial councils (see below), but for themselves, they retain the conventional consensus/unanimity rules. It seems the commitment to co-decision mechanisms is a device to be adopted selectively.

The frequency and formality of first ministers meetings is a necessary but not sufficient condition for whole-of-government coordination. Only by pursuing a coordinated agenda, tightly controlled and driven from the top, could the numerous vested interests in Commonwealth and state agencies be overcome.[3] For example, health care reform cannot be achieved unless the forum for negotiation is broader than the health ministers and their officials alone. Indeed, specific reforms in health and other areas may have stalled early on as a result of weak central oversight.[4] The lack of coordination became a more general problem after the 1996 election.

Effective coordination required the partnership of first ministers with their central agency officials. States with a poor commitment or lack of capability at the senior central agency level were unable to provide their political leadership with the necessary support to play an influential role. In this case, the leader was left to make judgments about the issues solely on political grounds and more likely to simply go along with what other states do. Yet if the bureaucrats get too far out in front of their leaders' commitment, the reform process risks being stalled at critical moments. Nonetheless, the dominance of the central agencies leaves the process open to charges of overcontrol and bureaucratization.[5]

Ministerial Councils and Co-Decision Mechanisms

Following from the first ministers' commitment to a whole-of-government approach is the attempt by governments to control and streamline the role of intergovernmental ministerial councils (MCS). COAG agreed to reduce the number of MCS from forty-three to twenty-one and approved a protocol and set of principles for their operation. Moreover, in seven cases (see table 8.1), governments have mandated formally a decision-making role for ministerial councils. These decisions range from approving the members of a new national agency to approving

Table 8.1 Institutions for Co-Decision in Australia

MINISTERIAL COUNCILS WITH LEGISLATED DECISION-MAKING MANDATES – INCLUDING VOTING RULES

- Australian Loan Council
- Australia-New Zealand Food Standards Council
- Ministerial Council on Corporations
- Ministerial Council on Financial Institutions
- Ministerial Council on the Australian National Training Authority
- National Environmental Protection Council
- Australian Transport Council
- Ministers authorized to act with respect to the mutual recognition scheme
- Ministers authorized to act with respect to the National Competition Council
- Ministerial Council on Reform of Financial Relations [GST]

policy recommendations from such agencies, mutual recognition of regulatory regimes, new uniform standards, and, most recently, overseeing the administration of the GST and approving changes to the tax base and rate.

The MC decision-making functions are spelled out clearly in each case in a formal intergovernmental agreement. These agreements have then been given greater legal standing through legislation in the Commonwealth parliament and (usually) all of the state and territorial parliaments. The normal case is for the relevant legislation to delegate continuing regulatory authority to the MCs. Examples include the *National Environmental Protection Council Act,* the *National Road Transport Commission Act* (for the Australian Transport Council), the *National Food Authority Act,* the *Australian National Training Authority Act,* and the *Australian Financial Institutions Commission Act.* In most cases, the agreements include a set of voting rules, which provide for decisions binding on all parties where there is a majority in favour. The nature of the majority required differs from a simple majority (50 per cent or more) to a qualified majority (most often two-thirds) to a combination of weighted votes (e.g., the MC for the Australian National Training Authority (ANTA) whereby the Commonwealth gets two votes plus the casting vote). The new GST agreement provides for a combination of unanimity and majority decisions by a ministerial council.

As discussed in chapter 4, the practice of delegating specific policy mandates onto ministerial councils with voting rules is not new in

Australia. The role of the Australian Loan Council since 1927, the Co-operative National Companies and Securities Scheme of 1980, and the National Crime Authority of 1984 are examples. Also, the presence of voting rules in Australian MCs may not make much immediate difference. One sees no evidence of votes actually occurring. As Painter points out, the pull of conventional consensus politics remains strong, mainly because it provides the parties with maximum individual flexibility.[6] However, the fact that votes could occur has likely changed the behaviour of governments and prevented reform laggards from delaying the overall process. They also provide safety in numbers for those who wish to proceed and probably increase the need for the states to meet among themselves before MC meetings with the Commonwealth.

The prospect of votes nonetheless raises the issue of their legitimacy. First, it is not clear that such votes would bind any government other than the current office-holders. Second, most formal voting in democratic institutions occurs in the open forums of parliaments and local government councils, where votes are registered and those doing the voting are held accountable for their actions. Ministerial councils operate in closed meetings – confidential if not secret. In this respect, the decision-making process is more akin to cabinets. Indeed, Commonwealth and state freedom of information laws treat them as such.

Mutual Recognition

A third reform in intergovernmental relations has been the adoption of mutual recognition as a joint policy instrument. Discussed in chapter 2 with respect to integration in the European Union, mutual recognition is the essence of a decentralized approach to harmonization. The Commonwealth had initially preferred a more uniform approach to negotiating new standards for the regulation of goods and occupations. However, the government of New South Wales argued successfully that such a process would be excessively time-consuming because an issue-by-issue review would unleash turf protection by each jurisdiction. The Commonwealth encouraged NSW to take the lead in developing the reform proposals. The result has been described by one of its architects as a "simple, elegant, and efficient solution to the positive task of regulatory harmonization."[7] The formal agreement on mutual recognition retains the objective of seeking uniform standards for health, safety, and environmental purposes, binding on all parties with a vote of a two-thirds majority in the ministerial council. In all other cases, however, mutual recognition becomes the default form of harmonization.

While not identical to the actual mutual recognition scheme, the device has also been applied to environmental policy. As part of the Intergovernmental Agreement on the Environment, one of the schedules provides for the option of mutual accreditation of land use decisions and approval processes (schedule 2) and environmental assessment processes (schedule 3). This would allow each state to pursue its own approach while meeting minimum national standards.

Uniform Legislation

Uniform legislation is another intergovernmental device used for national decision making. As shown in table 8.2, the governments have adopted joint or uniform legislation schemes across several policy areas.[8] The degree of centralization of legal authority and uniformity varies among the schemes. The most potentially centralizing would be "referral of powers" – i.e., invoking section 51 (XXXVII) of the constitution whereby one or many state parliaments transfer jurisdiction to the Commonwealth parliament.[9] Some states did refer powers for the mutual recognition scheme (i.e., New South Wales and Queensland referred both the initial act and its amendment; Tasmania referred the amendments only). Other states balked (Victoria, South Australia, and Western Australia). In the latter cases, any subsequent amendments to the Commonwealth legislation will have to be passed separately by those states' parliaments in order to apply. State concerns about further use of the referral of powers prevented its use in the implementation of the National Competition Policy.[10]

Otherwise, the governments have used either an "application of laws" or template approach, or a looser form of co-operative legislative scheme. In the former type, the typical pattern is for the Commonwealth to pass a law under its plenary jurisdiction over the territories and then for the states to adopt the law in their jurisdictions. This model has been used twice for companies and securities schemes. In the 1990s reform, a new interstate scheme has been adopted for nonbank financial institutions, introducing a state-based template, in this case Queensland. The most centralized result from this form of

Table 8.2 Joint or Uniform Legislation Schemes in Australia

FIELD	TYPE OF SCHEME
• Mutual recognition	• Referral of powers to Commonwealth (some states)
• Companies	• Adoption of uniform Commonwealth template
• Non-bank financial institutions	• Adoption of uniform Queensland template
• Disabilities services	• Complementary
• Competition	• Adoption of uniform New South Wales template – co-operative
• Road transport	• Co-operative

uniform legislation came when the states conferred power on the ACCC for the expanded scope of the Commonwealth's *Trade Practices Act*. In this case, the Commonwealth both administers and enforces the state legislation. The third type, termed "co-operative" or "complementary," is a looser arrangement whereby both orders of government must pass legislation for very specific new initiatives to proceed. The laws need not be uniform as such. This device was used in the cases of the disabilities agreement and road transport.

The significance in the variety of types of joint or uniform legislation measures is the willingness to apply different approaches to different problems – that there is not one right method of achieving harmoniza-tion or uniformity. Nonetheless, intergovernmental agreements on uni-form legislation leave very little, if any, room for subsequent parlia-mentary input. This is true with respect to the initial passage and the later amending of the scheme.[11]

New National Agencies

The creation of new national agencies is a third intergovernmental instrument used with renewed effect in the 1990s reforms. Table 8.3 lists eight new national agencies created by the intergovernmental reforms. These new agencies are the instruments for achieving harmo-nized or integrated regulatory regimes across a wide range of policy fields. However, they remain true to the spirit of reform in that "nation-al" interest is co-determined by the state and Commonwealth govern-ments. One of these is essentially a joint GBE: the Commonwealth and the states are shareholders of the National Rail Corporation. The other

Table 8.3 New National Agencies in Australia

Agency	Type
• Australian National Training Authority	• Commonwealth-state
• Australian Financial Institutions Commission	• States only
• National Food Authority	• Commonwealth-state
• National Environmental Protection Council	• Commonwealth-state
• Australian Competition and Consumer Council	• Commonwealth
• National Competition Council	• Commonwealth-state
• National Rail Corporation*	• Commonwealth-state
• National Road Transport Commission	• Commonwealth-state

* Shareholders

new agencies provide independent regulatory or policy advice to the governments collectively. In most of these cases, a ministerial council takes the final decision with respect to implementing a recommended measure. The National Environmental Protection Council is a hybrid, which has a mandate to provide regulatory advice to a ministerial council and to take legally binding regulatory measures of its own. Also, the two powerful institutions set up by the National Competition Policy, the ACCC and the NCC, do not report to or have decision-making oversight by ministerial councils. They are solely accountable through a federal minister to the Commonwealth parliament. The states do have a role in co-determining the work program of the NCC as well as the right to be consulted on the appointments to both commissions including the proviso that a majority of states must support any appointment.

Another important new role provided by some of these agencies is for increased private sector and general public input to the policy-making process. In the case of the NRTC, ANTA, and NFA, for example, the industry is represented on the agency board and thus has a formal role in the regulatory process. Therefore, these new agencies become important new players in the policy community.[12] Their presence reduces governmental dominance of the sector, but because of the multiple governments involved, it is unlikely to lead to industry "capture" and may keep the reform momentum going. The ACCC and NCC are set up to hear public views (including those of interest groups) on competition policy issues. Only the NEPC would appear to be more of an instrument for intergovernmental collaboration per se rather than an improved opportunity for public input on the environment.

Summary

The reform of intergovernmental relations of 1990–96 is a significant achievement in its own right. The process for collaborative policy-making made possible not only the substantive policy changes discussed in the next part of this chapter, but also may deliver a permanently more effective federal system. The chief characteristics of the reform may be summarized as follows:

- acquiring the personal, political interest, and involvement of all first ministers
- taking a whole-of-government approach to reform, requiring strong central direction within each government
- taking a broad and flexible approach to instruments of reform, borrowing liberally and adapting from past practice and relevant practice in other countries
- integrating and rationalizing the existing system of intergovernmental relations through the effective peak organization of COAG
- organizing ministerial councils more effectively, including establishing by legislation a decision-making mandate for policy collaboration in selected fields
- creating important new national agencies, some of which have the ability to expand the policy process to key community stakeholders
- proceeding with national reform by states and territories only when Commonwealth involvement is not forthcoming or desirable, including the role of the Leaders Forum

In sum, the reforms amount to a much greater ability of the federal system to produce national as opposed to federally determined policy. This means that the states have had to abandon a simplistic states-rights approach and consider the national perspective in a systematic way. For its part, the Commonwealth has had to abandon the reflex that a common solution must be a centralized one and have the patience to see through joint processes in the trust that more lasting and effective reform can be the result. Such attitudes and behaviours have not always been forthcoming and are difficult to sustain.

The last point raises the issue of whether these process reforms can or should become permanent features. A few cautions are worth noting in this respect. First, a more powerful and effective system of intergovernmental relations brings to the surface the long-standing problem that this executive-dominated and relatively closed process often leaves out parliaments and other public interests. This issue has been examined by legislative committees in Western Australia and Victoria.[13] Second, the process has been effective in producing the policy reforms required of it but may not be sustainable during a period of reduced emphasis on reform. The bureaucratic effort and political capital to be expended may not be considered to be worth it. Third, governments will not always want to pursue a collaborative approach. Martin Painter recently summarized the 1990s record of reform as follows: "intertwined with a growing area of collaborative policy-making was an evolving patchwork of state and Commonwealth reform initiatives and responses."[14] Collaboration coexists with competition. To the extent to which governments decide in the future to be more competitive, they will leave their newly created machinery unused. If the new machinery is not operated frequently, it may cease to operate altogether, leaving only the older machinery in place.

In conclusion, the comparison with Canada is striking. When executive federalism developed in both federal systems in the past thirty years, Canada led the way. It had experience going back to the mid-1970s, with First Ministers Conferences dealing with comprehensive policy agendas. So, too, the provincial premiers and territorial leaders have been meeting regularly for forty years. Yet attempts at modest efforts at formalization of peak intergovernmental bodies in the Meech Lake and Charlottetown Accords failed, leaving these institutions undeveloped and ad hoc. Australia's reforms – COAG, the rationalization of MCS, the broader use of voting rules, and the development of several new joint national agencies – demonstrate that it has now taken the lead in the formalization, innovation, and institution building of intergovernmental relations. Collectively, Australia's reforms provide the basis, if not the will, for effective "national" decision making. This is an important comparison in itself, but it must be combined with an assessment of the substantive policy outcomes to assess its significance fully.

The intergovernmental agenda had an original single focus in bundling fiscal and (mainly social) program "roles and responsibilities" issues, but this focus could not be sustained. As a result, the reforms in the fiscal and social policy area are not as extensive as the microeconomic reforms discussed in the next section; nor are they as significant to economic union reform as such. However, a concise analysis of the accomplishments will help to put the overall reform effort into perspective, particularly its impact on federalism in Australia.

Reform of fiscal relations went through three distinct phases: the first early discussion of comprehensive reform; a second period of no reform (just tinkering); and a third, late initiative of tax reform. In the first phase of reform under Hawke's leadership, the governments put a great deal of effort into a review of tax powers and tied grants. A working group on taxing powers proposed that the states get a guaranteed 6 per cent share of income tax revenues, up to $AUS10 billion, with the option of each state varying the rate on its share at a later stage. Financial Assistance Grants (FAGS) to the states would be reduced accordingly. The tied grants working group meanwhile surveyed a number of avenues for reform, including assumption by the states of full responsibility for certain programs and the Commonwealth for others (i.e., disentanglement), and consolidation and simplification of remaining conditional payments (SPPS). Since the mandate of these working groups ended with Hawke, nothing came of them initially, but at least all governments began a process of thinking through optional scenarios in the tax and program financing fields, with some ideas that would re-emerge later.

From 1991 to 1998, governments only tinkered with their fiscal relations. In 1992, the Commonwealth offered the states a "real terms revenue guarantee" to cover FAGS. This addressed the more acute revenue problems of the states but did not solve the chronic issue. In 1993, the states agreed with the Commonwealth on a renegotiation of the medicare arrangements in the absence of any major progress on the realignment of health care responsibilities. In 1995, the Commonwealth agreed to a set of payments to the states, totalling an estimated $2.4 billion over eight years commencing in 1997–98, as part of the National Competition Policy. The Commonwealth also renewed its commitment to maintain the real per capita guarantee of

FAGs on a rolling three-year basis (although in its first budget, the Howard government reneged on that guarantee).

Finally, and most significantly, is the Howard government's tax reform proposals, which will see the states eliminate several indirect tax sources in return for receiving, as a dedicated revenue, the proceeds of the new GST. Two developments in 1997 pushed tax reform into the limelight. First, the High Court in the *Ha v. New South Wales* and *Hammond v. New South Wales* cases ruled that the states' business franchise fees – on the sale of petroleum products, liquor, and tobacco – were unconstitutional. This outcome created a $5 billion hole in state revenues (16 per cent of total state revenues). As a temporary measure, the Commonwealth increased its own excise tax on these products in order to provide the states with a set of "revenue replacement" payments. However, the scheme could not last since it distributed the federal revenues according to past tax effort and thus unevenly across the states.[15]

Second, the court judgment contributed to increased calls for tax reform. The states had been urging the new government to proceed with tax reform since its election. Victoria and WA, in particular, undertook significant policy work on income tax sharing, payroll tax harmonization, as well as consumption tax reform.[16] Responding both to demands from the states and to policy imperatives of its own, the Howard government took the lead in August 1998 with a major reform proposal for a new GST.[17] As a whole, the states responded positively to the proposal, although Labor governments in NSW and Queensland were careful not to openly endorse the GST. Much had to be worked out, but the federal coalition government was able to go to the polls in October 1988 on a platform of tax reform with the tacit agreement of the states. Following its re-election, the Howard government convened a Special Premiers Conference in November 1998 to discuss the principles of agreement. At a COAG meeting in April 1999, all governments agreed to the complex terms. The government jumped its last major hurdle with the passage of legislation in the federal parliament in June 1999.

Under the terms of the April 1999 agreement, the Commonwealth would levy a new broad-based GST to replace its wholesale sales taxes and nine state taxes on various types of business transactions. In return for abolishing their taxes and committing to refrain from reintroducing them, the states would get all the proceeds of the new GST.

This guaranteed source of revenue would replace the existing FAGS as well as the replacement payments for the unconstitutional franchise fees. Moreover, the new GST rate, set at 10 per cent, would not be increased without the consent of all the states. Scheduled to go into effect by 1 July 2000, the GST would initially garner $32 billion for the states. The tax revenue would be distributed according to the horizontal equalization formula as recommended by the Commonwealth Grants Commission. In addition, the Commonwealth would pay three years of transition loans and grants to ensure that no state was worse off in its fiscal position than when the new tax began. Indeed, the Commonwealth expected that state revenues would improve.

The agreement covered many other intriguing aspects, which cannot be given their due here: the disentanglement of local government finance; issues of reciprocal taxation; price monitoring; the role of the ministerial council; and the details of the transitional payments, among others. More important is its significance for fiscal federalism more broadly. The agreement does not fix vertical fiscal imbalance (VFI) as such; indeed, by having the states get rid of tax sources over which they have full control in return for a new tax over which they have joint control, VFI is made worse. Also, individual states will have no power to vary the tax rate in their jurisdiction. Yet the states have received full access to a guaranteed source of revenue that will grow with the economy while ridding themselves of the FAGS and the annual battle over their calculation. What's more, they achieve co-decision not only over the base and rate of the new tax, but they have a substantial say over its administration. In the meantime, fiscal equalization is maintained, essentially by transferring it from the FAGS to the new GST revenue, adding health care grants to the pool. The Commonwealth stresses its commitment to continue the SPPs, although observers doubt that they will now grow.[18] In sum, the GST agreement delivers a significant reform, shoring up state financial security, reducing inefficiency in the tax system, and introducing a unique degree of co-decision to fiscal arrangements and tax policy.

As for the second part of the original reform agenda – the program "roles and responsibilities" exercise – governments have similarly made some piecemeal but not comprehensive progress in four program areas.[19] In 1991, the governments agreed to transfer responsibility to the states for most services to the disabled, with the Commonwealth paying all net additional costs. They held on-again, off-again discussions on housing programs, with a new interim agreement reached in 1997 for two years. Governments have been co-operating through the Australian National Training Authority set up in 1992 to regulate funding to the technical and further education (TAFE) institutions. Health and community services had also been slated for early review but got nowhere after the end of 1991. In the meantime, the governments renegotiated current arrangements such as medicare. At the April 1995 COAG, governments began a renewed attempt to flesh out wide-ranging reform of the organization, planning, and funding of health care services. Still, the issue of medicare funding per se remains highly contested.

Throughout all of these program areas, a common thread of public management reform is being woven. However, the objective of that reform remains in conflict. The Commonwealth tends to stress national planning, funding, and standard setting, but decentralized, often private, service delivery. The "national" function can be inter-governmental, but the goal is to sever the states from their monopoly over service provision. The states stress disentanglement in a purer sense, reducing the role of Canberra in program design and the con-ditionality of its funding.[20] The states' way lies in more diverse, state-based solutions and is thus integrally tied to fiscal relations reform to improve their autonomous fiscal position. It is thus no surprise that, in the absence of such fiscal reform, the Commonwealth's approach has been slowly gaining.

The Commonwealth's strategy differs markedly from that of the federal government in Canada. In the latter case, federal fiscal clout is con-siderably reduced from what it once was and is more balanced with respect to the provinces. The provinces have a stronger jurisdictional base to fend off federal conditions and encroachments, significantly reinforced by their relative fiscal autonomy. This equilibrium created the conditions for the Social Union Framework Agreement (SUFA) re-ferred to in chapter 6. The conditions for such a framework agreement do not exist in Australia, mainly because the Commonwealth govern-ment has the overwhelming advantage.

In summary, the piecemeal reform in fiscal and social policy fields demonstrates the lack of a common approach to program roles and res-ponsibilities. The sudden death of fiscal reform in late 1991 cut off fur-ther consideration of reform in health and housing especially. Renewed efforts since 1995 indicate some promise, but they have suffered from the interruptions of a change in government in 1996 and the lack of a concerted whole-of-government approach to reform since then. Only in environment – discussed below under microeconomic reform, not a social program area as such – was there a successful effort to delineate new roles and responsibilities. Finally, the tax reform initiative of the Howard government does not appear to be linked to a comprehensive reform of roles and responsibilities. But it is important in its own right and may yet open the way to a rationalization of program funding.

MICROECONOMIC AND RELATED REFORM

The third and last category of reforms is the most significant in policy terms. The microeconomic reforms represent an important improvement to the economic union. My assessment here focuses on seven sets of reform:[21]

1 National Competition Policy
2 Mutual Recognition of Standards
3 New National Standards
4 Transportation Reform
5 Utilities Reform
6 Environmental Regulation
7 National Benchmarking

National Competition Policy

Undoubtedly, the most sweeping and significant set of reforms has been the new National Competition Policy (NCP).[22] These reforms arose from a jointly agreed set of principles in 1991 that led to an independent inquiry, resulting in the Hilmer Report of 1993. Through these principles, governments sought to apply a common view of what constituted competitive and anti-competitive behaviour in the marketplace to all participants, regardless of business form and legal jurisdiction. They sought to apply a transparent assessment process to determine the public interest when anti-competitive practice occurred. And they sought to encourage a broad policy framework in which diverse federal and state public policies, regulations, and ownership structures could be harmonized.

The result of the negotiations in 1993–95, discussed above, was a set of six carefully crafted and linked elements. These are like a set of

Russian dolls, with the first being the core reform, broadened by the second, and so on.[23] The first element is the key legislative amendments to the Commonwealth's *Trade Practices Act* (TPA), mainly to extend part IV of the act. The second is the adoption by the states and territories of the extension of the TPA through "application of laws" legislation. The third is an agreed approach to the structural reform of public monopolies: a flexible national framework creating a more or less level playing field for the utilities and transportation sectors. The fourth is an agreed approach to ensure access for all market participants to essential infrastructure, helping to ensure that the newly competitive players can actually compete in a national market. The fifth is a new co-operative regime for price monitoring to protect consumer interests and to police the newly created national market. And the sixth is a legislative review to ensure that no stone is left unturned in the effort to apply the new competition principles to the totality of government jurisdiction and activity in the country.

The reform goals – those of the Hilmer Report, in particular – have been achieved in large measure. The private sector is covered uniformly by the new Competition Code (the TPA amendments) except where specific sectoral regulatory regimes apply. However, the application to the public sector of GBEs and monopolies is a more flexible regime, leaving significant room for state variation in approach. There is thus plenty of room for exceptions and exemptions. Such exceptions include those made under section 51 of the Competition Code (scheduled version of part IV, TPA in the *CPR Act, 1995*) which allows governments to specifically exempt any activity through legislation and authorization. For example, states have recently registered legislation covering the dairy industry, energy and forest developments, and gambling, among others. The states have agreed, however, to a transparent process of notification and justification of such measures in their "conduct code" agreement with the Commonwealth (COAG, 1995b: clause 2). The states also retain the ability to pursue their own agendas for price oversight reform, the application of competitive neutrality, the structural reform of monopolies, and the timetable and methods of legislative review. This is stipulated in the Competition Principles Agreement (COAG, 1995c: clauses 2, 3, 4, and 5) and will provide further room for special interest consideration. Nonetheless, the legislative review process, the last and biggest of the Russian dolls, is intended to put these exceptions and regionally diverse processes under the spotlight, encouraged by the watchful eye of the National Competition Commission (NCC). The clout of the NCC to keep exceptions to a minimum is strengthened by its role in determining whether the states have kept to the reform schedule and thus merit their payments under the financial compensation agreement.

The true measure of the NCP lies in its implementation. The policy framework is complex and by design, requires years to take full effect. However, its scope is so broad and its impact so potentially powerful that the NCP has been blamed (like free trade in Canada) for all manner of economic disruptions and injustices. Grievances seem especially sharp in rural regions where the reduced service obligations on GBEs hit hardest and where previous regulatory regimes incorporated a good deal of subsidization. Appealing partly to rural voters, the One Nation Party led by Pauline Hanson has been vociferous in its criticism, but also the ALP, Democrats, and many in the coalition parties (particularly the Queensland National Party) warn about the scope and bite of competition reform. Moreover, business and labour is nervous about extension of the NCP to industrial relations, and many sectors continue to resist the new policy, such as newsagents, dairies, and Australian Post.[24] These sorts of concerns, highlighted by a productivity council report and a Senate committee inquiry,[25] led COAG in November 2000 to agree to clarify some community interest aspects of the NCP and to extend the deadline for the legislative review and reform by eighteen months to mid-2002.

Nonetheless, from the initial reports of the two new national agencies established to monitor and enforce the policy, the ACCC and NCC, the implementation has been proceeding well enough in the first three years. The NCC has only once had to recommend that a state not get its full compensation payments – i.e., recommending a $10 million penalty to NSW for lack of reform of its domestic rice marketing monopoly.[26] The NCC has named but not penalized states for other practices in agricultural supply and price regulation and inconsistent and slow progress on interstate competition in the professions and gambling. Individual governments singled out as laggards include Western Australia with respect to gas; Queensland on electricity; Victoria on taxis; the Australian Capital Territory (ACT) on business hours; and even the Commonwealth for its sluggish tariff reduction program and restrictions on the number of physicians able to bill medicare. In sum, the serious implementation difficulties of microeconomic reform are not in the competition framework per se, but in specific sectors (some of which are discussed below). In this respect, they are exceptions that prove the new market rules.

Mutual Recognition of Standards

The mutual recognition agreement of 1992 is the second important reform achievement. The COAG arrangement with New Zealand in 1996 is also remarkable as a hybrid between an intergovernmental agreement and an international treaty. These agreements go a long way to create the conditions for free interstate trade. The scheme does allow exceptions; for example, it does not apply to regulations of trade in goods for purposes of health and safety and the environment. Also, certain types of goods for which a national market would not be in the public interest (firearms, pornography) are exempted permanently. Otherwise, the scheme is relatively comprehensive with respect to goods. It does not cover services.

The mutual recognition scheme has been working well for goods, although no specific monitoring takes place. Implementation is left entirely to the parties' individual regulatory reform apparatus, which one analyst suggests may make for protracted and inconsistent results.[27] The mutual recognition of occupations is said to have contributed to the development of national standards, but it is more difficult to tell if professional mobility has been improved. The Productivity Council recommends that the scheme should be extended to the regulation of all services and to local governments.[28]

New National Standards

Mutual recognition is a decentralized approach to integration, but governments have not been willing in all cases to forego more explicit attempts to harmonize regulations and standards. In fact, the mutual recognition agreements provide a process to determine national uniform standards where these are deemed appropriate and where the parties can reach co-decision on them (otherwise, mutual recognition of diverse standards becomes the norm). The governments have also launched a variety of separate efforts to create, through co-decision, new sets of national uniform standards. These include food standards, credit law and other regulatory aspects of non-bank financial institutions, road transport, and companies and securities. As discussed above under inter-governmental relations reform, the process for co-decision of new harmonized standards involves specially mandated ministerial councils and new national agencies (although the centralization of companies and securities regulation under the Australian Securities Commission took place in 1990, ahead of the other reforms).[29]

Transportation Reform

Advocates of microeconomic reform have long targeted the inefficient transport infrastructure and its protectionist state-based institutions and regulations. Every SPC and COAG meeting has discussed road and rail reform, but ports and shipping have not been the focus of similar inter-governmental attention. The agreement to establish the National Rail Corporation (NRC) with some states as shareholders has yet to produce its goal of a national privatized rail carrier. The NRC has been caught up in the lengthy and difficult process of rationalization and privatization of the different states' rail networks. Nonetheless, it has served the purpose to get that process moving. By late 1998, for example, the states had agreed on a variety of further measures on interstate rail reform and on the establishment of a new "one-stop-shop" corporation to own and manage interstate track and related assets. Reforms in road transport have also been difficult to achieve. The National Road Transport Commission, authorized to provide policy advice on uniform road charges and other regulations and vehicle licensing regimes, has worked much more slowly than had been hoped, as the state and territorial governments find more incentives to go their own way.[30] The Commonwealth is said to be considering a proposal for a more uniform legislative approach.

Utilities Reform

The reform objectives for the three utility sectors of electricity, water, and gas have been the same: to create a national or at least a multi-state market in basic utilities and to increase efficiency and competition in sectors in which there has been a set of state monopoly providers. While this process has taken much time and involved much conflict, the basic goals remain in sight. The National Grid Management Council, established in 1991, has laid the foundation for a national market in electricity. This now includes the National Electricity Code Administrator (NECA) and the National Electricity Market Management Company (NEMMCO). Regular wholesale electricity sales have begun between NSW, ACT, and Victoria, with Queensland and South Australia not far behind. This bald fact belies an enormous amount of political struggle – particularly among Victoria, New South Wales, and Queensland – over the respective status and comparability of their industry competition and structure. The Commonwealth has little leverage to impose a common framework over the very different paths to reform pursued by the three states.

Reforms in gas and water have taken longer. The significant commitments on water reform will take years to implement, involving complicated negotiations with local governments. Intergovernmental agreement at a national level can realistically provide a general framework only. On gas, governments finally reached a National Gas Pipeline Access Agreement in November 1997, and Commonwealth and state legislation followed. Agreement on the specific terms of a reform code had been difficult to achieve due to inter-industry differences, a reluctance of governments to reduce the rents they gain from publicly owned facilities, and an overly centralizing approach to regulation. Western Australia, in particular, has been keen to go its own way, although it did sign the 1997 agreement.[31]

Environmental Regulation

Another area of reform significant to the economic union is environmental regulation and process. The Intergovernmental Agreement on the Environment (IGAE), reached in 1993, is only a broad set of commitments and requires continuing negotiations for detailed implementation. Some of its schedules remain undeveloped. The National Environmental Protection Council (NEPC), established in 1994 under Commonwealth legislation, provides for intergovernmental co-decision covering a range of specified environmental matters including mandatory standards. The NEPC also oversees its administrative arm, the NEPC Service Corporation, and provides for consultation with the states before the ratification of any environmental treaty. Western Australia has chosen not to become a member of the NEPC.

In late 1997, COAG met to consider a revised agreement on federal and state roles, including a legislative proposal governing when the Commonwealth would intervene in environmental assessment and related matters with impacts of "national environmental significance." This phrase has since been defined in proposed Commonwealth legislation, which, among other things, determines the process for the Commonwealth to endorse state environmental approval regulation in place of its own. The federal government retains the capacity to return to its own process if the state process fails to meet framework requirements. The legislation also requires consultation with the states before federal determinations are made and encourages concurrency with state laws. These arrangements have been the result of difficult and dogged negotiations with the Howard government. If they stick, they will go a long way to reducing long-standing intergovernmental conflict and legal uncertainty in this field, contribute to industry and investor stability, and retain important elements of regionally diversity in environmental management.

National Benchmarking

Finally, one of the least heralded but potentially most significant areas of reform has been agreements to submit all GBEs and public service providers to processes of national performance monitoring or benchmarking-type exercises. Governments agreed in 1991 to proceed with the national monitoring for GBEs. As these enterprises become increasingly commercialized (as they approach privatization in many cases), the performance monitoring to nationally determined standards provides essential information to governments, investors, managers, and consumers. In a similar process, COAG agreed in 1994 to review Commonwealth and state government service provision, developing performance indicators for efficient and effective programs. The Productivity Council wants to see this process extended to local government.[32] In sum, performance monitoring contributes essential information, underpinning an overall commitment to transparency and accountability to the microeconomic reform. It is an article of faith among the advocates of reform that open information is the best recipe for change.

To assess whether these reforms have had an impact on the economic union in Australia, we return to the list of barriers identified in chapter four. Table 8.4 summarizes the post-reform state of the Australian economic union. The left-hand column lists the major barriers identified by reform advocates in the 1980s. Of the thirteen barriers listed, the Australian intergovernmental reforms removed ten of these in a substantive way, although in some cases, full implementation has yet to be reached. Only three of the thirteen are not covered – i.e., industrial and agricultural subsidies, industrial relations, and ports and shipping.[33]

Another way to assess the overall impact is to return to the idea of negative and positive integration as presented in chapter 2 and elsewhere. *Negative integration* refers to market rules imposed on all governments to refrain from certain forms of market intervention. In these reforms, negative integration is extended through the National Competition Policy and similar sectoral reforms in transportation and utilities. The NCP extends common competition principles to virtually the entire private sector as well as to GBES – covering both goods and services. However, competition in individual sectors such as rail, electricity, and gas depends on the further positive integration of a unified regulatory framework to ensure access and actual investment in the construction of a national infrastructure.

Positive integration refers to common policies that shape the way the market operates, in particular, to harmonize regulation. This is achieved in the Australian reforms through three sets of measures. First, mutual recognition is the most impressive means as it applies so broadly to all goods in trade as well as to professional occupations. Mutual recognition also creates necessary uniform standards right away and in the long run, contributes to natural harmonization.[34] It would be even more effective if it were extended to services.

The second major thrust of positive integration is the co-operative process for creating uniform standards, the joint regulation of specific sectors, and the agreement to create a single new regulatory agency under Commonwealth control. The governments have applied these harmonization devices across a wide set of economic sectors and regulatory policies, including fiscal policy. Some attempts have not worked well, such as road transport, but governments are doing better

Table 8.4   Microeconomic Reforms and the Australian Economic Union

NATURE OF EXISTING BARRIER	MICROECONOMIC REFORM PROVISIONS
GOODS	
• Different product standards by state.	• Mutual Recognition Agreement covers the sale of all goods. Harmonized standards for environment, health, and safety purposes proceeding.
• Poorly integrated state railway systems.	• National Rail Corporation established. Integration of rail freight systems proceeding.
• Differing highway regulations.	• Uniform schemes for heavy vehicle licensing and fees apply across some states and territories.
• GBES restrict trade and competition in energy, transport, and other infrastructure and utilities.	• National Competition Policy applies to most sectors of goods production. Separate but similar frameworks for reform agreed and being implemented for water, gas, and electricity.
• Industrial and agricultural subsidies.	• Not covered.
• Significant gaps in coverage of federal competition law coverage.	• Extension of coverage of federal *Trade Practices Act* to state jurisdiction for all private business, except where exemptions provided in law. Agreement with the states on principles and process to cover publicly owned GBES.
SERVICES	
• GBES restrict competition in state-owned and regulated banking and insurance.	• National Competition Policy applies to most state-regulated services.
• GBES restrict competition in electricity and other utilities and in transport.	• National Competition Policy requires states to apply access regimes for essential facilities (with a national access regime to be applied if state schemes do not follow national principles). Partial national market in electricity established. National freight rail network being established.
• Protective regulation of ports and shipping.	• Not covered.
• Differing regulation of non-bank financial sector.	• New national agency regulates states' non-bank financial institutions. Uniform regulations approved by ministerial council.
• Differing regulation of professional services.	• Mutual Recognition Agreement covers most professional occupational standards.

Table 8.4   Microeconomic Reforms and the Australian Economic Union
            (Continued)

NATURE OF EXISTING BARRIER	MICROECONOMIC REFORM PROVISIONS
CAPITAL • Inefficient and non-harmonized indirect consumption taxes across states.	• Single federal Goods and Services Tax to replace several state indirect taxes. Harmonization proceeding for some remaining state taxes.
LABOUR • Differing state regimes for industrial relations.	• Not covered as such. Victoria refers powers to Commonwealth. Differing regulatory frameworks continue to apply in other states.

in food, environmental protection, and some tax fields. Joint regulation is proceeding in the states-only non-bank financial sector, the environment, and companies and securities. And uniform regulation through a single new agency under Commonwealth control is proceeding through the expanded mandate of the new Australian Competition and Consumer Commission.

A third significant form of positive integration is the new national infrastructure to promote interstate trade and competition. The reform accomplishments in rail, electricity, gas, and water – some still unrealized – will be an important boost to the economic union.

There remain the three gaps in economic union reform, at least as far as intergovernmental co-operation goes. The governments have not yet taken a common approach to the reform of industrial and agricultural subsidies. The Industry Commission has released a study condemning state business subsidy practices, in particular, the destructive competing for investment promotion and facilitation. The Commonwealth has apparently proposed an agreement on subsidy guidelines, but nothing has come of it yet.[35] On shipping and ports reform and in industrial relations, the governments individually have been very active. Also, the competitive neutrality provisions of the NCP, among others, apply to state-owned port facilities. But despite some apparent discussion at COAG meetings, a specific multilateral co-operative approach to reform has never emerged. This is likely due to partisan differences and sensitivities, in particular, the significant divide between the ALP and conservative parties on their attitude toward organized labour.

In the meantime, industrial relations itself remains a major – if declining – arena for competitive federalism. At the beginning of the reform period in 1990–93, New South Wales and Victoria led the way to reform industrial relations. By 1993–94, however, the Commonwealth government under Keating introduced its own reform bills to provide many employer/union groups the option of choosing federal jurisdiction over the arbitration of wages and work conditions. This precipitated a steady bleeding away of industrial relations settlements from state to federal jurisdiction. Three states (Victoria, South Australia, and Western Australia) challenged the Commonwealth's legislation but lost in the High Court (the case is *Ex Parte Australian Education Union,* 1995).

The Howard government also proposed a scheme to harmonize industrial relations law in 1996, covering such policy as unfair dismissal, access to federal contract minimum standards, and freedom of association. Again, there was not sufficient consensus among the states to proceed. Thus, the Commonwealth proceeded on its own to reduce the jurisdictional scope of the Australian Industrial Relations Commission, establishing enterprise bargaining as the primary means to determine wage and working conditions. In response, and after several years of being ahead of the reform game, Victoria reached a bilateral agreement to refer its jurisdiction to the Commonwealth in November 1996.[36] It may be only a matter of time before most states cede their jurisdiction to the Commonwealth. It is a case of competition prevailing over co-operation but in which the long-term advantages seem to have been with the Commonwealth. The same may be true of shipping and port reforms. In any case, as Painter points out, the field of industrial relations demonstrates that older-style patterns of adversarial relations continue to coexist with the new collaborative relationships.[37]

In summary, and despite these gaps, the reform of Australia's economic union through intergovernmental means has been a significant achievement, with unique features to respond to unique conditions. As discussed in chapter 4, Australia has been a regionalized economy, politically organized for well over a century in what amounts to a set of city states. Strongly controlled and regulated out of state capitals, the regional economies of Australia had served the country well for many decades but did not provide the national economic integration required for global competition. Australia embraced internal microeconomic reform of its trade in goods and services and its infrastructure to achieve economic adjustment. This matched the commitments to lower tariff protection and to make the entire country more productive and competitive. It also sought to fundamentally transform the balkanization of large and crucial parts of economic activity in what has been perceived as overregulated, subsidized, and politically driven state and federal corporations (GBEs) and monopolies.

The reforms thus have potential to transform the Australian economy. Indeed, there is already evidence that microeconomic reform has boosted national productivity.[38] Moreover, some credit the reforms in part with Australia's easy ride in the Asian financial crisis of 1997–98. And international agencies such as the OECD, IMF, and World Bank now point to Australia as a useful international model for successful adaptation to the global economy.[39]

In comparison with Canada's economic union reform, Australia's microeconomic reforms are more unilaterally driven and respond to more diffuse integrationist pressures. Australia has had to undertake the difficult task of initiating internal reforms on its own, without the incentive of an institutional framework for regional integration (i.e., a free trade agreement). Through these reforms, Australia has achieved or is near to achieving a much more effective economic union, exceeding the degree of integration of the EU. In fact, by focusing on the competition among utilities and service providers, even where there is no interstate trade in the first instance, Australia is probably going further with reform than is Canada. (A more detailed comparison follows in the next chapter.)

But at what cost is the extensive intergovernmental activity and cooperative achievement? In many areas of the economy, the states' ability to creatively devise their own regulatory and fiscal solutions is being eroded – in some cases, eliminated. Where the states' autonomy is being ceded to the marketplace, it shares its fate with the Commonwealth. This is the case for all of the negative integration measures discussed above. The National Competition Policy, while having strong elements of regulatory centralization, is mainly about ending decades-old patterns of intervention in the marketplace. The same is true of the reform frameworks in transport and utilities. Other reforms, such as performance monitoring of GBEs and the agreement to maintain competitive neutrality, mean that even where governments retain ownership, their role must by and large conform to the new market rules.

Where the reduction of the states role is more unbalanced, with potential consequences for the federal system, is in the common movement to uniform standards. Uniformity is the immediate or long-term goal in many of the reforms, affecting regulations over food, securities, companies, non-bank financial institutions, road transport, training, and environmental protection. Support for such uniformity emerges strongly from the rationalist reform advocacy, but it is essentially anti-federal, depriving the states of their autonomy to produce diverse policy. Still, the states seem to be rediscovering the ability to slow down or disable the juggernaut of co-decision. There is evidence of this trend in road transport and rail. The trend to uniformity is also counterbalanced by the process of mutual recognition that allows for initial diversity, but which may lead to tighter harmonization over time.

ख

Thus, some of the reform processes have been more centralizing than others. The states are still leery of proposed schemes to invest new regulatory authority in the Commonwealth without their participation. They will continue to seek opportunities to inject into national policy frameworks the room for state flexibility in enforcement and implementation. To the extent to which they are successful, the worst aspects of the uniformity and centralization in these reforms may be controlled. Indeed, Martin Painter's recent study of the Australian reforms stresses, in the end, the limitations of collaborative federalism and the persistence of an overall "arm's-length relationships" in which the reforms are nested.[40] Our findings do not contradict that conclusion, but the same set of facts look somewhat different when one compares the relative degree of binding collaboration, centralization, uniformity, and therefore reduced flexibility in Australia with the economic union reform in Canada.

As shown in chapter 4, the Australian federal system as a whole tends to a more collaborative model, especially in comparison to Canada. This is due to Australia's concurrent distribution of law-making powers and the relative centralization of fiscal resources. The question is whether the institutions of Australian federalism as reformed in the past decade further configure the incentives in favour of collaboration, if not rationalization (compare table 3.1 in chapter 3), and, if so, in what relative degree in comparison with Canada? Which, if either, constitutes

the better response to economic globalization, and what can be concluded from these two federations' experience with reform for federal
systems more generally? These issues are addressed in the next and concluding chapter.

9 Conclusions: Market Rules and Federalism

This work began with one very large issue and three subsidiary ones. The big issue is whether federal systems at the end of the twentieth century are capable of adapting to the changes wrought by economic globalization. To deal with this question, one must examine three more. First is the nature of the challenge to federal systems from economic globalization. Throughout this book, I have focused on the process of global and regional integration impinging on the two federal systems of Australia and Canada, and of a relentless program of economic liberalization that has tended to accompany the new forms of integration. Thus, adapting to globalization in this context means, in the main, adjusting national economies to supranational integration and liberalization.

The second issue is the nature of the task of economic adjustment. Here, I have undertaken the case study of the reform of a set of market rules integral to federal systems – their economic unions. The latter form a regime – i.e., norms and institutions – which were crucial to the original founding of the two federations but had been taken for granted over time. In the new era of globalization, the economic union regimes came under close scrutiny. They were perceived as not promoting a sufficient degree of national competitiveness in the more liberal international environment and as not imposing sufficiently comprehensive market principles over the whole of the federation. In the process, long-standing political trade-offs imbedded in these economic unions – to balance integration and diversity, efficiency, and equity – became untenable.

The third issue is how to reform economic unions in federal states. The task is essentially concurrent, turning on the effectiveness of intergovernmental relations. In this study, I present a comparative case of the effectiveness of the two federal systems to achieve reform through intergovernmental means. In particular, the capacity for joint policy-making and co-decision is a key variable in the comparison.

In the process of exploring these issues, a fourth issue emerged: the significance of the changed circumstances of interdependence facing Australia, Canada, and other federal systems. In particular, I examine the effect of reformed economic unions on federalism itself. This final chapter pulls together the evidence and interpretation of the preceding chapters to answer these questions.

COMPARING THE POLITICS AND PROCESS OF REFORM

Australia and Canada face the world economy with remarkably similar circumstances. They both have highly advanced industrial economies with a strong measure of resource product dependency; relatively small populations in a huge territory; Anglo-American business culture; and a common history of evolution from British colonies to middle power federations. In both cases, a chief rationale for the original federation had been the creation of a single market – defined here as an economic union. These two economic union regimes came under increasing criticism in the 1970s and 1980s for allowing major gaps in their common market rules and as an inadequate basis for national competitiveness. State and provincial interests had resisted some aspects of economic integration, and all governments had intervened in the national economy for equity and other purposes. As both countries faced strong and growing exposure to international integration and liberalization, economic union reform became an important political issue.

Reform of economic unions is not merely policy change, however. As a wide-ranging set of market rules, economic unions encompass many different policy instruments and objectives. As noted in chapter 3, economic unions are regimes with characteristic norms and institutions. Thus, their reform is *institutional* reform – institutions that form an important part of federal systems and reflect underlying federal values. In the introductory chapter, I cited a study of institutional reform by Thelen and Steinmo in which they stressed the significance of moments of institutional change. Such moments illuminate underlying interests and power relations and lead to outcomes that "not only reflect but magnify and reinforce the interests of winners, since broad trajectories can follow from institutional choices."[1] Thelen and Steinmo note three sources for such change.

From the analysis in the first four chapters, I applied these to the economic unions of the two federations. Change occurs, first, when previously latent institutions become more noticed. Long taken for granted, the economic union suddenly became a political issue in the 1980s. Second, change also occurs when old institutions are put to new ends. The economic unions designed to promote interstate trade among sets of developing colonial economies had to adapt to much more intense and external competition and to the need for market rules that are compatible with integration beyond the federation's borders. Third, change occurs when the goals and strategies of institutions become transformed. Embedded in the economic unions of Australia and Canada were political bargains to balance integration goals with diversity and economic efficiency with equity. Prevailing ideas of neo-liberalism led reform advocates to call for a rebalancing, to stress uniformity and efficiency in a new set of market rules for the economic union.

Early in this work (chapter 2), I underlined the essential difference in the positioning of the two countries in the international political economy. Australia experiences diffuse market integration with its many trading partners and a low level of institutional integration within the region (e.g., APEC). This means that while competitive pressures on Australia are strong, no one competitor sets the market rules. This leaves Australia with considerable room to adjust to international integration and liberalization on its own terms. Its economic union reform agenda consisted, then, of unilateral microeconomic changes focused on improving the conditions of national competition. Canada, however, faces concentrated market integration and a more intensive form of institutional integration with its continental neighbour, the United States (i.e., the FTA and NAFTA). The market rules tend now to be set by the dominant partner, and, in any case, domestic adjustment is strongly influenced (and in part achieved) by the terms of regional free trade. Thus, economic union reform in Canada took place within a free trade paradigm, using trade policy devices and language and at a pace and scope largely set by the international agenda. The consequence of this distinction between "competition" oriented reform and "free trade" reform is explored below.

For our purposes, the ends of reform have been essentially an exogenous variable. This work has not attempted to test rigorously the assumptions of reform advocates or to delve too deeply into the interests at hand. This is not to suggest that there were not many subtle political factors in play that would give a more human face to the conceptual discussion here. Certainly reform advocacy was led by national business organizations interested in broad-brushed microeconomic reform and the entrenchment of neo-liberal policy. In both societies, these policy goals remain strongly contested. Public interest groups have sought to ensure that the interests of citizens, consumers, and the disadvantaged are not left out of the reform policies. Yet economic union reform as such was not a partisan political issue. There has been some debate on the margins in Australia and Canada about the precise extent and speed of reform but no serious questioning of the need for reform. Instead, the politics were expressed in process issues and in regional and jurisdictional conflicts. To these issues we now turn.

Proceeding with reform through intergovernmental negotiation and collaboration was not the only choice open to the governments involved. As set out in chapter 4, they faced three large avenues of options: (1) unilateral and potentially competing programs of reform undertaken by each order of government; (2) amendment of the specific constitutional terms of the economic union; and (3) intergovernmental co-operation. The choice of options is partly determined by the desirability of certain ends and gets at the heart of the politics of federalism.

The two federations' case provides ample evidence that central governments often, if not always, perceive economic union reform as an opportunity to increase their own power over the economy or, at the very least, to bind the states or provinces more restrictively to new rules than they would themselves. Recalling the distinction between negative and positive integration, reform to the former aims at extending the economic rights of citizens against governments. Still, such reform can be proposed in terms that privilege a federal government over a province, as shown in the proposed Common Market provisions (a revised section 121) in Canada. Measures for extending positive integration are even more open to charges of centralization such as the proposed new powers over the economy in the Australian constitutional proposals in 1988 and the Canadian counterparts in 1980 and 1991.

In both Australia and Canada, the first, unilateral route to reform remained a live alternative. Central governments can seek to extend unilaterally the scope of both negative and positive integration in a variety of ways, including aggressive challenges of state/provincial legislation and the introduction of their own legislation. The federal government in Canada extended the scope of its competition law through such means in the 1980s. As discussed in chapters 7 and 8, in Australia, the Commonwealth government pursued reform of corporations law and industrial relations in a similar way in the 1980s and 1990s. But such a route to reform entails large risks. It can backfire in the courts (e.g., the Commonwealth's loss in the *Incorporations* case), and it can backfire politically if the states and provinces can rally aggrieved interests under a banner of states rights.

Unilateral approaches to reform are thus risky. They are also rarely comprehensive. For comprehensive reform of the economic union, a joint approach is required. The new market rules had to be comprehensive and consistent if they were to truly form the basis for enhanced national competitiveness. Partial and incremental reform is also politically more difficult to achieve as reform costs are typically too concentrated. Thus, economic unions may be seen as a common property resource in which the same rules must bind everyone; otherwise, the benefits soon diminish. In this respect, the reform of economic unions constitutes a collective action problem in which the incentives to co-operate must be maximized if progress is to be achieved.[2] In Australia and Canada, the state and provincial governments did not have to be convinced of the need for comprehensive reform. They all recognized that economic union reform per se required a comprehensive, all-in approach. However, this consensus was a necessary but not sufficient condition for success. Governments shared similar views about the need for new market rules, but they did not agree on the precise means to achieve them nor the precise form they should take. The devil would be in the details.

Constitutional amendment can be a co-operative route to reform. Indeed, constitutional law is appropriate to the scale and symbolism of economic union regimes. However, constitutional reform in federal systems is notoriously difficult, often by design. One source of the difficulty is the common perception of constitutional politics as a zero-sum contest over power and federal balance. In any case, the constitutional amendment route to economic union reform closed early for Australians. Any proposal would have had to clear the hurdle imposed by the requirement for a double-majority referendum approval; historically Australian voters have rejected any referendum proposal seen as strengthening Commonwealth power at the expense of the states. The Commonwealth government chose wisely not to risk political damage in putting to the people a set of economic union proposals that clearly could have been targeted as overly centralizing.

Canadian constitutional amendment produced some reform of the economic union (e.g., the mobility rights in the *Charter,* 1982), but overall, it also failed as a reform vehicle. At the heart of this failure lies distrust of the ambitions of the other order of government. In Canadian constitutional mega-politics, reform proposals became instruments for symbolic and real conflict between strongly different visions of federalism. Also, outcomes hinged not on the design or policy merits of specific amendment proposals so much as their overall ability to shore up the legitimacy of the federal regime in the face of Quebec's sovereignty option. Canadian economic union reform became a victim of the mega-politics in two senses. First, it became a pawn in the end-game of constitutional negotiations in 1978–82 and 1991–92 in which other priorities prevailed. Second, the nearly thirty-year search for constitutional rebalancing (1964–92) focused Canadian governments' game strategies on the mega-game and thus prevented progress on a "mezzo" game of potential improvement in the institutions of intergovernmental relations. Progress on the latter could have led to more effective agreements concerning the economic union. Only when the constitutional reform game finally ran its course did Canadian governments turn to a non-constitutional solution, such as the Agreement on Internal Trade (AIT).

Thus, we come to the third route: reform by intergovernmental agreement. Both federations had considerable success with this process, and it is worth pointing out a few broad political and procedural prerequisites for that success. First, the agendas adopted for reform were comprehensive and bold in their scope. The AIT agenda in Canada covered the entire economy, exclusions being the exception rather than the rule. The Australian reforms were also broad in sweep, particularly the National Competition Policy (NCP) and mutual recognition. It is also important to note in Australia's case that the agenda set out to cover fiscal relations and program roles and responsibilities. These issues were not essential to a coherent set of new market rules but were important to get the states on board in the first instance.

Such comprehensiveness requires, however, a strong measure of central control and political leadership within each government if sectoral issues and departmental interests are not to delay the process and compromise the results. Australia maintained effective whole-of-government coordination, at least with respect to the economic regulatory agenda, mainly through the bipartisan commitment of first ministers and the effective coordination of their governments through the COAG process. Only when the federal government changed hands in 1996 and the new prime minister stopped using COAG for at least two years did coordination break down. Canada's AIT experience was less successful. First ministers did not devote significant effort to the process, leaving the Committee of Ministers on Internal Trade (CMIT) to do the job without the power to overrule resistance from other groups of ministers such as agriculture or environment. The lack of coordination contributed to a less coherent set of reforms.

The second broad prerequisite for success is that governments adopted a wide variety of devices to achieve their ends, partly to accommodate diverse interests and needs in different policy areas. Governments in both countries adopted four broad categories of mechanisms. First were a variety of consensus-building devices ranging from the talking shops of COAG and the general statements of intent in Australia (e.g., gas and water reform) to the ministerial councils and the dispute settlement process in Canada. Second were various types of intergovernmental agreements, not legally binding on legislatures, but in which governments make definitive commitments in what is essentially a joint policy framework. The entire AIT fits in this category, and as an omnibus agreement, it is itself an additional type of instrument of reform. In Australia, separate agreements cover government borrowing, training, financial institutions, securities, environment, food standards, road transport (among others), and the codes of conduct and competition principles agreements of the NCP. A variant on this instrument is agreement among the states only on a uniform or harmonized approach, such as for non-bank financial institutions in Australia.

A third broad category is mutual recognition. The hallmark of this device is harmonization without central control. Fourth and finally, governments occasionally created a wholly new, single authority to replace concurrent or multiple control. This occurred in Australia with uniform legislation schemes to extend the authority of federal competition legislation to impose uniform road fees and rules and to provide a unified regulatory authority for securities, competition, food standards, and some aspects of environment. By contrast, Canadian governments did not adopt this approach. The AIT is a new set of rules to which all governments agree, but there is no new central regulatory authority and only a co-operative dispute settlement process with non-binding effect. Within the AIT structure, however, there are a variety of consensus-building forums, harmonization processes, and dispute resolution procedures.

The use of a variety of instruments encompassing significantly different types of co-operative action is an obvious strength of the reform process. Some instruments are more or legally entrenched than others, some more or less uniform in the results achieved. Where each federation sits with respect to the balance of instruments employed illustrates differences in federal values and configures the future operation of the system and its capacity for co-operation and competition. This issue is taken up below.

Finally these cases illustrate the life cycle of reform processes: they seem to have a natural birth, maturity, and demise. Changes in political leadership, party agendas, and electoral timetables all intervened to dilute a common commitment to reform. These factors argue for a relatively brief window of opportunity. In Australia's case, this seemed most propitious in Prime Minister Hawke's last term of office in 1990–91 when a large bipartisan consensus on reform emerged. Still, Keating managed to sustain reform momentum after he took over Commonwealth leadership because by then, the states were committed to the key microeconomic reform issues. By early 1995, however, the concentrated effort and enthusiasm faded; the governments achieved little more once the NCP had been settled in April of that year. Many reforms stalled altogether after the 1996 election, which brought a complete change of government in Canberra. Bureaucratic inertia and political fatigue has since taken hold. This does not mean that the new market rules will be reversed, but it does mean that this episode of extending and reforming them has come to an end. In this sense, the Howard government's important GST reforms in 1999–2000 signal a new round, not a completion of the previous one.

In Canada, the time frame between the collapse of the Charlottetown Accord in October 1992 and the Quebec election in September 1994 also provided an opening to reach agreement. Yet the AIT leaves much unfinished business, hostage to the inevitably declining priority of reform. One cannot rule out another round of proposed unilateral federal action or even constitutional reform, but this AIT round is over as well. The conclusion in both cases is that reform movements are not sustainable indefinitely and, in the context of these two federations, have realistic lives that can be measured more in months than years. The prerequisite to success is to recognize this fact and to act and organize accordingly. It is a credit to the political and bureaucratic leadership in both countries that they did so to a reasonably effective extent.

The episodic nature of intergovernmental politics also reflects the constraints imposed by federal systems on intergovernmental co-operation. The political incentives are to deal with separate electoral constituencies and within conflicting political priorities and electoral time frames. To that extent, it fits a pluralist definition of politics in which the actors are rational players who co-operate when and how it suits them – this is Andrew Moravcsik's position with respect to the development of the European Union.[3] But as I have stressed throughout this work, the reforms under way in the two federal systems have the potential to change the conditions for co-operative action in the future, which may permanently alter the incentive structure in which individual government actions are taken. This can take two forms: first, the establishment of new market rules for the economic union, which is very much about constraining and shaping the activities of governments in the federation; and second, new principles for intergovernmental co-decision, which will affect the institutions of intergovernmental relations themselves and the extent to which they can be reformed to improve the capacity for future co-operation. Let us review each of these in turn.

New Market Rules for Economic Union

The evidence of new market rules constituting economic union reform can be assessed in a variety of ways. Here, I begin with a comparative assessment of the specific achievements of reform against the benchmarks that reform advocates set out in the 1980s and the European Union single market reforms. In order to assess the reforms and their impact as a whole, I apply to the three sets of economic union a common framework of economic integration. From these comparisons, I draw conclusions about the emerging nature of federal economic unions as a regime of norms and institutions and the role that economic union regimes now play in federal systems.

In both Australia and Canada, governments have achieved a significant degree of the reform of their economic unions as advocated in the 1980s. In chapter 4, I compared the degree of existing integration in the Australian and Canadian economic unions and the remaining barriers as identified by independent analysts (table 4.1). In that table, I also compared integration in Australia and Canada with the results of the internal market reforms in the EU completed in 1986–92. In later chapters, I assessed the effect of reform on these specific barriers. This is done with respect to Canada in table 5.1 on the effects of international liberalization and table 6.2 on the effects of the AIT. For Canada, one can conclude that of the twelve major barriers analysed (i.e., those on the left-hand column in tables 5.1. and 6.2), all are removed, in whole or in part, by these liberalization agreements. For Australia, I assess the effects of microeconomic reform on major barriers in table 8.4. Here, too, ten of the thirteen main barriers identified have been tackled, mostly with success, by intergovernmental means and two others by more competitive reform programs.

Still, it is difficult to see the forest for the trees just by counting barriers removed. It is useful therefore to focus at greater length on different aspects of the economic union to make some general points. In table 9.1, I return to a comparison across three economic union regimes – Australia, Canada, and the European Union – and present selected examples of aspects of economic union. The categories of integration in this table are drawn from Peter Leslie's five aspects of economic union as discussed in chapter 2 (see table 2.1). The five are:

1 Trade and Investment Union
2 Labour Market Union
3 Foreign Economic Policy Union
4 Monetary Union
5 Structural/Developmental Union

Table 9.1 compares how the 1990s reforms in the two federations and the Maastricht Treaty and other reforms in the EU have supplemented constitutional or treaty provisions for each of these aspects. The reforms in Australia and Canada cover mainly the first two aspects, but it is important to review all of them to see how economic union regimes are evolving.

Table 9.1 Comparing Reformed Economic Unions

ASPECTS OF ECONOMIC UNION	CANADA	AUSTRALIA	EUROPEAN UNION
TRADE AND INVESTMENT UNION • Basic statement of free trade in goods, services, and capital.	• Section 121 (*Constitution Act*, [CA] *1867*) prohibits fiscal barriers to trade in goods. • AIT general rules cover goods, services, and capital.	• Section 92 (*Constitution Act* [CA] *1900*) prohibits fiscal and direct regulatory barriers on all trade.	• Treaty of Rome, 1957 article 3c.
• Harmonization of product and other standards affecting goods and services.	• AIT chapter 8 provides for voluntary mutual recognition.	• Mutual Recognition Agreement (1992) provides for mandatory mutual recognition.	• *Single European Act*, 1987 provides for mandatory mutual recognition.
• Common competition rules.	• Single federal jurisdiction confirmed under trade and commerce power (section 92(1), [CA] 1867).	• National Competition Policy extends federal trade practices law to state jurisdiction; applies contestability, neutral access, and other competition principles to whole economy.	• Common Competition Policy.
• Non-discriminatory government procurement of goods and services.	• AIT chapter 5 prohibits discrimination and establishes a harmonized bid process. GBES not to be ordered to provide preferential purchasing.	• National Preference Agreement (1990) provides non-binding commitment against discrimination (GBES generally exempted).	• Commission directives provide formal non-discrimination of procurement, moving to a harmonized process.

Table 9.1 Comparing Reformed Economic Unions *(Continued)*

ASPECTS OF ECONOMIC UNION	CANADA	AUSTRALIA	EUROPEAN UNION
• Discipline of industrial and agricultural subsidies.	• AIT chapter 6 code disciplines some subsidies (agriculture not included). • AIT chapter 9 commits to review agricultural subsidies in line with WTO commitments.	• Not covered.	• Formal prohibition of subsidies (article 92, Treaty of Rome, 1957). Surveillance of member-state practice.
LABOUR MARKET UNION			
• Basic guarantee of labour mobility.	• Section 6, *Charter of Rights and Freedoms* (CA, 1982) guarantees labour mobility.	• Section 117 (CA, 1900) prohibits certain residency requirements.	• Treaty of Rome, article 3c and 48.1 establishes basic freedom of labour mobility.
• Harmonization of occupational standards.	• AIT chapter 7 provides for voluntary mutual recognition process.	• Mutual Recognition Agreement (1992) covers occupational standards.	• Process of mutual recognition attempts to cover occupational standards.
FOREIGN ECONOMIC POLICY UNION			
• Treaty implementation and consultation.	• Federal treaty power does not extend to implementation in provincial jurisdiction. Consultative mechanisms established.	• Federal treaty power does extend to implementation in state jurisdiction. Consultative mechanisms established (Treaty Council).	• EU treaty-making power rests with Commission, on co-decision by member-states in Council of Ministers.

Table 9.1   Comparing Reformed Economic Unions *(Continued)*

ASPECTS OF ECONOMIC UNION	CANADA	AUSTRALIA	EUROPEAN UNION
MONETARY UNION			
• Currency union and single monetary policy.	• Currency union since 1867; independent central bank since 1934.	• Currency union since 1901; independent central bank since 1959.	• Currency union and independent central bank in place for some member-states.
• Fiscal and budgetary harmonization.	• No formal budgetary harmonization; partial harmonization in income tax and consumption tax fields.	• Agreement on common budget reporting and other procedures; centralized income tax; harmonization in progress for consumption taxes.	• Maastricht Treaty requires high level of budgetary coordination for EMU. Harmonization of value-added tax.
STRUCTURAL/DEVELOPMENTAL UNION			
• Expenditure and regulatory measures to promote common economic infrastructure.	• AIT provides guaranteed access regime for telecoms and other common carriers. Agreement pending on electricity grid access.	• NCP applies to national and state common carriers. • Electricity grid and rail network being upgraded.	• Structural funds for less developed member-state economies.
• Regional redistribution and regional sectoral policies.	• Fiscal equalization; declining regional development programs.	• Fiscal equalization; increasing emphasis on rural/regional programs.	• Regional and sectoral policies; no formal fiscal equalization.

Trade and Investment Union

A trade and investment union entails the free movement of goods, services, and capital. The most powerful form of measures to guarantee these freedoms are constitutional in that they can be enforced by courts on governments and private actors – classic cases of negative integration. Australia and the EU now have the appropriate constitutional guarantees. Indeed, the High Court in *Cole v. Whitfield* has since 1988 reinforced and simplified Australia's section 92 *(Constitution Act, 1900)* as an economic union measure. Canada's failure to upgrade its original Common Market guarantee of section 121 *(Constitution Act, 1867)* can be judged as a continuing disability. The substitute in the form of the general rules of the AIT, while significant in scope and drawing from the best practices of international trade liberalization, depends in the end on political will and not the courts for its enforcement. Canada seems a long way from adopting rules that could lead to the kind of economic litigation witnessed in the European Court of Justice; Australia is closer.

Constitutional guarantees of free trade are not sufficient, however, to sustain a trade and investment union. Recent trends in international trade policy, including intra-EU policy, focus on going deeper with negative integration to prohibit or to discipline anti-competitive practices, discriminatory government procurement, and industrial and agricultural subsidies. On these measures, convergence between the three unions is more evident. On anti-competitive practices, Canada's economic union reforms did not have to address the issue because competition law is a federal jurisdiction, which the Supreme Court's 1989 ruling in *General Motors* confirms as part of the trade and commerce power. Still, the reach of that power does not extend to anti-competitive practices of publicly owned monopolies, as has been achieved by the NCP in Australia. Indeed, Australia's competition policy reforms go well beyond the narrowly and legally defined scope of antitrust law to encompass broadly sweeping forms of negative and positive integration. Perhaps Canada, with its intensive market competition with the United States, does not need to concentrate on forced competitive policy as a form of economic reform. In any case, Australia is closer to the cutting edge in this form of "deeper integration."[4] On the other hand, Canada's reforms focus much more squarely on ending non-discriminatory practices in procurement and disciplining government subsidies. In both these areas, liberalization was led by the FTA or WTO agreement. When combined with the provisions of the

AIT, Canada is ahead of the game in these two fields compared with Australia.

Regulatory harmonization – key to bringing down technical barriers to trade such as multiple product standards and conflicting consumer and environmental protection law – is an area in which the EU's practices have had the greatest exemplary effect. Australia has adopted the EU's mutual recognition process, although thus far, it applies only to trade in goods (and occupational standards, as noted below under labour mobility), not to services. Canada's application of mutual recognition is broader (i.e., to goods and services), but its adoption is limited by being voluntary. In the EU and Australia, mutual recognition is the default result when governments cannot agree on a new set of common standards. In Canada's mutual recognition process in the AIT, the default position is the status quo. The value of mutual recognition is that it preserves diversity and does not force a harmonization process that could only result in lowest common denominator results. In fact, over time, mutual recognition could contribute to an upward harmonization of standards.

Labour Market Union

The next aspect of economic integration is the labour market union. Once again, basic constitutional guarantees of negative integration are the most important sort of provisions that can be adopted. The EU's Treaty of Rome provides such a guarantee, although in the context of language and cultural diversity across the member-states, labour mobility has natural limits. Such guarantees are thus of greater use in the more potentially homogenous labour markets of the two federations. In Canada, labour mobility guarantees were enshrined in section 6 of the *Charter of Rights and Freedoms (Constitution Act, 1982)*. In Australia, section 117 *(Constitution Act, 1900)* provided a similar guarantee, reinforced by the High Court in the 1989 judgment of *Street v. Queensland Bar Association*.

As with trade and investment, negative integration measures for the labour market union are not a sufficient condition. In all three economic unions, governments have recognized the need to harmonize occupational standards if labour is truly to take advantage of employment opportunities throughout the union. The EU is moving slowly, through mutual recognition and other means, to harmonize these standards. In Australia, the mutual recognition agreement incorporates occupational standards. In Canada, chapter 7 of the AIT provides for a comprehensive process by which labour market ministers can achieve harmonization, although implementation has proven difficult. The Social Union Framework Agreement (SUFA) of 1999 also reinforces the commitment to these labour mobility measures.

Foreign Economic Policy Union

The other three aspects of economic union were not the focus of so much explicit reform in the 1990s, but they deserve brief attention. A foreign economic policy union is a form of common policy-making in which the members have created a single voice and actor for the purposes of extra-union economic policy. This is obviously important in the EU context in which a customs union and other aspects of trade policy had to be wrested from strongly developed nation-state members. Canada and Australia have been custom unions since the beginning. Therefore, tariffs on internal trade have always been prohibited. But in an age of non-tariff barriers to international trade, foreign economic policy extends much more deeply into domestic affairs. Non-tariff barriers imposed by the states and provinces become issues of negotiation with trading partners. In this respect, constitutional law is an important factor in comparing the two federations.

In Canada, the federal government can ratify treaties but can implement them only in subjects of federal jurisdiction *(Labour Conventions)*. In Australia, international treaties once ratified by the Commonwealth government may be used to uphold federal law in areas of state jurisdiction (*Tasmanian Dam* case). But having the legal clout is one thing; exercising it is another. In both federations, the central government has recognized the value (in the context of "two-level" games) of consulting the constituent governments on proposed trade agreement measures that would bind them. Australia adopted, as part of the COAG process, a set of consultative rules including a formal Treaty Council. This process is being used to provide state input to the WTO negotiations on government procurement, among other trade issues.[5] In Canada, as discussed in chapter 5, international trade negotiations led the domestic agenda on broader economic union reform, particularly in agriculture, energy, subsidies, and alcoholic beverages. In turn, the provinces entered into extensive consultation with Ottawa over its international trade negotiation position. Thus, the provinces played an important political role in the domestic mobilization of consent for the FTA and other trade agreements.[6] In this respect, the Canadian practice resembles more closely (even if not in a decision-making mode as such) the internal EU mechanisms by which the member-states, through the Council of Ministers, reach consensus on common trade policy.

Monetary Union

A monetary union is another aspect in which the basic features of integration have been in place in the two federations from the beginning. The characteristic tools of monetary union have been transformed since the nineteenth century to go beyond a single currency to include tighter and more uniform regulation of financial markets and the independent role of central banks in monetary policy. It is a matter of some debate whether monetary unions also require fiscal harmonization across the constituent governments of the union, particularly in an era when counter-cyclical macroeconomic policy is discredited.[7]

However, European Monetary Union (EMU) policies in the EU require a convergence of budgetary and interest rate policies preparatory to the introduction of the Euro. It is not clear that this is needed in federations, even though Australia has a strong degree of tax harmonization (further improved by the GST agreement of 1999). Canada's tax harmonization is not as tight – and may be getting looser[8] – but is still significant. The harmonization of regulation for financial institutions and the integration of financial services markets are another desirable, if not essential, part of monetary union. Australia has already achieved this through the co-operative legislative and common regulatory scheme for securities set up in 1990 and by the states through their non-bank financial institution agreements. In Canada, integration is still more limited and was largely excluded from the AIT.

Structural/Developmental Union

The last of Leslie's aspects of economic union is the structural/developmental union. This amounts to joint action or policy on economic development, as illustrated in the EU by the Common Agricultural Policy, other regional and sectoral policies, and by the structural funds for the less developed member-states. In more fully fledged federal states, this aspect of the union takes on a typically broader set of instruments and policies. This includes federation-wide social programs and fiscal relations to achieve redistribution, among other goals. This can be done both horizontally from rich states to poor ones and vertically among income groups by virtue of taxation and expenditure programs. As I have noted at various points in this book, these latter characteristics may be called a "social union."

Economic and social development was not a prime focus of the reforms in Australia and Canada. In Canada, the economic union issue was strongly linked to the concept of a social union in the Canada Round of constitutional debate in a context of anticipated fiscal and program decentralization. When those discussions ended with the demise of the Charlottetown Accord, the negotiations narrowed initially to the economic regulatory agenda only. Canadian governments eventually reached agreement with the SUFA in 1999. Some analysts continue to link economic and social union, and the SUFA did include a commitment to reinforce the AIT provisions for improving labour mobility. The SUFA is, however, a brief and rather general set of guidelines covering a few pages, compared with the much more specific and lengthy AIT agreement. It is too early to tell whether Canadians will adopt a new network of intergovernmental agreements to flesh out the SUFA.

In Australia, fiscal and program decentralization was on the agenda in the early stages, but after 1991, it played only a minor role. Economic development is promoted if one assumes that greater interstate competition will spur new infrastructure such as electricity grids, gas pipelines, and railways. However, Australian fiscal federalism and social program delivery is already considerably more centralized than in Canada. At this stage, therefore, Australia does not need a social union agreement – at least not for the same reasons as does Canada. However, if the entrenching of neo-liberal values by microeconomic reform has the effect of widening regional and social inequalities, the federation may ultimately have to seek ways to shore up its social union.

Finally, and more to the focus of this study, it is telling that the advocates of economic union reform in both federations sought not the extension of the redistributive union, but its constriction. By extending pro-competitive forces and restricting the room for government intervention, the reforms, in fact, reduce much built-in redistribution in economic policies. The consequences for the political balance between efficiency and equity, and diversity and integration, are discussed below.

≈

In summary, these comparative findings underscore the nature of integration in federal economic unions. It is not an all-or-nothing phenomenon; there are many degrees and shadings. The two federations fulfill almost all of the prerequisites for economic integration, significantly covering much ground in all five aspects of economic union, not fully completing the union in only a few respects. Peter Leslie makes the point that integration does not always proceed in a fixed pattern of stages.[9] The recent developments in Australia, Canada, and the EU confirm this. It seems that the more comprehensive the integration across the aspects of union, the more leeway there may be, politically and economically, for deviations in any given aspect. Thus, Canada and Australia, as federations, have both had strong or implied guarantees of freedom of labour mobility and monetary union from the beginning. The resultant contribution to market integration of labour and capital may provide a floor of economic integration on which one may tolerate some degree of deviation in terms of trade in goods and services. Similarly, the existence of a customs union in Canada means that the federation has been able to tolerate more easily the gaps in its foreign policy union (e.g., the inability or hesitancy of federal governments to implement treaties where matters fall under provincial jurisdiction). Conversely, the European Union does not have a well-developed labour market union nor (until very recently) a monetary union. Thus, it has had to fall back with even greater emphasis on its common competition and trade policies and its harmonization of regulatory measures to achieve the benefits of integration that would be gained by other aspects of integration.

One can take two possibly contradictory conclusions from this comparison. First, federal economic unions are indeed more comprehensive than confederal unions such as the EU; all of the hyperbole about the EU being more integrated than these two federal economies is just that. But second, the EU route to integration is different and maybe better in the sense that it is less reliant on fiscal and bureaucratic centralization. The labour and monetary unions of Canada and Australia are more complete than their European counterpart, but international competition has exposed the gaps in other aspects of integration, mainly trade and investment. In these areas – to tackle discriminatory government procurement, subsidies, state-owned monopolies, product standards, environmental regulation, and so on – the European Union's innovative approaches captured the imagination of reformers in Canada and Australia. The two federations did not adopt wholly the "community method" of integration, although the sweeping new sets of rules for negative integration have some parallels, as do devices such as mutual recognition. More significant differences lie in the much more elaborate central machinery in the EU for proposing and legislating directives for integration (the Commission and the Council of Ministers) and for enforcing them (the Court of Justice). This point is strongly demonstrated by the much more limited approach in Australia and Canada toward intergovernmental co-decision, discussed below.

It is more difficult to compare precisely the economic unions of the two older federations. The nature of the deficiencies in their single markets was different, reflecting different positions in the international political economy. Australia faces international integration in a diffused way, without North America's concentrated market competition. To compete internationally, it had to undertake reforms to enforce adjustment in a collusive, heavily interventionist, and regulated economy. Competition is the byword. And a common approach to competition requires a somewhat larger degree of positive integration, which is one reason why Australia's reforms are achieved more by way of centralized regulatory control. In Canada, the terms and instruments of integration were shaped by international trade policy. Free trade is the byword. And while the AIT provides much more by way of positive integration than the FTA and NAFTA, overall, there is more reliance on negative integration than in Australia, avoiding the creation of new centralized regulatory authority.

In both federations, the constitution and underlying federal values place certain limits to what reform can (many would say, *should)* achieve. As covered in the detail of the reforms in chapters 5 to 8 of this book, many holes appear in the new integration measures and their implementation. Some of the rules of negative integration are, in effect, compromises between integration and equity or regional autonomy objectives. Also, the positive integration measures entail processes of harmonization and reconciliation that will take some time to be fully implemented and will provide considerable room for backsliding and diversity. In Canada, the compromises take the form of exceptions and exemptions to the AIT rules and, in the fact, that the AIT is not self-executing or enforceable by the courts. If a government cheats on the rules or drags its feet on its commitments, the other parties can engage in only a non-binding dispute resolution process. The Australian reform agreements, generally backed up with specific legislation, are less easy to give the slip. Also, the creation of powerful new agencies such as the ACCC and NCC leaves less to chance for laggard state implementation. Even so, the governments did leave room for compromise with diverse state interests in the form of flexible reform timetables and other details left to state discretion (seen, for example, in the differing pace and direction of electricity market reforms in NSW, Queensland, and Victoria). And, more recently, the governments have extended some implementation deadlines.

If the nature of the specific problems and their solutions differed, the results in terms of the entrenching neo-liberal values are common. When taken as a whole, there can be no doubt that the economic union reforms in the two federations have changed not only the institutions by which economic integration is achieved, but also the norms – or, more precisely, the objectives to which integration is to be put. Earlier in this work, I stressed that there had been an implied equity bargain and integration/diversity trade-off in the economic unions until the 1980s. The point of balance between the two federations differed, with Australia being more committed to nation building and equity in uniform terms; Canada was more committed to provincial autonomy and equity in regional terms. That difference remains, but the point of balance in both economic unions is now one of greater efficiency and less equity. In Canada, I find that the international trade agreements provided an alternative to constitutional reform in entrenching neo-liberal values as well as continental integration. The AIT copied in domestic form many of the institutional forms and norms of those agreements. The Australian reforms, while diverse in form, achieve similar ends by pushing broad market principles to every corner of the economy.

As Pelkmans, Leslie, and other integration theorists contend, economic integration is as much an ongoing process as it is a static state of affairs. The effect of economic union regimes is not to fix results in the single market so much as to provide a point of equilibrium. Around this point are what Polyani termed "double movements" swinging one way toward social imperatives and another way toward economic ones. Robert Wolfe calls this a "characteristic tension and balance between politics and economics."[10] The new market rules of economic unions thus create a new equilibrium in which efficiency gains are made more possible and imposed equity solutions made more difficult.

As discussed in chapter 4, the design and development of the two federations significantly shapes their intergovernmental relations. In particular, the "working rules" have not been suited to comprehensive joint policy-making, such as required in economic union reform. Here, I return to the significance of the existing rules and then to the attempts in the two federations to deal with them, before reaching conclusions on the consequences for federalism and its adaptation in a world of multi-level governance.

The literature on rational choice and co-operation, as adapted to the working rules of intergovernmental relations, stresses that federal systems need to overcome collective action problems.[11] As Elinor Ostrom contends, "The central question ... is how a group of principals who are in an independent situation can organize and govern themselves to obtain continuing joint benefits when all face temptations to free ride, shirk, or otherwise act opportunistically."[12] Reform of intergovernmental relations itself can be a prerequisite for solving collective action problems by improving the capacity for joint policy-making and co-decision. A prominent benchmark for such reform, especially in the context of the collective action problems of economic union, is the experience of the European Union. Most notable in the EU approach is its "community method," incorporating qualified majority voting rules and the principles of mutual recognition, subsidiarity, and *"acquis communitaire"* (see my discussion in chapter 2).

Yet in the two federations of Australia and Canada, the pathways of historic institutional development remain deeply grooved.[13] Canada's more diverse federal society and coordinate distribution of powers has led to more competitive relations and a stronger emphasis on provincial jurisdictional and fiscal autonomy. These characteristics have been reinforced in recent decades by resurgent Quebec nationalism. Nonetheless, Canadian governments have had extensive experience in consensus building and low intensity collaboration. Institutional development such as First Ministers Conferences, Annual Premiers Conferences, and specialized intergovernmental agencies were arguably well ahead of Australian practice until the 1990s. Yet in comparison with Australia, the incentives to co-operate in the Canadian federal system are harder to find because the provinces have more diverse interests, are less fiscally dependent on the federal government, and have greater policy autonomy under the distribution of powers. On the whole, then, Canadian governments have been less inclined to co-decision. The political culture does not encourage it; intergovernmental processes, while extensive, remain informal; and intergovernmental agreements have little legal clout.

Australia has a more homogenous federal society with a greater nation-building ethos; this is matched with a more concurrent distribution of federal and state powers and a more centralized fiscal federalism. The states have a long history of co-operative schemes with the Commonwealth, including a tightly coordinated, often coercive, system of conditional grants. But until the 1990s, the states did not normally take to the national stage. As in Canada, governments maintain a degree of policy autonomy due to the fused power of the legislature and executive. However, the Commonwealth has overall greater capacity to impose unilateral results. Intergovernmental relations remain largely outside the formal constitution, but one sees signs of a capacity for co-decision emerging in the coordinating and deliberative roles of ministerial councils over the years.

My point is that, even with the differences just described, both federal systems approached the complicated co-operative task of economic union reform with institutions and processes that were better suited to more competitive relations and a more classical form of federalism in which interdependence is at a minimum. For Australia, Canada, and other federal systems, two problems have been especially difficult to resolve.

The first is how to avoid the effect of decision rules of consensus or unanimity that produce slow, lowest common denominator results and empower holdout governments. Institutional change in Canada continues to be limited by the requirement for unanimity in certain constitutional reform contexts (which prevailed in the Canada Round of negotiations, for example). Governments are also deeply suspicious of any move past consensus decision making in ordinary intergovernmental relations. Certainly, they did not get past them in the AIT round. In

Australia, consensus bargaining also dominated the main political forums of the SPCS and COAG. But the governments agreed to ease the decision rule constraints in a variety of specific settings, adopting various types of majority voting rules for some decisions of some ministerial councils.

Enforcement is the second major collective action problem. As discussed in chapter 4, intergovernmental agreements in the two federations are not enforceable in any legal sense unless they are specifically entrenched in statute law or constitutional amendment. In Canada, reforms to improve the capacity to entrench and thus enforce intergovernmental agreements died with the Charlottetown Accord. The AIT, though complex and drafted in legalese, remains a political document. Some legislatures have passed bills to implement the AIT, but no uniform approach has been adopted. This contrasts with Australia's approach to more enforceable commitments. The instrument used most often to achieve this result is joint or uniform legislation; in other cases, it is the establishment of new regulatory agencies that also require uniform legislation. However, governments in both Canada and Australia rely increasingly on monitoring and information exchange to provide more informal, political enforcement of their agreements. Such devices are prominent in the reporting requirements and dispute resolution mechanism of the AIT and in the performance benchmarking agreements and NCP legislative review in Australia.[14]

Apart from the institutional issues of decision rules and enforcement, certain other procedural practices contribute to an improved capacity for joint policy-making and co-decision. In the first part of these conclusions, I summarized practices that were important to the success of the economic reform episodes in the two countries. These include the adoption of a comprehensive agenda (at least with respect to coverage of the economy), whole-of-government coordination and central control within each government in the negotiations, and a broad tool kit of co-operative instruments.

The use of a diverse set of instruments is important as a negotiation tactic of trying multiple paths to the same end. It is also important to the politics of federalism. Reform would have been neither successful nor feasible if all the devices had led to uniform results across the federation or if regulatory authority over each sector had been centralized. Both federations achieved economic union reform, in part, through *non-centralizing* means. These are: negative integration through the adoption of new rules applicable to both orders of government; mutual recognition agreements; and state/provincial-only harmonization. These methods establish new market rules without upsetting the federal balance. Such characteristics of reform proved especially important in Canada. The provinces have long distrusted federal advocacy of economic union reform as a "power grab" in disguise. So long as reform stays out of the realm of creating enhanced central authority, strongly autonomist governments such as Alberta and Quebec can support it.

These considerations lead to the notion of *national* policy-making. In Australia, state leaders and several commentators have hailed the COAG and related processes as signalling a new era in which the national interest is defined not by the Commonwealth government and parliament alone, but in partnership with the states. The new processes brought state and territorial governments to the national stage, engaging them on more than just local issues. In this respect, a partnering role in national policy-making is seen as a trade-off for reduced state flexibility through tighter coordination. It is analogous to the pooling of sovereignty in the EU. Thus, for example, even in those instruments of reform that create new centralized regulatory agencies, national policy is partly co-determined by ministerial councils. Yet the new ethos is only partial. Both sides continue to resort to competitive or domineering modes. National policy-making is also crucially contingent on federal political leadership.

The notion of national policy-making remains contentious and partial in Canada as well. The term "national" has different meanings inside and outside Quebec, but even sanitized as "federation-wide," the notion of joint federal-provincial determination of the national interest has clear limits. Ironically, the idea has longer roots than in Australia. These are in the role played by provincial premiers on national issues since at least the mid-1960s, partly to compensate for an inadequate degree of regional representation in federal institutions. Interprovincial consensus building and the development of "national" policy-making without the federal government are also practised, although largely as a prelude to federal-provincial negotiation. However, on the whole, the issue of co-determination of national interest has been contested, particularly in the constitutional mega-politics of the past thirty years. Strongly entrenched and defensive provincial autonomy, especially in Quebec but also elsewhere, leads the provinces to shrink from national policy-making that entails binding decision processes. Even the federal government has seldom appeared enthusiastic about such reform. As shown in chapters 5 and 6 on the Canadian process, Ottawa remains conflicted between its desire for more central coordination of the economic union and the risk to national unity if it were to use all of its power to get it. Just as in the provinces, most policy-makers in Ottawa prefer independence of movement to national (i.e., intergovernmental) policy-making.

In summary, the efforts of governments in the Australian and Canadian federal systems to overcome collective action problems in order to reform their economic unions point to a new set of requirements for effective intergovernmental co-decision. These requirements are:

1 the selective use of majority voting so that policy decisions can be made more quickly and more substantively
2 improvement of enforcement mechanisms to make commitments legally enforceable or to increase the political costs of cheating
3 harmonization of policy through non-centralized policy instruments (e.g., mutual recognition)
4 consensus-building institutions based on the norm that national policy-making means joint federal-state/provincial collaboration

These principles could be drawn from federal theory as a priori features of an effective intergovernmental decision-making process. What is significant is that they may now be seen in actual federal practice in the EU, Australia, Canada, and possibly elsewhere. The EU is obviously at the leading edge of "best practice" of effective intergovernmental co-decision because it has no choice. It has no central government as such and does not appear to want one; but obviously, its member-states have built federal-type institutions with a strong capacity for co-decision. In more classic federal systems, the need for adjustment to global and regional integration brought to the fore the issue of the capacity for co-decision. In our two-federation case and very likely in many other federal systems, the task of multi-level governance and managing interdependence (discussed more fully below) is a concurrent one in which co-decision is increasingly required. Of the two, Australia has gone further in the development of the four requirements just listed. But it is by no means a foregone conclusion that all the requirements will be met in any comprehensive way in the near future. Canada lags behind even in the adoption of the machinery, but some elements of the norms underlying the required institutions are in place.

To explain why the adoption of effective intergovernmental co-decision is so hesitant and episodic in the two federations, one must return to the broader context of their federal institutions and values. Recall the typology of intergovernmental relations introduced in chapter 3 (see table 3.1) and applied to the pre-reform stage in chapter 4. In that typology, I contend that relationships in federal systems cover three types: competition, co-operation, and rationalization. During this century, intergovernmental relations in most federations tended to the co-operative mode, but since the 1970s, federal theory and practice have tried to break out of the collusive and overlapping web of co-operative federalism into either more competitive or more rationalized relations.

As noted throughout this work, Australian federalism is predisposed to the co-operative and rationalist modes. Many of the economic union reform advocates saw solutions in rationalist terms – i.e., to create a consolidated, single legal authority over key parts of the reform agenda. They succeeded in part. A rationalized approach is achieved in the creation of a single securities regime; consolidation of Commonwealth regulation of trade practices under the ACCC; and the establishment of new national agencies for food standards, road transport, training, and environment. But against this result, one must balance the continuing presence of reform agendas outside even a co-operative framework, such as the competitive approach to industrial relations. And as Martin Painter points out, a certain amount of backsliding on commitments and avoidance of rationalized machinery seems to have taken place in areas such as road transport and rail. Much of the rest of the reform initiatives fit most comfortably in the co-operation type. These include mutual recognition, the NCP codes of conduct, the role of ministerial councils, and the COAG process itself. It remains to be seen if, overall, these co-operative reforms will edge Australia into a form of "joint decision trap."[15] Given the present federal government's reluctance to use the co-operative machinery in any comprehensive way, a broad joint decision trap seems unlikely in the short term.

Canada has avoided altogether centralized, rationalist solutions to economic union reform. This is not surprising given the more firmly competitive style of Canadian federalism, even if many reform advocates would clearly have preferred greater central control. Instead, the AIT emphasizes negative integration through rules applicable to all governments and positive integration through voluntary harmonized initiatives overseen by weak institutional machinery. As noted above, these results do ensure that the federal balance itself is unchanged. However, the price is a stronger upfront commitment to common rules that entrench economic liberal values. One may continue to see individual governments cheating at the margins of the AIT or resisting excessively uniform measures in the harmonization process. Nonetheless, what is striking is the degree of convergence in economic policy expressed in the AIT. This convergence is especially noteworthy in view of the considerable conflict and competition in economic policy in the 1960s to 1980s. Voluntary co-operation has its clear limits in Canada, shown in the many loopholes and weak enforcement of the AIT, but one could hardly claim that it does not work at all. Indeed, one has to admit that within an admittedly strong competitive federal political culture, these reforms show that Canada is indeed capable of pursuing co-operative-type relations, and in the field of economic policy, is much more capable than in the recent past.

In both systems, then, federalism is alive and well. Economic rationalists have not successfully imposed centralizing solutions, at least not comprehensively. Governments are highly constrained by the path dependencies of the existing federal systems so that their responses to economic union issues continue to be bound by their differing institutional design and values.

FEDERALISM AND GLOBALIZATION

In this book, I have been undertaking what amounts to a comparative case study of the ability of federal systems of government to adapt in an era of globalization. The facets of globalization that have been examined are global and regional economic integration and accompanying economic liberalization. Globalization can also bring disintegration pressures, especially in the context of competing national and other identities within federal societies, but that is a subject for another study, not this one.[16] Rather, my task has been to see how and whether federations have made the economic policy adaptation and what that adaptation implies for the future of federal values. This study also is a test, if a partial one, of whether federal states are "strong" or "weak" as nation-states in the face of globalization.[17] I have taken economic union reform as a demonstration of the capacity of state institutions to successfully adapt to external economic, social, and political forces.

The critics of economic globalization, microeconomic reform, and/or free trade might argue at this stage that I have missed the point entirely.[18] It is not what the new market rules do to the finely tuned balance in federal systems or to how governments interact now and in the future that matters. What matters to them is that governments at all levels have given over their sovereignty to the market. As I have argued above, the new economic union rules in Australia and Canada do go a long way to extending and redefining economic integration to reduce the scope for equity and increase the emphasis on efficiency.

But I think it remains vital to federal societies that market rules, even if they are homogenizing of broad principles of economic policy, do not do so in centralizing terms. The new market rules remove some of the traditional brakes on the concentration of wealth and power that federalism is partly designed to disperse. Such concentration would be more severe if the market rules were achieved through an increase in federal legislative power as well. If there remains some room for local flexibility in the market rules, then there also remains room for greater or less emphasis on equity as local conditions and preferences require. Also, in the context of regionally differentiated economic structure, a more decentralized response is also likely a more efficient response. Thus, the extent to which economic union can be regulated by the non-centralized solutions of negative integration, mutual recognition, and national co-decision, so much the better.

Indeed, based on the evidence in Australia, Canada, and the European Union, federal systems can not only adapt well to the external policy requirements of globalization, but they can also preserve federal values while doing so. For federal systems encompassing a large and regionally diverse economic space – which is certainly the case for the two examined here – federalism is an essential aspect of effective economic adaptation. A rationalized set of uniform market rules covering all aspects of economic integration would be economically counterproductive in view of the regional economic diversity and politically dysfunctional, if not illegitimate, in view of the diverse federal society.

Federal values are sustained, in large part, by the ongoing process of decision making in a federal state. The experience of Australia and Canada to reform their economic unions provides a strong demonstration of this point. The governments collectively had three broad routes to reform: unilateral actions, constitutional amendment, and intergovernmental co-operation. Choice of one option for part of the reform agenda could leave room for alternative means to achieve other reforms and, as shown here, this is partly what took place in Australia and Canada. Unilateral actions remain attractive for all political leaders and their bureaucracies because they are simpler, more easily achieved, and respond more directly to citizen and voter demands. But apart from engendering inevitable conflict in a policy field as resolutely concurrent as the economic union, unilateral actions are also not comprehensive enough to deal with the task at hand. The governments in Australia and Canada recognized that. The second option of constitutional reform is thus also attractive for governments – and perhaps even more so for citizens and private actors in the marketplace – because it could establish comprehensive rules binding on the entire federation and its governments and protect economic citizenship. In symbolic terms, constitutions are especially appropriate vehicles for certain types of economic union guarantees, such as mobility rights. Yet constitutional reform inevitably places a strong role for continuing interpretation of policy in the courts, which, in the current political culture in both these federations, is a liability. And once made, constitutional provisions are very difficult to change. This difficulty is partly by design in governmental systems and has been demonstrated forcefully in Australian and Canadian experience. Ultimately, constitutional reform of the economic union became too hard to achieve.

This left the third option of ongoing intergovernmental co-operation. It has the virtue, born of necessity, of providing more easily attained goals than constitutional reform. However, governments in Australia and Canada deliberately chose intergovernmental co-operation because of the more coordinated, and therefore potentially more comprehensive, policy outcomes that could be achieved. They recognized that intergovernmental relations could achieve flexible rules and implementation schedules using a variety of policy techniques, including non-centralizing devices. While they sought new economic union regimes to last for some time, they produced results that could be more easily adapted in the future than could constitutional provisions. In sum, the recent Australian and Canadian experience demonstrates that intergovernmental co-operation is the best means to achieve economic union reform in these federal states, a conclusion that may stand for many other, if not all, federal systems.

More important, the method of intergovernmental collaboration establishes an important pattern of effective policy-making in an area of policy crucial to the federal state's response to globalization. If market integration continues its rapid growth, regional and global economic liberalization and political integration will follow. The European Union has been a harbinger of how nation-state economies can be integrated and how member-state governments of a federal-type union can co-operate to achieve that integration. Moreover, as international organizations across a wide range of policy fields seek greater functional integration to deal with the effects of global problems, all nation-states must enter into a future of multi-level governance. This is precisely what these federal states have been doing. Federal states (some more than others) have long experience with the kinds of multi-level politics and intergovernmental collaboration that multi-level governance implies. Rather than hindering the capacity of federal states to respond to global and regional integration, federal intergovernmental relations may become a comparative advantage for them among nation-states.

In conclusion, federalism can survive globalization. Yet that survival hinges on the ability of individual federal systems to adapt to economic and political integration in two vital aspects: the rules for their internal market or economic union, and their ongoing capacity for intergovernmental co-decision. Without upgraded economic unions, federated economies can have little hope to make a successful adaptation to wider regional and global economic integration. This task requires, however, a sophisticated capacity for intergovernmental co-decision, one which will equip federal systems for other multi-level governance tasks in the arena of global interdependence.

The new market rules in place in Australia and Canada have addressed, as summarized earlier in this concluding chapter, almost all of the significant barriers to trade and competition in the federated economic space. The resulting economic union regime (which includes elements that did not need to be reformed) gives now each of these two federations a broader and deeper degree of national economic integration than even the EU, which had been a model for reformers throughout the process. The new market rules do entrench neo-liberal principles and thus shift the equilibrium toward efficiency and away from equity, but they leave room for diversity and flexibility.

Australia and Canada have also demonstrated an improving capacity for intergovernmental co-decision. Australia is ahead of the game, nonetheless, in applying principles for effective intergovernmental policy-making that include the selective use of majority decision rules, improved enforcement, non-centralized harmonization processes, and institutions for national consensus building. Canada's intergovernmental relations are evolving more slowly.

Therefore, more than just surviving, federal states can be "strong" states in an era of globalization. As we enter the twenty-first century, governments in federal systems will still be autonomous actors but within a developing system of multi-level governance in which the capacity for intergovernmental co-decision will constitute a strong comparative advantage. Despite the many caveats inherent in the flawed reform outcomes and waning appetite for reform in Australia and Canada, these two federations have met the test of reform of their economic unions through intergovernmental means. This augers well for their future adaptability to the emerging conditions of economic globalization, even more so if they can continue to build toward the requirements of effective intergovernmental policy-making.

Appendix 1

Australia

1 Rationale and genesis of reform:
   - How did the process start?
   - How important is intergovernmental reform to overall economic reform?

2 Role of your government in the reform process:
   - What is the nature of overall commitment in your government (leader or laggard)?
   - How did you achieve internal coordination? Successful or not?
   - What are your priorities for reform?

3 Assessment of the reform process:
   - What were the most important process innovations?
   - Is the new process sustainable?

4 Assessment of substantive policy changes:
   - What are the major successes and failures and why?

5 Consequences for the federal system:
   - How do the reforms change the role of the states?
   - What effect do the reforms have on overall system openness and accountability?
   - What has been the impact on governmental innovation and competition?

6 Current Status:
   - How has the change of federal government in 1996 affected the

reform movement and its implementation?
- What is the continuing agenda for reform?

CANADA

For participants in Canada Round of constitutional negotiations:

1 What role did economic union reform play in the Canada Round?

2 What were your government's negotiation priorities for the round, and how did economic union fit into those priorities?

3 (To provinces): What was your reaction to the federal government's September 1991 reform proposals and why? (To federal government): What were your goals with respect to the proposals, and why did they take the shape they did?

4 Why did economic union issues get minimized in the final Charlottetown Accord, and what were the negotiation dynamics leading to that result?

Regarding Agreement on Internal Trade (AIT):

1 Rationale for the AIT:
   - What is your assessment of the economic importance of the trade barriers issue?
   - What is your specific business and other interest group advocacy?
   - Is provincial autonomy/ regional difference still important?

2 Negotiation of the AIT:
   - What is your government's negotiation position? Priorities? Deal breakers?
   - What is your specific position on the proposed form (architecture) of the AIT?
   - What is the nature of intra-government coordination of position? Is it successful or not?
   - What is the nature of institutional/negotiation "rules"? Can inter-governmental decision making be improved?

3 Assessment of the AIT:
   - According to your views on scope and coverage, what is left out and why?
   - Are the institutions of AIT effective?
   - What is the legal and political impact of the nature of agreement?

4 Implementation of the AIT:
   - What are the key issues for your government in the implementation process?
   - Is continuing negotiation a problem/necessity?
   - Are AIT institutions/dispute resolution mechanisms working?
   - Is AIT an ongoing priority of your government?
   - What is your linkage to international trade issues/policy?

Appendix 2

AUSTRALIA

Deputy secretary, Department of Premier and Cabinet, Government of Queensland, Brisbane, January 1997.

Former deputy secretary, Department of Premier and Cabinet, Government of Queensland, Brisbane, January 1997.

Professor Glynn Davis, School of Politics and Public Policy, Griffith University (formerly Department of Premier and Cabinet, Government of Queensland) Brisbane, January 1997.

Dr John Wanna, School of Politics and Public Policy, Griffith University, Brisbane, January 1997.

Former senior official, Department of Premier and Cabinet, Government of Queensland, Brisbane, January 1997.

Professor Kenneth Wiltshire, University of Queensland, Brisbane, January 1997.

Senior official, Business Council of Australia (formerly Department of Premier and Cabinet, Government of Victoria), Melbourne, March 1997.

Senior official, Department of Premier and Cabinet, Government of Victoria, Melbourne, March 1997.

---

* Interviewees names are not provided for current and former government officials, according to understandings reached with each interviewee.

Former secretary, Department of Prime Minister and Cabinet, Commonwealth government, Canberra, March 1997.

Robert Lim, Business Council of Australia, Canberra, March 1997.

Glenn Withers, Graduate School of Public Policy, Australian National University, Canberra, March 1997.

Assistant secretary, Department of the Treasury, Commonwealth government, Canberra, March 1997.

Deputy secretary and other senior official, Department of Prime Minister and Cabinet, Commonwealth government, Canberra, March 1997.

Assistant secretary and other senior official, Environment and Energy Branch, Department of Prime Minister and Cabinet, Commonwealth government, Canberra, March 1997.

Director and senior analyst, Intergovernmental and Financial Policy, Department of Treasury and Finance, Government of Tasmania, Hobart, April 1997.

Former secretary, Department of Premier and Cabinet, Government of Tasmania, Hobart, April 1997.

Senior officials, Policy Division, Department of Premier and Cabinet, Government of Tasmania, Hobart, April 1997.

Director general, Department of Premier and Cabinet, Government of New South Wales, Sydney, May 1997.

Gary Sturgess, consultant and former director general, Department of Premier and Cabinet, Government of New South Wales, Sydney, May 1997.

Senior official, Cabinet Office, Department of Premier and Cabinet, Government of New South Wales, Sydney, May 1997.

Ken Baxter, KPMG consulting and former director general, Department of Premier and Cabinet, Government of Victoria, Sydney, May 1997.

Assistant secretary, Department of the Treasury, Government of New South Wales, Sydney, May 1997.

Former senior official, Department of Premier and Cabinet, Government of Victoria, Melbourne, June 1997.

CANADA

Senior official, Internal Trade Division, Department of Industry, Science, and Technology, Government of Canada, Ottawa, October 1997.

Director, Policy and Research, Intergovernmental Affairs, Privy Council Office, Government of Canada, Ottawa, October 1997.

Former chief negotiator for AIT, Government of Newfoundland and Labrador, St. John's, October 1997.

Internal trade representative/trade policy advisor, Department of Industry, Trade, and Technology, Government of Newfoundland and Labrador, St. John's, October 1997.

Senior officials, Department of Mines and Energy, Government of Newfoundland and Labrador, St. John's, October 1997.

Deputy minister, Department of Economic Development, Government of New Brunswick, Fredericton, October 1997.

Internal trade representative, Department of Economic Development, Government of New Brunswick, Fredericton, October 1997.

Former chief negotiator and alternate chief negotiator for AIT, Government of New Brunswick, Fredericton, October 1997.

Assistant deputy minister, Department of Intergovernmental and Aboriginal Affairs, Government of New Brunswick, Fredericton, October 1997.

Former director general, Internal Trade Secretariat, Department of Industry, Science, and Technology, Government of Canada, Ottawa, December 1997.

Former deputy minister, Department of Justice, and constitutional advisor to Government of Canada 1990–92, Ottawa, December 1997.

Senator Michael Kirby, Senate of Canada, and former secretary, Federal-Provincial Relations Office, Government of Canada, Ottawa, December 1997.

Senior officials, Internal Trade Division, Department of Industry, Science, and Technology, Government of Canada, Ottawa, December 1997.

Tim Reid, president, Canadian Chamber of Commerce, Ottawa, December 1997.

Former director, Intergovernmental Affairs, Privy Council Office, Government of Canada, Ottawa, December 1997.

Assistant deputy minister, Ministry of Intergovernmental Affairs, Government of Ontario, Toronto, February 1998.

Assistant deputy minister, Strategic Policy, Ministry of Economic Development, Trade and Tourism, Government of Ontario, Toronto, February 1998.

Director and other senior official, Trade Policy Branch, Ministry of Economic Development, Trade and Tourism, Government of Ontario, Toronto, February 1998.

Former deputy minister, Ministry of Intergovernmental Affairs, Government of Ontario, Toronto, February 1998.

Former chief negotiator for AIT, Government of British Columbia, Victoria, March 1998.

Assistant deputy minister and other senior officials, Intergovernmental Relations Secretariat, Government of British Columbia, Victoria, March 1998.

Director, International Branch, Ministry of Employment and Investment, Government of British Columbia, Victoria, March 1998.

Former chief negotiator for the AIT, Government of British Columbia, Victoria, March 1998.

Former assistant chief negotiator for AIT/assistant deputy minister, Department of Intergovernmental and Aboriginal Affairs, Government of Alberta, Edmonton, March 1998.

Internal trade representative/director, Internal Trade, Department of Intergovernmental and Aboriginal Affairs, Government of Alberta, Edmonton, March 1998.

Senior official, Constitutional Affairs, Department of Intergovernmental and Aboriginal Affairs, Government of Alberta, Edmonton, March 1998.

Executive director, Federal-Provincial Relations, Executive Council, Government of Manitoba, Winnipeg, March 1998.

Executive director, Internal Trade Secretariat, Winnipeg, March 1998.

Secrétaire général associé, Secrétariat aux affaires intergouvernementales canadiennes, Gouvernement du Québec, Quebec, October 1998.

Secrétaire général adjoint and other senior official, Direction de commerce intérieur et des politiques hors Québec, Secrétariat aux affaires intergouvernementales canadiennes, Gouvernement du Québec, Quebec, October 1998.

Conseiller en affaires internationales, Ministère de l'Industrie, du Commerce, de la Science, et de la Technologie, Gouvernement du Québec, Quebec, October 1998.

Notes

CHAPTER 1: FEDERALISM, GLOBALIZATION, AND
ECONOMIC POLICY-MAKING

1 Wheare, 1963.
2 The competitive aspects of federalism are discussed in chapter 3. For a statement of the normative position, see Breton, 1985 and Ostrom, 1987.
3 The most often-cited such critique is that of Laski, 1939.
4 For discussion of pluralist and Marxist society-centred perspectives, see Alford and Friedland, 1985; Held, 1984; and Head and Bell, 1994.
5 See Skocpol, [1985] 1992: 461.
6 For an overview of the literature, see Wilks and Wright (eds.), 1987, citing, among others, Katzenstein (ed.) 1978; Dyson, 1980; Badie and Birnbaum, 1983; Krasner, 1978.
7 Peter Hall, 1986: chapter 1.
8 Andrew Gamble, 1988 and 1995.
9 Thelen and Steinmo, 1992: 27.
10 For example, Mancur Olson, 1965.
11 Cairns, 1986: 55.
12 Ibid.
13 Atkinson and Coleman, 1989: 189.
14 Davis, 1978.
15 For example, Livingston, 1967.
16 Watts, 1999: 1.
17 Bakvis and Chandler, 1987b: 5–9.
18 Przeworski and Teune, 1982 [1970]: chapter 2.
19 In Australia, this included, apart from the Commonwealth government, the state governments of Victoria, New South Wales, Queensland, and Tasmania. In Canada, apart from individuals in the federal government, I interviewed officials in Newfoundland, New Brunswick, Quebec, Ontario, Manitoba, Alberta, and British Columbia.

CHAPTER 2: GLOBALIZATION, LIBERALIZATION, AND INTEGRATION

1 This description has been influenced, among others, by Drucker, 1986; Ohmae, 1990; Nymark, 1991; Cable, 1995; and Bell, 1997.

2 Cf. Strange, 1994.

3 For a discussion of the concept of hegemony in international relations literature, see Keohane, 1984; Gilpin, 1987; Strange, 1994; and Leslie, 1996a. On Asia-Pacific, see Camilleri, 1995.

4 Hirst and Thompson, 1995.

5 On consumer sovereignty, see Ohmae, 1990; on the importance of liberalization to liberty, see the discussion in Head and Bell, 1994: 37-9, citing Milton Friedman.

6 For a survey of recent literature, see Hirst and Thompson, 1995.

7 Cable, 1995: 38.

8 Leslie, 1996a: 194.

9 Pentland, 1973.

10 Pelkmans, 1997: 2-3.

11 Balassa, 1961.

12 Leslie, 1998: 5.

13 Scharpf, 1996:15; cf. Tinbergen, 1965.

14 Pelkmans, 1997: 6; Leslie, 1998: 5.

15 Saunders, 1994a: xii.

16 The term "European Union" has been in use only since the ratification of the Maastricht Treaty in 1992; the union encompasses, but does not supersede, the European Community. The latter term, in turn, encompasses the European Economic Community founded by the Treaty of Rome in 1958, the Euratom of 1957, and the European Coal and Steel Community of 1951. In this book, I generally use the term European Union.

17 Confederal unions have traditionally been formed by treaty among formally sovereign countries in which common institutions have delegated powers only. The European Union, as it has evolved, is more of a hybrid between a confederal and a federal union (Cf. Forsyth, 1981).

18 Leslie 1996b: 9. For the reform rationale from the European Community perspective, see the 1985 White Paper, "Completing the Internal Market" [Commission of the European Communities (CEC), 1985]. On the specifically economic rationale, see Cecchini et al., 1988.

19 In the EU, qualified majority voting (QMV) is a decision rule whereby the Council of Ministers may approve a measure binding on all members by

using a special majority (almost three-quarters) consisting of votes cast by each member according to a weighted system whereby the more populous members receive more votes within a range. The only other decision rule is unanimity. QMV applies to most categories of decisions before the council, in particular most matters related to the internal market.

20 Tsoukalis, 1997: 261.

21 Leslie, 1996b: 20-1. See also Scharpf, 1996; Hall, 1986.

22 According to Pelkmans, 1997: 25, *acquis communitaire* is "Euro-jargon for the accomplishments of the EC thus far. This provision pre-empts retrogression. It is vital for mutual trust among member-states and for business confidence in the stability of the internal market rules."

23 Pelkmans, 1997: chapter 4. *Minimum approximation* refers to EU regulation issued by commission directive whereby essential regulatory requirements are established. Member-states are free to regulate at a higher level. It applies to technical standards for goods as well as to some services such as financial services. *Mutual recognition* is a process whereby member-states accept the regulatory regime of other member-states as equivalent to their own for the purposes of allowing trade in goods, services, and labour. The Court of Justice introduced and has enforced the principle. The long-term effect is to eliminate excess regulation.

24 I am indebted to Peter Leslie for pointing out the significance of the work of these two authors. For his written commentary, see Leslie, 1996a.

25 Moravscik, 1993; cf. Leslie 1996a: 200–1.

26 Moravscik, 1993: 507–17.

27 Pierson, 1996.

28 Ibid.: 126.

29 Ibid.: 158–9.

30 This is not to argue that Canada's "natural" economic development is necessarily north-south. See Creighton, 1937.

31 For one of the original characterizations of the Anglo-American versus continental European forms of capitalism, see Dyson, 1980. For a review of recent literature, see Wilks and Wright, 1987; see also Hall, 1986. The distinction has also been made between Anglo-American capitalism and Asian market economies. See the discussion in Bell, 1997: chapter 11, citing, among others, Thurow, 1992; Weiss and Hobson, 1995.

32 Hancock, [1930] 1961.

33 On the limits of corporatism in Canada, see Atkinson and Coleman, 1989; Panitch, 1979; 1986. Within the context of Canadian federalism, see Chandler and Bakvis, 1989: 70–1. On the role of Crown corporations, see

Laux and Molot, 1988.

34 See Cooper, Higgott, and Nossal, 1993.

35 Drucker, 1986.

36 For an insightful discussion of the impact of economic globalization on Australia and Canada, see Courchene, 1993 and 1996a. See also the brief discussions provided by Molot, 1994 and Higgott 1994.

37 See Kelly, 1994: 1–16; cf. Capling and Galligan, 1992: chapter 3; Bell, 1997: chapter 3.

38 At the completion of the Tokyo Round of tariff cuts in the mid-1980s, Australia's effective protection across manufactured products remained 25 per cent on average, compared to 8 per cent for Canada (IAC, 1983; ECC, 1988).

39 *Economist*, 17 March, 1984; cf. Kelly, 1994: 13–14.

40 At a declaration at Bogor in November 1994, APEC members committed themselves to a goal of "free trade" by 2010 for its industrialized members and 2020 for its developing members, as well as on a sort of standstill agreement on new protection. For a summary of what APEC has achieved and Australia's role in its formation, see Cooper, Higgott, and Nossal, 1993: chapter 4; and Ravenhill, 1997. Apart from the long-term commitment to trade liberalization among its members just noted, the most important achievements appear to have been: (1) to provide a broad regional stance on the multilateral trade negotiations (Uruguay Round) which appeared stalled when APEC was first formed in 1989; (2) to pursue a functional work program of practical co-operation in the areas of trade promotion, human resource development, telecommunication, tourism, fisheries, and energy; and (3) to exchange information on the respective economies and economic and financial policies of its members. As Cooper, Higgott, and Nossal indicate, Australia at least had hoped to model APEC somewhat along OECD lines but has been unable to achieve even that modest level of institutional support.

41 The absurdity of the "regional" nature of APEC was driven home to me in 1997 when Canada, as the host country for the year, convened a ministerial meeting in St. John's, Newfoundland, a city closer to Europe than it is to the Pacific, let alone Asia. For a critical view of APEC and Australia's role, see FitzGerald, 1997: 13–15. A more standard advocacy is provided in Garnaut, 1989. See also Cooper, Higgott, and Nossal, 1993: 98–105.

42 This discussion is drawn in part from Brown and Leslie, 1994. For other interpretations, see the orthodox economic history perspective of Aitken (1978 [1959]) and Innis and Easterbrook (1962). And for a more contemporary IPE approach, see Eden and Molot, 1993.

43 For more on the significance of this form of industrial relations and its reform to the Australian economy, see Bell, 1997: chapter 8.

44 Following the short-lived Reciprocity Treaty between the United States and the BNA provinces in 1854–66, there were unsuccessful attempts to renew free trade in 1874, 1911, and 1948–9. See Leyton-Brown, 1994.

CHAPTER 3: FEDERALISM, ECONOMIC UNIONS, AND INTERGOVERNMENTAL POLICY-MAKING

1 For essential differences between American capitalism and that practised in Canada and Australia, see Chandler and Bakvis, 1989: 70–1. On Thatcher's use of the strong state, see Gamble, 1988.

2 For a pessimistic assessment of the current possibilities of an industrial strategy, see Lang and Hines, 1993. For a more positive view, see Porter, 1990. On France, see Hall, 1986. On Sweden, see Milner, 1989.

3 For an excellent set of papers on this theme from a mainstream Canadian policy economics perspective, see Courchene and Purvis (eds.), 1993, especially Harris and Watson's essay, "Three Visions of Competitiveness: Porter, Reich and Thurow on Economic Growth and Policy." For Australia, see Garnaut, 1989; Dyster and Meredith, 1990; Marsh, 1995: chapter 6.

4 For an overview, see Jones, 1994; cf. Bell, 1997, chapter 6.

5 OECD, 1987: 34–47.

6 Gamble, 1988.

7 Courchene, 1993: 67.

8 Boeckleman, 1996; Deeg, 1996.

9 For a more radical perspective in which neo-liberal globalization threatens the room of subnational governments more generally, see Robinson, 1995.

10 Hirst and Thompson, 1995; Saunders, 1994a.

11 Cameron and Simeon, 1999:4. Cf. Marks et al., 1996; Pennock, 1959.

12 Saunders, 1995.

13 See Putnam, 1988; Higgott, 1991.

14 For surveys of the terms of federal economic unions, see Hayes, 1982; Bernier et al., 1986.

15 I draw these categories as elements of "regimes" from the discussion in Wolfe, 1998: 26–35.

16 The term "national" is adopted here to coincide with the sense of nation-state. It is a problematic term in Canada due to the multinational character of the federation and the widespread tendency in Quebec to refer to Quebec institutions as "national" and Canadian institutions as "federal."

Outside Quebec, the term "national" is more commonly used to refer to a Canada-wide context. This terminology problem does not occur in Australia. Elsewhere in this work, I generally use the term "federal" to refer to an institution that is Canada-wide or Australia-wide in scope.

17 ECC, 1991: 31–3. These sorts of benefits also apply to federations created from unitary states but would obviously not be among the reasons for adopting a federal form of government in the first place.

18 Maxwell and Pestieau, 1980: 15.

19 These issues are pursued in Canada, 1980: chapter 1; Canada 1985: 111–14; Cairns, 1986; Howse, 1992.

20 Cf. Polyani, 1944; Wolfe, 1998.

21 There has been considerable discussion of the nature of this trade-off in Canada. See Safarian, 1974; Maxwell and Pestieau, 1980; Prichard, 1983; Canada, 1985; ECC, 1991. On equity issues in particular, see Boadway and Flatters, 1982 and Leslie, 1996a.

22 See Biggs, 1996 and Cameron (ed.) 1997.

23 For overviews on the EU social policy framework, see Leslie, 1996a: 50–4; Leibfried and Pierson, 1996.

24 Elazar, 1966, 1987.

25 Fowler (ed.) *Concise Oxford Dictionary*, 1964.

26 My understanding of these terms is formed in part from their use by Wheare, 1963; Watts, 1970; Ostrom, 1987; and Galligan, 1995.

27 Ostrom, 1987: 106.

28 Ibid.: 129–30.

29 See Painter, 1991 and 1998: 93–7 with respect to Canada and Australia respectively; cf. Ostrom, 1990.

30 On trends in co-operative federalism in the United States, see Elazar, 1962; Wright, 1998; cf. Canada in Simeon and Robinson, 1990; Australia in Mathews, 1977.

31 Grodzins, 1966 cited in Wright, 1998.

32 Painter, 1998: 23. See also Watts, 1987 and 1989.

33 Evidence is mixed as to the effects of regulatory competition on whether standards race to the bottom or the top. For what he calls the "California effect" of US competitive federalism in promoting higher environmental and consumer regulatory standards, see Vogel, 1995. Vogel applies this effect, with some conditions, to international liberalization, arguing that nations can "trade up" standards.

34 Ibid.

35 Breton, 1985: 495–6.

36 Tiebout, 1956.

37 Kincaid, 1991: 91. See also Kenyon and Kincaid, 1991.

38 The concept of managerial rationalism applied here to federalism is drawn from analysis of the Australian system. See Fletcher and Walsh, 1991; Galligan, 1995; and Painter 1998.

39 Gordon Brown, 1994: 29-36.

40 Schecter, 1981: 136; q.v. in Wright, 1998: 426. Italics in original.

41 Kincaid, 1991: 110; Wright, 1998: 426-30.

42 In his study of collaborative federalism in Australia, Martin Painter (1998: 123) adopts a two-type model of intergovernmental relations, the "arm's-length" type and the collaborative type. He describes the types in terms of public choice institutional analysis. My typology is less specific on institutional rules but intends a broader scope for comparative analysis.

43 Sharman, 1991: 35.

44 Davis, 1978: 68.

CHAPTER 4: COMPARING PRE-REFORM ECONOMIC
UNIONS IN AUSTRALIA AND CANADA

1 The phrase is Aitken's (1959).

2 These were that trade among the states would be "absolutely free" (in wording, very similar to section 92 in the *Constitution Act, 1900*) and that the new central government would have exclusive power over customs duties.

3 For discussion, see Galligan, 1995: 166-7; Craven, 1992: 62. The misapprehension may have arisen from a too literal reading of the admittedly centralist terms of the *Constitution Act, 1867*. As early as the 1880s, political and judicial developments show a flexing of provincial rights. In later years, features such as federal disallowance and reservation of provincial laws, even if not extensively used, were enough for K.C. Wheare to class the Canadian system as only "quasi-federal" (Wheare, 1966: 20).

4 A discussion of Australian jurisprudence is found in Coper, 1988; Craven, 1992; Galligan, 1995.

5 Section 121, *Constitution Act, 1867* (originally the *British North America Act):* "All Articles of growth, Produce, or Manufacture of any one of the Provinces shall, from and after the Union, be admitted free into each of the other Provinces."

6 Full legal citations for all cases noted in this book are provided following the bibliography in a separate list.

7 Coper, 1983.

8 For commentary, see Blackshield et al., 1996: 686.

9 *Street v. Queensland Bar Association*, 1989: 502-3, 511.

10 This paraphrasing is from Hogg, 1996: 463.

11 See Howse, 1992: 56-8.

12 Coper, 1988: chapter 4; Galligan, 1995: 170-4.

13 Zines, 1992; Coper, 1988: 181.

14 Saunders, 1992b.

15 Ibid., 108.

16 On the notion of federal balance as a jurisdictional principle in Canada, see Lederman, 1975, cf. Laskin, 1947; Cairns, 1971; Hogg, 1996: 110-11. Concerning lack of federal balance in Australian jurisprudence, see Coper, 1988: 43-4, 171-7; Hogg, 1996: 335.

17 *Labour Conventions*, 1937: 354.

18 Zines, 1992: 71.

19 These issues are discussed in Walsh, 1991; Saunders, 1992b; Galligan, 1995.

20 Some of these redistributive aspects of the federal bargain have been entrenched by the constitutional revisions of the *Constitution Act, 1982* (Part III, section 36), entitled "Equalization and Regional Disparities." This section enshrines a general commitment by the federal and provincial legislatures to promote equal opportunities and to provide essential public services of reasonable quality to all Canadians and commits the federal parliament to the principle of equalization payments. According to Hogg (1996: 142), these provisions are probably not justiciable.

21 Courchene, 1996a: 9–21.

22 There has also been the impact of constitutional provisions, noted above, to prohibit the Commonwealth from engaging in discriminatory or preferential policies (sections 99 and 51(2) and (3)). For example, legislated direct industry assistance programs must be generally available throughout the country.

23 The Canadian summary relies heavily on the work published in ECC, 1991a. No such comparable overview exists for Australia.

24 Ibid., 34–44.

25 See Courchene and Telmer, 1998: 276–80; Statistics Canada, 1997.

26 ABS, 1998.

27 For discussion, see Fagan and Webber, 1994: 70–2; Courchene, 1996: 214–16.

28 Cohen et al., 1972.

29 See EPAC, 1989, 1990, and 1991; IAC, 1989; IC, 1992; Hawke et al., 1991; Keating, 1992; BCA, 1993; Hilmer, 1993.

30 The major studies are: Safarian, 1974; Canada, 1980; Hayes, 1982; Flatters and Lipsey, 1983; Trebilcock et al. (eds.) 1983; Canada, 1985; ECC, 1991a; CMA, 1991; Canada, 1991a; Howse, 1992; BCNI, 1992b.

31 Sharman, 1991.

32 Cf. Scharpf, 1988; Painter, 1991.

33 Painter, 1998: 22–4; cf. Ostrom, 1987.

34 Smiley, 1980: 91.

35 Sharman, 1991: 25.

36 Watts, 1989.

37 For these features, see Simeon, 1972; Smiley, 1979; Warhurst, 1987.

38 Scharpf, 1988; also Painter, 1991.

39 My discussion on the democratic critique of Canadian executive federalism is drawn from Smiley, 1979; Dupre, 1987; Breton, 1985; Brock, 1995. For Australia, see Saunders, 1984 and 1995; Uhr, 1995.

40 See Sproule-Jones, 1993: 84–90.

41 Olson, 1965; Scharpf, 1988; Painter, 1991; Sproule-Jones, 1993: 79–124.

42 Chandler and Bakvis, 1989.

43 This conclusion is reached by the following studies: Fletcher and Wallace, 1985 citing studies by Jenkin, 1983; Thorburn, 1984; Tupper, 1982; Brown and Eastman, 1981.

44 Cf. Moravscik, 1993 for his analysis of conditions in which intergovernmental bargaining produces substantive policy change. See also my discussion in chapter 2.

45 Cf. Thelen and Steinmo, 1992.

CHAPTER 5: REFORMING THE CANADIAN
ECONOMIC UNION, 1976–1992

1 Author's interview with Senator Michael Kirby, then senior federal strategist. A similar assessment is found in Sheppard and Valpy, 1982: 48–9 and Romanow et al., 1984: 68–9.

2 See Romanow et al., 1984: 99. The federal government had commissioned a groundbreaking study from Ed Safarian on economic issues (Safarian, 1974). For other contemporary analyses of economic union issues during the "patriation round," see Maxwell and Pestieau, 1980; Trebilcock et al., 1977; Shoup, 1977; Safarian, 1980; Canada, 1980; Haack et al., 1981; and Hayes, 1982.

3 Canada, 1980: 29.

4 See, for example, Canada, 1980: Annex A "Illustrative Survey" of restrictions

in which many federally induced barriers are missing (such as unemployment insurance, oil and gas pricing, subsidies to business, and freight rate regulation). Cf. Milne, 1986: 18.

5 The provinces' arguments are summarized in Romanow et al., 1984: 70-2; Sheppard and Valpy, 1982: 48-9; Hayes, 1982: 13-19.

6 Howse, 1992: 49-51.

7 Trebilcock et al. (eds.), 1983.

8 Trebilcock, Whalley, Rogerson, and Ness, 1983: 243-351.

9 See Canada, 1985: Vol. III, Chap. 22: 99–272. Further argument was presented in the background research volume published by the commission: Norrie, Simeon, and Krasnick, 1986.

10 Canada et al., 1985.

11 Knox, 1997.

12 CICS [APC], 1986.

13 For details, see Brown, 1991.

14 Canada, 1985: Vol. I: 368-73; Vol. III: 153.

15 Brown, 1991: 95.

16 Chapter references here are from the Canada-United States Free Trade Agreement, 1989. See also Canada (1987).

17 See Attorney General of Ontario, 1988; "Anonymous," 1988; and articles in Gold and Leyton-Brown (eds.), 1988.

18 For legal commentary, see Fairley, 1986; Whyte, 1987; Johnson and Schacter, 1988: 188-92.

19 Bill C-130, as passed, *An Act to Implement the Free Trade Agreement Between Canada and the United States of America, 1988.*

20 For diverse views, see Leslie, 1989; Shoyama, 1989; Courchene, 1990; Robinson, 1993.

21 The NAFTA text is cited in the references as Canada, 1993. For provisions on intellectual property, see chapter 17. On performance requirements of investors, see chapter 11, especially article 1106. On financial services, see chapter 14.

22 Kukucha, 1994: 31-6.

23 Data on interprovincial and international trade comparing 1981 with 1994 indicate that the value of international trade (combined exports and imports) had grown by 120 per cent in constant 1986 dollars, while interprovincial trade had grown by only 6.5 per cent (Courchene and Telmer, 1998: table 9.1, p. 279, using Provincial Economic Accounts data from Statistics Canada).

24 QLP, 1991.

25 QNA, 1991.

26 *Globe and Mail,* 14 December 1991.

27 See Johnston et al., 1993; Watts, 1993; cf. Boismenu, 1993.

28 Author's interview with senior federal official who was a former deputy minister, Department of Justice, and a constitutional advisor to the Government of Canada.

29 Author's interview with former deputy minister of Intergovernmental Affairs, Government of Ontario. The Ontario position was set forth in Ontario, 1991.

30 Miriam Smith, 1993: 90.

31 For an overview of the conceptual options, see Watts and Brown (eds.), 1991.

32 See, for example, Howse, 1992: 1-17.

33 See, for example, Courchene, 1991; Schwanen, 1992; Fallis, 1991.

34 Harris, 1991; see also ECC, 1991; Hartt, 1992; Leslie, 1991; McCallum, 1992.

35 Canada, 1991b: 17, 22.

36 Ibid.

37 Canada, 1991a: 29.

38 CICS, 1992d, item 6.

39 There was also significant debate in left circles on whether a justiciable social charter was in fact the best course. See Bakan and Schneiderman (eds.), 1992.

40 Fortin, 1991.

41 Russell, 1993: 217.

42 For disappointment on the substantive content of the Charlottetown Accord, see Purvis and Raynauld, 1992; David Brown et al., 1992; BCNI, 1992 c. On the virtue of proceeding through non-constitutional means, see ECC, 1991; Maxwell et al., 1991; Schneiderman, 1991; Meekison, 1993.

43 Author's interviews with senior negotiators in the Canada Round for the governments of Canada, New Brunswick, Ontario, Alberta, and British Columbia.

44 CICS, 1992d: item 6.

45 For their statements to this effect, see BCNI, 1992c; CMA, 1991; CCC, 1992; D'Cruz, 1992.

46 Russell, 1993: chapter 10; Monahan, 1993: 231-4; Segal, 1996: chapter 9. My views on the final negotiations have been formed also from information provided in interviews with officials (see note 43).

CHAPTER 6: CANADA'S AGREEMENT ON INTERNAL
TRADE, 1992–99

1   See CCPA *Monitor*, June 1994; Barlow and Cameron (eds.), 1995.
2   *AIT*, 1995: Article 101 and Annex 1813.
3   See Montreal *Gazette*, 2 July 1994; *Globe and Mail*, 28 June 1994; 19 July
    1994; *Toronto Star*, 18 July 1994.
4   *First Protocol of Amendment, AIT*, 1995; *Second Protocol of Amendment, AIT*, 1998.
5   Cf. Doern and MacDonald, 1997: 143-50; 1999: chapter 4.
6   Author's interviews with senior officials in Industry Canada, the Ontario
    Ministry of Economic Development and Trade, and the British Columbia
    Ministry of Employment and Investment and the former chief negotiator of
    AIT, British Columbia (see Appendix 2 for full list of interviewees). See also
    Doern and MacDonald, 1999: 68.
7   Author's interviews with senior officials in Industry Canada, the former chief
    federal official for internal trade, and senior officials from Ontario, Alberta,
    New Brunswick, Newfoundland, Quebec, and British Columbia.
8   Ibid., note 6.
9   Author's interviews with former assistant chief negotiator, AIT for Alberta
    and internal trade representative for Alberta.
10 Author's interviews with senior officials in Industry Canada and the
    provinces of New Brunswick, Ontario, and British Columbia.
11 Author's interview with senior Ontario government official.
12 Compare the typology adopted in Doern and MacDonald, 1999: chapter 4.
    My version differs mainly in nuance, stressing the conflicted position of
    Ottawa and the complex position of Ontario. See also Giles Gherson, *Globe
    and Mail*, 25 June 1994.
13 Author's interviews with senior officials of governments of Quebec, Ontario,
    and Alberta and former chief negotiator for Newfoundland.
14 See also Doern and MacDonald, 1997: 147; 1999: 24-5, 160.
15 Author's interviews with internal trade representative, Alberta; seniors offi-
    cial in government of Quebec, Industry Canada, Ontario, and British
    Columbia; and former assistant chief negotiator for Alberta.
16 *AIT*, 1995: Article 200.
17 Doern and MacDonald, 1999: 146.
18 Lenihan, 1995: 104-5.
19 Author's interviews with officials with governments of Newfoundland, New
    Brunswick, Canada, Ontario, British Columbia, and Quebec. Information
    also obtained from Alberta in 1996.

20 Author's interviews with officials in New Brunswick, Ontario, British Columbia, and Quebec and with a former official of the Privy Council Office, Government of Canada. See also Doern and MacDonald, 1999: 165.

21 *Globe and Mail*, 18 July 1994.

22 Author's interview with former chief negotiator for Newfoundland.

23 Carol Goar in *Toronto Star*, 18 July 1994; Doern and MacDonald, 1999: 63–4.

24 Quebec's negotiating position was to liberalize interprovincial trade on electricity as it fit in well with its strategy of free access to the American market, but this position does not mean that it wished to have such a sensitive area scrutinized during an election campaign.

25 Author's interviews with former chief negotiator for Newfoundland and assistant negotiator for Alberta.

26 Author's interviews with officials with governments of Ontario, Alberta, Quebec, and the federal government.

27 Doern and MacDonald, 1999: 26-9; 158-61.

28 Author's interviews with senior officials in Industry Canada and British Columbia.

29 Giles Gherson, *Globe and Mail*, 28 June, 1994; Barrie McKenna, *Globe and Mail*, 18 July 1994; also, author's interviews with former federal official and senior Ontario official.

30 Doern and MacDonald, 1999: chapter 2.

31 Swinton, 1995: 201-5. Doern and MacDonald (1999: 165) argue that while the AIT was not drafted for the purpose of legal interpretation, this may not prevent the agreement from being subjected to court scrutiny, as has happened to federal environmental assessment guidelines (see *Oldman River* case). However, one recent attempt to do so has failed thus far. The food processing firm Unilever has challenged Quebec's restrictive product specifications that margarine cannot be the same colour as butter. The firm requested that Ontario make a formal complaint against Quebec under the AIT, but Ontario did not take the dispute past the consultation stage (ITS, 1999). Unilever then took the Quebec government to court to try to enforce AIT provisions. It has lost its case in the Quebec Superior Court but may appeal (*Globe and Mail*, 27 May 1999).

32 Swinton, 1995: 201.

33 Howse, 1996: 4-5.

34 De Mestral, 1995: 95-7.

35 Kennett, 1997: 29-31, citing Cohen, 1995; Biggs, 1996: 15-19.

36 *Globe and Mail*, 15 June 1998; 16 July, 1998; Author's interviews with senior officials in Newfoundland, New Brunswick, Ontario, and Quebec.

37 Author's interview with senior official, Secretariat of Canadian Intergovernmental Affairs, government of Quebec.

38 Trebilcock and Behboodi, 1995: 56-7.

39 Lenihan, 1995: 117.

40 Easson, 1995.

41 Howse, 1995: 180. See also Howse, 1996; Biggs, 1996.

42 Miller, 1995: 152.

43 Monahan, 1995: 216.

44 Doern and MacDonald, 1999: 145.

45 See, for example, Howse, 1995; de Mestral; and to a degree, Schwartz, 1995.

46 Knox, 1998; Schwanen, 1998.

47 For documentary evidence, see ITS, 1998b, *[First] Annual Report of the Committee of Ministers on Internal Trade, 1994–96;* Clendenning and Associates, 1997; and ITS, 1998c, "Outstanding Obligations" on the AIT [web site report: www.intrasec.mb.ca]. For the views of independent analysts, see Howse, 1996; Schwanen, 1996; CCC, 1996; Knox, 1998; Schwanen, 1998.

48 Knox, 1998: 149–51. Author's interviews with New Brunswick and British Columbia officials.

49 *Globe and Mail*, 10 July 1998; ITS, 1998d.

50 Author's interviews with officials in Industry Canada, government of Alberta, and the executive director of the Internal Trade Secretariat; see also Doern and MacDonald, 1999: 163.

51 CCC, 1996: 18; see also CCC 1998.

52 Author's interviews with officials in the governments of New Brunswick, Ontario, British Columbia, and the executive director of the Internal Trade Secretariat.

53 Brodie and Smith, 1998: 94.

54 CICS, 1999. In the policy debates leading up to the SUFA, some analysts made explicit linkages with economic union issues. See Courchene, 1996b; Burelle, 1997; Kennett, 1998. See also articles in *Policy Options* Vol. 19, No. 9 (November 1998).

55 For discussion, see Gagnon and Segal (eds.), 2000.

CHAPTER 7: MICROECONOMIC AND
INTERGOVERNMENTAL REFORM IN AUSTRALIA, 1990–99

1 Detail is available from the communiqués and attached documents of the Special Premiers Conferences (SPCS), Council of Australian Governments (COAG), and Leaders Forum meetings. Reference to specific documents will

be made as required. Edwards and Henderson, 1995; Weller, 1995; and Painter, 1998 provide analytical overviews.

2 SPC, Communiqué 30–1 October 1990.

3 The summary of reform outcomes produced here is based in part on Edwards and Henderson, 1995: Attachment C. Unless otherwise noted, all references to the states implies the territories as well.

4 Painter, 1998 provides a more comprehensive discussion of these process issues. My analysis differs somewhat from his as noted in this chapter.

5 To the author's knowledge, there has been no comprehensive study of the role of interest groups or the broader policy community in the microeconomic reform movement in Australia. Elizabeth Harman's work on the National Competition Policy process is especially instructive. See Harman, 1996; also Bell, 1994; Gerritsen, 1994; Nelson, 1992.

6 The story of this relationship is well told in Kelly, 1994.

7 For an assessment, see Bell, 1994.

8 See EPAC, 1989, 1990, and 1991; IAC, 1989; IC, 1992.

9 Harman, 1996: 215–6.

10 The main sources of such reform advocacy were EPAC, 1989, 1990, and 1991; IAC, 1989; and IC 1992; Hawke et al., 1991; Keating, 1992; BCA, 1993; and Hilmer, 1993. For specific state perspectives, see Bannon, 1987; Greiner, 1990.

11 For an overview of this process, see Carroll, 1995b; Harman, 1996.

12 See the range of issues dealt with in the proceedings of the Australian Constitutional Convention (see reference for Australian Constitutional Convention, 1973–85), and the Constitutional Commission, Final Report (see reference for Commonwealth of Australia, 1988).

13 For an overview, see McMillan et al., 1983; Galligan, 1995: 122–6.

14 Coper, 1988: 357.

15 See Sharman, 1989; and Galligan, 1989.

16 See, in particular, report of Standing Committee 'A', 1978; Fiscal Powers Subcommittee report, 1984; Plenary report, Brisbane, 1985, all found in Australian Constitution Convention, 1973–85.

17 See Coper, 1988: 357–60; Galligan, 1995: 125; and comments by Saunders and Sharman in Galligan and Nethercote (eds.) 1989.

18 ACTNEM, 1987; Commonwealth of Australia, 1988.

19 Commonwealth of Australia, 1988: 810.

20 See Blainey, 1989; Sharman, 1989; and Galligan, 1989.

21 Commonwealth of Australia, 1988: chapter 11.

22 Galligan, 1995: chapter 5.

23 McMillan et al., 1983; Head, 1989.

24 Author's interviews with Professor Kenneth Wiltshire, Robert Lim of the Business Council of Australia, and Professor Glenn Withers, with the former secretary, Department of Prime Minister and Cabinet of the Commonwealth Government, the assistant secretary, Commonwealth Treasury and the former director general of the Premier's Office, State of NSW.

25 Painter, 1998: 34. See also Laffin and Painter, 1995; Forsyth, 1995a.

26 Nahan, 1995.

27 This point is stressed in think-tank reports: IAC, 1989; IC, 1990, EPAC, 1991; and in author's interviews with a former senior Queensland official and the assistant secretary, Commonwealth treasury. See also Carroll, 1995b: 80–90.

28 For more detail, see Forsyth, 1995a: 66–7; also Forsyth, 1995b; Walsh, 1992.

29 William Scales q.v. in FSRC, 1998: 70.

30 Author's interviews with Professor Ken Wiltshire and with the assistant secretary, Treasury of NSW. See also Fletcher and Walsh, 1991; Painter, 1998: 16–20.

31 My understanding of these dynamics has been drawn from interviews with former and currently senior officials and advisors for the Commonwealth government and the states of Queensland, Victoria, New South Wales, and Tasmania. They are also covered by Fletcher and Walsh, 1991: 19–24; Carroll and Painter, 1995a: 6–7; and Painter, 1998: 65–7.

32 Keating, 1991.

33 Based on author's interviews with senior officials with the Commonwealth Department of Prime Minister and Cabinet and Treasury, and state officials in Tasmania and NSW. See also Bell, 1997: 216–20.

34 Painter, 1998: 56–7.

35 Harman, 1996: 212.

36 Author's interview with Professor John Wanna; see also Harman, 1996: 222.

37 Author's interviews with senior officials in Department of Premier and Cabinet, Tasmania.

38 Author's interviews with Professor Ken Wiltshire, senior official NSW Treasury, former senior officials with Department of Premier and Cabinet in NSW and in Victoria. On Keating's terms for reform, see Keating 1994; on the states' sense of betrayal of fiscal issues, see Bannon, 1992; Court, 1994.

39 Author's interviews with former senior Commonwealth, Victoria, and Queensland officials. See also Kelly, 1994: 641.

40 Painter, 1995: 7.

41 Author's interviews with former senior officials of Victoria and NSW, and current assistant secretary of the Commonwealth Treasury.

42 See Painter, 1998: 49–52; Harman, 1996.

43 Harman, 1996: 208–9.

44 The latter approach had been advised by the Hilmer Report. See Hilmer, 1993: xxxvii–viii; 342–6.

45 These conclusions are drawn in part from Harman and Harman, 1996; and Nahan, 1995; and the author's interview with Professor Glynn Davis.

46 Author's interviews with Professor Glynn Davis, Gary Sturgess, and a senior Commonwealth Treasury official.

47 For more detail, see Painter, 1998: chapters 4 and 6.

48 *AFR*, 5 November 1996; *Australian* 11 November 1996; Alan Wood in the *Australian*, 3 March 1997; also author's interviews with former senior Victoria official and current senior NSW official.

49 *Australian*, 17 June 1997.

50 See editorials in *AFR*, 16 May 1998 and 20 June 1998.

CHAPTER 8: REFORM OUTCOMES IN AUSTRALIA

1 Painter, 1998: 90.

2 The Leaders Forum is assessed in *Intergovernmental News,* Vol. 8, No. 5, Spring 1995.

3 This point was reinforced in author's interviews with several state and Commonwealth officials and has been discussed by Weller, 1995; and Painter, 1995.

4 Author's interviews with Gary Sturgess, senior officials of Department of Prime Minister and Cabinet, Commonwealth, and senior officials in Tasmania and Victoria.

5 Author's interviews with former Queensland and Commonwealth officials. For discussion, see Weller, 1995; Charles, 1995.

6 Painter, 1998: 140–52.

7 Wilkins, 1995; see also Thomas and Saunders (eds.), 1995.

8 For a similar typology of legislative schemes, see WALA, 1994; and Working Party, 1996.

9 Referral of powers under section 51(XXXVII) has been done over thirty times by several states, over such diverse matters as air navigation, family law, trade practices law, and labour relations. (See Commonwealth of Australia, 1995: n.12, pp. 43–4).

10 Author's interviews with former deputy secretary, Department of Premier and Cabinet, Queensland; the assistant secretary of the Commonwealth Treasury; and the director general of the Department of Premier and

Cabinet, NSW. Uniform legislation is also discussed extensively in WALA, 1995 and 1996; and in *Intergovernmental News,* Vol. 6, No. 3, Spring, 1993; Vol. 6, No. 4, Winter 1994; Vol. 8, No. 2, Winter 1995.

11 See WALA, 1992; Pendal, 1995; and Working Party, 1996.

12 This point is emphasized in Painter, 1995 and 1998.

13 See Pendal, 1995; WALA, various reports, 1992–96; FSRC, 1998; and cf. Saunders, 1989.

14 Painter, 1998: 183.

15 *Intergovernmental News,* Vol. 9, No. 3, October 1997.

16 See LF, 1996; *Australian,* 11 November 1996; AFR, 20 June 20 1997; Victoria, 1997.

17 *Commonwealth of Australia,* 1998.

18 See comments by Alan Wood, *Australian,* 14 and 15 August 1998; and Michelle Gratton, *AFR,* 15 August 1998.

19 For more detail, see NCOA, 1996; FSRC, 1998: chapter 5; Painter, 1998: chapter 7.

20 Discussed in Painter, 1998: chapter 7.

21 For other overviews, see Carroll and Painter (eds.) 1995; Larkin and Dwyer, 1995; PC, 1996; and Painter, 1998.

22 The key NCP documents are Parliament of Australia, *CPR Act,* 1995; and COAG, 1995 b, c, and d. All of the documents are included as appendices in WALA, 1996. Detailed information is also available in the annual reports of the National Competition Council (NCC), 1996, 1997, and 1998.

23 Cf. WALA, 1996: Chart 1, p. 3.

24 See Katherine Murphy, *AFR,* 8 July 1998 and 29 January 1999; editorial *AFR,* 20 June 1998.

25 PC, 2000; Parliament of Australia, 2000.

26 NCC, 1998: 23, 50.

27 Carroll, 1995a: 42.

28 PC, 1997.

29 Details are found in Painter, 1998; Nelson, 1992; and Gray 1993.

30 Painter, 1998: 140–52.

31 See *AFR,* 24 September 1996; 2 February 1997; 1 May 1997; 23 May 1997; *Australian,* 28 August 1997; also Harman and Harman, 1996: 19–22.

32 PC, 1996.

33 I repeat the caveat made in chapter 6 with respect to the Canadian reforms. That is, a degree of judgment on my part is required to assess that barriers have or have not been removed and to what degree.

34 Carroll, 1995a, 1998.

35 *IC,* 1996; *AFR,* 24 February 1998.

36 The Kennett (Liberal-National coalition) government lost the Victoria election in October 1999. The new Labor government is renewing a more conflictual and competitive approach with respect to the Commonwealth government on industrial relations.

37 Painter, 1998: 183.

38 *IC,* 1997.

39 See *AFR,* 27 February 1999; Peter Hartcher "Australia: The Model Economy," *AFR,* 14 August 1999, citing John Edwards' report "The New Australian Economy" for the Hong Kong and Shanghai Bank (HSBC group).

40 Painter, 1998: chapter 8.

CHAPTER 9: CONCLUSIONS: MARKET RULES AND FEDERALISM

1 Thelen and Steinmo, 1992: 27.

2 For a discussion of this issue with respect to the EU, see Moravcsik, 1993: 496–507.

3 Moravscik, 1993. I have discussed his analysis in chapter 2 above.

4 For the link between "deeper integration" and competition policy, see Hines, 1996.

5 For more discussion, see FSRC, 1997.

6 Brown, 1991; see also Skogstad, 2000.

7 Cf. Commission of the European Communities [CEC], 1993, chapter 3.

8 See Brown (ed.), 2001.

9 Leslie, 1998.

10 Wolfe, 1998: 20; cf. Polyani, 1944.

11 See E. Ostrom, 1990; and for Canada and Australia, Painter, 1991 and 1998. I have discussed the concept of working rules in chapter 3.

12 E. Ostrom, 1990: 29.

13 Cf. Pierson, 1996.

14 Canada's Social Union Framework Agreement (SUFA) also relies on such "political" enforcement, requiring extensive reporting to, and consultation with, the public. For Canadian analysis on monitoring and information as a means of enforcing intergovernmental agreements in the proposed SUFA, see Burelle, 1995; Biggs, 1996; Courchene, 1996b; Kennett, 1998. See also SUFA text, part 3 (CICS, 1999).

15 The phrase is from Fritz Scharpf, 1988.

16 The paradox of integration and fragmentation is explored in Brown and Laforest (eds.), 1994.

17 See my discussion in chapters 1 and 3, citing among others, Wilks and Wright, 1987; Gamble, 1988; Hall, 1986; Chandler and Bakvis, 1989.

18 See, for example, Barlow and Campbell (eds.), 1995; Robinson, 1995; Bell, 1997.

Bibliography

ABBREVIATIONS

ACTNEM	Advisory Committee on Trade and National Economic Management
ABS	Australian Bureau of Statistics
ACC	Australian Constitutional Convention
ACCC	Australian Competition and Consumer Commission
AGPS	Australian Government Publishing Service
BCA	Business Council of Australia
BCNI	Business Council on National Issues
CCC	Canadian Chamber of Commerce
CCPA	Canadian Centre for Policy Alternatives
CEC	Commission of the European Communities
CICS	Canadian Intergovernmental Conference Secretariat
COAG	Council of Australian Governments
ECC	Economic Council of Canada
EPAC	Economic Planning Advisory Council
FRC/ANU	Federalism Research Centre, Australian National University
FSRC	Federal-State Relations Committee
IAC	Industry Assistance Commission
IC	Industry Commission
IIR/QU	Institute of Intergovernmental Relations, Queen's University
ITS	Internal Trade Secretariat
LF	Leaders Forum
MSS	Minister of Supply and Services, Canada
OEC	Ontario Economic Council
OECD	Organization for Economic Cooperation and Development
PC	Productivity Commission
PQ	Parti Québécois
QLP	Quebec Liberal Party
QNA	Quebec National Assembly
REC	Regroupement Économie et Constitution
SPC	Special Premiers Conference
WALA	Western Australia Legislative Assembly

Advisory Committee on Trade and National Economic Management [ACTNEM] (1987) *Report to the Constitutional Commission* (Canberra: AGPS).

Aitken, H.G.J. (1978 [1959]) "Defensive Expansion: The State and Economic Growth in Canada" in M. Watkins (et al.) (eds.) *Approaches to Canadian Economic History* (Toronto: Macmillan (Carleton Library No. 31)): 183–221.

Alberta Government (1992) *Improving Efficiency and Accountability: Rebalancing Federal-Provincial Spending Responsibilities* (Edmonton).

– (1996) "The Canadian Agreement on Internal Trade: Overview" (Department of Intergovernmental and Aboriginal Affairs, Trade Policy, October) (Edmonton: mimeo).

Alberta Legislature (1995) *Agreement on Internal Trade Statute Amendments Act* (1995), Bill 36 (passed 17 May).

Alexander, Malcolm and Brian Galligan (eds.) (1992) *Comparative Political Studies: Australia and Canada* (Melbourne: Pittman).

Alford, Robert R. and Roger Friedland (1985) *The Powers of Theory: Capitalism, the State and Democracy* (Cambridge: Cambridge University Press).

Anonymous (1988) "Canada-United States Free Trade: Issues of Constitutional Jurisdiction" in P.M. Leslie and R.L. Watts (eds.) *Canada: The State of the Federation, 1987–88* (Kingston: IIR/QU): 39–55.

Atkinson, Michael and William D. Coleman (1989) *The State, Business and Industrial Change in Canada* (Toronto: University of Toronto Press).

Attorney-General of Ontario (1988) *The Impact of the Canada-US Trade Agreement: A Legal Analysis* (Toronto: Government of Ontario).

The Australian (Sydney) 11 November 1996, 3 March 1997, 28 August 1997.

Australian Bureau of Statistics [ABS] (1998) *Census of Population and Housing: Population Growth and Distribution, Australia, 1996* (Canberra: ABS [Catalogue No. 2035.0]).

Australian Competition and Consumer Commission [ACCC] (1998) *Annual Report, 1997–98* (Canberra: AGPS).

Australian Constitutional Convention [ACC] (1973–85) *Proceedings* (Canberra: Queen's Printer).

Australian Financial Review [AFR] (Sydney) 5 November 1996, 24 September 1996, 2 February 1997, 1 May 1997, 23 May 1997, 24 February 1998, 16 May 1998, 20 June 1998, 8 July 1998, 15 August 1998, 29 January 1999, 27 February 1999, 14 August 1999.

Badie, Bertrand and Pierre Birnbaum (1983) *The Sociology of the State* (Chicago: University of Chicago Press).

Bakan, Joel and David Schneiderman (eds.) (1992) *Social Justice and the Constitution* (Ottawa: Carleton University Press).

Bakvis, H. and W. Chandler (eds.) (1987a) *Federalism and the Role of the State* (Toronto: University of Toronto Press).

Bakvis, H. and W. Chandler (1987b) "Federalism and Comparative Analysis" in Bakvis and Chandler (eds.) *Federalism and the Role of the State*: 3–11.

Balassa, Bela (1961) *The Theory of Economic Integration* (Homewood, Ill.: Irwin).

Bannon, John (1987) "Overcoming the Unintended Consequences of Federalism" *Australian Journal of Public Administration* 46(1): 1–9.

– (1992) *Cooperative Federalism: Good Policy and Good Government* (Canberra: ANU/FRC).

Banting, Keith G. (1984) "The Decision Rules: Federalism and Pension Reform" in D. Conklin (et al.) (eds.) *Pensions Today and Tomorrow: Background Studies* (Toronto: Ontario Economic Council): 189–209.

– (1987) *The Welfare State and Canadian Federalism* (2nd edition) (Kingston and Montreal: McGill-Queen's University Press).

Barlow, Maude and Bruce Campbell (eds.) (1995) *Straight Through the Heart* (Toronto: HarperCollins).

Beer, S. H. (1995) "Federalism and the Nation-State: American Experience" in Karen Knop et al. (eds.) *Rethinking Federalism: Citizens, Markets, and Governments in a Changing World* (Vancouver: UBC Press): 224–49.

Bell, Stephen (1997) *Ungoverning the Economy: The Political Economy of Australian Economic Policy* (Melbourne: Oxford University Press).

– and Brian Head (eds.) (1994) *State, Economy and Public Policy* (Melbourne: Oxford University Press).

Benz, Arthur (1987) "Regionalization and Decentralization" in Bakvis and Chandler (eds.): 17–46.

Bernier, Ivan (et al.) (1986) "The Concept of Economic Union in International and Constitutional Law" in Mark Krasnick (ed.) *Perspectives on the Canadian Economic Union* (Research Studies of the Royal Commission on the Economic Union and Development Prospects for Canada, Vol. 60) (Toronto: University of Toronto Press).

Bernier, Ivan et Andre Binette (1988) *Les provinces canadiennes et le commerce international* (Quebec: Centre québécois des relations internationals, Université Laval).

Biggs, Margaret (1996) *Building Blocks for Canada's New Social Union* (Working Paper No. F 02) (Ottawa: Canadian Policy Research Networks).

Blackshield, A., G. Williams and B. Fitzgerald (1996) *Australian Constitutional Law and Theory: Commentary and Materials* (Sydney: Federation Press).

Blainey, Geoffrey (1989) "What the Constitutional Commission Achieved: A Comment" in Galligan and Nethercote (eds.): 9–16.

Boadway, Robin and Frank Flatters (1982) *Equalization in a Federal State: An Economic Analysis* (Ottawa: Economic Council of Canada).

Boadway, Robin W. (et al.) (eds.) (1991) *Economic Dimensions of Constitutional Change* (Kingston: John Deutsch Institute for the Study of Economic Policy, Queen's University).

Boadway, Robin W. and Douglas G. Purvis (eds.) (1991a) *Economic Aspects of the Federal Government's Constitutional Proposals* (Kingston: Queen's University, John Deutsch Institute for the Study of Economic Policy).

Boeckleman, Keith (1996) "Federal Systems in the Global Economy: Research Issues" *Publius: The Journal of Federalism* 26(1): 1–10.

Boismenu, Gérard (1993) "When More is Too Much: Quebec and the Charlottetown Accord" in R.L. Watts and D.M. Brown (eds.) *Canada: The State of the Federation, 1993* (Kingston: IIR/QU): 45–60.

Bonin, Jean-Francois (et al.) (eds.) (1993) "Special Issue on European Subsidiarity" *National Journal of Constitutional Law* 3(3).

Boothe, Paul (ed.) (1996) *Reforming Fiscal Federalism for Global Competition: A Canada-Australia Comparison* (Edmonton: Western Centre for Studies in Economic Policy, University of Alberta Press).

Bradsen, John (1990) "Judicial Review and the Changing Federal Balance of Power" in John Summers, Dennis Woodward and Andrew Parkin (eds.) *Government, Politics and Power in Australia* (4th edition) (Melbourne: Longman, Cheshire).

Brennan, G. and J.M. Buchanan (1985) *The Reason of Rules: Constitutional Political Economy* (New York: Cambridge University Press).

Bressand, Albert and Kalypso Nicolaidis (1990) "Regional Integration in a Networked World Economy" in W. Wallace (ed.) *The Dynamics of European Integration* (London: Pinter/Royal Institute of International Affairs).

Breton, Albert (1985) "Supplementary Statement" in Canada (1985) Vol. 3: 486–526.

Brock, Kathy L. (1995) "The End of Executive Federalism?" in F. Rocher and M. Smith (eds.): 91–108.

Brodie, Janine and Malinda Smith (1998) "Regulating the Economic Union" in Leslie Pal (ed.) *How Ottawa Spends, 1998–99: Balancing Act: The Post-Deficit Mandate* (Toronto: Oxford University Press): 81–97.

Brown, David et al. (1992) "Common Market Proposal Would Enshrine Internal Trade Barriers in Canada's Constitution" *Backgrounder* (21 July) (Toronto: C.D. Howe Institute).

Brown, Douglas M. (1991) "The Evolving Role of the Provinces in Canadian Trade Policy" in Brown and Smith (eds.): 81–128.

– (ed.) (2001) *Tax Competition and the Fiscal Union* Proceedings of a Symposium at Queen's University, June 2000 (Working Paper Series)(Kingston: IIR/QU)

– (1993) "Canadian Integration and the Federal Bargain" *New Europe Law Review* 1(2): 321–50.

– and Julia Eastman (1981) *The Limits of Consultation: A Debate Among Ottawa, the Provinces and the Private Sector on an Industrial Strategy* (Discussion Paper) (Ottawa: Science Council of Canada).

– and Peter M. Leslie (1994) "Economic Integration and Equality in Federations" in Mullins and Saunders (eds.): 83–125.

– and Murray G. Smith (eds.) (1991) *Canadian Federalism: Meeting Global Economic Challenges?* (Kingston/Montreal: IIR/QU and Institute for Research on Public Policy).

– Dwight Herperger and Robert A. Young (eds.) (1991) *Constitutional Commentaries: An Assessment of the 1991 Federal Proposals* (Kingston: IIR/QU).

– and Guy Laforest (eds.) (1994) *Integration and Fragmentation: The Paradox of the Late Twentieth Century* (Kingston: IIR/QU).

Brown, Gordon R. (1994) "Canadian Federal-Provincial Overlap and Government Inefficiency" *Publius: The Journal of Federalism* 24(1): 21–37.

Brown-John, Lloyd (ed.) (1995) *Federal-Type Solutions and European Integration* (Lanham, Md.: University Press of America).

Burelle, André (1995) *Le mal canadien: Essai de diagnostique et esquisse d'une thérapie* (Montreal: Fides).

– (1997) "Canada Needs a Political and Cultural as well as a Social and Economic Covenant" in D. Cameron (ed.): 15–19.

Business Council of Australia [BCA](1993) *Australia 2010: Creating a Future Australia* (Melbourne: BCA).

Business Council on National Issues [BCNI] (1992a) *Canada's Constitutional Future* (Response to … [Federal] Proposals, January) (Ottawa: BCNI).

– (1992b) *Canada's Economic Union* (April) (Ottawa: BCNI).

– (1992c) *The Charlottetown Agreement* (October) (Ottawa: BCNI).

Butlin, N.G., A. Barnard and J.J. Pincus (1982) *Government and Capitalism: Public and Private Choice in Twentieth Century Australia* (Sydney: Allen and Unwin).

Cable, Vincent (1995) "The Diminished Nation-State: A Study in the Loss of Economic Power" *Daedalus* 124: (Spring): 25–53.

Cairns, Alan C. (1971) "The Judicial Committee and Its Critics" *Canadian Journal of Political Science* 4(3): 301–45.

– (1977) "The Governments and Societies of Canadian Federalism" *Canadian Journal of Political Science* 10(4): 695–725.

– (1986) "The Embedded State: State-Society Relations in Canada" in Keith G. Banting (ed.) *State and Society in Comparative Perspective (Research Studies of the Royal Commission on the Economic Union and Development Prospects for Canada,* Vol. 31) (Toronto: University of Toronto Press): 53–86.

Cameron, David R. (1994) "Post-Modern Ontario and the Laurentian Thesis" in Douglas M. Brown and Janet Hiebert (eds.) *Canada: The State of the Federation, 1994* (Kingston: IIR/QU): 109–32.

– (ed.) (1997) *Assessing ACCESS: Towards a New Social Union* (Kingston: IIR/QU).

–   and Richard Simeon (1998) "Multilevel Governance and Democratic Policy-Making" Paper delivered to Israel Association for Canadian Studies, Jerusalem.

Camilleri, Joseph A. (1995) "The Asia-Pacific in the Post-Hegemonic World" in Andrew Mack and John Ravenhill (eds.) *Pacific Cooperation: Building Economic and Security Regimes in the Asia-Pacific Region* (Boulder, Colo.: Westview Press): 180–208.

Canada (1980) *Securing the Canadian Economic Union in the Constitution: A Discussion Paper* (Ottawa: MSS).

–   (1985) *Report of the Royal Commission on the Economic Union and Development Prospects for Canada* [Donald Macdonald, chair] 3 Vols. (Ottawa: MSS).

–   (1987) *The Canada-U.S. Free Trade Agreement* (Ottawa: Department of External Affairs).

–   (1991a) [Privy Council Office] *Shaping Canada's Future Together: Proposals* (Ottawa: MSS).

–   (1991b) [Privy Council Office] *Canadian Federalism and Economic Union: Partnership for Prosperity* (Ottawa: MSS).

–   (1993) *North American Agreement on Labour Cooperation Between the Government of Canada, the Government of the United Mexican States and the United States of America* (13 September).

–   (1994) "Agreement on Internal Trade: Summary" (18 July) (Ottawa: mimeo).

–   (1996) *Renewing the Canadian Federation: A Progress Report* (Ottawa: Privy Council Office).

Canada, Parliament of (1992) *Report of the Special Joint Committee on a Renewed Canada* (Joint Chairmen: Hon. Gerald A. Beaudoin, Senator; Dorothy Dobbie, MP) (Ottawa).

–   (1996) *Agreement on Internal Trade Implementation Act*, 1996, c.17, 45 Elizabeth II.

Canada et al. (1985) *Intergovernmental Position Paper on the Principles and Framework for Regional Economic Development* (June) (Ottawa).

Canadian Centre for Policy Alternatives [CCPA] (1994) *Monitor* Vol. 1, No. 2 (June).

Canadian Chamber of Commerce [CCC] (1992) *Submission to the Special Joint Committee on a Renewed Canada* (12 January).

–   (1996) *The Agreement on Internal Trade and Interprovincial Trade Flows: Building a Strong United Canada* (Ottawa: CCC).

–   (1998) Text of Resolutions, 69th Annual Meeting of the Canadian Chamber of Commerce, Saint John, NB, 14 September (Ottawa: mimeo).

Canadian Intergovernmental Conference Secretariat [CICS] (1986) 27th Annual Premiers Conference [APC], *Communiqué: Trade*, Edmonton, 10–12 August.

–   (1991) Council of Ministers of Internal Trade [CMIT], *Press Release and Attachments re Intergovernmental Agreement on Government Procurement*, Moncton, 21 November.

–   (1992a) First Ministers Meeting on the Economy, *Outcome of Discussions: Interprovincial Trade*, Ottawa, 24–25 March.

–   (1992b) CMIT, *Press Release*, Winnipeg, 1 May.

–   (1992c) First Ministers Meeting on the Constitution [FFMC], *Consensus Report on the Constitution, Final Text*, Charlottetown, 28 August.

–   (1992d) FFMC, *Political Accords, Final* Charlottetown, 27–28 August.

–   (1992e) CMIT, *Press Release*, Toronto, 4 December.

–   (1993a) CMIT, *Press Release*, Montreal, 18 March.

–   (1993b) CMIT, *Press Release*, Vancouver, 8 June.

–   (1994a) CMIT, *Press Release*, Ottawa, 20 January.

–   (1994b) CMIT, *Press Release*, Ottawa, 7 April.

–   (1994c) CMIT, *Press Release*, Ottawa, 28 June.

–   (1997) 38th Annual Premiers Conference, *News Release: Agreement on Internal Trade*, St. Andrews, NB, 6–8 August.

- (1999) *A Framework to Improve the Social Union for Canadians* (Agreement between the Government of Canada and the Governments of the Provinces and Territories), Ottawa, 4 February.

Canadian Manufacturers Association [CMA] (1991) Canada 1993: A Plan for the Creation of a Single Economic Market (Toronto: mimeo).

Canadian Public Policy [CPP] (1986) "The Macdonald Report: Twelve Reviews" *Canadian Public Policy*, Supplementary Issue, Vol. XII (February).

Capling, A. and B. Galligan (1992) *Beyond the Protective State: The Political Economy of Australia's Manufacturing Industry Policy* (Cambridge and Melbourne: Cambridge University Press).

Carroll, Peter (1995a) "Mutual Recognition: Origins and Implementation" *Australian Journal of Public Management* 54(1): 35-45.

- (1995b) "Federalism, Microeconomic Reform and the Industry Commission" in Carroll and Painter (eds.): 76–96.
- (1998) "Globalisation and Policy Convergence: The Adoption of Mutual Recognition in the European Union and Australia" (unpublished paper).
- and Martin Painter (eds.) (1995) *Microeconomic Reform and Federalism* (Canberra: FRC/ANU).
- and Martin Painter (1995a) "The Federal Politics of Microeconomic Reform: An Overview and Introduction" in Carroll and Painter (eds.): 3–20.

Cecchini, Paulo (et al.) (1988) *The European Challenge 1992: The Benefits of a Single Market* (Aldershot: Gower).

CEPR (1993) *Making Sense of Solidarity: How Much Centralization for Europe?* (London: CEPR).

Chandler, William D. (1987) "Federalism and Political Parties" in Bakvis and Chandler (eds.): 149–70.

- and Herman Bakvis (1989) "Federalism and the Strong-State/Weak-State Conundrum: Canadian Economic Policy-Making in Comparative Perspective" *Publius: The Journal of Federalism* 19(1): 59–77.

Charles, Christine (1995) *"COAG and Microeconomic Reform: A South Australian Perspective"* in Carroll and Painter (eds.): 111–18.

Clayton, R., Conklin, P. and Shapek (eds.) (1975) "Policy Management Assistance – A Developing Dialogue" *Public Administration Review* 35: 693–818.

Clendenning and Associates (1997) *Internal Trade Barriers in Canada: Final Report* (Winnipeg: Internal Trade Secretariat).

Cohen, David (1995) "The Internal Trade Agreement: Furthering the Canadian Economic Disunion?" *Canadian Business Law Journal* 25: 257–79.

Cohen, M.D., J.G. March and J.P. Olsen (1972) "A Garbage Can Model of Organizational Choice" *Administrative Science Quarterly* 17(1): 1–25.

Commission of the European Communities [CEC] (1985) *Completing the Internal Market*, COM (85) 314 (14 June) (Brussels: CEC).

- (1993) *Stable Money – Sound Finances: European Economy* 53 (Directorate-General for Economic and Financial Affairs) (Brussels: CEC).

Commonwealth of Australia (1988) *Constitutional Commission: Final Report* (Canberra: AGPS).

- (1995) *Australia's Constitution* (Canberra: AGPS).
- (1998) *Tax Reform: Not a New Tax, a New Tax System* (Canberra: AGPS).

Cooper, Andrew, Richard Higgott and Kim Nossal (1993) *Relocating Middle Powers: Australia and Canada in a Changing World* (Melbourne: Melbourne University Press).

Coper, Michael (1983) *Freedom of Interstate Trade Under the Australian Constitution* (Sydney: Butterworths).

- (1988) *Encounters with the Australian Constitution* (Sydney: CCH).

- (1992) "The Economic Framework of the Australian Federation: A Question of Balance" in Craven (ed.): 131–50.

Costello, Hon. Peter (1999) "Second Reading Speech to the House of Representatives, on A New Tax System" (Commonwealth-State Financial Arrangements) Bill, [March].

Council of Australian Governments [COAG] (1992a) "Communiqué" Meeting of Heads of Government, Canberra, 11 May.

- (1992b) "Communiqué" Perth, 7 December.
- (1993a) "Communiqué" Melbourne, 8–9 June.
- (1993b) "Review of Ministerial Councils" June.
- (1994a) "Communiqué" Hobart, 25 February.
- (1994b) "Communiqué Attachment A: Water Resource Policy" 25 February.
- (1994c) "Communiqué Attachment B: Free and Fair Trade in Gas" 25 February.
- (1994d) "Communiqué" Darwin, 19 August.
- (1995a) "Communiqué" Canberra, 11 April.
- (1995b) "Conduct Code Agreement" Canberra, 11 April.
- (1995c) "Competition Principles Agreement" Canberra, 11 April.
- (1995d) "Communiqué Attachment A: Agreement to Implement the National Competition Policy and Related Reforms," Canberra, 11 April.
- (1996a) "Communiqué" Canberra, 14 June.
- (1996b) "Communiqué Attachment C: Principles and Procedures for Commonwealth-State Consultation on Treaties" 14 June.
- (1996c) "Communiqué Attachment D: Trans Tasman Mutual Recognition Agreement," Canberra, 14 June.
- (1997a) "Communiqué" Canberra, 7 November.
- (1997b) "Communiqué: Taxation Reform" Canberra, 6 November.
- (1997c) "Communiqué: Treaty Council" Canberra, 7 November.
- (1999) "Intergovernmental Agreement on the Reform of Commonwealth-State Financial Relations" 9 April.
- (2000) "Communiqué" Canberra, 3 November.

Courchene, Thomas J. (1983) "Analytical Perspectives on the Canadian Economic Union" in Trebilcock (et al.) (eds.): 51–110.

- (1990) *Forever Amber: The Legacy of the 1980s for Ongoing Constitutional Impasse* (Kingston: IIR/QU).
- (1991) "The Economic Union and Other Aspects of the Federal Proposals" in Brown, Herperger and Young (eds.): 36–46.
- (1992) "Mons Pays, C'est L'hiver: Reflections of a Market Populist" *Canadian Journal of Economics* XXV (4): 759–91.
- (1993) "Glocalisation, Institutional Evolution and the Australian Federation" in Galligan (ed.): 64–117.
- (1996a) "The Comparative Nature of Australian and Canadian Economic Space" in Boothe (ed.): 7–21.
- (1996b) "ACCESS: A Convention on the Canadian Economic and Social Systems" in D. Cameron (ed.) (1997): 77–112.
- with Colin Telmer (1998) *From Heartland to North American Region State: The Social, Fiscal and Federal Evolution of Ontario* (Toronto: Centre for Public Management, University of Toronto).
- and Douglas D. Purvis (eds.) (1993) *Productivity, Growth and Canada's International Competitiveness: Proceedings of a Conference Held at Queen's University 18–19 September 1992* (Kingston: John Deutsch Institute for the Study of Economic Policy, Queen's University).

Court, Richard (1994) "Rebuilding the Federation: An Audit and History of State Powers and Responsibilities Usurped by the Commonwealth in the Years Since Federation" (speech delivered in Perth, Australia).

Craven, Greg (1992) "The States – Decline, Fall or What?" in Craven (ed.): 49–69.

– (ed.) (1992) *Australian Federation: Towards the Second Century* (Carlton: University of Melbourne Press).

Creighton, Donald (1937) *The Commercial Empire of the St. Lawrence, 1760–1850* (New Haven: Yale University Press).

Daley, John (1992) "Economic Unions in Canada and Australia" (unpublished paper).

Davis, S. Rufus (1978) *The Federal Principle: A Journey Through Time in Quest of Meaning* (Berkeley: University of California Press).

Dawson, Sir Daryl (1992) "The Founders' Vision" in Craven (ed.): 1–13.

D'Cruz, Joseph R. (1992) *Interprovincial Trade Barriers and Canadian Competitiveness: Report on a Survey by the Canadian Chamber of Commerce* (Ottawa: CCC).

Deeg, Richard (1996) "Economic Globalization and the Shifting Boundaries of German Federalism" *Publius: The Journal of Federalism* 26(1): 27–52.

DeMestral, Armand (1995) "A Comment" in Trebilcock and Schwanen (eds.): 95–7.

Denoon, Donald (1983) *Settler Capitalism: The Dynamics of Dependent Development in the Southern Hemisphere* (Oxford: Clarendon Press).

Dicey, A.V. ([1885] 1982) *Introduction to the Study of the Law of the Constitution* (Indianapolis: Liberty Fund).

Doern, G. Bruce (1991) *Europe Uniting: The EC Model and Canada's Constitutional Debate* (Canada Round Papers No. 7) (Toronto: C.D. Howe Institute).

– and Brian Tomlin (1991) *Faith and Fear: The Free Trade Story* (Toronto: Stoddard).

– and Mark MacDonald (1997) "The Liberals' Internal Trade Agreement: The Beginning of a New Federal Assertiveness ?" in Gene Swimmer (ed.) *How Ottawa Spends 1997–98: Seeing Red: A Liberal Report Card* (Ottawa: Carleton University Press): 135–58.

– and Mark MacDonald (1999) *Free-Trade Federalism: Negotiating the Canadian Agreement on Internal Trade* (Toronto: University of Toronto Press).

Drache, Daniel and Duncan Cameron (eds.) (1985) *The Other Macdonald Report* (Toronto: Lorimer).

Drucker, Peter (1986) "The Changed World Economy" *Foreign Affairs* (Spring): 3–17.

Duchacek, Ivo (1987) *Comparative Federalism: The Territorial Dimension of Politics* (Lanham, Md.: University Press of America).

Dupre, J. Stefan (1987) "Reflections on the Workability of Executive Federalism" in Bakvis and Chandler (eds.): 236–58.

Dyson, Kenneth (1980) *The State Tradition in Western Europe* (New York: Oxford University Press).

Dyster, Barry and David Meredith (1990) *Australia in the International Economy* (Cambridge and Melbourne: Cambridge University Press).

Easson, Alex (1995) "Harmonization of Legislation: Some Comparisons between the AIT and the EEC Treaty" in Trebilcock and Schwanen (eds.): 119–50.

Economic Council of Canada [ECC] (1988) *Adjustment Policies for Trade-Sensitive Industries* (Ottawa: MSS).

– (1991a) *A Joint Venture* (Ottawa: MSS).

Economic Planning Advisory Council [EPAC] (1989) *Promoting Competition in Australia* (Council Paper No. 38) (Canberra: AGPS).

– (1990) "Commonwealth-State Overlap of Functions and Regulations" in *Towards a More Cooperative Federalism?* (Discussion Paper 90/04) (Canberra: AGPS): 1–41.

– (1991) *Competitiveness: The Policy Environment* (Canberra: AGPS).

Economist (London) 17 March 1984.

Eden, Lorraine and Maureen Appel Molot (1993) "Canada's National Policies: Reflections on 125 Years" *Canadian Public Policy* XIX (3): 232–51.

Edwards, Meredith and Alan Henderson (1995) "COAG: A Vehicle for Reform" in Carroll and Painter (eds.): 21–51.

Elazar, Daniel J. (1962) *The American Partnership: Intergovernmental Cooperation in the Nineteenth Century United States* (Chicago: University of Chicago Press).

– ([1966] 1984) *American Federalism: A View from the States* (3rd edition) (New York: Harper and Row).

– (1987) *Exploring Federalism* (Tuscaloosa: University of Alabama Press).

– (1993) "International and Comparative Federalism" *PS: Political Science and Politics* 26(2): 190–95.

– (1994) *Federalism and the Way to Peace* (Kingston: IIR/QU).

Fagan, R. and M. Webber (1994) *Global Restructuring: The Australian Experience* (Melbourne: Oxford University Press).

Fafard, Patrick (1994) "Confederalism as an Alternative Form of Governance: Some Lessons from the European Community" Paper presented to Canadian Political Science Association, University of Calgary.

Fairley, Scott (1986) "Constitutional Aspects of External Trade Policy" in Mark Krasnick (ed.) *Case Studies in the Division of Powers* (Research Studies of the Royal Commission on the Economic Union and Development Prospects of Canada, Vol. 62) (Toronto: University of Toronto Press): 1–51.

Fallis, George (1991) *The Costs of Constitutional Change: A Citizen's Guide to the Issues* (Toronto: Lorimer).

Federal-State Relations Committee [FSRC] Parliament of Victoria (1997) *International Treaty Making and the Role of the States (First Report of the Inquiry into Overlap and Duplication)* (Melbourne: Government Printer).

– (1998) *Australian Federalism: The Role of the States (Second Report of the Inquiry into Overlap and Duplication, October 1998)* (Melbourne: Government Printer).

FitzGerald, Stephen (1997) *Is Australia an Asian Country?* (St. Leonards, NSW: Allen and Unwin).

Flatters, F.R. and R.G. Lipsey (1983) *Common Ground for the Canadian Common Market* (Montreal: Institute for Research on Public Policy).

Fletcher, Christine (1991) "Rediscovering Australian Federalism by Resurrecting Old Ideas" *Australian Journal of Political Science* 26(1): 79–94.

– (1992) *The Australian Territories and New Federalism* (Discussion Paper No. 13) (Canberra: FRC/ANU).

– (ed.) (1994) *Aboriginal Self-determination in Australia* (Canberra: Australian Institute of Aboriginal and Torres Strait Islander Studies, Australian National University).

– and Cliff Walsh (1991) *Intergovernmental Relations in Australia: Managerialist Reform and the Power of Federalism* (Discussion Paper No. 4) (Canberra: FRC/ANU).

Fletcher, Frederick J. and Donald C. Wallace (1985) "Federal-Provincial Relations and the Making of Policy in Canada: A Review of Case Studies" in R. Simeon (ed.): 125–205.

Forsyth, Murray (1981) *Unions of States: The Theory and Practice of Confederation* (Leicester: Leicester University Press).

– (1995) "The Political Theory of Federalism: The Relevance of the Classical Approach" in J.J. Hesse and V. Wright (eds.) *Federalising Europe? The Costs, Benefits and Preconditions of Federal Political Systems* (Oxford: Oxford University Press): 25–45.

Forsyth, Peter (1995a) "Microeconomic Reform in a Federal System: Constraints and Incentives" in Carroll and Painter (eds.): 63–75.

– (1995b) *The States, Microeconomic Reform and the Revenue Problem* (Discussion Paper No. 27) (Canberra: ANU/FRC).

Fortin, Pierre (1991) "The Constitutional Proposals, Social Efficiency and the Quebec Problem: Suggested Amendments" in Boadway and Purvis (eds.): 73–79.

Fournier, Pierre (1990) "L'échec du Lac Meech: Un point de vue québécois" in Watts and Brown (eds.): 41–68.

Fowler, H. W. and F. G. Fowler (eds.) (1964) *The Concise Oxford Dictionary* (5th edition) (London: Oxford University Press).

Gagnon, Alain-G. (1993) "The Political Uses of Federalism" in Michael Burgess, and Alain G. Gagnon (eds.) *Comparative Federalism and Federation: Competing Traditions and Future Directions* (New York: Harvester, Wheatsheaf): 15–44.

– and Hugh Segal (eds.) (2000) *The Canadian Social Union Without Quebec* (Montreal: Institute for Research on Public Policy).

Galligan, Brian (1989) "The 1988 Referendums in Perspective" in Galligan and Nethercote (eds.): 118–46.

Galligan, Brian (1995) *A Federal Republic: Australia's Constitutional System of Government* (Melbourne: Cambridge University Press).

– and Richard Mulgan (1994) "Closer Political Relations for Australia and New Zealand: Towards an Asymmetrical Federal Association" in Bertus De Villiers (ed.) *Evaluating Federal Systems* (Cape Town: Juta and Company): 333–44.

– (ed.) (1993) *Federalism and the Economy: International, National and State Issues* (Canberra: FRC/ANU).

– and J.R. Nethercote (eds.) (1989) *The Constitutional Commission and the 1988 Referendums* (Canberra: ANU/ Centre for Research on Federal Financial Relations and Royal Australian Institute of Public Administration).

– Owen Hughes and Cliff Walsh (eds.) (1991) *Intergovernmental Relations and Public Policy* (Sydney: Allen and Unwin).

– and Christine Fletcher (eds.) (1992) "Special Issue: Australian Federalism: Rethinking and Restructuring" *Australian Journal of Political Science* 27.

– Bob Lim and Kim Lovegrove (eds.) (1993) *Managing Microeconomic Reform* (Canberra: ANU/FRC).

Gamble, Andrew (1988) *The Free Economy and the Strong State: The Politics of Thatcherism* (Basingstoke: Macmillan Educational).

– (1995) "The New Political Economy" *Political Studies* XLIII: 516–30.

Garnaut, Ross (1989) *Australia and the Northeast Asian Ascendancy* (Canberra: Australian Government Publishing Service).

Gazette (Montreal) 2 July 1994.

Gilpin, R. (1987) *The Political Economy of International Relations* (Princeton: Princeton University Press).

Globe and Mail (Toronto) 14 December 1991, 25 June 1994, 28 June 1994, 2 July 1994, 18 July 1994, 19 July 1994, 15 June 1998, 10 July 1998.

Gold, Marc and David Leyton-Brown (eds.) (1988) *Trade-Offs on Free Trade* (Toronto: Carswell).

Goss, Wayne (1995) *Restoring the Balance: The Future of the Australian Federation* (Canberra: FRC/ANU).

Gray, A.M. (1993) "Non-Bank Financial Institutions Reform" in Galligan, Lim, and Lovegrove (eds.): 84–96.

Gray, Gwendolyn (1991) *Federalism and Health Policy: The Development of Health Systems in Canada and Australia* (Toronto: University of Toronto Press).

Greiner, Nick (1990) *Physician Heal Thyself: Microeconomic Reform of Australian Government* (Press Release of Speech, National Press Club, Canberra).

Grodzins, Murray (1966) *The American System: A New View of Government in the United States* (New Brunswick, NJ: Transaction Books).

Haack, R.E., D.R. Hughes, and R.G. Shapiro (1981) *The Splintered Market: Barriers to Interprovincial Trade in Canadian Agriculture* (Toronto: Lorimer).

Hall, Peter (1986) *Governing the Economy: The Politics of State Intervention in Britain and France* (Cambridge: Polity Press).

Hamilton, Stuart (1995) "The Intergovernmental Agreement on the Environment: Three Years On" in Carroll and Painter (eds.): 185–90.

Hancock, W.K. ([1930]1961) *Australia* (Brisbane: Jacaranda Press).

Harman, Elizabeth (1996) "The National Competition Policy: A Study of the Policy Process and Network" *Australian Journal of Political Science* 31(2): 205–33.

– and Frank Harman (1996) "The Potential for Local Diversity in Implementation of the National Competition Policy" *Australian Journal of Public Administration* 55(2): 1225.

Harris, Richard G. (1991) "The Federal Constitutional Proposals and the Economic Union" in Boadway and Purvis (eds.): 13–25.

– and Douglas D. Purvis (1991) "Economic Union and Policy Coordination: Some Economic Aspects of Political Restructuring" in Boadway (et al.) (eds.): 189–211.

– and William Watson (1993) "Three Visions of Competitiveness: Porter, Reich and Thurow on Economic Growth and Policy" in Courchene and Purvis (eds.): 233–80.

Hart, Michael (1994) *Decision at Midnight: Inside the Canada-United States Free Trade Negotiations* (Vancouver: University of British Columbia Press).

Hartt, Stanley H. (1992) "Sovereignty and the Economic Union" in S. Hartt et al.: 3–30.

– et al. (1992) *Tangled Web: Legal Aspects of Deconfederation* (Canada Round Series No. 15) (Toronto: C.D. Howe Institute).

Hawke, R.J. (1990) "Towards a Closer Partnership" (Canberra: Press Release of Speech, National Press Club).

– et al. (1991) *Building a Competitive Australia* (Canberra: AGPS).

Hayes, John (1982) *Economic Mobility in Canada* (Ottawa: Canadian Government Publishing Service).

Head, Brian (1989) "Federalism, the States and Economic Policy: A Political Science Perspective" in B. Galligan (ed.): *Australian Federalism* (Melbourne: Longman, Cheshire): 239–59.

Head, Brian and Stephen Bell (1994) "Understanding the Modern State: Explanatory Approaches" in Bell and Head (eds.): 25–74.

Held, David (1984) *Political Theory and the Modern State: Essays on State, Power, and Democracy* (Cambridge: Polity).

Helliwell, John F. (1998) *How Much Do National Borders Matter?* (Washington, DC: The Brookings Institution).

Higgott, Richard (1991) "The Politics of Australia's Economic Relations: Adjustment and Two-Level Games" *Australian Journal of Political Science* 26(1): 2–28.

– (1994) "Australia and the Pacific Region: The Political Economy of 'Relocation'" in Stubbs and Underhill (eds.): 524–36.

Hilmer, Frederick, M. Rayner and G. Taperell (1993) *National Competition Policy* (Report of the Independent Committee of Inquiry) (Canberra: AGPS).

Hines, W.R. and Associates (1996) *Discussion Paper Concerning the Convergence of the Domestic and International Trade Policy Agendas* (Ottawa: mimeo [prepared for Industry Canada]).

Hirst, P. and G. Thompson (1995) "Globalization and the Nation-State" *Economy and Society* 24(3): 408–42.

Hogg, Peter W. (1985) *Constitutional Law of Canada* (2nd Edition) (Toronto: Carswell).

– (1996) *Constitutional Law of Canada* (4th student edition) (Toronto: Carswell).

Howard, John (1997) "Media Release" 13 August.
- (1999) "Media Release" 9 April.
Howse, Robert H. (1992) *Economic Union, Social Justice and Constitutional Reform: Towards a High but Level Playing Field* (North York: York University, Centre for Public Law and Public Policy).
- (1995) "Between Anarchy and the Rule of Law: Dispute Settlement and Related Implementation Issues in the AIT" in Trebilcock and Schwanen (eds.): 170–95.
- (1996) *Securing the Canadian Economic Union: Legal and Constitutional Options for the Federal Government* (Commentary No. 81) (Toronto: C.D. Howe Institute).
- and Michael Trebilcock (1991) "Proposals for the Economic Union and Division of Powers" in Boadway and Purvis (eds.): 26–35.
Ikenberry J. (1986) "The State and Strategies for Industrial Adjustment" *World Politics*, 29: 53–77.
Innis, H.A. and W.T. Easterbrook (1962) "Fundamental and Historic Elements" in J.J. Deutsch (et al.) (eds.) *The Canadian Economy: Selected Readings* (Toronto: Macmillan): 363–71.
Industry Assistance Commission [IAC] (1983) *Annual Report, 1982–83* (Canberra: AGPS).
- (1989) *Annual Report, 1988–89* (Canberra: AGPS).
Industry Commission [IC] (1990) *Annual Report, 1989–90* (Canberra: AGPS).
- (1992) *Pro-Competitive Regulation* (Discussion Paper) (Canberra: AGPS).
- (1994) *Annual Report, 1993–94* (Canberra: AGPS).
- (1996) *State, Territorial and Local Government Assistance to Industry* (Report No. 55) (Canberra: AGPS).
- (1997) *Assessing Australia's Productivity Performance* (Research Paper) (Canberra: AGPS).
Intergovernmental News [Quarterly] (1988–96) (Melbourne: Centre for Comparative Constitutional Studies, University of Melbourne), Vol. 6, No. 4 (Winter 1984), Vol. 8, No. 2 (Winter 1995), Vol. 8, No. 5 (Spring 1995), Vol. 9, No. 3 (Spring 1997).
Internal Trade Secretariat [ITS] (1998a) "Press Release" Ottawa, 20 February.
- (1998b) *[First] Annual Report of the Council of Ministers on Internal Trade, 1994–96* (Winnipeg: ITS).
- (1998c) "Outstanding Obligations" (Winnipeg: ITS web site: www.intrasec.mb.ca).
- (1998d) *Report of the Article 1704 Panel Concerning a Dispute Between Alberta and Canada Regarding the Manganese-Based Fuel Additive Act* (Winnipeg: ITS).
- (1999) "Summary of Disputes/Complaints – Tracking Tables" (Winnipeg: ITS web site: www.intrasec.mb.ca/eng/table.htm).
Jackson, John (1989) *The World Trade System: Law and Policy of International Economic Relations* (Cambridge: MIT Press).
Jenkin, Michael (1983) *The Challenge of Diversity: Industrial Policy in the Canadian Federation* (Background Study 50, Science Council of Canada) (Ottawa: MSS).
Johnson, Jon R. and Joel S. Schacter (1988) *The Free Trade Agreement: A Comprehensive Guide* (Aurora, Ont.: Canadian Law Books).
Johnston, Richard, André Blais, Elisabeth Gidengil and Neil Nevitte (1993) "The People and the Charlottetown Accord" in Watts and Brown (eds.): 19–43.
Jones, Ross (ed.) (1994) *Australian Microeconomic Policies* (4th edition) (Sydney: Prentice-Hall).
Julien, Germain and Marcel Proulx (1978) *Les chevauchements des programmes fédéraux et québécois* (Quebec: École national d'administration publique).
Katzenstein, Peter (ed.) (1978) *Between Power and Plenty* (Madison: University of Wisconsin Press).
- (1985) *Small States in World Markets: Industrial Policy in Europe* (Ithaca: Cornell University Press).

Keating, Paul (1991) "The Commonwealth and the States and the November Premiers Conference" (Press Release of Speech, National Press Club) 22 October.
– (1992) *One Nation* (Policy Statement, 26 February) (Canberra: AGPS).
– (1994) "Reshaping Australian Institutions" (Speech to Australian National University, Canberra).
Kellow, Aynsley (1995) "Federalism and Environmental Policy Reform: Micro Economics and Macro Politics" in Carroll and Painter (eds.): 200–15.
Kelly, Paul (1994) *The End of Certainty: Power, Politics and Business in Australia* (St. Leonards, NSW: Allen and Unwin).
Kennett, Steven A. (1998) *Securing the Social Union: A Commentary on the Decentralized Approach* (Research Paper No. 34) (Kingston: IIR/QU).
Kenyon, Diane and John Kincaid (1991) "Introduction" in Kenyon and Kincaid (eds.) *Competition Among States and Local Governments: Efficiency and Equity in American Federalism* (Washington, D.C.: Urban Institute Press): 1–33.
Keohane, R. O. (1984) *After Hegemony: Cooperation and Discord in the World Political Economy* (Princeton: Princeton University Press).
Kincaid, John (1991) "The Competitive Challenge to Cooperative Federalism: A Theory of Federal Democracy" in Kenyon and Kincaid (eds.): 87–114.
Kirchner, E.J. (1992) *Decision-Making in the European Community: The Council Presidency and European Integration* (Manchester: Manchester University Press).
Knop, Karen, Sylvia Ostry, Richard Simeon and Katherine Swinton (eds.) (1995) *Rethinking Federalism: Citizens, Markets, and Governments in a Changing World* (Vancouver: UBC Press).
Knox, Robert H. (1997) "Economic Integration in Canada Through the Agreement on Internal Trade" (draft paper).
– (1998) "Economic Integration in Canada Through the Agreement on Internal Trade" in Lazar (ed.): 137–67.
Krasner, Stephen (1978) *Defending the National Interest: Raw Materials Investment and U.S. Corporate Interests* (Princeton: Princeton University Press).
Kukucha, Chris (1994) "International Economic Regimes, Canadian Federalism and the NAFTA Side Deals – the Role of the Provinces" Unpublished paper presented to Canadian Political Science Association, University of Calgary.
Laffin, Martin and Martin Painter (eds.) (1995) *Reform and Reversal: Lessons from the Coalition Government in New South Wales, 1988–1995* (Melbourne: Macmillan).
Laforest, Guy (1992) *Trudeau et la fin d'un rêve canadien* (Sillery, Que.: Septendrion).
Landau, Martin (1973) "Federalism, Redundancy and System Reliability" *Publius: The Journal of Federalism* 3: 173–96.
Lang, T. and C. Hines (1993) *The New Protectionism* (London: Earthscan).
La Presse (Montreal, 7 December 1991).
Larkin, J.T and T.M. Dwyer (1994) *Refocussing Microeconomic Reform* (Melbourne: Business Council of Australia).
Laski, Harold (1939) "The Obsolescence of Federalism" *The New Republic* 3 (May): 367–69.
Laskin, Bora (1947) "Peace, Order and Good Government Re-Examined" *Canadian Bar Review* 25: 1054–87.
Laux, Jeanne Kirk and Maureen Appel Molot (1988) *State Capitalism: Public Enterprise in Canada* (Ithaca: Cornell University Press).
Lazar, Harvey (ed.) (1998) *Canada: The State of the Federation, 1997: Non-Constitutional Renewal* (Kingston: IIR/QU).
Leaders Forum [LF] (1994) "Communiqué" Sydney, 29 July.
– (1996) "Communiqué" Melbourne, 27 September.

Lederman, W.R. (1975) "Unity and Diversity in Canadian Federalism: Ideas and Methods of Moderation" *Canadian Bar Review* 53: 597–620.

Leibried, Stephan and Paul Pierson (1996) "Social Policy" in Helen Wallace and William Wallace (eds.) *Policy-Making in the European Union* (Oxford: Oxford University Press): 185–207.

Lenihan, Donald G. (1992) "Economic Union: Notes on the Federal Proposals" *Network Analyses* (No.1, December).

–   (1995) "When a Legitimate Objective Hits an Unnecessary Obstacle: Harmonizing Regulations and Standards in the AIT" in Trebilcock and Schwanen (eds.): 98–118.

Leslie, Peter M. (1987) *Federal State, National Economy* (Toronto: University of Toronto Press).

–   (1989) "The Peripheral Predicament: Federalism and Continentalism" in Leslie and Watts (eds.): 3–36.

–   (1991) "Options for the Future of Canada: the Good, the Bad and the Fantastic" in R.L. Watts and D.M. Brown (eds.): 123–40.

–   (1994) "Economic Union, Social Union, and Political Union: Reflections on the State of the Canadian Federal System" Paper presented at conference "Federalism in Practice," Brussels.

–   (1996a) "Asymmetry and Integration: The Emergence of Regional Hegemonic Systems" in W. Schutze and J. Bingen (eds.) *Europe at the end of the '90s* (Oslo: Europa Programmet): 191–235.

–   (1996b) *The Maastricht Model: A Canadian Perspective on the European Union* (Kingston: IIR/QU).

–   (1997) " 'Governing the Economy' within Economic Unions: Canada, the EU and the NAFTA" Paper at ECPR-APSA workshop, Bern, Switzerland.

–   (1998) "Abuses of Asymmetry: Privilege and Exclusion" Paper delivered to the International Political Science Association, Brussels, February.

–   and R.L. Watts (eds.) (1989) *Canada: The State of the Federation, 1987–88* (Kingston: IIR/QU).

Leyton-Brown, David (1994) "The Political Economy of North American Free Trade" in Stubbs and Underhill (eds.): 352–65.

Lisée, Jean-François (1994) *The Trickster: Robert Bourassa and the Quebecers, 1990–92* (Toronto: Lorimer).

Livingston, William S. (1967) "A Note on the Nature of Federalism" in A. Wildavsky (ed.) *American Federalism in Perspective* (Boston: Little, Brown): 33–47.

March, James G. and Johan P. Olsen (1989) *Rediscovering Institutions: The Organizational Basis of Politics* (New York: Free Press).

Marks, Gary, F. Scharpf, P. Schmitter and W. Streech (eds.) (1996) *Governance in the European Union* (London: Sage).

Marsh, Ian (1995) *Beyond the Two-Party System: Political Representation, Economic Competitiveness and Australian Politics* (Melbourne: Cambridge University Press).

Marshall, T.H. (1964) *Class, Citizenship and Social Development* (New York: Doubleday).

Mathews, R.L. (1977) "Innovations and developments in Australian federalism" *Publius: The Journal of Federalism* 7(3): 9–19.

Maxwell, Judith and Caroline Pestieau (1980) *Economic Realities of Contemporary Confederation* (Montreal: C.D. Howe Institute).

Maxwell, Judith, Caroline Pestieau and Harvey Lazar (1991) Submission to the Joint Committee of Parliament on a Renewed Canada (Ottawa: Economic Council of Canada: mimeo).

McCallum, John (1992) "An Economic Union or a Free Trade Agreement: What Difference Does It Make?" in S. Hartt et al.: 54–9.

McMillan, John, Gareth Evans and Haddon Storey (1983) *Australia's Constitution: Time for Change* (Sydney: Law Foundation of New South Wales and George Allen and Unwin).

McRoberts, Kenneth (1985) "Unilateralism, Bilateralism and Multilateralism" in R. Simeon (ed.) *Intergovernmental Relations* (Research Studies of the Royal Commission on the Economic Union and Development Prospects for Canada, Vol. 63) (Toronto: University of Toronto Press): 71–129.

– (1997) *Misconceiving Canada: The Struggle for National Unity* (Toronto: Oxford University Press).

Meekison, Peter J. (1993) "Let There Be Light" in Watts and Brown (eds.): 61–85.

Miller, Irving (1995) "Dispute Resolution: An Interprovincial Approach" in Trebilcock and Schwanen (eds): 151–69.

Milne, David (1986) *Tug of War: Ottawa and the Provinces Under Trudeau and Mulroney* (Toronto: Lorimer).

– (1991) "Asymmetry or Equality: Why Choose?" in Watts and Brown (eds.): 285–307.

Milner, Henry (1989) *Sweden: Social Democracy in Practice* (New York: Oxford University Press).

Molot, Maureen Appel (1994) "The Canadian State in the International Economy" in Stubbs and Underhill (eds.): 511–23.

Monahan, Patrick J. (1993) "The Sounds of Silence" in K. McRoberts and P. Monahan (eds.) *The Charlottetown Accord, the Referendum and the Future of Canada* (Toronto: University of Toronto Press): 222–48.

– (1995) " 'To the Extent Possible': A Comment on the Dispute Settlement in AIT" in Trebilcock and Schwanen (eds.): 211–17.

Moravcsik, Andrew (1993) "Preferences and Power in the European Community: A Liberal Intergovernmental Approach" *Journal of Common Market Studies* 31:4 (December): 473–524.

Mullins, Anne and Cheryl Saunders (eds.) (1994) *Economic Union in Federal Systems* (Sydney: The Federation Press).

Nahan, Michael (1995) "Competitive and Uncompetitive Approaches to Competition Policy and Microeconomic Reform" in Carroll and Painter (eds.): 233–42.

National Commission of Audit [NCOA] (1996) *Report to the Commonwealth Government* (Canberra: AGPS).

National Competition Council [NCC] (1996) *Annual Report, 1995–96* (Canberra: AGPS).

– (1997) *Annual Report, 1996–97* (Canberra: AGPS).

– (1998) *Annual Report, 1997–98* (Canberra: AGPS).

Nelson, Helen (1992) "Recipes for Uniformity: The Case of Food Standards" *Australian Journal of Political Science* (B. Galligan (ed.) Special Issue on Federalism) 27: 63–77.

Newfoundland House of Assembly (1995) *Agreement on Internal Trade Amendment Act S.N. 1995, c. A–5.1.*

Nordlinger, Eric (1981) *On the Autonomy of the Democratic State* (Cambridge: Harvard University Press).

Norrie, Kenneth, R. Simeon and M. Krasnick (1986) *Federalism and Economic Union in Canada* (Research Studies of the Royal Commission on the Economic Union and Development Prospects for Canada, Vol. 59) (Toronto: University of Toronto Press).

Nova Scotia Legislative Assembly (1996) *Internal Trade Agreement Implementation Act, S.N.S. 1996, c.8.*

Nymark, Alan (1991) "Globalization: Lessons for Canadian Investment Policy and the Federation" in Brown and Smith (eds.): 183–95.

Offe, Claus (1984) *Contradictions of the Welfare State* (Cambridge: MIT Press).

Ohmae, Kenichi (1990) *The Borderless World* (London: Collins).

Olson, Mancur (1965) *The Logic of Collective Action* (Cambridge: Harvard University Press).

– (1982) *The Rise and Decline of Nations: Economic Growth, Stagflation and Social Rigidities* (New Haven: Yale University Press).

Ontario (1990) Premier David Peterson, "Securing Ontario's Future in a Changing Canada" (Toronto: mimeo).

– (1991) *A Canadian Social Charter – Making Our Shared Values Stronger* (Toronto: Ministry of Intergovernmental Affairs).

– (1992) "Ontario's Proposal for a Social Charter for Canada" (13 February) (Toronto: mimeo).

Ontario Economic Council [OEC] (1977) *Intergovernmental Relations: Issues and Alternatives* (Toronto: OEC).

Organization for Economic Cooperation and Development [OECD] (1987) *Structural Adjustment and Economic Performance* (Paris: OECD).

Ostrom, Elinor (1990) *Governing the Commons: The Evolution of Institutions of Collective Action* (Cambridge: Cambridge University Press).

Ostrom,Vincent (1987) *The Political Theory of a Compound Republic: Designing the American Experiment* (2nd edition) (Lincoln: University of Nebraska Press).

Padoa-Schioppa, T. (et al.) (1987) *Efficiency, Stability and Equity: A Strategy for the Evolution of the Economic System of the European Community* (Brussels: European Commission).

– (1995) "Economic Federalism and the European Union" in K. Knop et al. (eds.): 154–65.

Painter, Martin (1991) "Intergovernmental Relations: An Institutional Analysis" *Canadian Journal of Political Science* 24: 269–88.

– (1995) *The COAG and Intergovernmental Cooperation: Competition or Collaborative Federalism?* (Discussion Paper No. 28) (Canberra: FRC/ANU).

– (1996) "Federal Theory and Modern Australian Executive Federalism" in John Halligan (ed.) *Public Administration under Scrutiny: Essays in Honour of Roger Wettenhall* (Canberra: Centre for Research in Public Sector Management, University of Canberra): 77–96.

– (1998) *Collaborative Federalism: Economic Reform in Australia in the 1990s* (Melbourne: Macmillan).

Panitch, Leo (1979) "Corporatism in Canada?" *Studies in Political Economy* 1 (Spring): 43–92.

– (1986) "The Tripartite Experience" in K. Banting (ed.) *The State and Economic Interests* (Research Studies of the Royal Commission on the Economic Union and Development Prospects for Canada, Vol. 32) (Toronto: University of Toronto Press): 37–119.

Parliament of Australia, *Commonwealth Disabilities Services Act, 1991.*

– *Competition Policy Reform Act [CPR Act] 1995*, Bill No. 88.

– *Environment Protection and Biodiversity Conservation Act 1998 [EPBC Act].*

– *National Food Authority Act 1991 [NFA Act]* No. 118.

– *National Rail Corporation Act 1992 [NRC Act]*, No. 26.

– *National Road Transportation Commission Amendment Act 1992 [NRTC Act]* Bill 149.

– (2000) *Jobs for the Regions* (Report of the Senate References Committee on Employment, Workplace Relations [etc.]) (Canberra: Parliament of Australia).

Parti Québécois [PQ] (1991) *Programme du Parti Québécois* (Montreal).

Pelkmans, Jacques (1997) *European Integration: Methods and Economic Analysis* (Harrow: Addison, Wesley, Longman).

Pendal, Phillip (1995) "Intergovernmental Agreements, Uniform Legislation and the Parliamentary System" in Carroll and Painter (eds.): 255–66.

Pennock, J. R. (1959) "Federal and Unitary Government – Disharmony and Reliability" *Behavioural Science* 4(2): 147–57.

Pentland, Charles (1973) *International Theory and European Integration* (London: Faber and Faber).

Pierson, Paul (1996) "The Path to European Integration: A Historical Institutionalist Analysis" *Comparative Political Studies* 29(2): 123–63.

Polyani, Karl (1944) *The Great Transformation: The Political and Economic Origins of Our Time* (Boston: Beacon Press).

Porter, Michael (1990) *The Competitive Advantage of Nations* (London: Macmillan).

Premiers and Chief Ministers Meeting [PCM] (1991) "Communiqué" Adelaide, 21–22 November.

Prichard, J.R.S. with Jamie Benedickson (1983) "Securing the Canadian Economic Union: Federalism and Internal Barriers to Trade" in Trebilcock et al. (eds.): 3–50.

Productivity Commission [PC] (1996) *Stocktake of Progress in Microeconomic Reform* (Canberra: AGPS).

– (1997) *Impact of Mutual Recognition on Regulations in Australia: A Preliminary Assessment* (Information Paper)(Canberra: Office of Regulatory Review, Productivity Commission).

– (2000) *Annual Report, 1999–2000* (Canberra: AGPS).

Przeworski, A and H. Teune (1982 [1970]) *The Logic of Comparative Social Inquiry* (New York: Wiley).

Purvis, Douglas D. (1991) "The Federal Proposals and the Economic Union" in R. Boadway and D. Purvis (eds.) 1–12.

– and André Raynauld (1992) "Lament for the Canadian Economic Union" in D. Brown and R. Young (eds.) *Canada: The State of the Federation, 1992* (Kingston: IIR/QU): 129–43.

Putnam, Robert (1988) "Diplomacy and Domestic Politics: The Logic of Two-Level Games" *International Organization* 42(3): 427–60.

Quebec Liberal Party [QLP] (1991) *A Quebec Free to Choose: Report of the Constitutional Committee of the Quebec Liberal Party* [Allaire Report] (Montreal: QLP).

Quebec National Assembly [QNA](1991) *Commission on the Political and Constitutional Future of Quebec* [Bélanger-Campeau], *Report* (March) (Quebec: NAQ).

– (1996) *An Act Respecting the Implementation of the Agreement on Internal Trade, 1996* (Bill 15).

Ravenhill, John (1997) "Foreign Economic Policies" in Brian Galligan, Ian McAllister and John Ravenhill (eds.) *New Developments in Australian Politics* (South Melbourne: Macmillan Educational): 213–30.

Regroupement Économie et Constitution, Le [REC] (1992) "Submission to Joint Parliamentary Committee" (Montreal: mimeo).

Riker, W.H. (1964) *Federalism: Origin, Operation, Significance* (Boston: Little, Brown).

Rivlin, Alice M. (1992) "A New Vision of American Federalism" *Public Administration Review* 52: 319.

Robertson, Gordon (1979) "The Role of Interministerial Conferences in the Decision-Making Process" in R. Simeon (ed.): 78–88.

Robinson, Ian (1993) "NAFTA, the Side-Deals and Canadian Federalism: Constitutional Reform by Other Means?" in Watts and Brown (eds.): 193–227.

– (1995) "Trade Policy, Globalization, and the Future of Canadian Federalism" in Rocher and Smith (eds.): 234–69.

Rocher, François and Miriam Smith (eds.) (1995) *New Trends in Canadian Federalism* (Peterborough, Ont.: Broadview Press).

Romanow, Roy, John Whyte and Howard Leeson (1984) *Canada ... Notwithstanding: The Making of the Constitution 1976–82* (Toronto: Methuen).

Rossiter, Clinton (ed.) (1961) *The Federalist Papers* (New York: New American Library, Mentor).

Russell Peter H. (1993) *Constitutional Odyssey: Can Canadians Become a Sovereign People?* (2nd edition) (Toronto: University of Toronto Press).

Safarian, A.E. (1974) *Canadian Federalism and Economic Integration* (Ottawa: Information Canada).

– (1980) *Ten Markets or One? Regional Barriers to Economic Activity in Canada* (Toronto: Ontario Economic Council).

Saunders, Cheryl (1984) *The Impact of Intergovernmental Relations on Parliament* (Papers on Federalism No. 1) (Melbourne: Centre for Comparative Constitutional Studies, University of Melbourne).

– (1989) *Intergovernmental Arrangements: Legal and Constitutional Framework* (Papers on Federalism No. 14) (Melbourne: Centre for Comparative Constitutional Studies, University of Melbourne).

– (1992) "Fiscal Federalism: A General and Unholy Scramble" in Craven (ed.): 101–30.

– (1994a) "Introduction" in Mullins and Saunders (eds.): VII–XVIII.

– (1994b) "Australian Economic Union" in Mullins and Saunders (eds.): 1–26.

– (1995) "Intergovernmental Relations: National and Supranational" in Carroll and Painter (eds.): 52–62.

Sbragia, Alberta (1992) "Thinking about the European Future: The Uses of Comparison" in A. Sbragia (ed.) *Euro-Politics: Institutions and Policymaking in the "New" European Community* (Washington, DC: The Brookings Institution): 257–91.

Scharpf, Fritz (1988) "The Joint-Decision Trap: Lessons from West German Federalism and European Integration" *Public Administration* 66: 239–78.

– (1991) *Crisis and Choice in European Social Democracy* (Ithaca and London: Cornell University Press).

– (1996) "Negative and Positive Integration in the Political Economy of European Welfare States" in Gary Marks (et al.) (eds.) 15–39.

Schecter, Stephen (1981) "On the Compatibility of Federalism and Intergovernmental Management" *Publius: The Journal of Federalism* 11: 127–41.

Schneiderman, David (1991) "The Market and the Constitution" *Constitutional Forum/Constitutionnel* Vol. 3, No. 2 (Winter): 40–44.

Schwanen, Daniel (1992) "Open Exchange: Freeing the Trade of Goods and Services within the Canadian Economic Union" in David Brown, Fred Lazar and Daniel Schwanen *Free to Move: Strengthening the Canadian Economic Union* (Toronto: C.D. Howe Institute):1–37.

– (1996) *Drawing on Our Inner Strength: Canada's Economic Citizenship in an Era of Evolving Federalism* (The Canadian Union Papers) (Toronto: C.D. Howe Institute).

– (1998) "Canadian Regardless of Origin: 'Negative Integration' and the Agreement on Internal Trade" in H. Lazar (ed.): 169–202.

Schwartz, Bryan (1995) "Assessing the Agreement on Internal Trade: The Case for a 'More Perfect Union' " in D.M. Brown and J.W. Rose (eds.) *Canada: The State of the Federation, 1995* (Kingston: IIR/QU): 189–217.

Segal, Hugh (1996) *No Surrender: Tales of a Happy Warrior in the Tory Crusade* (Toronto: HarperCollins).

Self, Peter (1993) *Government by the Market: The Politics of Public Choice* (Basingstoke: Macmillan).

Sharman, Campbell (1989) "The Referendum Results in their Context" in Galligan and Nethercote (eds.): 105–17.

– (1991) "Executive Federalism" in B. Galligan et al. (eds.): 23–38.

Sheppard, Robert and Michael Valpy (1982) *The National Deal: The Fight for a Canadian Constitution* (Toronto: Macmillan).

Shoup, Carl (1977) "Interregional Economic Barriers: The Canadian Provinces" in OEC: 81–100.

Shoyama, Thomas K. (1989) "The Federal-Provincial Social Contract" in P.M. Leslie and R.L. Watts (eds.): 159–66.

Simeon, R.E.B. (1972) *Federal-Provincial Diplomacy* (Toronto: University of Toronto Press).

– (ed.) (1979) *Confrontation and Collaboration: Intergovernmental Relations in Canada Today* (Toronto: Institute of Public Administration of Canada).

– (ed.) (1985) *Division of Powers and Public Policy* (Research Studies of the Royal Commission on Economic Union and Development Prospects for Canada, Vol. 61) (Toronto: University of Toronto Press).

– (1987) "Inside the Macdonald Commission" *Studies in Political Economy* (Spring): 167–79.

– (1990) "Why Did the Meech Lake Accord Fail?" in Watts and Brown (eds.): 15–40.

– and Ian Robinson (1990) *State, Society and the Development of Canadian Federalism* (Research Studies of the Royal Commission on the Economic Union and Development Prospects for Canada, Vol. 70) (Toronto: University of Toronto Press).

Singleton, Gwynneth (1992) "'New Federalism' and Industrial Relations" *Australian Journal of Political Science* (Special Issue) 27: 127–42.

Skocpol, Theda (1985) "Bringing the State Back In: Strategies of Analysis in Current Research" in Bernard Susser (ed.) (1992) *Approaches to the Study of Politics* (New York: Macmillan): 457–97.

Skogstad, Grace (2000) "External Trade Policy and Canadian Federalism: A Constructive Tension?" Paper delivered to conference "Canadian Federalism in the New Millennium," University of Toronto, May.

Smiley, Donald V. (1979) "An Outsider's Observations of Federal-Provincial Relations Among Consenting Adults" in R. Simeon (ed.): 105–13.

– (1980) *Canada in Question: Federalism in the Eighties* (3rd edition) (Toronto: McGraw-Hill Ryerson).

– (1987) *The Federal Condition in Canada* (Toronto: McGraw-Hill Ryerson).

– and Ronald L. Watts (1985) *Intrastate Federalism in Canada* (Research Studies of the Royal Commission on the Economic Union and Development Prospects for Canada, Vol. 39) (Toronto: University of Toronto Press).

Smith, Miriam (1993) "Constitutionalizing Economic and Social Rights for Democracy" in Susan D. Phillips (ed.) *How Ottawa Spends 1993–94: A More Democratic Canada ...?* (Ottawa: Carleton University Press): 83–108.

Special Premiers Conferences [SPC] (1990) "Communiqué" Brisbane, 30–1 October.

– (1991) "Communiqué" Sydney 30 July.

Sproule-Jones, Mark (1993) *Governments at Work: Canadian Parliamentary Federalism and Its Public Policy Effects* (Toronto: University of Toronto Press).

Statistics Canada (1997) "1996 Census of Canada – Population and Dwelling Counts" *The Daily*, 15 April (Ottawa: Statscan).

Steinmo, Sven, Kathleen Thelan, and Frank Longstreth (eds.) (1992) *Structuring Politics: Historical Institutionalism in Comparative Analysis* (Cambridge: Cambridge University Press).

Stevenson, Garth (1982) *Unfulfilled Union* (3rd edition) (Toronto: Gage).

Strange, Susan (1994) *States and Markets* (2nd edition) (London: Frances Printer).

Stubbs, Richard and Geoffrey Underhill (eds.) (1994) *Political Economy and the Changing Global Order* (Toronto: Macmillan).

Susser, Bernard (ed.) (1992) *Approaches to the Study of Politics* (New York: Macmillan).

Swinton, Katherine (1995) "Law, Politics and the Enforcement of the AIT" in Trebilcock and Schwanen (eds.): 196–210.

– (1997) "The Enforcement of Intergovernmental Accords" in Cameron (ed.): 21–5.

Thelen, Kathleen and Sven Steinmo (1992) "Historical Institutionalism in Comparative Politics" in Steinmo (et al.) (eds.): 1–32.

Thomas, T. and C. Saunders (eds.) (1995) *The Australian Mutual Recognition Scheme* (Melbourne: Centre for Comparative Constitutional Studies, University of Melbourne).

Thorburn, Hugh G. (1984) *Planning and the Economy: Building Federal-Provincial Consensus* (Toronto: Lorimer).

Thurow, Lester (1992) *Head to Head: The Coming Economic Battle between Japan, Europe and America* (Sydney: Allen and Unwin).

Tiebout, Charles M. (1956) "A Pure Theory of Local Expenditures" *The Journal of Political Economy* 64(5): 416–24.

Tinbergen, Jan (1965) *International Economic Integration* (2nd edition) (Amsterdam: Elsevier).

Toronto Star 18 July 1994.

Treasury Board Secretariat of Canada (1991) *Federal-Provincial Overlap and Duplication: A Federal Program Perspective* (Ottawa: Treasury Board Secretariat).

Trebilcock, Michael J. (et al.) (1977) "Restrictions on the Interprovincial Mobility of Resources: Goods, Capital and Labour" in OEC: 102–22.

– J.R.S. Prichard, T.J. Couchene and J.Whalley (eds.) (1983) *Federalism and the Canadian Economic Union* (Toronto: Ontario Economic Council).

– John Whalley, Carol Rogerson and Ian Ness (1983) "Provincially Induced Barriers to Trade in Canada: A Survey" in Trebilcock et al. (eds.): 243–51.

– and Rambod Behboodi (1995) "The Canadian Agreement on Internal Trade: Retrospect and Prospect" in Trebilcock and Schwanen (eds): 20–89.

– and Daniel Schwanen (eds.) (1995) *Getting There: An Assessment of the Agreement on Internal Trade* (Toronto: C.D. Howe Institute).

Trudeau, Pierre E. (1968) *Federalism and the French Canadians* (Toronto: Macmillan).

Tsoukalis, Loukas (1997) *The New European Economy Revisited* (Oxford: Oxford University Press).

Tupper, Allan (1982) *Public Money in the Private Sector: Industrial Assistance Policy and Canadian Federalism* (Kingston: IIR/QU).

Uhr, John (1995) "Parliament and the Political Management of Federalism" in Carroll and Painter (eds.): 267–85.

Vaillancourt, François (1991) "An Economic Assessment of the Canadian Federal Proposals for Constitutional Reform: Plus Ça Change, Plus C'est Pareil" in Boadway and Purvis (eds.): 66–72.

Victoria (1997) Office of the Treasurer "Press Release" 29 August.

Vogel, David (1995) *Trading Up: Consumer and Environmental Regulation in a Global Economy* (Cambridge: Harvard University Press).

Walsh, Cliff (1991) *Reform of Commonwealth-State Relations: No Representation Without Taxation* (Occasional Paper 2) (Canberra: FRC/ANU).

– (1992) "Federal Reform and the Politics of Vertical Fiscal Imbalance" *Australian Journal of Political Science* (Special Issue) 27: 19–38.

Warhurst, John (1987) "Managing Intergovernmental Relations" in Bakvis and Chandler (eds.): 259–76.

Warnick, Leigh (1988) "State Agreements" *Australian Law Journal* 62: 878–906.

Watts, Ronald L. (1970) *Multicultural Societies and Federalism* (Studies of the Royal Commission on Bilingualism and Biculturalism, No. 8) (Ottawa: Information Canada).

- (1986) "The Macdonald Commission Report and Canadian Federalism" *Publius: The Journal of Federalism* 16 (Summer): 175–99.
- (1987) "Divergence and Convergence: Canadian and U.S. Federalism" in Harry N. Schreiber (ed.) *Perspectives on Federalism: Papers from the First Berkeley Seminar in Federalism* (Berkeley: Institute of Governmental Studies, University of California): 179–213.
- (1989) *Executive Federalism: A Comparative Analysis* (Kingston: Queen's University, IIR/QU).
- (1993) "Overview" in Watts and Brown (eds.): 3–15.
- (1999) *Comparing Federal Systems in the 1990s* (2ⁿᵈ edition) (Kingston: IIR/QU).
- and Douglas M. Brown (eds.) (1990) *Canada: The State of the Federation, 1990* (Kingston: IIR/QU).
- and Douglas M. Brown (eds.) (1991) *Options for a New Canada* (Toronto: University of Toronto Press).
- and Douglas M. Brown (eds.) (1993) *Canada: The State of the Federation, 1993* (Kingston: IIR/QU).

Weiss, L. and Hobson, J.M. (1995) *States and Economic Development* (Cambridge: Polity Press).

Weller, Patrick (1995) *Commonwealth-State Reform Processes* (Canberra: Department of the Prime Minister and Cabinet).

Western Australia Legislative Assembly [WALA] (1992) *Report of the Select Committee for Parliamentary Procedures for Uniform Legislation Agreements* (Perth: State Law Publisher).
- (1994) *Standing Committee on Uniform Legislation and Intergovernmental Agreements, Second Report: Structures* (Perth: State Law Publisher).
- (1995) Standing Committee on Uniform Legislation and Intergovernmental Agreements, *First Annual Report: A Year's Experience (34ᵗʰ Parliament)* (Perth: State Law Publisher).
- (1996) Standing Committee on Uniform Legislation and Intergovernmental Agreements, *Twelfth Report: Competition Policy: Consideration of the Implementation of a National Competition Policy (34ᵗʰ Parliament)* (Perth: State Law Publisher).

Whalley, John (1983) "The Impact of Federal Policies on Interprovincial Activity" in Trebilcock et al. (eds.): 201–42.

Wheare, K.C. (1963) *Federal Government* (4ᵗʰ edition) (Oxford: Oxford University Press).
- (1966) *Modern Constitutions* (2ⁿᵈ edition) (Oxford: Oxford University Press).

Whyte, John (1985) "Constitutional Aspects of Economic Development Policy" in R. Simeon (ed.): 29–69.
- (1987) "Federal Powers over the Economy: Finding New Jurisdictional Room" *Canadian Business Law Journal*, Vol. 13: 257–302.

Wildavsky, Aaron (1976) "A Bias Towards Federalism: Confronting the Conventional Wisdom on the Delivery of Governmental Services" *Publius: The Journal of Federalism* 95–120.

Wilkins, Roger (1995) "Federalism and the Regulatory Process" in Carroll and Painter (eds.): 216–22.

Wilks, Stephen and Maurice Wright (eds.) (1987) *Government-Industry Relations: Western Europe, the United States and Japan* (Oxford: Clarendon).

Wilks, Stephen and Maurice Wright (1987) "Conclusion: Comparing Government-Industry Relations: States, Sectors and Networks" in Wilks and Wright (eds.): 274–313.

Williams, Shirley (1991) "Sovereignty and Accountability in the European Community" in R. Keohane and S. Hoffman (eds.) *The New European Community: Decision-Making and Institutional Change* (Boulder, Colo.: Westview): 155–76.

Wiltshire, Kenneth (1986) *Planning and Federalism: Australian and Canadian Experience* (St. Lucia: University of Queensland Press).

– (1990) "Barriers to Reducing State-Commonwealth Overlap" in EPAC, *Towards a More Cooperative Federalism?* (Canberra: AGPS).

Wolfe, Robert (1998) *Farm Wars: The Political Economy of Agriculture and the International Trade Regime* (London: Macmillan).

Working Group on Tied Grants [WGTG] (1991) "Draft Report and Appendices" 9–10 October.

Working Party on Taxing Powers [WPTP] (1991) "Report: Taxation and the Fiscal Imbalance Between Levels of Australian Government: Responsibility, Accountability and Efficiency," 4 October.

Working Party of Representatives of Scrutiny of Legislation Committees Throughout Australia (1996) *Scrutiny of National Schemes of Legislation: Position Paper* (Canberra: Parliament of Australia).

Wright, Deil S. (1998) "Federalism, Intergovernmental Relations and Intergovernmental Management: The Origins, Emergence and Maturity of Three Concepts Across Two Centuries of Organized Power by Area and by Function" in J. Rabin (et al.) (eds.) *Handbook on Public Administration* (2nd edition) (New York: Marcel Dekker Inc.): 381–447.

Young, R.A., Phillippe Faucher and André Blais (1984) "The Concept of Province-Building: A Critique" *Canadian Journal of Political Science* 17(4): 783–818.

Zines, Leslie (1990) "Federal Constitutional Powers over the Economy" *Publius: The Journal of Federalism* 20 (Fall): 19–34.

– (1992) "The Commonwealth" in Craven (ed.): 70–100.

Case Citations

CANADA

- *Attorney-General of Canada v. Attorney-General of Ontario* **(Labour Conventions)** (1937) AC 326
- *Attorney-General of Canada v.* **CN Transportation** (1983) 2 SCR 206
- *Citizens' Insurance Co. v.* **Parsons** (1881) 7 App Cas 96
- **General Motors** *v. City National Leasing* (1989) 1 SCR 641
- *Friends of the* **Oldman River** *Society v. Canada (Minister of Transport)* (1992) 4 DRL 88
- *MacDonald v.* **Vapor** *Canada* (1977) 2 SCR 134

Index

aboriginal title in Australia, 183, 185

acquis communitaire, principle in the European Union, 29, 257

Agreement on Internal Trade (AIT), Canada, 15, 112, 133, 137, 143–4, chapter 6 passim, 241–51, 259, 262–3; architecture of agreement, 155, 161, 162–4; code on incentives, 172–4; constitutional jurisdiction for, 171, 175–6; dispute settlement procedures, 157–8, 168–70, 173–4; exceptions and derogations, 156–7, 167; implementation, 172–8; institutions of, 157–8, 169–70, 172–3; negative integration, 164–7; negotiations for, 147–8, 151–62; positive integration, 167–8; provisions, 148–50, 171–2, 246–8, 253; secretariat, 157, 173

agriculture, 126–9, 133, 157, 164, 174, 246

Alberta, 73, 90, 95, 124, 136, 139, 152–8, 160, 163, 175, 260

alcoholic beverages, including beer, 126–7, 131, 164–5, 251

Allaire Report, 135, 138

Annual Premiers Conference, Canada, 119, 122, 258

Asia-Pacific Economic Cooperation (APEC), 41, 238

Australia: basic characteristics, 10–11, 34ff.; colonial development, 34–5; federal origins, 71–2; relations with Asia, 35, 38, 40–1, 233; territory, 73–4

Australia-New Zealand Closer Economic Relationship (ANZCER), 41

Australian Capital Territory (ACT), 74, 224

Australian Competition and Consumer Commission (ACCC), 184, 202–3, 215, 224, 231, 256

Australian Constitutional Convention (ACC), 180, 192–3

Australian Council of Social Services (ACOSS), 202

Australian Council of Trade Unions (ACTU), 188–9

Australian Labor Party (ALP), 188–9, 191–2, 199, 201, 220, 224

Australian Loan Council (ALC), 81, 106, 108, 185, 212

Australian Local Government Association (ALGA), 182

Australian "settlement," 39

Atkin, Lord, 83

Bakvis, Herman, 10, 110

Balassa, Bela, 22–3, 25, 52

Bloc Québécois, 145

Bouchard, Lucien, 145

Bourassa, Robert, 135

Breton, Albert, 3n., 63

British Columbia, 73, 90, 92, 124, 133, 136, 152–8, 160, 166, 173–5, 200

British Empire, 34–7, 39

Brown, Gordon, 65

business: role in economic union reform, 138, 144, 175, 189, 196, 202

Business Council of Australia (BCA), 189, 196, 202

Business Council on National Issues (BCNI), 138

Cable, Vincent, 19

Cairns, Alan, 8

Cameron, David, 49

Canada: basic features, 10–11, 34ff.; colonial development, 34–5; federal origins, 71–2; territory, 73–4

Canada, Government of (federal government): effect of policies on economic union, 86, 115, 120; economic union reform proposals, 1991, 140–2; free trade negotiations, 123–5; internal trade negotiations, 153–8, 161–2, 175ff., 260–1

Canada Pension Plan, 108

Canada Round of constitutional negotiations, 134–45, 171

Canada-United States Free Trade Agreement (FTA or CUSFTA), 23, 43–4, 78, 92, 111, 118, 122–9, 133–4, 146, 150, 163, 238

Canada-United States relations, 35–7, 41–3, 71, 100, 118–19, 123–5

Canadian Chamber of Commerce, 175

capitalism: compared in Australia, Canada, and other countries, 36, 38–9, 46–7

central agencies: Australia, 197, 210

Chandler, William, 10, 110

Charlottetown Accord, 136, 141–6, 192, 217, 243, 253

Charter of Rights and Freedoms, Canada, 75, 113–17, 141, 163; section 6: mobility rights, 117, 241, 247, 250

Chrétien, Jean, 145, 147

Clark, Glen, 160

Clark, Joe, 144

Coalition, Liberal-National, 185, 192, 194, 199

co-decision, intergovernmental, 15, 107–9, 140–2, 203, 208–212, 216, 220, 225, 257–63, 266–7

Cole v. Whitfield, 76, 89, 194, 249

Committee of Ministers on Internal Trade (CMIT), Canada, 125, 147, 158, 169, 173–4, 241

Commonwealth Government of Australia (federal government): power and position in relation to states, 83–4, 87–8; role in intergovernmental negotiations, 1990–99, 180–7, 188, 190–9, 200–6, 216, 218–20

companies and securities legislation, Australia, 108, 195–6, 212, 226

comparative analysis of politics in general, 9, 12

comparative analysis of Australia and
Canada, 10–12, 34–5; competitive
conditions, 35ff.; economic union
design, 70–89; economic union
conditions in 1985, 89–101;
federal economic powers, 77–89;
intergovernmental relations,
101–11, 177–8, 217, 257–63;
provincial/state economic powers, 81–4; Senates, 106
comparative federalism, 10, 103
competition: role in economy, 99,
196, 238, 249; comparing role in
Australia and Canada, 38, 93,
240, 246, 249
competition policy: Australia, 93,
196, 222–5, 246, 249 (*see also*
National Competition Policy);
Canada, 93, 246; European
Union, 93, 246
Competition Act, Canada, 78, 240, 249
competitive federalism and intergovernmental relations, 60, 62–4,
66–8, 103–5, 217, 232, 234,
262–3
competitiveness, 40–7, 119, 137,
196, 238
concurrent federalism and intergovernmental relations, 59ff., 102–5,
236
concurrent powers in constitutions:
Australia, 60, 79, 104; Canada,
104–5, 116
Constitution Act, Australia, 75; corporations power, 80, 194, 240;
external affairs power, 80; section 92, 75ff., 93, 193–5, 246,
249; trade and commerce,
79–80, 249

Constitution Acts, Canada, 74; *Act,
1867*, 74; *Act, 1982*, 108,
113–14, 116–17, 141; *Charter of
Rights and Freedoms (see Charter of
Rights and Freedoms);* powers over
the economy, 77–9, 114–16, 140;
section 6 of Charter: mobility
rights, 117, 241, 247, 250; section 36, *Constitution Act, 1982*,
117, 142; section 91, *Constitution
Act, 1867*, 77–9; section 92,
Constitution Act, 1867, 77, 81–2;
section 121, *Constitution Act,
1867*, 74–5, 114, 120–1, 140–2,
156, 176, 239, 246; trade and
commerce power, 114, 176
Constitutional Commission, 180,
193–4
constitutional reform: in Australia,
180, 191–5, 205, 239, 240–1; in
Canada, 112–17, 134–45, 239,
241; as means of reform of economic union, 239–41, 265
Coper, Michael, 80
co-operative/collaborative federalism
and intergovernmental relations,
61–3, 66–8, 103–5, 107, 199,
217, 234, 262–3.
coordinate federalism, 59, 66–7, 191
coordination, whole-of-government,
159–62, 203, 208–10, 216, 241
corporations power. *See Constitution
Act*, Australia
Council of Australian Governments
(COAG), 162, 182–6, 198, 201–4,
208–10, 216–17, 219, 221, 224,
225, 228, 241, 251, 259, 262
Council of the Federation proposal,
Canada, 140–2

federal theory, 10, 49; and confederalism, 28
federal values: Australia and Canada
compared, 104, 255–8, 262–3
federalism: as reform vehicle, 196,
264; defined, 3, 10; effects of economic union reform on, 233–5,
264; and European Union, 3,
28–9, 264; and globalization, 4,
16, 56–7, 263–7; and the Great
Depression, 3; and integration,
25–6, 263ff.
Federalist Papers, 60
federations, features of, 54–5;
Australia, 10–11, 60–9, 71–84;
Canada, 10–11, 53, 60–9, 71–84;
distribution of powers in, 56,
6off., 72; Germany, 26, 49, 52,
68, 87, 103; India, 11;
Switzerland, 52
Financial Premiers Conference,
Australia, 182, 185
financial services, 94–5, 128, 183,
213, 230
First Ministers Conferences (FMC)
and meetings: Australia, 208–10
(see also Council of Australian
Governments (COAG); Financial
Premiers Conference; Leaders
Forum; Special Premiers Conference; Treaty Council); Canada,
110, 119, 121, 134–5, 148, 160,
217, 241, 258 (see also Annual
Premiers Conference)
fiscal arrangements, intergovernmental: Australia, 182, 184, 203,
218–22; Canada, 85
fiscal federalism: reform in Australia,
182, 192, 197, 200–1, 205,
218–22, 241, 253. See also tax
reform; Goods and Services Tax
(GST)
foreign economic policy union:
applying Leslie's concept of, 24,
96, 247
free trade: general concept, 20, 42ff.,
71, 118 ff. (see also liberalization);
as paradigm for economic union
reform in Canada, 146, 152, 172,
238
French language and culture in
Canada, 34–6, 71, 73, 86, 90,
135, 257

Galligan, Brian, xiii, 195
Gamble, Andrew, 48
General Agreement on Trade and
Tariffs (GATT), 18, 37–8, 42, 114,
123, 126, 127–9, 141, 143, 146,
156, 163–4, 169–70.
General Motors case, 78, 79, 249
globalization, 17–20, 47–9, 57, 137,
236, 263–7
Goods and Services Tax (GST),
Australia, 189, 211, 219–20, 231,
243, 252. See also fiscal federalism; tax reform
government business enterprises
(GBES), 37, 93–8, 127–9, 157,
166, 190, 203, 214, 223–31, 246

Hancock, W.K., 32
Hanson, Pauline, 204, 224
Harman, Elizabeth, 188–9
harmonization of regulations, 63,
167–8, 229–30, 246, 250, 252
Hawke, Robert, 180–2, 188, 190–2,
194, 197, 201, 218, 243

High Court of Australia, 74, 75–6, 79–81, 84, 183, 194, 196, 219, 232, 249–50

Hilmer Report, 202, 222

Howard, John, 185–7, 198–9, 203, 219–22, 228, 232, 243

Howse, Robert, 54n., 139n., 163, 169

Industry Commission, 189, 231

industrial relations, Australia, 39, 87, 194–5, 231–2, 262

industrial strategy, 51. *See also* economic adjustment and federalism

integration: economic and political, 18–26, 48–9, 57, 236–7; in Europe, 21–2, 26–34; in federal systems, tension with diversity and equity, 55–6, 84ff.; of markets, 22, 44–5, 91, 238; negative, 23, 51–2, 74–7, 126, 229, 249, 255–7, 259; positive, 23, 51, 126, 229, 255–6; regional, 38–45, 57, 233, 236; theory of, 21–6, 32–4; typology of, 22–5, 51–2

intergovernmental relations (*see also* competitive federalism and intergovernmental relations; co-operative/collaborative federalism and intergovernmental relations; concurrent federalism and intergovernmental relations); agreements, enforcement of, 109, 163–4, 177, 242, 259; Australia, 102ff., 257 ff.; Australian reform of, 183, 185, 186, 207–17; Canada, 102ff., 177–8, 257ff.; consensus in, 242, 257–9; European Union, 34–5, 59, 103, 208, 252, 261; reform

of, in general, 15, 257ff.; effectiveness in, 261–3; role in economic union reform, 5, 50, 101–3, 109–10, 120–2, 177, 195–6, 205, 239, 265–6; theory of, 5, 32–3, 49–50, 58–9; typology of, 66–9, 103–5, 107, 109, 234–5, 262; working rules of, 61, 257

international political economy, 34, 38; comparing positions of Australia and Canada in, 38–45, 237–8

international trade agreements: role of provinces in, 123–5, 247, 251–2; jurisdictional conflict about, 136, 163

interprovincial trade in Canada, 89–92, 116, 123; barriers to, 53, 86, 92–7, 99, 119–21, 124, 126–9; costs of barriers to, 119–22, 139–40; effects of Canada-US free trade on, 133–4, 253–4, 264

interstate trade in Australia, 86–8, 90–7, 98–100, 190

interviews: as research material, 14, 269–76

institutional change, 7–8. *See also* neo-institutional analysis

investment, code on (AIT), 126–9, 132, 166, 172

Johnson, Daniel, 158

joint decision trap: Scharpf's concept of, 104, 106, 205–6, 262

Judicial Committee of the Privy Council, United Kingdom (JCPC), 77, 82, 130

Keating, Paul, 181–2, 188–9, 197, 200–2, 232, 243
Kelly, Paul, 39
Kennett, Jeff, 199
Kincaid, John, 64
Knox, Robert, 153, 173

Labour Conventions case, 82–3, 130, 251
labour market union: Leslie's concept of, 24, 96, 247, 254
labour mobility, 89–91, 115; AIT provisions, 166, 176–7, 247; Australian reforms, 235, 247
Laski, Harold, 3n.
Lazar, Harvey, xiii
Leaders Forum, Australia, 183, 186, 208–9, 216
Lenihan, Donald, 167
Leslie, Peter, 21–4, 26–7, 28, 51–2, 98, 245, 254, 256
Liberal-National Coalition, Australia. *See* Coalition
liberalization, economic, 18–26, 48–9, 57, 137–8, 172, 237–9, 263

MacDonald, Mark, 156, 159, 161n., 170
Macdonald report/Commission, Canada, 120–2, 124, 146
Madison, James, 60, 64
managerialism, 64–5, 190–1
Manitoba, 73, 90, 124, 136, 152, 154–5, 175
Manley, John, 153, 157, 161, 176
markets as institutions, 7
market rules, for economic unions, 244–57, 264–7
Mauro, Arthur, 147, 153

Maxwell, Judith, 53
Meech Lake Accord, 104, 122, 132, 134–5, 138–9, 142, 160, 192, 217
mega-game or mega-politics: constitutional reform as, 138, 241, 260
Melbourne, 91, 199
microeconomic policy/reform: agenda for reform in Australia, 43, 190, 198; general concept, 7–9, 188, 233; negotiations, Australia, 180–7, 201–2; outcomes in Australia, 222–8, 233
ministerial councils, Australia, 210–2, 217
Monahan, Patrick, 170
monetary union, including Leslie's concept of, 24, 52, 95, 97, 248, 254
Moravcsik, Andrew, 32–3, 244
Mulroney, Brian: and government led by, 118, 121, 123–4, 126, 137, 143–4, 147
multi-level governance, 49–50
mutual recognition, 32n., 242, 250–1, 260; in Australia, 182–3, 186, 212–14, 225, 229–30, 246–7, 250–1; in Canada (AIT), 168, 172, 250; in European Union, 32, 96, 168, 212, 246–7, 250–1, 257

national (intergovernmental) agencies, Australia, 225–6
National Competition Council (NCC), 184, 203, 211, 215, 224, 256
National Competition Policy (NCP), Australia, 15, 184–5, 189, 198,

201–4, 205, 213, 222–5, 229–30, 233, 241–2, 246, 249, 259, 262

National Energy Policy (NEP), Canada, 117–18, 124, 126

National Farmers Federation, 189, 202

National Policy, Canada, 41–2

national policy-making by intergovernmental means, 260

national standards, Australia, 225–6

national unity and economic union reform in Canada, 137–9, 144–7, 151, 153–4, 158–61, 176, 241

negative integration. *See* integration

neo-institutional analysis: applied to federalism, 6–9, 33, 110, 237–8, 257ff.

New Brunswick, 73, 124, 152, 157, 173

Newfoundland, 73, 90, 92, 124, 139, 152, 157, 159, 163

New South Wales, 71, 87, 91–2, 196–7, 199, 201, 212–13, 219, 226, 232

New Zealand, 13, 41, 74, 186, 225

non-centralization, as type of reform, 259–60

non-tariff barriers to trade: general concept, 86, 92, 98–9. *See also* interprovincial trade in Canada; interstate trade in Australia

North American Free Trade Agreement (NAFTA), 43–4, 118, 124–9, 131–4, 137–8, 146, 150, 163, 238

Northern Territory, Australia, 74, 182

Nova Scotia, 73, 90, 124, 152, 163

One Nation Party. *See* Hanson, Pauline

Ontario, 71, 85, 90, 92, 115; and AIT negotiations, 152, 155–8, 175; and Canada-US free trade, 124, 130–1; and Canada Round of constitutional negotiations, 133, 137–9

Ontario Economic Council: studies on Canadian economic union, 119–20

Organization for Economic Cooperation and Development (OECD), 37, 48, 57, 90, 233

Ostrom, Elinor, 61, 257

Ostrom, Vincent, 3n., 60, 64

overlap and duplication, 64–5

Painter, Martin, 62, 104n., 105, 196, 201, 208, 217, 232, 234, 262

Parti Québécois, 112, 139, 145, 147

patriation round of constitutional negotiations, Canada, 112–17, 138

Pelkmans, Jacques, 22, 24, 256

performance monitoring: as reform method, 181, 228

Pestieau, Caroline, 53

Peterson, David, 130

Pierson, Paul, 33–4

policy communities, role in economic union reform: Australia, 188–90, 194, 215; Canada, 161

policy-making, analysis of, 12

political accords, Canada, 141, 143–4

political requirements for reform, 205–6, 237–44

Polyani, Karl, 56n., 256

positive integration. *See* integration

Prince Edward Island, 73, 124, 152

procurement, 93–4, 127, 133, 164–5, 172, 174, 246, 251

product standards, 93, 181

public choice theory, application of, 7, 32, 61, 244, 257

qualified majority voting, European Union, 28–9

Quebec, Government of, 54, 71, 85–6, 90, 92, 95, 101, 112–14, 117, 123–4, 134–6, 138–9 (*see also* French language and culture in Canada); and AIT negotiations, 152, 154–61, 163, 167, 175, 243, 260; and Canada Round negotiations, 134–9, 141–2; and free trade with USA, 123–4; and referendums on sovereignty, 136, 145, 147; secession and sovereignty, 101, 117, 145, 159; and Social Union Framework Agreement, 176–7

Quebec Liberal Party (QLP), 135, 138, 154

Queensland, 90, 92, 199, 213, 224, 226

Rae, Robert, 138–9

rationalization in intergovernmental relations, 63–6, 67, 262–3

Reagan, Ronald, 65, 131

reform fatigue, 198–9, 204, 243–4

regional disparities and development, 115, 120, 131, 157, 167, 224, 232, 248

regional diversity and equity, 55–6, 84ff.

regional integration. *See* integration

roles and responsibilities: reform of government, Australia, 182, 187, 197, 200–1, 241, 253

Russell, Peter, 142

Saskatchewan, 73, 124, 152, 154, 157

Saunders, Cheryl, xii, 25, 50, 80

Scharpf, Fritz, 23–5, 104n., 106

Schecter, Stephen, 65

secession of Quebec. *See* Quebec, Government of

Senate: of Australia, 106; of Canada, 106, 135–6

Sharman, Campbell, 67, 104

Skocpol, Theda, 6n.

Simeon, Richard, 49

Single European Act, 27–9, 246

Smiley, Donald, 105

Smith, Adam, 7, 27

Smith, Miriam, 138

social charter. *See* social union

social interest groups, role in economic union reform debate: Australia, 190–1; Canada, 131, 137–8, 144, 146–7

social union: concept of, 57–8, 138, 253; Australia, 87–8, 187, 253; Canada, 57–8, 85, 136, 138–9, 142, 144, 253

Social Union Framework Agreement (SUFA), Canada, 58, 144, 147, 176–7, 221, 251, 253

South Australia, 91, 200, 213, 226, 232

sovereignty: pooled, concept of, 260; Quebec. *See* Quebec, Government of

Special Premiers Conference (SPC),
  Australia, 180–1, 198, 201, 208,
  219, 259
states, Australian: positions in intergovernmental negotiations,
  188–9, 196–7, 199–206, 210,
  216, 218–22; powers over economy, 81–4
state-society relations: general theo-
  ries of, 8–9
Steinmo, Sven, 7, 110n., 237
Street v. Queensland Bar Association,
  76–7, 250
strong/weak state dichotomy, 46,
  263, 267
structural/developmental union:
  Leslie's concept of, 24, 97, 248
subsidies to industry, 93, 95, 127–9,
  132–3, 230–1, 246, 251
Supreme Court of Canada, 82, 130,
  135, 163, 249
Swinton, Katherine, 163
Sydney, 91–2, 199

Tasmania, 87, 91, 200, 213
Tasmanian Dam case, 80, 83, 130,
  251
tax powers: Australia, 80ff.; Canada,
  79, 82
tax reform, Australia, 185–6, 198,
  201, 204, 219–20. *See also* Goods
  and Services Tax (GST)
territorial governments: Australia,
  213, 256; Canada, 154, 176
Thatcher government, United
  Kingdom, 48
think-tanks, role in reform of economic union, 190–1
Thelen, Kathleen, 7, 110n., 237

Tiebout, Charles, 64
trade and commerce power in constitution. *See Constitution Acts,*
  Australia and Canada
trade and investment union: Leslie's
  concept of, 24, 93–5, 246–7
Trade Practices Act (TPA), Australia,
  80, 184, 203, 214, 223, 230
transportation: reform of, Australia,
  93–4, 181, 226, 230
treaty-making: role of
  provinces/states in, 251–2. *See
  also* foreign economic policy
  union
Treaty Council, Australia, 186,
  208–9, 247, 251
Trudeau, Pierre, 113, 116, 118
Tsoukalis, Loukas, 27

uniform legislation, Australia, 163,
  213–14, 242
uniformity, as a value in federal systems, 234–5
unilateral reform of economic
  union, 239–40; Australia, 191,
  195–6, 231, 239–40; Canada,
  113–15, 121, 130–1, 161, 175–6.
  See also economic union
United States of America, 35–7. *See
  also* federations
utilities reform: gas and water,
  Australia, 185–6, 226–7, 230. *See
  also* electricity trade and markets

vertical fiscal imbalance, Australia,
  80, 190, 201, 220
Victoria, state of, 71, 82, 91–2, 196,
  199, 201, 213, 217, 219, 224,
  226, 231–2, 256

Vogel, David, 62n.
voting rules in intergovernmental
    relations, 108. *See also* co-decision

Watts, Ronald, xiii, 10
Western Australia (WA), 87, 90, 92,
    174, 185, 199–200, 213, 217,
    219, 224, 227

Wheare, K.C., 3n.
Wolfe, Robert, 256
World Trade Organization (WTO),
    118, 125–6, 127–9, 132–3, 146,
    164, 246, 249

Zines, Leslie, 79, 83